WITCHCRAFT

Published by Geddes & Grosset,
David Dale House, New Lanark, ML11 9DJ, Scotland

© 2005 Geddes & Grosset,

Published 2005

ISBN 1 84205 535 6

Printed and bound in Poland

POLSKABOOK

Contents

Chapter 1

Introduction

From childhood we all have a clear, preconceived idea of what a witch looks like – an ugly old woman wearing a black cloak and a tall, pointed, wide-brimmed hat, who gets around by flying through the air on a broomstick and who is frequently to be found cackling wickedly while stirring some foul-smelling brew in a black cauldron or casting evil spells. The picture is often extended to include a black cat that goes everywhere with her and a tumbledown cottage.

Unfortunately the clarity of our perception of the traditional witch does not extend to witchcraft. We know that it is traditionally associated with magic and sorcery but, after that, vagueness sets in. This is perfectly understandable as the word has been used to describe different concepts at different points in history.

Margaret Murray and the Pagan Theory

The confusion over the exact nature of witchcraft was far from helped by the writings of Margaret Murray, a British anthropologist, archaeologist and Egyptologist, who was born in 1863 and died in 1963, and who became interested in witchcraft in the course of her study of Egyptology. It was her contention, as set out in her book, *The Witch-cult in Western Europe*, published in 1921, that the history of witchcraft was an ongoing one, that witchcraft was originally an old pagan, organized religion dating back to earliest times and that the witchcraft which was the centre of so much hysteria in the Middle Ages and the Renaissance was a remnant of this ancient religion.

Some of Murray's conclusions were based on *The Golden Bough*, written by Sir James Frazer and published in 1890, in which the author raised the question of witchcraft having Palaeolithic origins. Murray, however, took the matter much further and maintained that there was a strong connection between what was known about some of the early pagan religious practices and the rites that were described by those confessing to witchcraft during the period of witchcraft hysteria, part of her research having included written records of witchcraft trials. According to her way of thinking, the supposed old religion of witchcraft had been alive, in part, all the time but had been driven underground by Christianity. The theory was that the old rituals had survived because of the meetings of a series of covens throughout the ages.

Murray's suggestion that witchcraft represents a continuing and continuous pagan religion was the subject of much controversy. Her theory is upheld by many modern witches but much of it has been rejected by modern scholars on the grounds of lack of evidence. She did not do her credibility much good by the publication of *The Divine King* in England in 1954 in which she contended that from William the Conqueror on every English king as far as James I and VI was a closet witch and also alleged that over the centuries many statesmen had been killed by witch's ritual rather than by the presumed means.

Murray's theories of witchcraft as an unbroken, secret, pagan religion that had suddenly become more prominent and more public during periods noted for their witchcraft hysteria did not take into account the part that the Church played in this hysteria. Nor did it place enough emphasis on the fact that the confessions that were a major part of the basis of her research were completely contrived. A great many such confessions were extracted by some form of enforced distress, whether this took the form of excruciating torture by some terrible device or some more subtle form, and the similarity that was a feature of these even from country to country was largely because of the degree of standardization of the questions. The similarity in witchcraft trials in different countries was far greater than might be supposed because of the existence of *Malleus Maleficarum*, a book on witchcraft first published in Germany in 1486 and known as the 'Hammer of the Witches', a kind of guidebook to witchcraft and the prosecution of witches, which was adopted as a kind of guidebook for witchcraft trials throughout Europe and later England.

Inquisition

The role that the Church played in the supposed rise of witchcraft is an important one. This role was an extension of its role as an exterminator of heretics. The Roman Catholic Church's vigorous campaign to stamp out heresy in Christian parts of the world began early in the thirteenth century. It was part of this campaign to establish tribunals, known as the Inquisition, an institution that acquired and has retained throughout history a reputation for the use of great cruelty and torture in pursuit of its aims to identify all heretics and to punish them, often by death and often by burning to death.

Before the Church courts, and the Inquisition in particular, turned their attention towards witchcraft there had been people accused of being involved in magic of various kinds. An interest in magic and sorcery has been part of sections of most societies from earliest times. However, an association with magic was not thought to be among the more heinous of crimes, being usually punished by fines or imprisonment.

Canon Episcopi

The problem for witchcraft was that it became designated as a form of heresy and former attitudes changed dramatically. It might confidently have been assumed that witchcraft was safe from such charges because there was in existence an important and respected religious document of unknown origin and uncertain date, called *Canon Episcopi*, that stated that witchcraft was a delusion and a belief in it the act of an infidel. This had been incorporated into canon law around the middle of the twelfth century. Thus it was thought at this time that it was not witchcraft that was heresy, since this was simply the result of a fevered imagination, but belief in such a thing.

Although the *Canon Episcopi* denied the existence of witchcraft it unwittingly helped to promote the movement against it. It referred to deluded women who thought that they had the ability to ride on animals to night-time services dedicated to their mistress, the pagan goddess Diana, and some of the imagined activities of witches described in the Canon were part of the basis of future charges against accused witches.

The *Canon Episcopi* was a much respected document for a long time but gradually attitudes to witchcraft changed. The views of the Dominican theologian Thomas Aquinas (1226–74) did much to foster the Church's change in attitude. It was his belief that, among other things, witches could fly through the air, change shape, raise storms, have implicit pacts with the devil and have sexual intercourse with demons. It was also part of his belief that demons and the devil tempt people.

Witchcraft as Heresy

Aquinas was an important figure in theology and much attention was paid to his views. These were to have a great effect on the thinking of those involved in the later prosecution of witches and they markedly influenced the Church's views on witchcraft.

There remained the matter of the *Canon Episcopi*, but ways around this were sought and it began to be discredited. There was a gradual but marked move to label witchcraft as both a reality and a form of heresy, and many people were prosecuted and burnt as witches in southern France in the first part of the fourteenth century, such action also spreading to Italy, Germany and Switzerland

These anti-witchcraft activities were given a tremendous boost in 1484 when Pope Innocent VIII issued a papal bull that emphasized the importance of the Inquisition and its zeal against heretics, referred to wicked acts being carried out in northern Germany and elsewhere, and condemned the people allegedly performing such acts as blasphemously renouncing their faith. The acts referred to included consorting with demons and using spells to bring harm to people, crops or animals.

Members of the Inquisition were delighted by the papal action, which meant that they could officially view witchcraft as a form of heresy and treat accused witches in the same way that they treated accused heretics. In any case, they were running out of heretics, so many people having been accused and burned to death by this time. Two years later was published the *Malleus Maleficarum* (*see* page 6 and Chapter 4, page 172), compiled by two Dominican members of the Inquisition, known as the Hammer of the Witches, a kind of guidebook to witchcraft and the prosecution of witches, which was to have a powerful influence on those who identified accused witches and prosecuted and sentenced them.

Thus began the spate of witchcraft trials described in Chapter 2 and based on the methods already established by the Inquisition in heresy trials. Because of the supposed connection between witchcraft and heresy, a great number of people were submitted to extreme torture and lost their lives. Witchcraft hysteria was at its peak between 1560 and 1660, although it lasted to a lesser degree for about another ninety years. At the height of the Inquisition witchcraft trials, the worst persecution took place in France and in Germany.

The Inquisition itself was responsible for few of the trials after 1500, later trials being conducted either by other ecclesiastical courts or secular ones. By the 1730s the persecution of accused witches, whether by the church or by the state, had largely reached an end in Europe, Britain and America. However, the last executions on the grounds of witchcraft did not take place in France until 1745, and in Bavaria Anna Maria Schwagel was the last person to be executed for witchcraft – she was beheaded.

Witchcraft in England

It has to be remembered that the Inquisition's activities against accused witches were confined to continental Europe. The torture that was seen as a necessary part of the trials was banned in England and witchcraft was regarded as a civil crime. In addition, the *Malleus Maleficarum* was not translated into English until 1584, and so it exerted an influence on witchcraft trials that happened nearly a hundred years after it had been compiled. In England execution for witchcraft was by hanging not burning.

In England witchcraft hysteria did not come into its own until much later than it did in continental Europe. There was an act passed by Henry VIII in 1542 that allowed for accused witches to be tried and punished by the state, but the aim of this Witchcraft Act was to prevent supposed witches from inflicting harm on others, not to have them tried for heresy. In fact this law brought the trial of only one person and even this resulted in a pardon, and the act was repealed in 1547 by Edward VI.

In 1563, however, Queen Elizabeth passed another Witchcraft Act that was to mark the beginning of witchcraft hysteria in England. Although the tenets of the act were not as severe as the legislation in Europe, they did allow for the death penalty for those found guilty of murder by witchcraft or sorcery. It is thought that Elizabeth was much influenced by some of her bishops, who had witnessed some of the European trials and consequent burnings, and by the fact that there were rumours of witchcraft plots against herself. In addition, fears about witchcraft were affecting the general public, rumours about what was happening on the Continent having reached England. Thus, although witchcraft hysteria in England had nothing directly to do with charges of heresy it did indirectly, news of the European trials having brought fear and unrest about the potential presence of witchcraft.

Another more stringent act was passed in 1581, but it was nothing like as stringent as the Witchcraft Act passed by James I of England (and VI of Scotland) in 1604. Many of the most important English witchcraft trials were conducted under the terms of this act. It allowed for the execution by hanging of anyone found guilty of trying to cause harm to someone else by means of witchcraft, whether or not the person at the receiving end of the witchcraft had actually died. It also made it a felony to consort with any evil spirits.

The worst of the English witchcraft hysteria occurred in the 1640s, when the country was in the grip of political and social unrest and in a mood to look for scapegoats. This was the period during which the notorious witch-finder Matthew Hopkins operated (*see* Chapter 2, page 34). The 1604 act remained in force until 1736. In the latter half of the seventeenth century the witchcraft hysteria gradually tapered off. The last person to be executed on charges of witchcraft in England was Alice Molland in Exeter in 1684. The last person to have a serious indictment brought against her was Jane Clarke in Leicester in 1717 but the case was thrown out of court, despite the large number of people wishing to testify against her.

There was much more of an archetypal witch in England than in Europe. There was more variation in the nature of the suspect in Europe, and it was the case with some European courts that they set their sights on the wealthy, since people convicted of witchcraft had to pay for their own trials and executions and had any remaining estate confiscated. In England the typical accused witch was a strange-looking, solitary elderly woman of eccentric habits and low social standing, who kept a cat. Such people were easy to intimidate and few would bother to come to their aid. There were, of course, exceptions to the rule.

Witchcraft in Scotland

In Scotland accused witches were treated much more brutally than they were in England. Indeed, their treatment was on a par with many of the European countries. Although the Inquisition was not involved, many of their methods were and the Presbyterian Church, as well as the secular courts, exhibited a zeal to stamp out witchcraft.

Witchcraft hysteria took some time to reach Scotland but when it did it was exceptionally strong. As was the case with England, the Inquisition with its charges of heresy was not the direct cause of the witchcraft trials in Scotland but it was an indirect cause since what was happening in Europe affected Scotland even more than it did England, Scotland's European links then being the stronger. A fear of witchcraft was therefore communicated to the people of Scotland.

Mary Queen of Scots in 1563 introduced tougher legislation against witchcraft than had formerly been the case. However, it was not until the coming to the throne of James VI, who was later also to become James I of England, that witchcraft hysteria in Scotland came into its own. He has been blamed for having added much fuel to the fire of this hysteria but it has been claimed that this was an unfair accusation and he was simply a product of his times as far as witchcraft was concerned, his views simply reflecting the prevalent views of the day.

However, James did have much contact with the Continent and was aware of the attitude to witchcraft there and of the trials that were going on. He was apparently originally sceptical of the confessions of some of the witches in the North Berwick Witchcraft Trials in 1590 (*see* Chapter 2, page 21), but his interest in witchcraft grew and his studies on the subject led to a book on the subject being written by him. Entitled *Daemonologie*, it appeared in 1597 and is claimed, at the very least, to have brought attention to and reinforced the then prevailing attitude to witchcraft and, at worst, to have fanned the flames of witchcraft hysteria among the general public. By

1604 James was also king of England and the act that was passed there (*see* Witchcraft in England, page 9) was also valid in Scotland. It is said that, despite his interest in the subject, his belief in many of the alleged acts of witchcraft and his defence of the test of swimming (*see* Chapter 2, page 46), he tried to calm some of the hysteria when it grew excessive.

Witchcraft trials in Scotland were notorious for the use of barbaric forms of torture that were banned in England. These included the use of devices of torture, such as thumbscrews (known in Scotland as pilliwinks) and boots as well as more subtle forms of torture such as sleep deprivation (*see* Chapter 2, page 50). Scotland was more like Europe in its manner of execution and convicted witches were burnt.

After around the year 1700 the number of witchcraft trials tapered off. The last actual trial specifically on the grounds of witchcraft took place in June 1727 when Janet Horne was convicted and put to death in Dornoch. The manner of her death illustrates the brutality of the Scottish witchcraft proceedings. She was placed in a burning barrel of pitch.

Witchcraft in the American Colonies

Witchcraft hysteria in the American colonies, although Salem (*see* Chapter 2, page 23) has gone down in history because of the hysteria there, never reached anything like the level of intensity that it did elsewhere. Witchcraft trials did not begin in the American colonies until the 1640s, the time when the witch-hunts were reaching their peak in England. As far as attitudes to witchcraft were concerned, the colonies were affected by what was happening in England but to a much lesser extent. Apart from those executed at Salem there are recorded as being around only twelve executions on charges of witchcraft in New England.

Witchcraft in Ireland

Despite its long connection with legends of the supernatural and its mystic Celtic connections, Ireland remained free of the hysterical attitude to witchcraft that pervaded mainland Europe, England and Scotland. It has been suggested that this was largely owing to the fact that Ireland was more inaccessible from mainland Europe than were Scotland and England and had fewer European contacts.

Alice Kyteler

The first recorded witchcraft trial in Ireland took place in 1324. It concerned a rich aristocratic woman, Alice Kyteler, who lived in Kilkenny and had amassed a great deal of wealth on the death of her three husbands. When her fourth husband, Sir John Le Poer, was taken ill, he and his children, who did not want their father's money to go to Alice, suggested to the local Franciscan bishop, Richard de Ledre, that Poer's illness was attributable to Alice and possibly to witchcraft.

The bishop, who may well have encountered the European stance on witchcraft during his years of religious training in France and who probably had a view to confiscating Alice's estate should she be found guilty, agreed with the suspicions of the family. Alice was accused among other things of consorting with a demon, holding sacrilegious services, leading a group of devil-worshippers and murdering her first three husbands.

Alice Kyteler had powerful friends, and the bishop had the disadvantage in Ireland of being English-born. He had great difficulty in bringing charges against her and when he eventually succeeded it was to find that she had escaped to England. In her absence she was found guilty of witchcraft and heresy but she lived out the rest of her life in England.

Unfortunately some of those accused of being associated in witchcraft with Kyteler were not so lucky. Her maid, Petronilla, was flogged senseless repeatedly until she confessed that the charges against her and Kyteler were true. She was then excommunicated as a heretic and burned alive on charges of witchcraft in November 1324. Some others who had been accused with Kyteler are said to have been found and variously punished, some being executed by burning.

Magee Island Witches

This might have established a pattern in Ireland and been the start of witchcraft hysteria, but this did not prove to be the case. There are records of only a few trials, around eight, taking place between the first, as described above, in 1324 and the last in 1711 (*see* Chapter 3, Magee Island Witches, page 99). A Witchcraft Act was passed in Ireland in 1586 and was not repealed until 1821 but it was not brought into play very often.

Modern Witchcraft

The second part of the twentieth century witnessed a renewal of interest in witchcraft, but it is a different kind witchcraft and is often known as Wicca to differentiate it. Most of the practitioners of modern witchcraft claim that their cult is purely concerned with benevolent magic and reject any connection with its malevolent counterpart. Although modern witchcraft and Satanism are frequently confused, often because of how the former is portrayed in works of literature, plays and films, there is no connection between the two. Unlike Satanism, or alleged traditional witchcraft, modern witches do not claim any kind of alliance with the devil.

Modern witchcraft, or Wicca, is often described as a neo-pagan movement. Some members of the movement have been influenced by the writings of Margaret Murray (*see* page 5), which are described above, and regard their organization as having an continuous link with an early organized pagan witchcraft movement, driven underground by the advent of Christianity. However, Margaret Murray's theories on this have largely been discredited.

Some of the rituals of Wicca are reminiscent of some pagan beliefs and rituals, and it is thought that isolated groups throughout the centuries kept these alive without belonging to an organized witchcraft movement. For example, the object of worship of modern witches is the goddess, sometimes in partnership with her consort, the horned god (*see* Chapter 4, pages 135, 136). Wicca, however, is essentially a modern movement.

Modern witchcraft owes its existence in no small part to Gerald Gardner (*see* Chapter 3, page 82). His writings, which drew on folklore, ancient pagan rites and ceremonial magic, caused many people in Britain to develop an interest in witchcraft. He set up his own coven after the repeal of the witchcraft Act in 1951 and many others followed suit. At the time that Gardner was writing, Murray's theory had not yet been discredited and Gardner claimed to be keeping the old witchcraft cult alive by making it known to potential members.

Interest in modern witchcraft grew stronger throughout the 1960s and 1970s and spread to America, where it generated much activity. Many of the original members were women who were also interested in feminism and so a connection was established between the two. At first what was known as the Gardnerian tradition was followed but then Alexander Sanders founded his own tradition, although it too relied heavily on Gardner's rituals.

There are various traditions in the modern movement, and these are ever evolving and changing. They are essentially autonomous and there is no cohesive structure or central authority. The covens within each tradition are also autonomous, each with its own 'book of shadows' (*see* Chapter 4, page 159), which describes the coven's rituals, rules, etc. The modern witchcraft movement, which is imbued with a great respect for Nature, tends to be rather fragmented and, since many covens regard secrecy as being important, it is difficult to judge the extent of it.

Although modern practitioners of modern witchcraft claim that their practices are entirely harmless, there remains a good deal of suspicion directed at them. The word suggests the practices with which accused witches were charged in the period of witchcraft hysteria in Europe, England and Scotland, and the association remains in the minds of people. Also, Gardner was associated with the performance of ritual sexual acts and, although these are now mostly symbolic rather than actual, an image of witchcraft as an orgiastic movement remains.

Chapter 2

Witchcraft Trials and Executions

Witchcraft was regarded as an extremely serious offence, particularly in Europe, and was treated as a crime that was on a par with heresy. Indeed, in Europe it was often viewed as a type of heresy. Like heresy, it was seen as a crime against God himself since people found guilty of witchcraft were assumed to have made a pact with the devil and to have turned their backs on God. In fact, in the earlier witch trials the proceedings were seen as a matter for the church, and the trial was conducted by the ecclesiastical courts, the secular authorities becoming involved only at the punishment stage. The first secular witchcraft trials were held in Paris in 1390.

In several European countries the heresy trials conducted by the Inquisition were used as models for witchcraft trials. There was therefore very little value placed on proof, people being convicted on supposed voluntary confessions and the flimsiest of circumstantial evidence. It was assumed by the authorities from the start that the accused was guilty and it was just a matter of going through the motions, although these could be very savage indeed.

Little or no help was given to the accused. Witnesses for the defence were often not allowed to enter the courtroom. In fact, there were not many defence witnesses anyhow, since speaking up in defence of an accused witch was likely to result in a charge of witchcraft being made against the speaker. Those witnesses who were called to speak for the prosecution had the right to remain anonymous, a fact that made it very difficult for the accused to reply to their evidence. The accused often had to speak for themselves at their trials since it was common to debar them from having lawyers representing them.

Much emphasis was placed on confession, particularly in the continental courts. Most people who were accused of witchcraft did not lightly confess to this, and the courts resorted to torture to extract admissions from the accused (*see* Tests, Confession and Torture, page 43). The value placed on confession did much to encourage the witch hysteria that swept Europe, since many of those who were forced to make confessions with regard to their associates simply named anyone who came to mind. Thus people lived in fear of a representative of the authorities calling on them with an accusation of involvement in witchcraft.

The witchcraft trials were a source of terror wherever they were held. Because of the number of people that were named in the supposed voluntary confessions forced out of the accused, the number of people put on trial in any one place could be very substantial indeed. Given the reputation enjoyed by the courts of mainland Europe for almost always obtaining a conviction and therefore an execution, the witchcraft trials frequently resulted in mass slaughter.

Famous European Witchcraft Trials

Bamberg Trials

Of the European witchcraft trials, among the most notorious took place in the German principality of Bamberg. It was under the rule of Bishop Johann Gottfried von Aschhausen, which lasted from 1609 until 1622, that the persecution of people accused of witchcraft began. Between three and four hundred people at least were said to have been executed during this time, but this was nothing compared to what was to come. In 1623 Gottfried Johann Georg II Fuchs von Dornheim, who ruled until 1633, began a reign of terror in the area. He established an extremely efficient and extremely cruel campaign under the supervision of the suffragan bishop, Friedrich Forner, with the aim of eradicating any traces of witchcraft from the state.

Local people were encouraged to inform on each other on the least suspicion of witchcraft, and often this information was based on nothing at all, simply being an act of vengeance or an attempt to turn away attention and charges from the informers themselves. The witch-hunts were extremely thorough, and special prisons had to be built to accommodate the huge numbers of accused witches. Von Dornheim had a vested interest in trying and executing as many people as possible, since the estates of those executed for witchcraft were confiscated and the proceeds given to him after the expenses of the trial, torturing and execution had been deducted.

The most shocking aspect of the Bamberg trials was the use of the most barbaric and agonising forms of torture. Professional torturers skilled in the art were invited to Bamberg, and they used a wide range of devices in the torturing process, including the use of thumbscrews, boots, the rack and strappado (described below under Torture by Device, page 83). In addition, the accused were immersed in boiling hot baths to which lime had been added, placed upon a roasting hot iron chair, forced to kneel on a spiked board and placed in stocks fitted with iron spikes. There seemed no end to the savagery to which the Bamberg courts would put their victims.

As was usually the case in the European courts, the whole trial system was stacked against the accused persons. They were not allowed to have lawyers represent them and they were often not told the exact nature of the charges against them or the identity of their accusers. It was simply a question of getting them to make a supposed voluntary confession and torturing them until they did so. Even after they were condemned to death, the torture would not be stopped and was continued even while they were on the way to the place of execution.

The great in the land were not even exempt from this reign of terror, probably because von Dornheim had his eye on their wealth, much of which would go to him when they were executed. Anyone who dared to protest, either on behalf of an individual suspect or against the whole terrible process in general, was seized and charged with witchcraft.

Hysteria and panic reigned. People tried to escape but many were intercepted. Help was sought from the Holy Roman Emperor, Ferdinand, but von Dornheim paid no attention to his attempts at intervention and, although Ferdinand issued mandates in 1630 and 1631 banning the persecution, the situation did not really improve until von Dornheim died in 1632.

Trèves Trials

Germany was noted for the extent of its witchcraft hysteria. One area where this was particularly extensive in the late sixteenth century was Trèves, now Trier. The situation was at its worst from 1582 on and was largely instigated by Prince-Bishop Johann von Schonenberg, with the help of Johann Zandt, the governor, a notary, Peter Ormsdorf, and Suffragan Bishop Peter Binsfield.

The reign of terror began with von Schonenberg attacking Dietrich Flade, one of the civil judges who officiated at witchcraft trials, for being too lenient. Flade was tried as a witch and executed, and there began a whole spate of trials. Attempts made by a priest, Cornelious Loos, to bring attention to the lawless trials that were taking place were in vain as the church refused to act and, indeed, banished Loos to Belgium.

Between the years of 1587 and 1594 around six thousand people were accused, and there was general hysteria. Hardly any of the accused escaped torture and many were executed. Of those tried and found guilty, a great many were prominent affluent citizens. As was the case in Bamberg, money was a great motivator when it came to accusing witches because their estates were confiscated by the state after the expenses of their trial, torture and execution had been met.

Würzburg Trials

Germany was infamous for the severity of its witchcraft trials. Some of the worst of these occurred in Würzburg in the early seventeenth century. Between 1623 and 1633, during the rule of Prince Bishop Philip Adolf von Ehrenberg, nearly one thousand witches were executed. This slaughter was largely at the instigation of the Jesuits, and, as was the case in Bamberg and Trèves, many of the people executed were affluent, thus swelling the state coffers and those of the Jesuits when their estates were confiscated.

There was widespread hysteria and terror, and the situation was changed only when von Ehrenberg's heir, Ernest Ehrenberg, was suddenly seized, subjected to a secret trial for involvement with witchcraft and summarily executed. The Prince Bishop, who had not been informed, seems to have come to his senses at this point, although up until then he had gone along with the evil work of the Jesuits. He became more lenient and moderate in his views, but it was in fact the prospect of war that finally reduced the witchcraft mania. A Swedish army was approaching with a view to invading Würzburg and the authorities had to concentrate on military matters rather than on witchcraft.

Famous English Witchcraft Trials

Chelmsford Witchcraft Trials

The Essex town of Chelmsford was much associated with witchcraft, and it was the scene of several witchcraft trials. The best known of the mass trials that took place there was the most shocking. The trials took place in 1645 and the notorious English witch-finder, Matthew Hopkins, was much involved.

The trials began with the interrogation of Elizabeth Clarke, who was an old woman with one leg and a natural candidate for being accused of witchcraft, her mother having been hanged as a convicted witch. Elizabeth Clarke confessed to witchcraft and implicated several others, who in turn implicated others, and so on, until thirty-eight people were summoned to appear before the county courts on 29 July 1645. This kind of chain reaction of accusations was tragically common in witchcraft trials.

The Chelmsford trials are notorious partly for the scale and nature of the methods that were used to extract confessions. The use of physical torture inflicted by instruments was banned in England and so the accused were not subjected to such cruel devices as thumbscrews, the rack, strappado, etc. They were, however, mercilessly subjected to forms of what was known as induced torture. They were deprived of sleep, made to sit cross-legged on a stool for hours on end, and made to walk up and down continuously until they collapsed from exhaustion. Such methods were repeated until a confession was made, and they were employed largely at the instigation of Matthew Hopkins.

The trials are also infamous for the number of deaths. Of the thirty-eight people who were sent for trial only two were acquitted. Some of the others were imprisoned and some reprieved but seventeen of the women were executed by hanging.

For further details *see* Chapter 3, Chelmsford Witches, page 69.

Pendle Witchcraft Trials

One of the most notorious of the English mass witchcraft trials involved people from the Pendle Forest area of Lancashire, the trials taking place in Lancaster in 1612. At that time it was the largest witchcraft trial ever to have taken place in England. The trial was remarkable not only because of the numbers involved but because many of the accused were members of the same two feuding families.

Many of the charges were typical of those found in other English witchcraft trials. Several of them related to the killing of people by witchcraft, others to the harming of animals and others. An unusual slant was added to the trials by the fact that, shortly after the arrests, a rumour began to be circulated to the effect that members of the two families had got together in order to hatch a plot to blow up Lancaster Castle with a view to releasing their relatives imprisoned there.

Another remarkable feature of the trial was that one of the accused, Elizabeth Devine, was convicted largely on the evidence of her own children. These were a son in his twenties, who was of very limited intelligence, and a daughter aged nine, who was legally too young to give evidence, although such ineligibility on the grounds of age was often overlooked by the courts.

Both Elizabeth Devine's son and daughter testified to the fact that their mother had caused deaths by means of witchcraft and that she was known to have familiars, that is, supposed supernatural spirit companions in the form of animals. It was extremely easy in those days to find oneself in a situation in which one could be accused of either of these crimes. In the case of the second, all one had to do was a possess a cat or dog, have a cat or dog pass one's house or be so unfortunate as to have a hare appear in a field near one's house or a toad appear in one's garden.

At the end of the trials, ten of the accused were sentenced to death in Lancaster by hanging on 20 August 1612, despite the fact that most of them were still protesting that they were innocent. One, Elizabeth Sowthern, had died in prison and another, Jennet Preston, had been hanged in her home town of York.

For further details *see* Chapter 3, Pendle Witches, page 105.

Warboys Witchcraft Trial

The main reason for the fame of this trial was the high social standing of those involved. The trial of Alice Samuel and her husband, John, and daughter, Agnes Samuel, took place at Huntingdon. They were charged with bewitching the five daughters of Robert Throckmorton, a wealthy squire from Warboys in Huntingdonshire.

The case had several of the elements that were later to characterise the notorious Salem Witchcraft Trials in the American colonies. At the heart of both trials was a group of girls who were suffering from strange fits and who blamed the accused for having caused these by means of witchcraft. In neither case could any medical diagnosis be made to account for their condition.

As in the case with Salem but on a lesser scale, hysteria developed, and other people began to claim to have been bewitched by the trio. Fear of witches was widespread. Other charges of causing death and harm to people and livestock, charges that were to be common in future witchcraft trials, were added to the original accusations.

The most serious of these charges concerned the death of Lady Cromwell, wife of the Throckmorton's landlord, Sir Henry Cromwell, and grandmother of Oliver Cromwell. She had tried to remove the influence that Alice Samuel was said to have over the girls and, although the attempt failed, she had offended Alice. Later Lady Cromwell complained of having nightmares in which she was attacked by Alice Samuel and her cat. She died about fifteen months later, and the Throckmortons laid her death at the door of the Samuels and their witchcraft.

Alice Samuel eventually confessed to being involved in witchcraft and to having consorted with the devil. She and her husband and daughter were all found guilty and hanged, their property being confiscated. Sir Henry Cromwell used this to fund an annual sermon against witchcraft to be preached in Huntingdon and this custom lasted until 1814.

Famous Scottish Witchcraft Trials

Aberdeen Witchcraft Trials

These trials, which took place in the Scottish city of Aberdeen, were noted for their sheer scale and the hysteria behind the witch-hunts that resulted in the trials. Pressure was used on the accused to get them to confess to a series of crimes traditionally associated with witchcraft, such as causing death by witchcraft, harming people and livestock by witchcraft, raising storms, etc, and also to cavorting with the devil and demons and indulging in lewd behaviour with them.

The pressure that was put on the accused included the use of the swimming test, by which the accused were bound hand and foot and cast into a stretch of water. If he or she floated, the accused was deemed to be guilty since the devil was assumed to be giving assistance, and if he or she sank, the accused was deemed to be innocent, although often dead (*see* Tests, Confession and Torture, page 43).

By April 1597 twenty-three women and one man had been put to death. They were first strangled at the stake and then burnt to ashes. Some of those taken before the court and imprisoned were so afraid of the treatment that would be meted out to them and the execution that might well be awaiting them that they took their own lives in prison. Even then they were not safe from the vengeance of the authorities. Their bodies were dragged through the streets until they were torn to pieces. Those who ended up with a verdict of not proven were punished also, having their cheeks branded and being banished from the city.

North Berwick Witchcraft Trials

These trials, held 1590–92, concerned a group of people supposed to belong to a coven that met at North Berwick, a town down the east coast of Scotland from Edinburgh. The trials were notable for several reasons. Among these was the high social standing of some of the accused and the fact that the king, James VI of Scotland, later James I of England, was involved, although as a prosecutor not as a defendant.

James was involved in two ways. First, some of the accused, supposedly aided by the Earl of Bothwell, were alleged to have used witchcraft to make attempts on his life, which, of course, amounted to treason. Second, he took a personal interest in the trials and insisted on taking part as an interrogator. The king had developed an interest in, and an antipathy to, witchcraft, and his involvement did much to encourage the hysteria that surrounded the trials. *See also* entries for Gilly Duncan (page 77), John Fian (page 79), Effie MacLean (page 98), Barbara Napier (page 102).

The trials were also noted for the use of savage torture. Witchcraft trials in England were barred by law from the use of physical torture, but this was not the case in Scotland. In these particular trials, several means were used, including thrawing – the jerking of the head violently and suddenly by means of a rope; thumbscrews or pilliwinks, by which the thumbs were crushed; and the use of a witch's bridle, which was placed round the head and attached to a cell wall by a very short chain so that the accused was unable to lie down and so was deprived of sleep. The trials also saw the use of turcas, a pair of pincers used to pull out the fingernails.

Apart from the royal involvement and the use of torture, the trials were noted for the sensational nature of the details revealed in the confessions of some of the accused, especially the details of the orgies indulged in at sabbats and of the attempts to murder the king by witchcraft contained in the confession of Agnes Sampson. The details supplied by her confession and those of some of the others were considered by some as to be so preposterous as to be completely incredible. The king, however, became very angry at any suggestions that the accused should be acquitted because their supposed confessions were so extremely unlikely.

At the end of the trials, Margaret Thomson had died under torture, and three people, Agnes Sampson, John Fian and Effie Maclean, were all executed. The first two were strangled and then burnt at the stake but Effie Maclean, although of high social standing, being the daughter of Lord Cliftonhall, was refused the leniency of strangling and was burnt alive. This was very possibly a result of her connections with the Earl of Bothwell, who was believed to be behind plots on the king's life.

Bothwell himself was imprisoned for a time in Edinburgh Castle, but he had many supporters in the city and he escaped the death penalty. Although he had seen himself as a potential heir to the throne, he finally realised that he had failed to remove James from the throne and left Scotland to go into exile.

For further details *see* Chapter 3, North Berwick Witches, page 103.

Pittenweem Witchcraft Trial

This trial centred on a group of accused witches from the small fishing town of Pittenweem in Fife, Scotland, in 1704. It was remarkable for the ill-treatment of the accused, although there were no official executions, and for the fact that one of the accused was killed by an unruly mob after escaping. It was also notable for the fact that the original accuser, Patrick Morton, an apprentice blacksmith, who charged the first of the accused, Beatrice Laing, with causing him to suffer from fits and other ailments was later exposed as a fraud, having been helped in his deception with Patrick Cowper, the local minister, who was wont to warn his congregation of the dangers of witchcraft.

The accused included Mrs Nicholas Lawson, Janet Cornfoot, Isobel Adam, and Thomas Brown, as well as Beatrice Laing. Laing was subjected to sleep deprivation by the method known as watching and waking, by which the accused was subject to constant surveillance so that he or she would not fall asleep and to abrupt waking if sleep did occur. After being forced to confess by this means and thereafter having retracted her confession, she was cast into solitary confinement in a dark dungeon for around five months.

Thomas Brown was subjected to food deprivation and died in prison of starvation.

Cornfoot was also forced to confess under the influence of torture, and she also withdrew her confession. She was then cruelly imprisoned in a steeple but escaped. A more dreadful fate awaited her, however, although not at the hands of the authorities. While hiding out at the house of another suspected witch, she was seized by a mob of people who were furious that she had escaped punishment. They angrily took the law into their own hands and beat her and strung her up so that they could pelt her with stones. She was then placed under a heavy door, which was then covered with heavy stones until she was pressed to death. Finally a horse and cart were driven back and forth over her corpse in case there were any vestiges of life left in it. No legal action was taken against the mob for this barbaric treatment, probably because the authorities were in sympathy with their action.

See Chapter 3, Pittenweem Witches, page 107.

Famous American Witchcraft Trials

Salem Trials

By far the most famous of the New World witchcraft trials took place in Salem in Massachusetts between 1692 and 1693. At their centre was the extraordinary behaviour of a group of girls and young women. A group of them, between the ages of twelve and twenty, began having fits, making strange noises and contorting their bodies. The group included eleven-year-old Abigail Williams and her cousin, nine-year-old Elizabeth Parris, the first two girls to become affected by the strange fits, eighteen-year-old Elizabeth Booth, seventeen-year-old Elizabeth Hubbard, nineteen-year-old Mercy Lewis, eighteen-year-old Susan Sheldon, twenty-year-old Mary Warren, sixteen-year-old Mary Walcott, twenty-year-old Sarah Churchill and twelve-year-old Ann Putnam. Later the hysterical behaviour spread to others.

Cause of the Hysteria

There seemed no reason for the girls' strange behaviour. After consulting with some other ministers of the church, the local minister, Samuel Parris, father of one of the earliest of the girls to be affected and one of the youngest, decided to call in the local doctor, William Griggs, who was the employer of another of the affected girls, Elizabeth Hubbard. Griggs was unable to come up with any medical diagnosis for the condition of the girls and finally stated that it was his belief that they had been bewitched.

In order to cure the girls, it was believed that whoever had been responsible for casting spells on them had to be identified and punished. The girls were approached, questioned and asked to tell the authorities who was responsible for their bewitched state. The real cause of the girls' behaviour remains unknown, although various suggestions have been put forward, ranging from repressed sexuality to the repression of women, to local politics and feuds, to the presence of a cereal disease, known as ergot, in the flour (which could have given rise to a form of food poisoning, causing hallucinations), to simple mischievous deception and a desire for attention. A popular and plausible suggestion is that Elizabeth Parris and Abigail Williams had become interested in the occult from stories about voodoo told to them by Tituba Indian, a servant who had been brought with him by the Reverend Parris from Barbados. Whatever the real reason, the girls appear to have been happy to go along with the witchcraft theory and lost no time in pointing the finger of suspicion at several local women.

Salem was not unique in having young girls at the centre of accusations of witchcraft. There were cases in England of young girls going into fits, sometimes later assumed to be epileptic fits, and then blaming their condition on some woman in the area, usually someone who had offended the accuser or her family in some way. In Salem it was the scale of the accusations, both in terms of the numbers of accusers and accused, that was remarkable. As to the acceptance of children's statements in witchcraft trials, this was not unique either. Although it was frequently disallowed by law, the presence of such a law was frequently deliberately overlooked.

The girls and young women who were the accusers lived in a small, relatively closed community and all knew each other well. They would have been used to telling each other stories and exchanging secrets. Conditions were therefore ripe for their affecting each other with their hysteria, especially if they had been dabbling in the occult. Once they began with their accusations, the whole thing took on a life of its own, and it would have been difficult for them to put a stop to it, even if they had wanted to. The speed with which the witchcraft hysteria spread was terrifying, and several factors contributed to this – feelings of political unrest, hostile raids by the Native American Indians, a harsh winter that had resulted in poor crops and a smallpox epidemic. Salem was ready for a scapegoat and found it in witchcraft.

First Suspects

The girls were clever in their first choice of suspects. The first three to be named were not people whom the community would rush to defend since they were all in their own way on the very fringe of society and none was a member of the church. Tituba Indian, not surprisingly was the first to be named. She and her husband had been brought from their native Barbados by the Reverend Parris to be his servants, and she was already popularly supposed to have powers connected with the occult and had probably told her young charges, Elizabeth Parris and Abigail Williams, tales of voodoo and witchcraft from her native country. Next to be named by the girls were Sarah Good and Sarah Osborne. The former was a beggar woman and the latter an elderly cripple who had shocked the local community by allowing one of her servants to live in her house before marrying him.

Spectral Influences

These three outcasts of society were arrested and appeared at a preliminary before local magistrates John Hawthorne and Jonathan Corwin. The women were questioned and their accusers were allowed to be present at these interrogations. It was then that the occurrences began that were to make the Salem trials so remarkable. The girls were actually standing in front of the accused and patently obviously not being touched by them, yet they claimed that they were being pinched and bitten by them. It was the girls' contention that the women's spectres were harming them, although such spectres were visible only to the girls. They put on a convincing performance of being physically tormented and often pointed to some creature in the room, such as a bird in the rafters, as being the embodiment of the spectre of one of the accused.

Tituba's Confession

At the hearing Sarah Good and Sarah Osborne both denied any connection with witchcraft but, unfortunately for them, Tituba decided to make a confession associating herself with witchcraft. Worse, she identified Good and Osborne as fellow witches with whom she had attended meetings. Then she went on to claim that there was a coven of witches in Massachusetts led by a tall man dressed in black who had made her sign a book in blood. This was taken as evidence that Tituba had fulfilled one major condition for being a proven witch – she had signed a pact with the devil.

Tituba was the least likely of the accused to be acquitted on a charge of witchcraft. Even before the girls' behaviour and naming of names there had been rumours in the village about her connection with the occult. It is likely that she confessed to witchcraft thinking that by doing so she would save her life, it being the case in the American colonies, although not in mainland Europe, that making a confession would save one from execution.

The confession of Tituba and her talk of a coven struck fear into the hearts of local people. This was in part because of rumours that had circulated some years previously to the effect that Salem Village would be destroyed by a group of witches and that the household of the local minister would in some way be connected to this. As if in response to Tituba's confession and the increasing unease, the girls extended their range of accused. They appear to have been aided and abetted in this by Mrs Thomas Putnam, the mother of Ann Putnam, one of the accusers.

Accusations against the Godly

By this point the magistrates were much more inclined to believe the girls than they had been originally. In fact they were among those who encouraged the girls to name other names and did not question the veracity of their accusations, even when well-respected women in the village were accused. Among these were Martha Corey and Rebecca Nurse.

Martha Corey was acknowledged to be of excellent character, a devout Christian and regular churchgoer and wife of a local landowner. Nurse was one of the most respected people in the community and a regular churchgoer. Had such people been among the first of those accused by the girls, the magistrates and others would have been much more likely to look with incredulity on the claims of the girls. However, by this stage in the proceedings, there was no such thing as incredulity. The court simply accepted anything that the girls said, and they began accusing people from outside

Salem Village itself, twenty-two communities being eventually involved. By this time several other adults had joined Mrs Putnam in claiming that they were being attacked by spectres of witches. Among these was John Indian, husband of Tituba.

There was often an element of vengeance in accusations of witchcraft. Such an element was very probably inherent in the charging of John and Elizabeth Proctor. They, too, were upstanding members of the community, but John Proctor had greatly offended one of the group of girls, Mary Warren. She was a servant in the Proctors' household and had been beaten by her master when she first started suffering from fits and accusing people of being witches. Following the beating, her fits and strange behaviour mysteriously disappeared. The other girls would not have looked on this kindly, and, indeed, they named Mary Warren as a witch also, which action acted as a warning to the other accusers not to change sides. As for Mary, she simply confirmed the girls' accusations and became one of them again.

Yet another unlikely person was accused by the girls. This was George Burroughs, a minister who had officiated at the church in Salem from 1680 until 1682. He had once lodged with the Putnam family and had incurred their hostility. He was accused by the girls of having his spectre bite and pinch them, and it was alleged that it was substantiation of this claim that the bite marks matched his teeth. Another serious accusation made by the girls was that he had made some of them sign a book supplied by the devil, thereby making them sign a pact with the devil. He was also accused of bringing them effigies, or poppets, representing people so that the girls could stick pins in them and therefore bring harm to the people concerned. More serious accusations, including murder and performing blasphemous rites mimicking Puritan services, were made against him. In fact, the conclusion was reached that he was the head of the coven described by Tibuta.

Doubts

And so the hysteria continued, and more and more people were implicated. When a Justice of the Peace, Dudley Bradstreet, began to be concerned at the scale of the accusations and at the calibre of the people against whom they were levelled, he refused to sign any more arrest warrants. It was a sign of the times that he himself was promptly accused of witchcraft, but he was fortunate enough to escape before he could be tried.

In a similar category was John Willard. A local farmer, he was a deputy constable who had been involved in the arrest of the first suspects. However, as time went on and the whole thing appeared to be getting out of hand, he had second thoughts and was heard to say that the real guilty ones were the girls who had originally made the accusations. This was talk that was not to be tolerated and, having had wind of impending accusations against him, he fled. He was, however, not so lucky as Bradsheet and was captured, charged and hanged.

Second Thoughts and Retraction

As the hysteria continued, some of the girls appear to have had second thoughts and to have shown signs of admitting deception. Sarah Churchill actually admitted at one point to deceiving the court when her employer, George Jacobs, was arrested and interrogated. Mary Warren also began to indicate that deception had been involved when her employers, the Proctors, were thrown in prison, having had their property seized, leaving her in charge of their five children. Under threats from their co-accusers, however, both girls changed their minds and retracted their statements of deception.

Torture and Giles Corey

The Salem witchcraft trials, in common with others in the American colonies and in England, did not involve the horrendous physical torture by instruments that were such a feature of the trials conducted in mainland Europe. There was, however, at least one exception to this absence of torture, and this was the torture of a Massachusetts landowner, Giles Corey.

The reason for his harsh physical torture was that he refused to plead and remained silent during the reading of the indictment against him. He thought that if he did not answer to the charge he could not be tried and convicted. It is possible that he was conscious of the fact that if he were to be convicted his property would be confiscated and thought that if he could avoid trial and conviction his property would remain his.

The authorities took a very dim view of his refusal to cooperate and decided to punish him into answering the accusation. The punishment was cruel and severe, especially in view of the fact that he was an old man of eighty. Corey was taken to a field, where he was held to the ground, naked, by a series of stakes. He was then covered by a large wooden plank on which were gradually placed more and more heavy stones. Corey still refused to cooperate and he was crushed to death. At one point the weights were so heavy that his tongue was pushed out of his mouth but Sheriff George Corwin simply pushed it back in with his cane.

Such cruel treatment was actually against the law in the American colonies, and because of this and because of the fact that there was still a degree of humanity in some members of the community, there was some concern expressed about what had happened to Corey. However, people were generally afraid to speak out and, in any case, the Putnam family brought new evidence against Corey and nothing was done.

Corey's treatment was thankfully unusual but, although those accused of witchcraft in Salem were not subjected to actual physical torture, their plight was nevertheless desperate. They were left to languish in prison, usually chained up, for months on end, not knowing what their fate was to be but fearing the worst, worrying about their families outside and all the while witnessing yet more people joining their ranks.

Politics and Trials

The length of time the accused were imprisoned before trial was in part a result of politics. In 1629, when Massachusetts Bay was established as a Puritan colony, it enjoyed the advantages of self-rule. However, in 1684 its independence was greatly restricted by the revocation of its original charter by the English courts. On the overthrow of its governor in 1688, when William and Mary ascended the British throne, the colony lost the authority that it needed to try capital cases. No trials of this nature could be held unless Massachusetts obtained a new charter conferring on it its former powers. Thus all the accused had to endure the misery of prison without a formal trial for a long time.

Finally, in May 1692, a new governor of Massachusetts was appointed by the Crown. His name was Sir William Phips, and he arrived having in his possession a new charter conferring the requisite authority to try capital cases. Thus the witchcraft trials of Salem could begin.

The Trials Begin

The new governor established what was known as a Court of Oyer and Terminer, literally a court formed 'to hear and determine'. There had been much delay up until then but from 2 June, when the court first sat, little time was lost in trying and sentencing the accused witches. Indeed, the first of the accused, Bridget Bishop, was hanged on 10 June.

Spectral Evidence

As has been described above, the accusers claimed that the spectres of the accused appeared to them, sometimes in changed shape, and harmed them by biting and pinching them. Other people could not see these spectres unless the girls decided that a passing bird or animal was actually the spectre of one of the accused, but much credence was given to this spectral evidence

There were people who were worried about the use of such evidence. It was extremely unusual, and concern was raised about it from a theological as well as a legal point of view. The local ministers considered the matter and advised the courts against placing too much value on spectral evidence alone. This advice was by no means always taken by the court, many of whose members felt that their ability to harm the girls in spectral form was simply an extension of the pact that witches were traditionally supposed to make with the devil. In any case, the other forms of supposed evidence advocated by the ministers were neither factual nor reliable. Everything depended on the behaviour and claims of the accusers.

Falling at the Sight

One example of evidence of guilt concerned the behaviour of the accusers in the presence of the accused. If one of the accused looked at one of the accusers and the accuser collapsed, usually writhing in a fit, this was taken as clear evidence that the accused was a witch. No thought seems to have been given to the fact that this was simply an extension of the girls' hysteria and could easily be faked.

The Touch Test

Another supposedly reliable test involved the accusers being touched by the accused. If the accusers, who were still regularly afflicted by fits and attacks of gibbering, were touched by one of the accused in the course of a fit and immediately fell still and quiet then the accused was held to be a witch. Again this supposed evidence left the accused entirely at the mercy of the accusers.

Unjust Trials

Like many witchcraft trials elsewhere, the Salem trials could hardly be called just. Apart from the treatment meted out to Giles Corey (*see* page 28), there was an absence of physical torture. However, the accused were often convicted purely on unlikely evidence supplied by the accusers. Efforts were supposed to be made to obtain corroborative evidence, but such evidence was usually suspect. For example, if someone died in pain not long after having an argument with one of the accused, this could be taken as a clear indication that the accused had used witchcraft to bring death to his or her enemy as an act of vengeance. Anyone accused by the girls was thrown in prison to await trial, and after that conviction was almost a certainty.

For the most part the accused were denied the right to be represented by a lawyer. During interrogation, questions were expressed in such a way that made it almost impossible for the accused not to incriminate himself or herself. People were urged to confess on the grounds that such confessions would earn them a reprieve or at least save them from execution.

A case that illustrates the lack of justice involves Rebecca Nurse. This much respected member of the community was accused and tried but acquitted. On hearing the verdict, the girls, who were, as always, present at the trial, went into fits. The judge, Chief Justice Stoughton, was impressed with the reaction of the girls and immediately asked the jury to reconsider their verdict. Doubtless worried for their own safety, the members of the jury obliged the judge by reconsidering their decision and bringing in a verdict of guilty. Rebecca Nurse had many loyal friends, and they took a petition on her behalf to the governor to seek a reprieve. Initially this was granted, but later it was rescinded and Nurse was executed on 19 July 1692, along with Sarah Good, Sarah Martin and others.

Salem Confessions

The confessions were mostly acquired by means of question and answer sessions, which were standard elsewhere in witchcraft trials. Thus the Salem questions bore a resemblance to confessions obtained in the course of witchcraft trials in other parts of the world. Standard elements included consorting with the devil, signing a pact with him and flying to coven meetings on a broomstick.

Salem Executions

Those condemned to death on having been found guilty of witchcraft were executed by hanging. Their bodies were then placed in a shallow grave on Gallows' Hill, it being the accepted opinion that witches were consorts of the devil and so were not suitable candidates for Christian burial.

As has been mentioned above, Bridget Bishop was the first to be hanged, on 10 June. She was followed by Rebecca Nurse, Sarah Good, Sarah Martin, Elizabeth How and Sarah Wilds on 19 July. Further hangings followed on 19 August when John Willard,

John Proctor, Reverend George Burroughs, Martha Carrier and George Jacobs met their deaths.

Burroughs caused much consternation when, just before his execution, he faultlessly recited the Lord's Prayer to the assembled crowd. It was a traditional sign of witchcraft for the accused not to be able to carry out such a feat. There were immediate demands for the minister's release. These were not satisfied by the girls' claims that the devil had helped him, because there was an accepted belief that reciting the Lord's Prayer was a deed beyond the capability of the devil. However, the Reverend Cotton Mather succeeded in convincing the crowd that the work of the devil was afoot, and Burroughs was hanged.

There were further executions on 22 September. Those who were hanged then included Martha Corey, Alice Parker, Mary Parker, Mary Esty, Margaret Scott, Ann Pudeater, Samuel Wardell and Wilmott Redd. Samuel Wardell had been so intimidated by the whole trial process that he had confessed to having signed a pact with the devil. To no avail did he retract his confession, and he was sent to the gallows. During the execution process he choked on smoke from the executioner's pipe, an act that was claimed by the girls to be prompted by the devil to prevent him from confessing.

In all nineteen people were executed. Even more were sentenced to death but for various reasons did not actually go to the gallows. These included Elizabeth Faulkner and Abigail Faulkner, who were reprieved on the grounds of pregnancy, and Ann Foster and Sarah Osborne, who died in prison.

The Beginning of the End

By the time of the above executions, the girls and others who had joined the ranks of the accusers were in a position of extreme power, but the scale of the accusations was beginning to worry a great many people. The girls, however, were unperturbed and quite clearly felt that they could accuse anyone and get away with it. In this assumption they were quite wrong. Their credibility was called into serious question when they had the temerity to accuse the wife of the governor, Sir Williams Phips.

This was a step too far, and on 29 October the governor dissolved the court that had been trying the supposed witches. There remained the problem of what to do about the many accused witches who were languishing in jail awaiting trial. A new court was established and deprived of the right to admit spectral evidence.

The debarring of spectral evidence was an extremely important measure. Without it most of the accused were acquitted by the various juries. A major problem with the new court from the point of view of the accused was that it still had William Stoughton as chief justice, and he had been zealous in making convictions. To some extent his influence was negated, but three people were convicted and he rapidly signed the warrants for their execution so that there would be no time for them to be reprieved. He also signed warrants for the execution of five people who had been convicted in September of the previous year.

Stoughton had hoped to have these executions carried out before anyone could prevent them. However, the governor was anxious to avoid more bloodshed and reprieved all the condemned people. The court sat for the last time on 9 May. All those accused were acquitted, and the Salem witchcraft hysteria was finally at an end.

Atonement

When the trials ended, many people began to question whether they should ever have taken place. In the absence of hysteria, what had gone on was viewed in the cold light of day. In 1696 many of the jurors made a public confession admitting that they had been guilty of error. They confessed that there had in fact been insufficient information relating to the cases and insufficient understanding on their part as to what was going on. They also begged forgiveness of the relatives of those who had been put to death.

Steps of atonement were taken by the clergy and state. A day of fasting and public apology, known as the Official Day of Humiliation, was held in 1697. In 1703 the colonial legislature of Massachusetts began to issue retroactive amnesties to the convicted and the executed and began in 1711 to grant a degree of financial compensation to the victims and their families.

As for the girls who were at the centre of the accusations and convictions, they were lucky enough to escape punishment. In general they appear not to have shown any desire to repent or ask forgiveness. Only the younger Ann Putnam seems to have been moved to make any form of reparation. It took her a long time to get around to this, fourteen years in fact, and the confession when it came was a little less than wholehearted. Delivering it in Salem Church, she laid much of the blame for 'the guilt of innocent blood' on Satan, claiming that he had deluded her.

The Aftermath

Salem never did shake off its notorious connection with witchcraft. More than three hundred years later the hysteria is still remembered and speculated over. The trials were terrible but Salem and the town of Danvers have benefited from them in that each year many tourists visit the area.

See also Chapter 3, Salem Witches, page 110.

Witch-finders

The witch-finder was an essential part of the witch trial. Sometimes witch-finders were officials appointed by the court involved in setting up witch trials, but often they were independent entrepreneurs who made a business out of the identification of witches. Motivated by a desire to make money out of their calling, and often by an inherent zeal to root out witchcraft by any means, they made it their business to acquaint themselves with the lore of witchcraft so that they could best catch their prey.

It was the witch-finders who gave the investigators the information that they needed to set the wheels of their investigations in motion. They tended not to be involved in the actual trials but spent a great deal of time snooping around villages and towns in which there was the slightest suggestion of witchcraft, listening to local gossip. Witch-finders were an itinerant breed, travelling from area to area as occasion called, and as soon as witchcraft was suspected the local authorities would call them in.

It was very much in the interests of the witch-finders to find evidence of witchcraft. Witch-finding was a well-paid profession, and it was common for them to be paid according to their success rate. Thus they were very unlikely to leave a place before having failed identified several witches and to having obtained confessions using such investigative methods as swimming (*see* page 46). Having identified as many as possible supposed witches in the area and seen them safely committed for trial, most witch-finders left the area and moved on to pastures new to find other rich pickings. The actual trials were not their concern.

However, they were inclined to direct their zeal at people of relatively low social standing or at people already known to be at odds with the authorities. They did not wish to antagonise local communities or local authorities by accusing popular or distinguished local residents. On the other hand, they were very much aware of the fact that the wealthier an accused witch was, the more money would come into the coffers of the courts and investigators and thus the more money they themselves would be likely to receive. (DE LANCRE, Pierre *see* Witchcraft Trial Judges, page 37.)

Matthew Hopkins

Witch-finders were particularly active in the German states in the early part of the seventeenth century, but they also operated elsewhere. Of the English witch-finders the most notorious was Matthew Hopkins, who gave himself the title of Witch-finder General and operated in the middle part of the seventeenth century in East Anglia and neighbouring areas. He is credited with having been the instigator of the conviction or execution of at least 230 accused witches, this figure representing more than all the other witch-finders together achieved during the years of witchcraft hysteria in England.

Hopkins studied law and was making a modest living as a lawyer in Ipswich when he had the idea of becoming a witch-finder. He moved to Manningtree in Essex, the latter having a tradition of being associated with witchcraft. At that point in the mid-1640s he knew little about witchcraft, although he had read *Daemonologie*, written by James I. However, he advertised his services to anyone who wished to root out witchcraft in his or her town or village.

He had chosen a good time at which to capitalise on witchcraft. It being in the middle of the Civil War (1642–48), the country was in the grip of political unrest and was looking for a scapegoat for its many ills. Witchcraft was as good a candidate as any. In addition, Puritan society already had a fear and hatred of witchcraft.

Hopkins' modus operandi was to collect local gossip and listen to tales of local feuds. The gossip and tales he would then try to turn into formal accusations of witchcraft and inform the authorities. His first victim was Elizabeth Clarke, an old crone from Manningtree with only one leg – (*see* Chapter 3, Chelmsford Witches, page 69). She was old and strange, and that made her an obvious candidate for being accused of witchcraft. Hopkins soon tortured her into confessing to consorting with the devil and to having familiars and also into naming others.

They in turn named others, and soon thirty-eight people had been charged, with many local people coming forward to give supposed evidence at Hopkins' instigation. By this time Hopkins had acquired an assistant, John Stearne, and now he took on four more, one of whom was Mary Phillips, and set to extend his witch-finding empire throughout other parts of England, such as Suffolk, Cambridgeshire, Huntingdonshire, Norfolk, etc.

By this time he was making an extremely good living since he charged extremely high fees, arguing that witch-finding was a very skilled task and that he was very successful. No elderly woman of strange looks or behaviour was safe from him, and his success at getting charges brought was phenomenal. His success was in great part due to his cruel methods, and he was greatly feared.

He was excessively zealous in many of the tortures, which stopped short of the use of torturing devices, banned in English courts. The tortures, applied in order to obtain confessions, included many of those mentioned above as induced torture – looking for the devil's mark and much given to the painful use of pricking to identify insensitive areas. His victims were also deprived of food and sleep, sleep deprivation being achieved by watching and waking. They were also made to walk up and down constantly until they fell down with exhaustion.

Hopkins showed both zeal and cunning when interrogating people with a view to getting them to confess to witchcraft. He and his assistants were adept at phrasing questions and in interpreting the answers in such a way that it was almost impossible for them not to incriminate themselves. The crimes of which he accused his victims were largely the traditional ones associated with witchcraft – death or injury of people or livestock by witchcraft, the keeping of familiars, the use of a broomstick to fly to coven meetings or sabbats, etc – and Hopkins was particularly fond of the crime that involved the accused signing a pact with the devil.

Hopkins' zeal was particularly successful in the town of Bury St Edmunds. There he was responsible for the accusation of nearly two hundred people. Nearly seventy of them are thought to have been executed. Among these was an old man, named John Lowes, who had been a Royalist and a member of the clergy. He was subjected to sleep deprivation until he confessed, one of the charges brought against him being that he had used witchcraft to sink a ship, although no motive was established.

The witch-finder went on to be responsible for other deaths in other counties, but his career, although terrible, was short. He began to come in for quite a lot of criticism. First his use of swimming was condemned and he was forced to stop using this method of obtaining confessions. He continued with his other methods, such as sleep deprivation and starvation, but soon he was publicly criticised for his excessive zeal in applying these and for his excessive fees.

In April 1646 the Reverend John Gaule, minister at Great Staughton in Huntingdonshire, objected to the presence of Hopkins and his assistants and publicly spoke against their investigations, saying that no wrinkled old woman was safe from them, however innocent. Hopkins ceased his witch-finding activities after that but wrote a pamphlet entitled *The Discovery of Witches* in defence of himself and his methods in 1647.

After that he is surrounded by mystery. Various possibilities have been put forward as to what happened to him but it is all a matter of speculation. Possibly the most likely explanation is that supplied by his assistant, John Stearne. He gave it as his opinion in 1648 that Hopkins had never enjoyed good health and had died of consumption in Manningtree in 1647.

Hopkins was such an important and hated figure that his seeming disappearance gave rise to various legends. One of these was quite possibly simply the result of wishful thinking on the part of those with cause to hate him. This legend has it that he was himself accused of witchcraft and subjected to the swimming test. He floated, thereby indicating his guilt, and was chased out of town, although one version of the legend has it that he was hanged.

According to another legend, he found England so hostile to him that he decided to follow some of his fellow Puritans and go to New England. Indeed, there has even been some unlikely speculation that as an old man he was involved in the Salem Witchcraft Trials.

There has also been speculation about what Hopkins' motives were. Certainly he charged a great deal of money, but greed alone was not thought to have motivated him. He appears to have genuinely believed in witchcraft and to have been filled with a religious-like zeal to stamp it out. On the other hand, he also appears to have enjoyed the power that his post of witch-finder gave him and the fear that people felt for him.

Witchcraft Trial Judges

Many of these were particularly cruel and many of them were simply interested in finding as many people as possible guilty. Few made the effort to establish by absolute proof the guilt of the accused and few showed clemency.

Pierre de Lancre

One of the most notorious of such judges, in fact arguably the most notorious, was Pierre de Lancre, who conducted his operations in the Basque region of France. He was a French lawyer who was ordered by the king, Henri IV, in 1609 to go to the locality of Labourd, which it was claimed was being plagued by witches. It was de Lancre's task to eradicate this supposed plague of witches, and he took his task very seriously indeed, often combining the roles of witch-finder and trial judge.

De Lancre was convinced that the Basques, with their strange language and customs and their remote location, were exactly the kind of people who would be affected by witchcraft. He was also already convinced both of the actuality and dangers of witchcraft and filled with a determination to eradicate it.

He saw witchcraft everywhere and secured convictions on the slightest of evidence. Sometimes this supposed evidence comprised only completely uncorroborated accusations by children as young as five years old. Indeed, his judgements relied heavily on the testimony of children and on the use of torture to extract confessions.

De Lancre was particularly interested in gathering evidence of nocturnal orgiastic sabbats at which the devil was supposedly worshipped amid much merriment, nudity and lewd behaviour. It has been suggested that he was in fact fascinated by the descriptions of these and by the women who were supposedly involved in them.

Indeed, he is said to have had some of the condemned witches dance for him while he played the flute during court intervals. Nevertheless, he punished harshly those confessing to being involved in sabbats.

He was also particularly interested in the potions and poisons supposedly brewed by those accused of witchcraft and in the shape-changing traditionally associated with witchcraft. The devil appears to have been something of an obsession with de Lancre, and there are various stories about claims that he is said to have made with reference to being attacked by the devil and witches in his bedroom.

The judge was infamous for the speed with which he processed trials and executions and for the number of people involved in these. He is said to have had executed as many as six hundred people by the time he was recalled in 1610, and it is not surprising that terror reigned in the area while he was present.

It was bad enough that de Lancre was so zealous and unreasonable in his attitude towards witchcraft but his attitude affected others. He wrote the details of his investigations and trials in three books, one published in 1612, one in 1622, and one in 1627, and these acted as guides to other witchcraft trial judges. He died in Paris in 1631.

Witch-hunts

The determined efforts to identify and root out witchcraft were known as witch-hunts, and these were pursued with remarkable zeal, particularly by professional witch-finders. No one, however innocent, was safe when full-scale witch-hunts were in progress, and they did much to incite the hysteria that was such a feature of the witchcraft period in history.

Although the word 'witch-finder' remained restricted to describing those who set about seeking out and accusing witches, the word 'witch-hunt' took on a more general meaning than its literal one. It came to mean an orchestrated campaign to identify and get rid of anyone holding dissenting or unorthodox views, this supposedly being done in the public interest. Later the expression was used in an even more general way to mean simply an orchestrated campaign to get rid of someone from a post, etc.

Charges of Witchcraft

The reasons for people being charged with witchcraft were often extremely nebulous. Since it was extremely difficult to define the exact nature of witchcraft, so it was even more difficult to prove it. Fortunately for the courts, proof was not something that bothered them overly much and people were charged on the flimsiest of evidence. The basis of many of the charges was often simply vengeance, the result of a local feud or simply chance if a determined witch-finder was at work. In continental Europe the basis of a charge was not important since confession was of prime importance, but in England confessions were supposed to be backed up by supposed proof. Therefore there were many traditional bases for charges.

Appearance

Often people had a preconceived idea of what a witch looked like – female, elderly, unattractive, solitary and strange. Thus any old woman who lived alone and was ugly or misshapen and indulged in strange behaviour, such as talking to herself, was a prime target. This was particularly true in England and Scotland. In continental Europe it was by no means unusual for young women to be selected as targets for accusations of witchcraft, especially if they came from wealthy families.

The archetypal old woman of the English witchcraft tradition was very vulnerable when it came to undergoing persuasion to extract a confession. She might have been already in poor health, whether mentally or physically, at the time of torture and likely to agree to anything. There is certainly reason to believe that the level of detail in some of the confessions relating to sabbats suggests mental problems.

Familiars

An old woman living alone in a village would be very likely to keep a pet. Alas this fact could only add to the likelihood of her being charged with witchcraft. It was part of witchcraft lore, especially in England and Scotland and later in the American colonies, that witches kept familiars. These were demons or imps supposedly assigned to witches by the devil to assist them in their witchcraft. Their outward appearance, however, was such as to enable them to blend into the background.

They often took the form of domestic animals, especially cats, but also dogs, and thus any old woman alleviating her loneliness by keeping a pet stood in great danger of being accused of witchcraft. Owning several cats was most unwise. However, it was not necessary actually to own a cat or dog in order to be accused of having a familiar. One passing the door was good enough to warrant a charge of keeping a familiar.

Virtually any creature, especially if it was relatively small, could be suspected of being a familiar. The hare was a particular favourite, and it was unfortunate indeed if a hare made an appearance in a field near the home of someone already suspected of witchcraft. Another creature much associated with witchcraft was the toad, and it was as well not to have one pop up in one's garden. The crow and the blackbird were other favourites, but a creature such as a mouse, rat, ferret, hedgehog, or even a bee, grasshopper or ant could be suspect also, and there were more unusual ones. Since it was impossible never to come into contact with a small animal the charge of having a familiar was a common one.

Witches were popularly believed to take good care of their familiars, often baptising them, feeding them well and rewarding them with drops of their own blood. This blood was thought to be sucked by the animals from the fingers of the witches or from protuberances or spots on the skin. Some witches were even thought to have an extra nipple for this very purpose.

Familiars were traditionally held to be able to disappear at will and to have the capability of taking on more than one shape. Their function was to help their owners carry out their various acts of bewitchment. They were supposedly able to execute such deeds as turn milk sour and injure livestock. Sometimes they were alleged to substitute for broomsticks to enable witches to fly through the air to coven meetings.

Healing

It was common before the days of chemical medicines, and indeed becoming relatively common again now, for people to use things gathered from the countryside to try to heal or cure illness or wounds. There was often one person in a village who was particularly skilled in the making of herbal medicines and ointments. Sometimes he or she would have acquired particular skills in healing.

Such skills were useful to the community, but having a reputation for possessing them was very unwise during the period of witchcraft hysteria. Having the ability to heal in any way was seen as evidence of the supernatural. Anyone with a reputation for healing or for supplying medicinal herbs or potions was likely, indeed, to be accused of witchcraft.

Prophecies and Fortune-telling

Anyone who was credited with being able to foretell the future was at risk of being accused of dabbling in witchcraft. Divination was held to be supernatural and so probably a gift from the devil.

Causing Death, Injury or Damage by Witchcraft

It was common for someone to be accused of using witchcraft to kill someone. The accused killer did not have to be anywhere near the victim when death occurred. That was the beauty of witchcraft. At particular risk of such a charge was someone who had a particular reason for disliking someone who died or was killed.

Sometimes it was not death but injury or illness that occurred. For example, a person could be accused of witchcraft if someone started having fits, as was the case in the celebrated Salem Witchcraft Trials. It was not always people who were involved in accusations of death or injury by witchcraft. Often the basis of an accusation was that someone had killed or caused injury or illness in farm livestock. Hens that stopped laying or cows that ceased to yield any milk were enough for this charge to be made.

The failure of crops could also be conveniently blamed on alleged witches.

Storm-raising

The problem with many of the charges made against supposed witches was that, although they were impossible to prove, they were often difficult to disprove, and it was common to assume an alleged witch guilty until proved otherwise. If someone accused of witchcraft lived by the sea and a storm occurred that resulted in the wreck of or damage to a ship, he or she could readily be accused of storm-raising, a common traditional feat of witches. It was particularly dangerous for the accused if there was someone on board the ship who for some reason was disliked by him or her.

Storm-raising was a favourite charge in communities near the sea where seafaring was a regular part of life, but charges of storm-raising could also be brought against people who lived in inland communities. If storms destroyed crops, a suitable candidate for being accused of storm-raising was sought out.

Flying by Broomstick

The broomstick was traditionally held to be the preferred form of transport for witches. Questions relating to this were a standard part of the interrogation process carried out in order to elicit confessions. The standard confession would thus contain an admission of flying by broomstick. Occasionally neighbours would claim that they had seen the accused fly out of her window on a broomstick.

Devil's Pact

Admitting that he or she had entered into a pact with the devil, traditionally written in blood taken from the witch's left hand, was a standard part of an accused witch's confession, elicited by standard interrogation and usually by torture. The instigators of the Inquisition in continental Europe were particularly keen on pacts with the devil since these were a clear sign of heresy, and they were anxious to see witchcraft viewed as a form of, or as an extension of, heresy. The fact that so many people, under the influence of terrible torture, eventually confessed to signing pacts with the devil gave credence to the belief that such a thing actually existed and was an essential part of witchcraft.

There were two possible reasons for supposedly signing such a pact with the devil. One of these, and the one that was most common in the case of witchcraft, was that the devil, in return for the signing of the pact and so declaring allegiance to him, would help the witch in any way possible with the pursuit of his or her magic. The supplying of a familiar was often part of the deal, and the magic often was assumed to be a means of causing harm to others. The other reason to sign such a pact was the Faustian one where someone supposedly signed a pact with the devil giving the devil his or her soul in exchange for unbridled pleasure, wealth, power, etc.

The idea of signing a pact with the devil was of great importance in the witchcraft trials in mainland Europe where people could be convicted of witchcraft on the basis of confession alone. In England worries about witchcraft concentrated on the harm that witches could do rather than on the fact that they had turned their back on God. Thus the devil's pact as such did not play a major role in most English witchcraft trials, although the witch-finder Matthew Hopkins (*see* page 34) did obtain confessions of signed pacts and used these as evidence.

The pact could be either oral or written, but the latter was more popular as a reason for levelling an accusation of witchcraft. The signing ceremony might take place privately, sometimes under the auspices of another witch, or it might take place publicly at a sabbat. The courts much preferred the public ceremony because then they might acquire not only the confession of the person who did the signing but supposed proof from others who had attended the sabbat and allegedly witnessed the signing. Conveniently for the courts, it was apparently traditional for the devil to keep the signed pact and so it could not be produced as physical proof of an association with witchcraft.

Attendance at Sabbats

It also became a standard part of a witch's confession that he or she had attended a sabbat (*see* Chapter 4, page 185), a great celebratory gathering of witches, usually held in some remote location and characterised by feasting, drinking and dancing, often in the nude, uninhibited, indiscriminate sexual encounters and worship of the devil. Having a witch confess to having attended a sabbat was a good opportunity for the courts to illustrate just how lacking witches were in morality and piety.

Tests, Confession and Torture

At the height of the witch trials, the cruellest tortures imaginable were used on people accused of witchcraft in order to force a confession out of them and in order to make them give the names of their accomplices in the black art or to identify other people whom they suspected of witchcraft. It was deemed that justice demanded that a person accused of witchcraft should not be executed unless he or she confessed to the crime. Furthermore, by confessing, the supposed witches would be saving their mortal souls. Therefore all manner of means were used to make sure that people did confess, and this was far from being justice.

The tortures themselves must have been agonising beyond comprehension. Many of the devices of torture imposed such unbearable pain that people would agree to anything, including confessing to witchcraft, in order that the torture and pain would stop, although some of the accused retracted these confessions on cessation of the pain. Furthermore, many of the people accused of witchcraft were elderly and their bodies and minds were far from being able to withstand even the mildest of such tortures. The tortures themselves often resulted in serious injury, death or madness. Others of the accused were already mentally unstable and the tortures were almost guaranteed to send them insane.

The prevalence of torture varied from area to area. Although there was some torture inflicted on the accused in the Salem Witch Trials, this was on a far lesser scale than in Europe and in general torture was not much used in witch trials in America.

In England and Wales, where instruments of torture were not allowed according to the common law of the countries, the level and the nature of the torture was considerably less extreme than it was in such countries as Germany, although forms of it were more widely used than in America. Scotland, however, did not fare so well, and barbarous forms of torture were used there, particularly in the reign of King James VI, later James I of England.

It was in Germany, France, Switzerland and Italy that the worst tortures took place. The crime of witchcraft was deemed to be a crime against God, and the Inquisition had already established a frightening range of tortures against suspected heresy before attention was turned towards witchcraft. Witchcraft was added to the list of heresies in 1320, and Pope Innocent VIII issued a papal bull against witchcraft in 1484. Persecution of witches was then widespread and the ruthless inquisitorial system well in gear.

A major guide to the inquisition of witches was *Malleus Maleficarum*, compiled by the Dominican Inquisitors of Pope Innocent VIII, Heinrich Kramer and James Sprenger. They emphasised the need for confession and the need to employ torture in order to extract this. There were guidelines and set procedures laid down for the courts to follow.

Tests

There were a number of tests undertaken to identify supposed witches. They were not categorised as tortures but some of them caused much pain and distress. Tests used to establish an association with witchcraft included the following.

Shaving and Probing

The accused was first of all asked to confess. Sometimes even at this stage people were so aware of the kind of ordeal that lay in front of them that they simply gave in and confessed to witchcraft, although they had absolutely no connection with it. If such confession was not forthcoming then he or she was stripped naked and shaved. This procedure may not have been construed as torture but it certainly caused embarrassment and humiliation and, in the case of women, was not infrequently carried out by a member of the opposite sex. The accused were shaved partly in case a demon might have hidden in their body hair with a view to helping them in the course of a trial and partly because a charm with magical powers might have been similarly secreted. For these same reasons the accused had to submit to have having all their orifices probed.

The Devil's Mark

Then the accused were often subjected to a search for evidence of the devil's mark. It was the belief of those zealously intent on seeking out and exterminating witchcraft that the devil made a permanent mark on the bodies of those who had sworn allegiance to him, although there was a school of thought that he made such a mark only on those whom he considered to be unreliable. The search for such a mark was one of the major tests for the presence of witchcraft.

The devil was popularly held to mark the body of his initiates in a number of ways. These included licking, kissing or touching a particular spot, raking his claws across the body or branding it with a hot iron. Such marks were frequently thought to be difficult to locate and required the most rigorous and embarrassing of searches. They were thought to be often located under the armpits, under the eyelids, and in any of the body cavities. Such a mark was considered to be definite proof of being a witch, but if the investigator was a particular zealous one and bent the rules a bit then practically any mark on the body could be construed as being a devil's mark. This was bad news indeed since few of us have mark-free bodies.

Supposed experts on the subject claimed that a mark which could be categorised as a devil's mark was easily distinguishable from harmless body blemishes, but the categorisation system was not all that foolproof, even if such a thing as a devil's mark had actually existed. It was believed that the devil's mark was insensitive to pain or incapable of bleeding and that the best way to locate such a spot was to prick the accused person all over with a sharp pin or lance until such a spot, which might be a wart, cyst, mole, scar, callus or thickened area of skin, was identified. A particularly nasty trick consisted of cutting someone so painfully on one part of the body so that all attention was focused on that and any other pain in another part of the body went unnoticed.

All in all it was unusual for an accused person to escape having an insensitive area or an area that would not bleed identified on his or her body.

There was another less common form of devil's mark. This supposedly took the form of a shape or figure. This could be a cloven hoof, traditionally associated with the devil or a hare, often connected with witchcraft, or even something seemingly innocuous such as dormouse. Since with a bit of imagination such a mark on the body could be said to resemble just about anything, this was a very easy way in which to incriminate supposed witches (*see also* Chapter 4, page 163).

Pricking

If no mark could be found, and it was rare for a zealous investigator to admit defeat, then this was not always the end of the story. Conveniently for the investigators intent on discovering evidence of witchcraft, it was believed that the devil did not always leave a mark when claiming someone for his own. Apparently he sometimes just made a small area of the body of his devotee insensitive. Being searched for such an area could be extremely painful as pins were jabbed into the body all over and it was unlikely that the investigators employed gentle tactics. This was known as pricking.

The devil's mark test was a very common one in the identification of witches and the finding of anything that could possibly be construed as one was taken as proof positive of witchcraft. Evidence of such a mark and an accusation of witchcraft were often enough to convict, and many people were executed simply because they had blemishes on their bodies.

Margaret Murray (*see* page 5) put forward the theory that devil's marks did actually exist. She did not maintain that the devil had put them there but suggested that they might have been a form of tattoo with which people practising witchcraft marked themselves. This was part of her wider theory that witchcraft actually did flourish at the time of the witch trials and was part of an organised pagan religion with its roots in very early times, having been driven underground by the coming of Christianity. Her theory is now largely discredited by historians, although they were accepted by several of her contemporaries, but many modern people who describe themselves as witches still believe that witchcraft is an ongoing ancient religion with its own established rites.

Lord's Prayer

One of the tests for witchcraft consisted of getting the accused to recite the Lord's Prayer. This had to be repeated accurately and without stumbling. If any mistakes or pauses occurred, the accused was held to be unable to complete this holy task because of his or her association with the devil. Since most of the accused would likely be trembling with terror and incapable of thinking or speaking clearly, the number of people who failed to pass this test was very high.

Swimming

Technically, swimming was not an official test of an accused witch's guilt. In England, indeed, the swimming test was declared illegal by Henry III in 1219. However, it was often used as a kind of unofficial initial test when suspicions about a person's association with witchcraft first arose and was frequently conducted by a mob of villagers with absolutely no legal backing. Sometimes the courts regarded swimming as a valuable first step in a witch trial and turned a blind eye to the fact that it was illegal.

Swimming, also known as ducking, was an ancient test of guilt that had its origins in Babylonia and was used in England pre-1219 for a range of suspected crimes before becoming associated with witchcraft.

This test of guilt consisted of binding the accused's hand and foot, often with the right thumb bound to the left big toe and vice versa, before throwing him or her into a stretch of water, such as a pond, lake or river. If the accused floated then it was taken as a sign of guilt, the theory being that the devil was helping his own to survive. If on the other hand, the accused sank, then it was supposed that the person was innocent. This, however, was often small comfort since many of the accused who sank drowned before they could be helped out of the water. Sometimes the plight of the accused was even worse because he or she was sewn into a sack before being thrown into the water.

The swimming test grew more popular in England after it was commended by James VI of Scotland and I of England in his book *Daemonologie* (1597). James was convinced that there was witchcraft abroad in his kingdom and he was determined to root it out. Swimming, he felt, would help him to do this. He was convinced that the reason people who floated were considered to be guilty of practising witchcraft was that the water would not receive into it people who had been baptised in water as Christians and then renounced this sacrament when they began associating with the devil.

Confession

Having had supposed evidence of the devil's mark found on them, the accused was usually given the opportunity to confess. It was considered an essential part of the witchcraft investigation process that the accused admitted to being a witch, as opposed to being allegedly proved to be one. The Continental courts were reluctant to sentence a supposed witch to be executed unless a confession had been obtained, although they do not appear to have been unduly concerned about whether there was any actual proof that witchcraft was involved. In England the situation was rather different since the courts usually required some form of proof, however flimsy, to back up the confession.

Since the barbarity of the witch trials, especially in mainland Europe, gradually became well known there were those who felt that they might as well make a voluntary confession right away, thinking that if they were going to be tortured into confessing anyway they could save themselves a great deal of pain. Their logic, however, tended not to pay off.

The investigators were not disposed to look kindly on these instant confessions. They felt, rightly, that they had been made to avoid pain and might well be false.

They frequently were false but not in the suspected way. It was a case of innocent people confessing to witchcraft to avoid torture, but the investigators assumed them to be guilty but to have given false details in their confessions. The only way to make sure that the correct details were given, they reasoned, was to torture these instant confessors into giving the 'real' details.

As an aid to the obtaining of a so-called voluntary confession, details of the kind of ordeal to which the accused would be subjected in order to secure an eventual confession were often relayed by the investigators, doubtless with glee.

The threat of torture, especially when it was graphically described, was quite enough to have some of the accused, although there appear to have been surprisingly few of these, agreeing to make a confession that was then deemed to be voluntary. If no voluntary confession was forthcoming then it was a case of proceeding to the next stage of the trial – the torture.

The use of the most remarkably brutal torture was common in Europe, although not so in England or the American colonies. Basically the policy of the European courts appears to have been that the accused be tortured until a confession was made. The physical agony was such that many died in the course of torture, a blessed relief for them, although it was the aim of the investigators to keep them alive. Others were driven to 'confess' to crimes that they had never committed just to have the pain stop. Many were probably driven mad.

Throughout the various tortures the accused was asked to confess. Various questions were put, and these often followed a formula, concentrating on such issues as meeting the devil, causing death by casting spells on the victim and the use of broomsticks as transport to sabbats. It is because the questions were formulaic that the confessions were so formulaic, thereby often closely resembling one another.

In order to be valid in court, the confession had to be documented. With this in mind a clerk recorded the proceedings when the inquisitor was putting his questions and demanding a confession. It was the fact of confession rather than the details that had to be recorded. There were so many accused and the questions so formulaic that the accused's confession was very rarely recorded in any detail.

Having confessed while being tortured, the accused then had to confirm the confession after a time of recovery from the torture. This was apparently to avoid any suggestion that the confession had been extracted by force – which of course it had.

It was not uncommon for confessions to be made just before the scheduled time for an execution. This was often done to lessen the pain of death. Most witches who had confessed fully to their association with witchcraft were accorded the supposed leniency of being strangled to death before they were burned at the stake. While hardly a pleasant death it was preferable to the slow agony of being burnt alive. Confession at the stake proved popular with the crowds who gathered at the place of execution as it added to the drama of the occasion.

One of the remarkable features of confessions to witchcraft is the extent to which many of them implicated other people. Perhaps this was because the confessor cherished a hope, which usually proved vain, that appearing to be helpful to the authorities would persuade them to show a degree of clemency. Perhaps there was an element of vengeance relating to past quarrels. Perhaps the naming of names was done in the spirit of wishing others to share the same misfortune as the confessor was experiencing. Or perhaps it was just part of the formulaic question and answer sessions which typified many of the witchcraft trials. At any rate, fear must have struck people's hearts if anyone they knew was charged with witchcraft.

Not confessing, even under the duress of the most severe torture, was certainly not regarded as evidence of innocence. Quite the reverse. Being able to withstand the level of physical pain to which the accused was subjected was held to be extremely unnatural and clear evidence that the devil was at work helping his initiate. In the end, if torture failed the only solution that offered itself to the investigators was execution.

Retraction

It was by no means unknown for people to try to withdraw their confessions after they had stopped being tortured and had had time to reflect on what had happened. This rarely did them any good. Usually the retraction of a confession simply resulted in renewed torture until they withdrew their retraction. Recanting was seen as evidence that the devil was using his wiles to encourage the accused to adopt delaying tactics and prevent the due process of the law. Just as some of those accused of witchcraft confessed just before execution, so did some of them chose that moment to withdraw their confessions. Again this usually resulted in more torture being administered.

Induced Torture

The degree of torture and the nature of it varied. In England physical torture using barbaric instruments of torture was not nearly as common as elsewhere. This was in part because the Inquisition, which was behind much of the torture imposed on accused witches in mainland Europe, had never made much ground in England. Its lack of success was to a great extent owing to the tenets of the English law, which debarred the courts from accepting confessions unsupported by other proof and disallowed the forms of torture that were a major part of the Inquisition's investigations.

Instead, in England what was known as induced torture was used. This was an insidious form of torture not requiring much in the way of instruments but was nevertheless capable of causing much pain and distress. Such forms of torture included depriving the accused of food or water. Sometimes they were fed a diet of salty food and then deprived of water so that they suffered the distress of terrible thirst. In particular there were two extremely common forms of this type of torture – watching and waking, and walking.

Watching and Waking

This was an example of induced torture and was much used in England, especially by Matthew Hopkins, the notorious English witch-finder, the more extreme forms of torture practised in Germany and elsewhere being not allowed. Its aim was to deprive the accused of sleep until a confession was obtained.

Everything was done to prevent the accused from sleeping. Sometimes it was just a question of the guards roughly waking people who were clearly about to sleep, but some of the methods used were more cruel. For example, those whom the guards wanted to keep awake might be rendered unable to lie down or even to sit down to sleep because of being chained to the cell wall by means of an iron bridle attached to the head and a very short iron chain. Another cruel way of keeping people from sleeping was to make them sit cross-legged on a stool for hours on end.

Walking

This was another form of induced torture. It does not sound anything like as horrific as some of the methods of torture allowed on the continent but it had a terrible effect on those who were subjected to it and was frequently efficacious in obtaining confessions. As the name suggests, this particular torture involved the accused being forced to walk up and down all the time, sometimes for days at a time, without any rest until exhaustion and collapse set in.

Torture by Device

In mainland Europe the use of barbaric methods of torture using various devices was widespread. It is for that reason that courts there had such a reputation for obtaining convictions. In the light of the pain experienced by the accused it was virtually impossible to maintain and prove one's innocence. There were degrees of torture, and if the accused successfully tolerated one form then the investigators simply moved on to one further up the scale of agony and terror.

Ironically, the cost of administering the torture, including the travel and accommodation expenses of the torturer, and also of mounting the witch trial generally, was met by the accused. If a person on trial for witchcraft had enough money then his or her funds were seized or the estate confiscated after execution. On the other hand, if the accused was impoverished or did not have enough money to pay for the considerable expense of being tried and tortured for witchcraft, then the authorities simply made the accused's relatives responsible for meeting the bill.

Rack or Ladder

The rack was not used either in England or in Scotland, which had quite a reputation for savage torture, but was used throughout Europe, particularly in France. It was a device for stretching the victim to an agonising extent. The prisoner would be laid horizontally on the rack or ladder and have his or her limbs bound to it with ropes tied with a tourniquet knot. This knot could then be tightened by gradually twisting it, the ropes controlled by it stretching the accused's arms and legs and thus the whole body. The rack, which often broke bones and tore muscles, was a horrendous form of torture but by the standards of Inquisition-style torture it was by no means the worst and tended to be used in the relatively early forms of torture to give the accused a taste of what was to come.

Boots

Known also as Spanish boots, bootikins or cashielaws, the device called boots was also a stretching instrument. It consisted of lengths of wood bound together lengthways. These lengths of wood were fitted on the legs of the accused from the ankles to the knees and were either gradually tightened by hand or knocked together with a wooden mallet. The result was broken bones and torn flesh and muscles and often legs that never walked again.

Thumbscrews

This form of torture did for the thumbs what the boots did for the lower limbs. They consisted of vices on which the thumbs of suspected witches were crushed by gradual tightening of the vices unmercifully until blood spurted. A variation on this theme of torture was the application of such vices to the toes.

Spider

The spider was a sharp iron fork used in torture. Many of those accused of witchcraft were women and the spider was used to cause injury to their breasts.

Red-hot Irons and Pincers

Much had been learnt by the practitioners of the Inquisition about inflicting pain and they were certainly not unaware of the agony to be inflicted by the use of red-hot instruments. Red-hot pincers were used to tear flesh unmercifully and were even used to tear off women's breasts.

Red-hot irons were used to burn flesh and to gouge out eyes but were also used to insert into the vagina or rectum. There was also a red-hot iron test for witchcraft. Accused witches were told to grab hold of a red-hot iron. If they succeeded in holding it they were deemed to be guilty but, by this stage in the torture proceedings, they had been subjected to such pain that they had acquired a certain amount of insensitivity to pain.

Turcas

This device was used to tear out fingernails, the torture being made severe by driving needles into the quicks after the application of the turcas. Although England was largely free of the more extreme forms of torture, particularly those that employed devices of torture, because of restrictions imposed by the legal system, this was not so true of Scotland. As an example of this, Scotland allowed the use of turcas, the device being used in the trial of John Fian (*see* Chapter 3, page 79).

Thrawing

This form of torture, popular in Scotland, involved the head being bound with ropes. It was then jerked from side to side, causing much pain and damage to the neck. An exceptionally painful refinement of this had the ropes attached to a collar studded with spikes.

Strappado

This was a more extreme form of torture, extensively practised in mainland Europe. It involved tying the hands of the accused behind their backs prior to attaching them to pulleys. The accused were then hoisted to the ceiling, heavy weights sometimes being attached to the legs or feet to increase the pain and injury. The result of this form of torture was the dislocation of shoulders and other joints. In order to increase the agony imposed by this torture it was often combined with the use of thumbscrews.

Squassation

This refers to an extreme form of strappado used on those accused who had refused to succumb to other forms of torture. The victims of this were treated to the same initial process as for strappado, heavy weights being strapped to their lower limbs as a matter of course. Then the pulley ropes holding them were suddenly released and the accused fell to the floor, only to have the fall suddenly brought to a halt by the tightening of the ropes. People who were subjected to this form of torture were lucky to escape with any undislocated bones.

Water Torture or Ordeal

A particularly barbaric form of torture involved forcing the accused to swallow great quantities of water, sometimes boiling water to add to the pain, along with lengths of knotted cord or cloth. The cord or cloth was then yanked back up violently and suddenly, and this often had the effect of disembowelling the accused.

Other Forms of Torture

There were several other forms of torture, for there was really no limit to the lengths the investigators would go to in continental Europe to ensure a conviction. Hands and ears were cut off, burning feathers dipped in sulphur were applied to sensitive areas such as the armpits and groins, fingers were immersed in pots of boiling oil and bodies were immersed in boiling-hot baths treated with lime.

Post-confession Torture

Those of the accused who confessed did so because they were driven to this action by the agony of the ordeal of torture. They probably thought that such confessions would bring an end to their pain until they faced their executioners. Frequently this was not the case, especially in mainland Europe. Those skilled in the techniques of the Inquisition were not likely to let their victims go lightly. Thus it was quite common for those condemned to die for supposed witchcraft to be subjected to flogging or branding on their way to the place of execution. At this time also, fingers, hands and tongues were sometimes cut off and nailed to the gallows. Presumably this was meant to act as an extra grisly warning to others not to become involved in witchcraft.

The End of Torture

By the middle of the seventeenth century the full horror of the savage torture to which accused witches in Europe were subjected began to be appreciated by those in power. Several German rulers, notably the Duke of Brunswick, abolished the use of torture in the areas ruled over by them and also made efforts to get other rulers to follow suit.

Execution

The Inquisition had established burning at the stake as an appropriate punishment for heretics and the same punishment was frequently meted out to witches. Witches were regarded in much the same light as heretics since they were presumed to have turned their backs on God in favour of the devil. Fire was seen as a means of purification, and in addition it was thought that only by burning witches to ashes could all remnants of their powers be destroyed. Even children sometimes were punished in this way, although many of them were punished by imprisonment or flogging rather than execution.

Burning at the stake was a very painful death, particularly if the wood used was green and therefore slow to kindle and burn, resulting in a slow as well as agonising death. In Italy and Spain witches were often subjected to the agony of being burnt alive at the stake. In other countries, such as France, Germany and Scotland, they were either strangled at the stake or hanged before being burnt, but this clemency could be revoked if the accused retracted a confession of witchcraft at the time of execution. Courts in England and the American colonies usually ordered those found guilty of witchcraft to be hanged and they were burned alive only if found guilty of what was regarded as treason.

The execution of a witch was a major public occasion, and crowds would gather enthusiastically to view the spectacle, which was meant to serve as a warning to others as well as punishment to the person condemned. People facing execution were often expected to repeat their confession or otherwise confirm their guilt after having had read out a list of the crimes of which they had been found guilty. Sometimes they added to the excitement of the crowd by withdrawing their confession and thus deprived themselves of the privilege of being hanged or strangled before going to the stake.

Usually the execution took place shortly after the sentencing, indeed as soon as an executioner was summoned and the fire built. Local people were advised of the coming event by the tolling of church bells or by the blaring of trumpets. As was the case with the expenses for the trial and torture, the expenses of the execution were paid out of the condemned person's estate or by relatives.

In Scotland the execution was not so speedy. The days before the burning of a witch were often taken up by fasting and preaching. The condemned witch was usually first strangled and then burnt but not too much care was taken to check that death by strangling had actually occurred. It was not unknown for the condemned person simply to be unconscious or semiconscious when committed to the fire. If they were still alive and attempted to get out of the fire there were many willing helpers to push them back in again.

Summary

At the time when witchcraft mania was at its height it was all too easy to be accused of witchcraft. In England, if you were a poor, elderly, solitary, rather ugly woman and slightly strange, the outlook was bleak. If you had as a pet a cat or a dog and were interested in herbal medicine and natural healing then you were exceptionally at risk. In parts of Europe it was not poor, elderly women who were at risk but the affluent. The courts and state were very conscious of the fact that the estates of those accused of witchcraft would be forfeited if they were convicted and executed.

Even if you fulfilled neither of these criteria you were not safe. In fact hardly anyone was safe from accusations of witchcraft. When people were tortured into confessing, either by the horrific devices common in mainland Europe and in Scotland or by the more subtle means common in England, they mostly showed a tendency to name others. If you knew any of the accused, if you had offended any of them, or even if you were just known to them, you were at risk of being named as a witch. People who had been repeatedly tortured until they made a confession of something with which they probably had no association were in no mental state to be rational.

Once you had been charged, the outlook was indeed black. It was particularly bad if you were in one of the mainland European countries, particularly France or Germany, and Scotland was not very far behind them in this respect. All these countries allowed physical torture by horrific devices, and the mainland European countries allowed convictions and executions on the basis of confession only. Given the fact that people were tortured until they did confess, and the fact that if they somehow managed to withstand the torture and refused to confess they were executed since this was taken as a sign that the devil was helping them, the vast majority of those accused were convicted and most of them executed.

In England things were not quite so bad in that the horrific devices of torture were not allowed and in that the accused were not supposed to be convicted on the basis of confession alone. However, there was much turning of a blind eye to some of the practices that were undertaken when the hysteria was at its height. These included letting underage children testify. When the notorious English witch-finder, Matthew Hopkins, was at work it is said that he used extremely cruel means to obtain a confession, such as swimming, starvation and sleep deprivation, and that he recommended that people be charged on the flimsiest of supposed proof, such as the fact that they kept cats as pets. Also it appears that he was not above recommending conviction by confession only.

All the advantage was on the side of the accusers when it came to the trial. Often the accused were debarred from being legally represented and often they were not told the actual substance of the accusations against them nor the identity of their accusers. People were reluctant to offer to speak on behalf of the accused because they were likely to be assumed to be his or her associates and themselves accused of witchcraft. Those who were brave enough to volunteer to give evidence for the defence were often not allowed to testify in the actual courts.

The period of witchcraft hysteria was among the most tragic in history. Huge numbers of people were subjected to the most inhumane of tortures. A vast number of people were convicted of something that was at best nebulous, and a great many of these were executed. It was indeed a case of the slaughter of the innocents and a blot on the history of Europe and, in some cases, on that of the American colonies.

Chapter 3

Witches and Magicians:
The Accused and Self-Confessed

Aberdeen Witches

This was the name given to a group of people accused of witchcraft in the Aberdeen area in 1596–97. Most of the accused were elderly women and included Janet Wishart (page 124), Isobel Cockie (page 72), Margaret Ogg (page 104) and Helen Rogie (page 109). They were accused of a number of crimes that were regarded as a traditional part of witchcraft. These included causing death by witchcraft, harming people and livestock, turning milk sour and raising storms. In addition they were charged with cavorting with the devil and his demons and with indulging in lewd behaviour with them.

The scale of the witch-hunt and subsequent trials amounted to widespread hysteria and the trials were noted for their severity, twenty-four people being executed.

See Chapter 2, Aberdeen Witchcraft Trials, page 21.

Abramelin the Mage

A native of Würzburg in Germany, Abramelin (1362–1460) is now best known for the influence that he has had on other magicians and witches through the ages. He claimed to have been instructed how to conjure up demons and make them do his bidding and also how to raise storms. He also claimed that those who instructed him in these arts were none other than angels. It was his theory that everything in the world was the work of demons working under the instructions of angels and that each person had both an angel and a demon as a familiar.

Details of Abramelin's magic is said to be found in a manuscript written in French in the eighteenth century but claiming to be a translation of an original manuscript composed by Abramelin in Hebrew and dated 1458. It was translated into English as *The Sacred Magic of Abramelin the Mage* by S. L. MacGregor Mathers around the beginning of the twentieth century. Abramelin's work is said to have greatly influenced Aleister Crowley (page 75).

Isobel Adam

One of the Pittenweem Witches, named by Beatrice Laing (page 96) as a fellow-witch in her confession, Adam then confessed herself and spoke of selling her soul to the devil for wealth, having encountered him in Laing's house. She also confessed to having been involved with other witches, whom she named, in strangling a man. Despite this, she did not suffer the terrible fate of other witches, both supposed and self-confessed. Clearly she had connections with someone in authority because she was allowed to go free on payment of a small fine.

Agrippa

Agrippa (1496–1535), short for Henry Cornelius Agrippa von Nettesheim, is best known now for the influence that he has had on later followers of the occult. He was originally interested in knowledge generally and was a great scholar but he soon developed a particular fascination for alchemy and magic. He conducted extensive research into the state of the occult at that time and summed it up in *De Occulta Philosphia* (*On Occult Philosophy*, although this was not published until twenty years later).

Many people associate witchcraft, magic and the occult generally with the devil but Agrippa did not do so. It was his contention that the gift of magic was dependent on naturally occurring psychic gifts and he believed firmly that the mind had ascendancy over the body.

Agrippa had a chequered career, partly because of his beliefs but also because of his hot temper, and he had a succession of jobs throughout Europe, usually ending in disaster. People's suspicions of his beliefs hardened when he successfully defended a woman in Metz accused of witchcraft seemingly on the sole grounds that her mother had been burned as a witch. He won the case but gained a few more enemies and a reputation for being a supporter of witches. It was rumoured that he, himself, was a witch.

Various stories surround Agrippa. He is said to have been always accompanied by a black dog, which was widely taken to be his familiar. It is alleged that he had the ability to raise demons and that on one occasion he conjured up the spirit of the famous orator Tully to give a speech for him.

The charm of magic wore off as far as Agrippa was concerned. By the time of the publication of his book on the occult, written twenty years earlier, he had become disillusioned with magic and had turned to theology instead. After more unfortunate adventures, more quarrels with people and more wandering, he died in greenbelt in

1535. It is said that on his deathbed he renounced all his work on magic and attributed the many misfortunes in his life to this work.

Albertus Magnus

Born in Swabia in Germany, Albertus Magnus (1193?–1280) was a Dominican theologian and scholar who believed not in black magic but in the good magic that is naturally associated with nature, with plants, precious stones, etc. He was also a firm believer in the possibility of turning base metals into gold and wrote a book on alchemy.

There are many legends associated with Albertus Magnus. In one of the most famous he is credited with creating an android in the form of a man and with the gift of speech. The android, supposedly created using natural magic with some help from astrology, became his servant.

Albertus Magnus was a philosopher and a theologian. For his services to religion he was beatified in 1622 and canonised in 1932.

Alphonsus de Spina

A Spanish Franciscan monk who died in 1491, he was the author of the earliest work to be published on witches.

Charles Arnold

Arnold is noted for being the prime mover in getting Wicca, or witchcraft, legally recognised in Canada in December 1987. This was the result of lengthy negotiations, which began in April 1986 when Arnold applied unsuccessfully to his employers, the Humber College of Applied Arts and Technology, for leave at the Wiccan festivals of Beltane, celebrated on 1 May, and Samhain, celebrated on 31 October.

Arnold was born in Washington DC in 1947 and moved to Canada after his discharge from the US army, having served in Vietnam. He began practising witchcraft in the late 1970s.

Anne Baites

One of the Morpeth Witches who, with Anne Forster (page 81), was accused of attending sabbats. The main accuser, Anne Armstrong, claimed to have seen Baites take on various animal shapes, such as that of a cat and that of a hare, in rapid succession for the entertainment of the devil at one of the sabbats. She pleaded not guilty to this and other charges.

The trials of the Morpeth Witches are not very conclusive but it seems likely that they were acquitted and did not suffer the horrific fate of others accused of witchcraft.

Bamberg Witches

Some of the worst of the hysteria surrounding witchcraft in the sixteenth and seventeenth centuries occurred in Germany. Some of the worst hysteria and consequent witch-hunts and trials occurred in the small state of Bamberg (*see* Chapter 2, Bamberg Trials, page 16), especially during the rule of Prince-Bishop Gottfried Johann George II Fuchs.

A huge number of people were accused of witchcraft and found guilty on the flimsiest of supposed evidence at the most perfunctory of trials. Terror reigned and many more would have been accused, found guilty and executed had they not fled the country. Many prominent and wealthy citizens were among those accused of being Bamberg Witches. It was in the interests of the accusers and the state to accuse the wealthy because money was deducted from the estates of those found guilty to defray the cost of their trials, tortures and executions, while the residue went to the ruler-bishop.

One of the best remembered victims of the Bamberg witch mania was the Vice-Chancellor of Bamberg, George Hahn (page 93), who was so horrified by the slaughter going on around him that he felt compelled to protest. This action led to his own conviction for witchcraft and his forced confession implicated other local dignitaries.

Margaret Barclay

Most women accused of witchcraft were elderly but Margaret Barclay, who lived in Irvine in Ayrshire in the early seventeenth century, was a young woman. She was originally accused not of witchcraft but of theft, the charge being made by her brother-in-law, John Deans. The charges were unfounded, a fact verified by the church court, and, although things seemed to have been smoothed over, Barclay remained extremely annoyed about the whole affair.

When she heard that her brother-in-law was about to set off on a voyage as captain of a merchant vessel, people claimed that they heard her say that she wished that the ship might sink with the captain in it. Unfortunately for Margaret, the ship failed to return to shore at the time it was expected and rumours started. Now people said that she had been seen throwing pieces of hot coal into the sea, which piece of magic was meant to make the ship run aground. At this point a beggar, John Stewart (page 116), supposedly endowed with the gift of clairvoyance, stated that he had discovered by means of this gift that the ship was lost. When factual verification of this was made and the ship was found to have sunk off Cornwall, Stewart was arrested.

He immediately pointed the finger of suspicion at Barclay and at two other women whom he claimed were her accomplices, the women being Isobel Insh (page 95) and Isobel Crawford (page 75). In an effort to save himself, he told the authorities that he had been asked by Barclay to provide her with a curse that would have the effect of bringing destruction to the vessel. He further claimed that he knew that Barclay and her accomplices had met together to make clay figures of John Deans and some of his fellow sailors, this being a favourite charge against supposed witches, and had thrown them into the sea with a view to causing the men's ship to founder. On receiving the clay figures the sea had become very stormy and had turned red.

On hearing this perceived damning evidence, the authorities ordered Barclay to be arrested and set upon the process of making her confess. There were many horrific ways of dragging confessions from people accused of witchcraft (*see* Chapter 2, Witchcraft Trials), and it was Barclay's lot to have heavy iron bars placed on her legs until she could bear it no more and confessed to witchcraft. As was extremely common in the case of forced confessions, her confession was retracted after she had recovered slightly from the trauma of her torture. Her retraction was repeated in court but made no impression on the jury. She was found guilty, then first of all strangled and then burned at the stake.

Francis Barrett

The author of *Magus*, a book devoted to the occult and magic, published in London in 1801, Barrett was an eccentric who gave lessons in the art of magic. His book deals with such subjects as the natural magic inherent in plants and stones, alchemy, numerology and ceremonial magic, and had a significant influence on Eliphas Levi (page 97), a French occultist who did much to revive an interest in magic in the nineteenth century.

Elizabeth Barton

Known as the Maid of Kent, Elizabeth Barton (*c.* 1506–34) was a domestic servant who was accused of being a witch and of having committed treason after she made prophecies warning of a disaster that would befall Henry VIII after he divorced Anne Boleyn. This was clearly an unwise thing to do in respect of any monarch, let alone Henry VIII, and Barton paid the ultimate price by being condemned to death on charges of treason and being duly hanged at Tyburn.

Before her death she admitted that the prophecies were a piece of trumped-up deception and had no basis whatsoever. She laid the blame at the door of others who had got to hear of her supposed powers as a foreseer of the future and manipulated her for their own ends.

She acquired her fame as a prophet after making a seemingly amazing recovery from a series of violent fits at the chapel of a priest in Aldington in Kent. She claimed that her recovery was a gift from the Virgin Mary, who had also endowed her with the gift of prophecy. News of this spread, and people flocked to be told what she perceived their future to be. The chapel that was the scene of her recovery and the granting of her gift became a place of pilgrimage.

Naturally the priest of the chapel was delighted that his place of worship had become so famous. However, it was to emerge that his good fortune was far from accidental. Barton's fits were simply pretence and it was the priest who had instructed her to fake them.

Barton was a naive serving girl and when she was feted by those wishing to profit from her supposed powers was flattered into making more and more false prophecies. Eventually her claims came to the notice of the king's critics and they thought to make use of her with a view to discrediting the king. Barton's succumbing to this particular piece of flattery cost her life.

Basque Witches *see* Pierre BOCAL.

Elizabeth Bennet

One of the St Osyth Witches (page 109), Bennet was one of those accused by Ursula Kempe (page 95). She confessed to having two familiars, a creature resembling a dog, called Suckin, and one resembling a lion, called Lierd, and was charged with murder by means of witchcraft.

She was accused of having killed a farmer called William Byet because he had refused to sell her milk and had called her rude names. Furthermore, she was also accused of killing Byet's wife and two other people. Bennet was found guilty and executed by hanging.

Chatrina Blanckenstein

An elderly widow from Naumburg in Saxony, Chatrina Blanckenstein (1610–80) was accused of witchcraft. Her case, and later that of her daughter, serves to illustrate the fact that to be accused of witchcraft in the witch-obsessed years of the seventeenth century all you had to do was to be a woman and to be rather elderly.

Blanckenstein was accused of the murder of a child by witchcraft. The hysteria surrounding witchcraft at that time was such that hardly any misfortune was held to occur naturally – it had to be laid at a witch's door. The old woman's only connection with the dead child was that her daughter, being short of fuel, had exchanged some of this for some jam made by her mother. The child ate this and died four years later. The child's parents promptly accused the Blanckenstein household of witchcraft.

There followed one of the commonest and saddest aspects of witchcraft charges. At the slightest suggestion of witchcraft previously friendly neighbours would accuse each other, seeking to add credence to their accusations by pointing to various occurrences or phenomena supposedly associated with witchcraft. They had seen a hare running from the scene, where dead livestock were found, towards the door of a particular neighbour, proving supposedly that the hare was the neighbour returning from killing the livestock by means of witchcraft. Or the neighbour was always seen with a black dog and this was bound to be the devil in disguise, her helper in her nefarious practices.

The things supposedly associated with witchcraft (*see* Chapter 4) were well known. It simply took an overactive imagination, a predisposition to hysteria, a spirit of revenge or ill-will towards a neighbour, or simply a desire to point the finger of suspicion at somebody else before it could be pointed at oneself for people to be convinced that there was a witch in their midst and to name her.

After the allegations by her fellow-villagers Blanckenstein was charged with infanticide by means of witchcraft. Despite protestations of total innocence, she was imprisoned and subjected to a range of the horrific tortures that were a regular part of witch trials (*see* Chapter 2, Witchcraft Trials). The very sight of some of the instruments of torture were enough to terrify some accused witches into confession but Blanckenstein remained adamant about her innocence even when the worst of these were applied to her. Finally, when she had somehow survived unbelievable torture, her tormentors let her go. In this she was fortunate because often they took the inability to be broken down by torture as a sign that the tortured person was being helped to sustain the pain by the devil.

The charges were dropped and she was released. However, she did not go scot-free. Ironically, she was forced to pay to the authorities the cost of her tortures.

This was not, alas, the end of the family's suffering. There was a deep-seated belief that witchcraft ran in families. The article on Agrippa, given on page 58, tells how he defended a woman in Metz on charges of witchcraft seemingly based solely on charges that her mother was burned as a witch. People were generally suspicion of the relatives of anyone who had been accused of witchcraft.

So it was that Blanckenstein's daughter suffered the cruel fate that her mother had avoided. In 1689, some years after her mother had died, the daughter was accused of being involved in the death of another baby. This time the authorities were determined not to let her go but, in any case, she was not made of such stern stuff as her mother and was moved to confess to charges of witchcraft at the sight of the torturing equipment that they proposed to use on her.

She confessed to being involved in the murder of the child and to various other charges relating to witchcraft, such as killing livestock and denying God and Christ. As was very frequently the case in forced confessions, she also named supposed accomplices. Having made her confession, she then tried to commit suicide by hanging herself by her belt in prison. Her tormentors were not to let her take such a way out, however, and they resuscitated her with the intention of making her death much more painful. They burned her alive, a common way to put witches to death.

John Blymire

Blymire was the central figure in a murder trial in York County, Pennsylvania, in January 1929. The case attracted a great deal of attention because it was widely held that the case had strong connections with witchcraft, although the authorities insisted that the motive for murder was robbery.

In the early part of the twentieth century there was still a strong belief in witchcraft in the York area of Pennsylvania. Blymire was born into a family of German extraction and many of its members were meant to have the power to heal and to bewitch people. Such powers were known locally as powwowing, after the North American Indian word for a ceremonial meeting for discussion.

As a boy Blymire appeared to be suffering from a wasting disease that neither his father or grandfather, noted witches and healers, could cure. Consequently he was taken to another witch, Nelson Rehmeyer, a few miles away, to be cured. A cure was duly effected and later Blymire was employed by Rehmeyer on his farm.

Gradually the young Blymire began to develop a reputation for his healing skills. He was not very bright, was physically unattractive and had few friends, but people began to seek him out as a healer and he had some spectacular success. Shortly after he had drawn attention to himself by stopping a mad dog in its tracks and curing it instantly of rabies, Blymire became ill and appeared once again to be suffering from a wasting disease.

Nothing seemed to go right for him, and Blymire, who was at that time still a youth, became obsessed with the notion that someone had put a spell on him. He gave up his job in a cigar factory and began to roam from place to place, taking short-term jobs and making some money from healing but all the while trying to find someone who could break the spell that he was convinced had been placed on him.

In 1917 he got married and for a while his health and luck appeared to improve. After the deaths in infancy of two of his children, however, his health took a turn for the worse and he lost his job. His obsession with the notion of a spell on him returned and he consulted yet more witches to find the source of his bewitchment. By this time he was suspecting everyone, including his wife, and a psychiatrist arranged for him to be admitted to mental hospital.

He was there for only a short time and in June 1928 he consulted another witch, one Nellie Noll, a very old woman whose powers were held in great regard. After a few sessions she told Blymire, whose wife by this time had divorced him, that she had succeeded in identifying the person who was at the centre of his misfortune. She named Rehmeyer, the healer who had cured Blymire as a boy and his ex-employer. Blymire at first was disinclined to believe this but was eventually convinced and vowed vengeance on Rehmeyer.

An important book in local witchcraft lore was *Powwows*, or *Long Lost Friend*, written by John Hohmar and containing suggested cures, spells, etc. Noll told her client that he could break the spell cast on him in one of two ways. He could cut a lock of his tormentor's hair and bury it deep in the ground or he could remove his copy of *Long Lost Friend* and bury it.

By this time Blymire had teamed up with a youth named John Curry, who blamed his unhappy childhood on a spell of unknown origin. They were now joined by Wilbert Hess, son of a farmer whose crops and livestock were in a poor way and who was convinced that this was also the result of a spell laid on him. The father had originally consulted Blymire professionally but he secretly consulted Noll on behalf of the Hess family and Curry. She again pointed the finger of suspicion at Nelson Rehmeyer.

Now it took a great deal of courage to confront Rehmeyer because he was a huge man with the reputation of being able to conjure up demons. After an unsuccessful visit, the three returned to Rehmeyer's house and demanded 'the book'. He claimed ignorance of what they were talking about. His attackers succeed in felling the huge man and in getting a rope round his neck to choke him. They then beat and kicked him to death. Before they left they ransacked his house for money but this amounted to very little.

The attackers were soon found and arrested, and Blymire was proud to proclaim his part in the murder of the person whom he claimed had put a spell on him and ruined his life. In most parts of America witchcraft was not an issue by this time and the press made the most of the stories of witchcraft. The judge in charge of the case, Ray Sherwood, did not want to have the area dubbed a backward place ruled by superstition and instructed the lawyers involved in the case that it would be dealt with as summarily as possible and that no mention of witchcraft was to be made in the course of the trial.

Instead of witchcraft, the official motive for the crime was to be robbery. This was not really credible, since the amount stolen was thought to be less than three dollars. Blymire's defence lawyers disagreed with the judge's ruling but were forced to go along with it. It was their feeling that Blymire stood a better chance with the jury, whose members were likely to share his belief in witchcraft, if his motive for murder could be shown to be witchcraft rather than robbery.

However, the official motive for murder remained robbery, and all three accused were found guilty of murder. Blymire and Curry were given life sentences and Hess twenty years. After serving nearly twenty-four years, Blymire was released at the age of fifty-six and returned to live in York.

Pierre Bocal

The Basque region of the Pyrenees was at several points in history considered to be a centre of witchcraft. When Christianity came to the region, which had tended to retain its own culture separate from the rest of France and Spain, the old beliefs concerning the old gods to some extent became entangled with the new beliefs. As in other parts of the world, the pagan beliefs exercised some influence on the new religion and in some cases the old beliefs lived alongside the new beliefs.

The Basque region in Spain received particular attention from the authorities during the time of the Spanish Inquisition (from around 1480). They were determined to root out witchcraft and, as was usually the case, where witchcraft was suspected ways and means were found to prove it, whether or not there was any actual objective evidence. The man in charge of the witch-hunt was a lawyer, Pierre de Lancre, and he was completely ruthless and obsessive

The assiduousness of the Spanish Inquisition in rooting out witchcraft in the Spanish Basque region had greatly impressed the French, and in the early seventeenth century, they set about doing the same in the French Basque region. Their commitment was, if anything, greater than the Spanish, and their activity amounted to slaughter. There was the usual series of tortures and forced confessions and invitations to some to implicate neighbours in order to achieve immunity for themselves. Many children were involved in reporting that they had seen relatives and neighbours flying through the air, working spells, etc. Huge numbers of people were alleged to be attending sabbats, or gatherings of witches arranged in order to reaffirm allegiance to the devil and to indulge in orgies of an obscene nature.

Best known among the victim's of de Lancre's excesses was a young priest who was accused of witchcraft because it was rumoured that he officiated not only over Christian rites but over pagan rites, the pagan element in religion still being very much in evidence in the Basque region. When he was found wearing a goat's-head mask at a pagan ceremony, he was assumed to be involved in witchcraft and was burned alive. The people were shocked that such treatment had been meted out to a priest, and one so young – he was twenty-seven.

Three more priests were burned and the slaughter of others continued. Eventually the local populace were shocked into protest and went on the rampage. De Lancre was forced to give up his terrible witch-hunts.

Christine Boffgen

A native of Rheinbach, a village in Germany, Boffgen was one of the most famous victims of Franz Buirmann, who acted as a kind of itinerant judge at witchcraft trials and who was notorious for the severity of his tortures. As was often the case with those accused of witchcraft, the person at the heart of the charges, namely Boffgen, was an elderly woman, and a very respected one at that.

Her accusers were people who were already in jail on charges of witchcraft, it being very common for those making forced confessions to implicate other people who were quite innocent, as indeed they themselves probably were. First she was blindfolded and shaved and was then subjected to a series of the most cruel tortures routinely used in witchcraft trials (*see* Chapter 2, Witchcraft Trials). In particular, she was subjected to the use of boots, vises designed to enclose the legs of the accused that were then tightened until the bones of the legs were crushed and the flesh torn. One can only guess at the scale of the agony endured by people subjected to this heinous torture and sympathise with the wretches who confessed to crimes that they had never committed and to connections with a way of life that they had never had just to stop the excruciating pain.

With the worst of the pain abated, many of the accused came to enough of their senses to realise that agony had forced them into false confessions and they recanted. This is what happened in the case of Boffgen. However, her tormentors did not accept this and simply ordered more physical torture. By this time her body was too weak to sustain any more punishment and after four days of it she died in 1631.

Great shame was felt in the village and the sense of shame was to last for an extremely long time. As recently as the early part of the twentieth century, masses were still being said for her in the local church.

Raymond Buckland

Born in England in 1934, Buckland went to live in America in 1962 and is credited with having done much to introduce contemporary witchcraft there. His father was of gypsy blood and one of his uncles interested him in spiritualism from an early age. He then went on to develop an interest in the occult and witchcraft.

He was greatly influenced by *Witchcraft Today* by Gerald Gardner (page 82) with whom he corresponded regularly while establishing a coven. The two men met in 1964, after Buckland's initiation into witchcraft. Later he turned his back on some of Gardner's teachings and formed a new tradition of witchcraft with Saxon connections, known as Seaxa-Wica. He has written extensively on witchcraft.

George Burroughs

One of the Salem Witches (page 110, *see also* Salem trials, page 23), Burroughs had been parish minister at Salem from 1680 until 1682. The Putnam family were hostile to Burroughs since he had formerly been their lodger and had fallen out with them. By this time he was a resident of Wells, Maine, but he was accused and brought to Salem on the grounds that he had asked some of the girls to sign devil's pacts. His spectre was accused of biting the girls and Tituba (page 117) accused him of being head of a coven to which she belonged. In addition, he was accused of murder. He absolutely refused to accept that there was such a thing as witchcraft and was found guilty and hanged with John Proctor (page 108) on 19 August 1692. Even the fact that he was able to say the Lord's Prayer (page 46) just before his death did not save him, although witches were not meant to be able to do this. Some of the crowd grew restive but they were persuaded that Burroughs was indeed a witch and in any case would have been too terrified to try to prevent the execution for fear of reprisals.

Chelmsford Witches

Chelmsford in Essex was the centre of much witchcraft hysteria from the mid-sixteenth century until about a century later. The first person executed (July 1566) under the tenets of the Witchcraft Act, passed in 1563, was an alleged Chelmsford witch. This was Agnes Waterhouse (page 121). Also accused of witchcraft in Chelmsford were Joan Waterhouse (page 121), daughter of Agnes, and Elizabeth Francis (page 81).

Another wave of witchcraft hysteria hit Chelmsford in 1579. Elizabeth Francis was again involved in this, as were Ellen Smith (page 115), Alice Nokes (page 102) and Margery Stanton.

This was far from being the end of Chelmsford's association with witch trials. In 1582 it was the venue of the trial of the St Osyth Witches and in 1589 nine women and one man were put on trial. Several charges of murder were made and many of the witnesses for the prosecution were children. Of the ten accused, four were executed and three of them went to the gallows within two hours of a guilty verdict having been reached. The three were Joan Cony, Joan Prentice and Joan Upney, and in the last hour before they were hanged all three confessed to the crimes of which they had been tried, although they had denied them up until then. Doubtless this was an attempt to be shown clemency or granted a pardon but the attempt was in vain.

In 1610 Chelmsford was again to be the scene of another witch trial. This time the accused was Katherine Lawrett from Colne Wake in Essex. Harm done to animals by means of witchcraft was a common charge and such was the nature of the accusation made against Lawrett. She was charged with having used her supposed magic to bring about the death of a valuable horse belonging to a man called Francis Plaite.

Chelmsford's association came to prominence again in 1645. That year saw the start of a notorious mass trial, thirty-two women being put on trial in July. Five of these were named by the first of these supposed witches to be questioned and tortured, Elizabeth Clarke (page 72) of Manningtree. These five in turn named others, and so it went on. It was an unfortunate aspect of witch trials that once someone was arrested he or she seemed only to eager to implicate others, perhaps in an attempt to curry favour with, and so receive clemency from, the authorities or perhaps from a determination not to suffer alone.

Seventeen of the accused were hanged, one of these being Clarke, two were acquitted and various fates befell the others. The trial was notorious for the methods used to obtain confessions, these including depriving the accused of sleep for days at a time, forcing them to walk back and forwards continuously until they fell down with exhaustion, compelling them to sit cross-legged on a stool for hours at a time and submitting them to the swimming test. This last involved throwing the accused into a stretch of water, such as a pond or river, having first bound him or her hand and foot. If the accused person floated then it was assumed that help was being given by the devil and the person was deemed to be guilty of witchcraft. If the person sank then innocence was assumed but this was often of small comfort since the person often drowned.

Organising the initial proceedings that led to these trials was the notorious witch-finder Matthew Hopkins, totally relentless in his efforts to identify, prosecute and execute anyone supposedly associated with witchcraft. It is likely that his attitude affected that of the trial judges (*see* Chapter 2, Chelmsford Witchcraft Trials, page 18).

Elizabeth Clarke

One of the Chelmsford Witches (page 69), Clarke was tried during the fourth wave of witch trials to be held in Chelmsford. The trials took place in 1645 and were largely at the instigation of the notorious witch-finder Matthew Hopkins, who called himself Witch-finder General. They were noted for the extremity of the torture used to extract confessions.

Clarke was the first of this series of accused witches to be charged. She was an elderly woman, which alone made her a prime target for being accused of witchcraft. She also had only one leg and was rather strange-looking, which confirmed her status as prime target. Finally, as if she needed any other factors against her, she was the daughter of a convicted witch – and a hanged witch at that.

Hopkins the witch-finder was exceptionally eager to find supposed evidence against anyone accused of witchcraft and claimed that he had seen various of Clarke's supposed familiars in various shapes, including a legless spaniel called Jarmara and a polecat called Newes. The old woman confessed to having a series of familiars, after having been tortured, and also confessed to having had intercourse with the devil over a period of several years. Given the severity of the tortures that were associated with the 1645 Chelmsford trials, it is hardly surprising that Clarke confessed. She was found guilty and hanged.

Elizabeth Clauson

One of the Stamford Witches (page 115), Clauson was the first to be accused. She was an extremely well-respected person in the community and it was a great surprise to everyone when Katherine Branch, a servant girl, accused the woman of being the cause of the fits and visions from which she was suffering. However, she and Branch's employer's wife, Mrs Westwood, had been involved in a long-term quarrel over some flax and there could have been an element of revenge in the girl's claim.

Other people were also accused, principally Mercy Disborough (page 76). Clauson and Disborough and three others were made the subject of a court of inquiry in May 1692.

Apparently Mrs Westwood felt that her servant might well be lying but she was powerless to do anything. On being searched for evidence of the devil's mark, by which the devil was supposed to imprint those who had vowed allegiance to him, Clauson was found to have only a wart, which was deemed to be harmless. Meanwhile the servant girl continued to have regular fits.

Clauson and Disborough were imprisoned and the trial began in September. Disborough insisted on being subjected to the swimming test to prove her innocence and Clauson also had to undertake it. This was an ordeal, common elsewhere but not in America, involving a suspected witch being bound hand and foot and thrown into a stretch of water, such as a pond or river, to see if he or she would float or sink. If the accused floated, it was deemed to be a sign of guilt, and if he or she sank it was a sign of innocence, although it was also often a cause of death.

Both women survived and were thus deemed to be guilty of witchcraft. Numerous people were found to testify against Clauson but at first no one could be found to testify in her favour. This was not surprising, as people giving testimony on behalf of an accused witch were liable to be accused of witchcraft themselves and charged with being accomplices.

Such was Clauson's standing in the community, however, that two of her neighbours risked the wrath of the court and did indeed testify in her favour. Perhaps thinking that there was safety in numbers, others then followed suit, and soon seventy-six of the townspeople had indicated that they were willing to testify as to Clauson's character and conduct.

In the light of this, the jury felt unable to reach a verdict and five ministers were called in to investigate the evidence that had been taken in the course of the trial and also the trial records. As has been mentioned above, the ordeal of swimming as a test for witchcraft was not usually used in America, and the ministers decided to disallow the evidence deduced from it, saying that the test was not only illegal but sinful. In addition they suggested that Branch might either be guilty of deception or have inherited a physical condition from which her mother had suffered.

The court was reconvened in October and further testimony was put forward. By this time the Salem witchcraft trials were at their height. Clauson was found not guilty and was set free. She died in Stamford in 1714 at the age of eighty-three. The Stamford trials were conducted with considerably more restraint than those at Salem.

Isobel Cockie

One of the supposed witches involved in the witch trials in Aberdeen in 1596 (pages 37, 93). She was accused of putting a spell on livestock so that they failed to produce milk, lay eggs, etc. Such a charge was very common among those seeking to charge someone with witchcraft.

Cologne Witches

Germany in the seventeenth century was the scene of much witchcraft hysteria and of relentless witch-hunts and cruel tortures. Cologne was by no means one of the worst areas and indeed had a reputation for enlightenment. However, there were two periods when Cologne was affected by witch mania, one between 1625 and 1626 and another between 1630 and 1636, but even then the authorities were disposed to be lenient.

Several witches were put on trial during the first of these periods. Of these Cologne Witches the most discussed was Catherine Henot (page 94). She was accused of putting a spell on some of the nuns of the St Clare order. Around 1929 many people were accused of witchcraft by Christine Plum, who claimed to have been possessed by demons conjured up by the accused.

Yet more people were accused of witchcraft after 1631 when there was an exodus of inhabitants from Leipzig to Cologne after their native city became caught up in a war with Sweden. This had an unfortunate effect on Cologne since Leipzig had had a great number of witch-hunters, dedicated to rooting out witchcraft, and these turned their attention to their new home city. Many people were accused of witchcraft and prosecuted, the situation only calming down in 1636 after papal intervention.

The last witch to be executed according to official records was killed in 1655.

Connecticut Witches

The title refers to a number of people accused of witchcraft throughout the northeastern part of America around the period 1647–62. New England had recently been settled and the settlers were much influenced by the mores of their mother country, England. Part of this influence took the form of an attitude to witchcraft that bordered on paranoia and hysteria. In 1642 legislation against witchcraft was passed in Connecticut, and this led to several executions. *See* Rebecca Greensmith (page 91), Katherine Harrison (page 94), Mary Johnson (page 95), Mary Parsons (page 105), Alice Young (page 126).

Mrs Corbyn

Known as the Fressingfield Witch, Corbyn had the distinction of being accused of witchcraft after her death. She died on the day in 1890 that also saw the death of a child to whom she was step-grandmother. Corbyn is said to have announced on her deathbed that she felt that the child was not likely to outlive her for long.

At the inquest into the sudden death of the child, the medical examiner gave the opinion that the child had died of shock, this having been in response to the application of some kind of irritant that could not be identified. Immediately the child's parents claimed that the child's death was the result of witchcraft practised by Corbyn. The dead woman's husband then said that he had always had the suspicion that his wife was a witch and had been scared to annoy her throughout their married life lest she use her black art to harm him.

Giles Corey

One of the Salem Witches (page 110), Giles Corey was the husband of Martha Corey (page 73) and he had thought her guilty of witchcraft. When he himself, as an old man of eighty, was accused of witchcraft he refused to plead to the charge. It is thought that he did so because he knew that the property of convicted witches was confiscated by the Crown and because he believed that his property could not be confiscated if he refused to plead and so could not be convicted.

His case is unique in America in that physical torture was used on him and he was pressed to death despite the act of 1641 that forbade inhuman or cruel punishment. Furious that he would not speak, the authorities forced him to lie on the ground with a large wooden plank covering him. Heavy boulders were then placed at intervals on the plank with a view to forcing him to beg for mercy and plead guilty – or even to plead at all. However, he somehow withstood the terrible torture for two days and then died.

Martha Corey

One of the Salem Witches (page 110), Martha Corey was an upstanding member of the community and a pious church member, but this did not save her from the hysterical claims of the girls who claimed that her spectre regularly attacked them. They put up such a convincing show that even Martha Corey's husband, local landowner Giles Corey (page 73), thought her guilty of witchcraft. She was found guilty and hanged on 22 September 1692.

Janet Cornfoot

One of the Pittenweem Witches, Cornfoot was named by Beatrice Laing (page 96) as a fellow-witch in her confession, confessed after torture and withdrew the confession after recovering from the distress of the torture. She was locked up in a steeple rather than in the gaol because the authorities were worried that she would persuade other inmates of the gaol who had confessed to witchcraft to withdraw their confessions.

She succeeded in escaping from the steeple and sought help and shelter from the local minister, Patrick Cowper, not being aware of the fact that he had been instrumental in getting the charge of witchcraft brought against Laing in the first place. He was very much concerned in stamping out witchcraft, so was quite the wrong person to ask for help. She had no choice but to seek refuge in the house of someone who was a suspected witch.

This simply exacerbated the situation, and she was set upon by an angry mob early in 1705 and severely beaten. Worse, the mob strung a rope between a ship and the shore and hanged her from it so that they could pelt her with stones. Following this they took her down and submitted her to a terrible death by covering her with a heavy door and piling boulders on this until she was crushed to death.

As was often the case with the kind of agonising deaths suffered by witches, no punitive action was taken against the perpetrators. The authorities simply turned a blind eye, glad to be rid of another supposed witch.

Mrs Julian Cox

A beggarwoman, she was charged with witchcraft and tried at Taunton in Somerset in 1663. Her accuser was a servant girl who accused Cox of putting a spell on her after she refused to give her any money. Revenge was often put forward as a motive for someone practising witchcraft on another.

Cox was accused of a number of activities traditionally associated with witchcraft. She was charged with putting a spell on a neighbour's livestock in order to harm them, in particular with putting a spell on a neighbour's cows to drive them mad. She was also charged with flying around on a broomstick, a traditional form of transport for witches, and was supposedly seen flying in through her own window on it. It was traditional for a witch to have a familiar and Cox was said to keep a pet toad.

Cox was claimed to be particularly skilled at shape-changing, another common activity supposedly associated with witches. In particular she had a reputation for turning herself into a hare. One person who accused her of such an ability claimed that his hounds had chased a hare into a large bush. When he tried to get at the hare, the creature vanished and its place stood a woman whom he instantly identified as Cox. He was absolutely terrified but was able to ask her how she came to be in the bush. He reported that the woman was so out of breath that she could not answer him, and this led him to suppose that this breathlessness was a result of being chased by his hounds in the shape of a hare.

The accused did not do her case any good by claiming that she herself had seen two witches and a black man, presumed to be the devil, flying low to the ground on broomsticks.

One of the more lenient ways of trying supposed witches was to get them to say the Lord's Prayer (page 46). If they could not, or made any mistake, this was seen as evidence of consorting with the devil and so of witchcraft. Cox almost passed the test. She made one serious mistake, however, that proved fatal. In the line from the Lord's Prayer 'And lead us not into temptation' she omitted the word 'not'. This was taken as definite evidence of guilt rather than just an unfortunate accidental slip, and she was found guilty and executed. On such tenuous evidence were many witches sent to their deaths.

Isobel Crawford

One of the alleged accomplices of Margaret Barclay (page 60), Crawford was named as an accomplice both by Barclay in her forced confession, it being a common practice among people being tortured to try to get a confession out of them to implicate others, and by John Stewart (page 116). She protested her innocence vehemently but in vain. Even after being subjected to horrific torture she refused to confess to witchcraft and was burnt at the stake.

Aleister Crowley

A British occultist, Crowley was born in 1875 into a family of Plymouth Brethren, a strict religious sect, and he appears to have rebelled against his strict upbringing at an early age. He became interested in the occult and devoted more time to his study of this at the University of Cambridge than to his conventional studies, being influenced by a book entitled *The Book of Black Magic and of Pacts*, written by Arthur Edward Waite.

Leaving Cambridge without graduating, he became a member of the Hermetic Order of the Golden Dawn, a society devoted to the study of the occult, led by Samuel Liddell. However, Crowley was determined to achieve greatness, fell out with Liddell, with whom he then conducted a feud, and was expelled from the group. Crowley then travelled widely to learn more about the occult and mysticism.

In Egypt he supposedly had communications with a spirit called Aiwass. Allegedly the spirit was endowed with a voice and dictated to Crowley the information that was to form his most famous book, *The Book of the Law*, which contains the law 'Do what thou wilt shall be the only law'. Aiwass apparently also announced the dawning of new age, the Age of Horus, of which Crowley was the prophet.

Crowley has been variously hailed as a renowned magician who achieved great feats and as a man of great wickedness. His reputation as a magician was much marred for many by his sexual excesses, which were associated both with his person relationships and his magic rituals. He had become involved with a German occult movement, called the Order of the Temple of the Orient, which practised sex magic, and his interest in this grew.

He moved to America in 1915 and lived there until 1919, after which he went to Sicily and founded the Abbey of Thelema, which he hoped to make an international centre for occult studies. However, stories of his sex ceremonies spread and he was ordered to leave Sicily. He took to his travels again, became addicted to heroin and fell into financial difficulties. He eventually died in England in 1947.

Dalkeith Witch *see* Christine WILSON.

Madeleine Demandolx *see* Louis GAUFRIDI.

Elizabeth Device

One of the Pendle Witches (page 105).

Mercy Disborough

One of the Stamford Witches, Disborough, with Elizabeth Clauson (page 70), was one of the main accused, having had the finger of suspicion pointed at her by Katherine Branch, a servant girl who blamed her fits and visions on witchcraft practised by some of the women in the town. With Clauson, she was searched for evidence of the devil's mark. In the case of Disborough, the searchers claimed success, saying that they had found unnatural marks that qualified as devil's marks.

Disborough was duly charged and brought to trial, the trial opening on 14 September 1692. Although such a test for witchcraft was uncommon in America, but usual elsewhere, Disborough asked for the swimming test to be applied. This test involved binding the accused hand and foot and casting him or her into a stretch of water. If the accused floated, then guilt was assumed, it being supposed that witchcraft had come to his or her aid. On the other hand, sinking was thought to be a sign of innocence, although this presumed innocence was often paid for by the accused's death from drowning.

Disborough and Clauson both floated and were thus found to be guilty of witchcraft. However, partly because a great number of people came forward to testify to the good character and conduct of Disborough's co-accused, Clauson, the trial jury, after long deliberation, found themselves unable to reach a verdict.

A committee consisting of five ministers was called in to review the evidence that had been given in the course of the trial and also to review the trial records. They decided to disallow the results of the swimming test, deeming it to be both unlawful and sinful. They also disallowed the evidence supplied by Disborough's supposed devil's marks, unless the marks that had been found on her skin should be so described by a competent physician after investigation. The five ministers also cast doubt on Branch's allegations by suggesting that she might be guilty of deception or that she might be suffering from the same physical condition from which her mother had suffered.

The court was reconvened on 28 October and more evidence was heard. This time the jury found Disborough guilty and she was sentenced to death, although her co-accused, Clauson, was found not guilty and released. In the end Disborough's execution did not take place. After the trial her friends made application to the court that the second session of the court was not lawful in light of the fact that one of the original jurors was not present. She was reprieved, thus having her life saved by a technicality.

Gilly Duncan

The woman who sparked off the witchcraft trial surrounding the North Berwick Witches (page 77) of 1590–92, Duncan was a servant girl in the employment of an local dignitary, David Seaton, in the town of Tranent in East Lothian near Edinburgh. He became suspicious of her when she began to be involved in healing people, his assumption being that these skills were inspired by the devil rather than God. His suspicions deepened when it came to his attention that she was leaving the house at night on mysterious nocturnal visits.

Seaton had legal authority, being a deputy bailiff, and he took it upon himself to exert his official powers in his own home. Not only did he exercise his powers of questioning but he exercised extremely painful forms of torture on the girl. He is said to have made use of the process known as thrawing, in which the accused's head was jerked violently by a rope. This would obviously have been extremely painful, and it was followed by use of the 'pilliwinks' or thumbscrews. This instrument of torture consisted of a vice in which the thumbs of suspects were crushed, and it is a testament to the severity of the other forms of torture used in witchcraft trials that this was considered one of the less severe tortures.

These tortures having been carried out, Duncan was then subjected to a body search for signs of the devil's mark with which the devil was meant to imprint in various ways, such as by touching or kissing the bodies of those who promised to serve him. It could be in any part of the body and the search for it was often humiliating. Also, since hardly anyone has a flawless body, a great many naturally occurring marks were said to be proof of the devil's involvement.

This being the case, it was not surprising that a devil's mark was supposedly found on Duncan's body – on her throat. After the finding of the devil's mark and after enduring the various tortures, Duncan had had enough and agreed to give a formal confession admitting to an association with witchcraft and the devil. She was determined not to go down alone, however, and set about implicating other people. This was an extremely common feature of witchcraft trials. It may have been the result of not wishing to face something alone, it may have been an act of vengeance or it may have been a result of a belief that naming accomplices would involve the accused being treated more leniently.

Whatever the reason, Duncan provided a significant list of people who had shared her involvement in witchcraft. These included Agnes Sampson (page 110), whose revelations in the trial, including efforts to bring about the death of the king, King James I of Scotland, were so sensational that many people disbelieved them, two women of noble connections, Effie Maclean (page 98) and Barbara Napier (page 102), and John Fian (page 79), a schoolteacher.

Susanna Edwards

One of the Exeter Witches (page 79) who voluntarily confessed to witchcraft and were hanged in 1682. Edwards, who in common with her co-accused, Temperance Lloyd (page 98) and Mary Trembles (page 118), was impoverished and elderly, openly claimed to have been recruited to witchcraft by the devil himself.

In the course of her trial she shocked the people attending it by her account of her meeting with the devil, who had taken on the guise of a gentleman dressed in black. She is said to have given independent evidence of her guilt by glaring at her guard in jail until he fell down in a fit. She was found guilty with the others and they were hanged in August 1682.

Exeter Witches

The Exeter witches consisted of Susanna Edwards (page 79), Temperance Lloyd (page 98) and Mary Trembles (page 118). Their trial for suspected witchcraft in Bideford in 1682 was one of the last major witchcraft trials to be conducted in England.

The women, all poor, elderly and often seeming confused were accused of belonging to a coven. Their actions did not help their case. All three women gave voluntary confessions of such a shocking nature that the people of Exeter were virtually baying for their blood. As was often the case with witchcraft trials, the start of the case saw several people bringing charges against the accused, although these had never been mentioned before. These charges, as was not unusual, were vague in the extreme, one of them being based on the fact that someone had claimed to have seen a cat jump in at the window and had assumed it to be the devil.

It is said that the judge felt quite sorry for the women but, in the light of public opinion against them, he could take no other course of action than to find them guilty. They were duly sentenced to death and hanged in August 1682.

John Fian

Mostly it was women who were accused of witchcraft but Fian was an exception. A respected schoolmaster, he was one of the people accused of belonging to a coven known as the North Berwick Witches. He was one of those whom Gilly Duncan (page 77) named as one of her accomplices when she confessed to witchcraft. Fian was found guilty and put to death by strangling and burning at the stake.

Dietrich Flade

A civil judge appointed to officiate at the wholesale trials of the Trèves Witches (page 118), he was accused of leniency in his judgements and dismissed from his post. Later he himself was accused of witchcraft, found guilty and executed.

Joan Flower

An English peasant who was unusual among women accused of witchcraft in that she admitted to some of the charges without torture, although she later retracted the confession before her death in 1618. Flower had been widely suspected of being a witch for some considerable time before she was tried and was also considered to be a particularly unpleasant person.

The events that led to her being charged began when one of her daughters, Margaret, who worked as chief laundress at Belvoir Castle, home of Francis, sixth earl of Rutland, was dismissed on charges of stealing food and of staying out at night. The outraged Margaret immediately sought her mother's help in seeking vengeance.

The mother first rather foolishly cursed the earl in public. She then asked her other daughter, Philippa, who worked as an occasional cleaner at the castle to try to obtain some of the personal possessions of the earl's family. In this way she is alleged to have obtained a glove belonging to the earl's eldest son, Henry, and to have used her magic to treat it in various ways before burying it. This was supposedly done in order to bring misfortune to the owner of the glove. Henry died a few years later and his two surviving brothers became ill, supposedly after Flower had subjected them to similar magical feats.

These and other misfortunes that befell the earl and his family reminded some local people of the curse that Flower had put on the earl and witchcraft was suspected. These suspicions were strengthened by the fact that Flower and her daughters did not try to conceal that they had plotted for the undoing of the earl's family. They were duly arrested and were committed for trial in the company of others accused of being accomplices. During the trial they admitted to being members of a coven and confessed to other misdeeds associated with witchcraft.

Too late did Flower realise where their confessions were leading. Not wishing to be executed, she is said to have retracted any confession of association with witchcraft and to have declared her innocence. It is said that she reached for a piece of dry bread and put it in her mouth, declaiming that the bread might choke her if she were guilty of the charges. Alas for her – she choked to death in front of the judges of the court. It was unfortunate also for her daughters. Not only did they lose their mother but the seeming proof of her guilt led the judges to declare them and their co-accused guilty also and they were hanged in Lincoln in March 1619.

Anne Forster

The main suspect at the heart of witchcraft trials in Morpeth in 1673, Forster was accused by Anne Armstrong, a local servant girl. Armstrong claimed that she had been forced to carry Forster to a sabbat, an orgiastic gathering of witches, the woman having supposedly having put a bridle over Armstrong's head, this being a popular part of witchcraft lore. Having been put under a spell so that she was devoid of will she was forced to carry her load cross-legged to the sabbat.

Later she was forced to carry other members of the coven to sabbats. Her supposed attendance at the sabbats gave her ample opportunity to recognise and name more people whom she claimed to be present. Armstrong went into great detail about the activities of the witches at the sabbats, claiming that there were several covens present and a long black man on horseback whom she took to be the devil.

As well as accusing Forster of attending sabbats, Armstrong claimed that she had performed a number of misdeeds associated with witchcraft, such as using her black art to put spells on the livestock belonging to anyone whom she disliked. Accusing people of deeds linked to witchcraft often seems to have created a chain reaction, and soon others followed Armstrong's example, Forster being accused, among other things, of bringing about the death of a neighbour's child.

Three of the other people accused with Forster were Anne Baites (page 59), Dorothy Green (page 91) and Mary Hunter. They all denied the charges, and although the trial records do not shed much light on the case it is likely that the trial was a great deal milder than many witch trials. It is likely that all the accused were acquitted, although two of the supposed coven spent some time in prison.

Elizabeth Francis

One of the early Chelmsford Witches, Francis was accused at the same time as Agnes Waterhouse and her daughter, Joan, in 1566. Like the Waterhouses, she was a resident of Hatfield Peverel in Essex, and in fact, although the charges against Francis and the Waterhouses were quite separate, there was a connection between them relating to the details of the trial. The cat, known as Sathan, which at time of her trial was owned by Agnes Waterhouse and which was accused of being her familiar and accomplice, had once been owned by Francis and had been given by her to Waterhouse. Indeed the cat's ownership was even more complicated than that, since it had been inherited by Francis from her late grandmother, known as Mother Eve.

Francis was accused of having caused illness in people by means of sorcery, two of the people in question being William Auger and Mary Cocke. It was also alleged that she had enlisted the help of her cat Sathan to punish a wealthy man who had refused to marry her, first by ruining him financially and then by killing him. His name was Richard Byles, and he did indeed soon lose first his wealth and then his life.

The enterprising cat then supposedly found Francis another husband, one Christopher Francis, but it appears that all was not well with the marriage. A baby appeared on the scene and this was not part of Elizabeth Francis's plan. Consequently she got Sathan to kill the baby. Christopher Francis apparently was not measuring up to his wife's expectations and again she enlisted the help of her trusty cat. This time he assumed the shape of a toad and hid in the husband's shoe so that he was able to come into contact with the man's foot and so cause lameness. Toads were not to be meddled with in witchcraft lore.

After this, Francis gave the cat to Agnes Waterhouse. The reason for the gift is not known. It seems strange that such a helpful companion was given away. However, it appears that Sathan continued to play havoc.

In the trials of 1566 Francis was more fortunate than Agnes Waterhouse. She was found guilty but her life was spared and her punishment confined to terms of imprisonment and appearances in the pillory. She was not so fortunate, however, in the Chelmsford trials of 1579. Francis confessed to charges of witchcraft, having previously said that she had been taught the basics of the art at the feet of her late grandmother, known as Mother Eve, the original owner of Sathan (page 114). She was duly judged guilty of witchcraft and hanged along with Ellen Smith (page 115) and Alice Nokes (page 102).

Gerald Gardner

Born near Liverpool in 1884 into a family of Scottish descent, he played an extremely large part in reviving witchcraft in the twentieth century. The family claimed as an ancestor Grizell Gairdner, who had been burnt as a witch at Newburgh in Scotland in 1640, and Gerald Gardner's grandfather had married a woman who was reputed to be a witch.

He worked for a considerable time in the Far East and became interested in the spiritual beliefs of some of the local people. When he retired and returned home to

Britain in 1936 he developed his interest in archaeology and became interested in witchcraft. He and his wife lived in the New Forest area and became members of a coven there in 1939. In 1946 Gardner was introduced to Aleister Crowley (page 75).

It was Gardner's wish to write about witchcraft, but at that time witchcraft was still illegal in Britain, the law banning it not being repealed until 1951. He had to content himself with writing about witchcraft in a novel based on witchcraft rituals until the witchcraft ban was lifted and he was able to write *Witchcraft Today*, published in 1954, which presented modern witchcraft as the survivor of an ancient pagan religion. Gardner was much influenced in his theories by the work of Margaret Murray, who put forward the theory that witchcraft was a continuation of a pagan religion in her book *The Witch-cult in Western Europe*, published in 1921 (*see* page 5).

The publication of Gardner's book aroused much interest in witchcraft, and many people wrote to him asking for advice. Numerous covens were set up, some of them scandalising people by gathering in the nude in the open air and performing sexual acts as part of their rituals.

In 1951, the year in which Gardner set up his own coven, he went to the Isle of Man to become manager of a museum of magic and witchcraft, which he extended and later bought. He continued to write on the subject of witchcraft, his works including *The Meaning of Witchcraft*, published in 1959. He also helped to compile a book of witchcraft rituals, known as a book of shadows. This is the name given to a book of beliefs, rituals, spells, etc, which acts as a guide for the practice of witchcraft. There is no definitive work, and each tradition and coven can adapt it for their particular use. Gardner was helped in his compilation of his book of shadows by Doreen Valiente, a member of his coven. The book became known as the standard guide to the Gardnerian tradition of witchcraft.

Shortly before his death he met Raymond Buckland (page 68), with whom he had corresponded and whom he had influenced greatly so that Buckland introduced the Gardnerian tradition of witchcraft to America. Gardner died aboard ship in February 1964 on his way back from a journey to the Lebanon and was buried in Tunis.

Louis Gaufridi

Gaufridi was a priest accused of bewitching nuns in a convent in Aix-en-Provence. The case bears some similarities to the later case of Urbain Grandier (page 88), and it is thought that Gaufridi's case was taken as a kind of precedent for Grandier's. At any rate, both involved a priest, both involved nuns and charges of demonic possession, and both had distinctly sexual elements.

Gaufridi, who came from Marseilles, was, like Grandier, an exceptionally handsome man. He was friendly with a wealthy family named Demandolx, and when he was thirty-four he showed this friendship by trying to help the family's thirteen year-old daughter, Madeleine, who appears to have been suffering from mental problems. He began to spend a great deal of time with the girl and, despite her youth and the age difference between them, rumours being to circulate as to the nature of their relationship.

The priest was advised by his superiors of the rumours and cautioned him to limit his visits. In 1607 the situation appeared to resolve itself when Madeleine went to the Ursuline convent at Marseilles to begin her noviciate. On arrival there, she confessed that she had had a full-blown affair with Gaufridi and she was despatched to a sister convent in Aix-en-Provence to try to prevent any further meetings.

At the end of 1609 Madeleine began to suffer fits and went on to claim to being possessed by demons at the instigation of Father Gaufridi. Attempts were made to exorcise the demons but her fits and allegations continued. Meanwhile Madeleine grew more insistent that she had had a sexual affair with the priest and gave more and more detailed accounts of this. Gaufridi denied any such sexual involvement with her.

It was common in accusations of witchcraft or demoniac possession for people to affect each other, especially if the accusers were young girls or members of a close community. True to form, Madeleine's hysterical outbursts began to be copied by other nuns, of whom Louise Capel was the worst affected.

Madeleine and Louise were ordered to appear before the Grand Inquisitor in Avignon. The two young women gave colourful details of the demons that were meant to possess them. Attempts to exorcise these failed. Gaufridi was then asked to conduct a session of exorcism, a procedure that was to be repeated in the case of Urbaine Grandier.

The process was not successful and the priest was imprisoned. There being little evidence of witchcraft or demoniac possession against him, he was released and appealed to the head of his church, the Pope, to take some action against the girls and their fraudulent claims. Madeleine was ordered to be subjected to supervision, but her hysteria worsened, and her speech and actions became very lewd.

Eventually the case came to trial in 1611. Madeleine's behaviour was, to say the least, unstable. Sometimes she was on the side of Gaufridi, denying her claims and asking him for forgiveness, and sometimes she was on the side of the prosecution, raving about demonic possession and sexual perversions.

Meanwhile Gaufridi had been languishing in jail. Having been inspected for evidence of the devil's mark, a mark, often a mark of insensitivity, supposedly imprinted by the devil on the bodies of those who had sworn allegiance to him, and this almost inevitably having been found since practically any mark could be so categorised, he was formally charged. After severe torture, in sheer desperation, he admitted to the charges, agreeing that he had signed a pact with the devil in order to satisfy his lust for Madeleine and other women.

He later retracted these charges, but he was found guilty and sentenced to death. His body was subjected to terrible torture before execution in order to try to force him to name accomplices but he did not do so. He was strangled and burnt to ashes on the stake.

In 1642, and again in 1652, Madeleine herself was accused of witchcraft. Evidence of the devil's mark was found upon her body and she was imprisoned for life. She died in 1670.

Sarah Good

One of the Salem Witches (page 85), Sarah Good was one of the first to be accused by the girls. She was a poor woman who begged to keep her family alive, her husband being shiftless. Given her circumstances, no one protested much at the accusations against her. Furthermore, Tituba (page 117) claimed that she had travelled through the air with her to coven meetings and that she kept a familiar in the form of a yellow bird. She was found guilty and executed on 19 July 1692 alongside Rebecca Nurse (page 104).

Alice Goodridge

Accused of witchcraft in 1596 on the evidence of Thomas Darling, known as the Burton Boy because he lived in Burton-on-Trent, she faced the charges simply because she had the misfortune to meet the boy in local woods on a day when he later fell ill. People suspected that his illness might have been caused by witchcraft when he began to have fits and to speak of seeing visions of the devil and other demons, especially one in the form of a green cat.

When asked if he had seen anyone in the woods on the day he had been taken ill, Darling racked his brains and remembered that he had had an encounter with an elderly woman. He remembered the incident because she complained when he broke wind in her presence and recited a poem that indicated that because of his action she would go to heaven and he would go to hell. His description of her clothes and of three warts on her face led his relatives to deduce that the person whom he had met was Goodridge, who lived nearby.

Goodridge, whilst readily admitting that she had met the boy in the woods, gave an entirely different version of events. She claimed that he had taunted her with abuse, saying that she was a witch. Her claims were to no avail, as Darling's fits and visions increased in intensity when Goodridge was brought near to him. She was subjected to various tests for witchcraft, and her failure to recite the Lord's Prayer was regarded as proof of her guilt. This supposed proof was underlined by the fact that a local man claimed that she had bewitched his cow. It was extremely common when anyone was accused of witchcraft for others to rush in with tales that made her plight worse.

She was submitted to tortures in order to make her confess, one of these forms of torture including the placing of her feet in shoes and the positioning of her feet so close to a fire that the shoes grew quite unbearably hot. Despite this extreme discomfort and pain, she refused to make a confession but did admit to keeping a dog that had been given to her by her mother. This was taken by the authorities to be a familiar of the kind regularly kept by witches. Because there was a deep suspicion that witchcraft ran in families, especially in the female line, Goodridge's mother, Elizabeth Wright (page 126), was also accused of witchcraft.

Goodridge was duly declared guilty of witchcraft but before the death sentence could be carried out she died in Derby jail. As was often the case with those who brought charges of witchcraft, Darling was later to admit that he had made the whole thing up in order to draw attention to himself.

Isobel Gowdie

A young and attractive self-confessed witch, Gowdie lived in Auldearn in Morayshire in Scotland. She made her confessions in 1662 without any threat of the tortures that were usually used to extract confessions from supposed witches. Quite why she confessed to witchcraft so readily is not known, although various possibilities have been put forward.

The suggestions include that she was mad, that she was desperately bored with her rather uninteresting farmer husband, and consequently with her childless marriage, and craved the excitement and attention that was brought to her by her explicit claims of sexual intercourse with the devil – huge genitals and semen like ice – and her accounts of orgiastic meetings of her coven of thirteen witches. One can deduce something of her relationship with her husband from the fact that, when she was out at one of her coven meetings or enjoying one of her sexual sessions with the devil, her husband was completely convinced that she was in bed beside him, she having had the forethought to substitute a broomstick, a symbol of witchcraft, for her body.

Gowdie also gave detailed descriptions of the activities of the coven to which she belonged. These included transforming themselves into various animals, such as cats and hares; raising storms by beating wet rags frenziedly on stones while reciting spells; making clay models of enemies with a view to bringing about their destruction; ruining farmers' crops by burying the bodies of unchristened children in their manure heaps, the bodies having been specially dug up for the occasion; aiming elf-arrows at people, these magic arrows being designed to cause illness and misfortune in both humans and animals; and making previously fertile land barren by using a miniature plough pulled by toads to dig it up.

All the activities admitted to by Gowdie were those traditionally associated with witchcraft. She further sought to establish her status as a witch by claiming to have the devil's mark an area of the body, in her case the shoulder, from which the devil was said to have sucked blood or otherwise marked his witch followers, often traditionally by raking his claw over them, licking them, burning them with a hot iron, etc, in a symbolic gesture to seal their pledge to be his servants. Although Gowdie gloried in having such a mark, many accused witches had cause to regret the presence of scars or natural blemishes since these were assumed by the authorities to be devil's marks. It was claimed that experts, such as were supposedly used as inspectors in witch trials could differentiate between a birthmark, scar or natural blemish and the mark of the devil but this was far from true. Not many people enjoy unblemished bodies and a surprising number of women accused of witchcraft were found by the experts to have been marked by the devil.

Whatever the reason for Gowdie's remarkable claims, and whatever the state of her sanity at the time, there is no doubt that she was a positive gift to the authorities since she claimed to encompass the whole range of activities associated with witchcraft. She seemed to welcome the punishment that she knew would accompany confessions of witchcraft, remarking that she deserved tortures such as being stretched on an iron rack or having her body torn asunder by wild horses. Perhaps she was also some kind of masochist.

What happened to Gowdie is not indicated by any records, as the trial proceedings are for some reason incomplete. It seems likely, however, that she suffered the fate suffered by others found guilty of witchcraft and was put to death, her body having been burned to ashes. It is likely, also, that those accomplices whom she had named in her confession, as was part of the tradition of witch trials, were also painfully executed.

Urbain Grandier

Appointed parish priest of St-Pierre-du-Marche in Loudun, a town in Poitiers in France, in 1617, Urbain was handsome and fond of women. It was alleged that this fondness for the opposite sex went beyond what it should have done, given his vows of celibacy. He was popularly supposed to have had relationships with several young women and he was suspected of being the father of the child of Philippa Trincant, whose father held an administrative post in the town. In addition, he was assumed to have taken as his mistress Madeleine du Brou, whose father was also part of the town's administration.

In 1630 he was arrested on charges of immorality, tried by the Bishop of Poitiers and found guilty. Although Urbain had made powerful enemies he also had powerful friends and was reinstated to his post within a year. Urbain so far had survived despite his reputation, but Jeanne des Anges, Mother Superior of the Ursuline Convent, was to be his undoing.

It is not entirely clear whether the hysteria in the nuns, which was identified as demonic possession caused by Grandier, was Jeanne's idea or whether it was suggested to her by Father Mignon, father confessor to the nuns and an enemy of Grandier, being related to Trincant, whose baby Grandier was suspected of fathering. Certainly it was obvious that Mignon wished Grandier harm but it may well have been that Jeanne, who had turned her back on fleshly pleasures, wished to make Grandier pay for his lust and lack of celibacy. The Mother Superior of the convent, formerly Madame de Beclier, before becoming a nun, was of a wealthy family and was supposedly extravagant and even wild in her secular life before settling down to a life of piety.

Whatever the truth behind the plot to bring about the downfall of Grandier, Jeanne began to claim that Grandier was appearing to her in her dreams and was trying to seduce her into sexual acts and other vices. She began to rave and throw fits, and some of the other nuns followed suit. Mignon and his assistant were brought in to exorcise the nuns, and Jeanne claimed that she and some of her fellow nuns were possessed by two demons, Asmodeus and Zabulon, whom she claimed had been conjured up by Grandier sent to her in a bouquet of roses that had been thrown over the convent wall.

News of the nuns' condition and supposed demonic possession spread through the town, and Grandier could see that things were not looking too good for him. In an effort to counteract the damage being done to him by the nuns' ravings, he approached his friend the Archbishop of Bordeaux for help. The archbishop ordered the nuns to be examined by his doctor who found no evidence of possession and declared the nuns to be fakes. At this the archbishop ordered Mignon's exorcism to be brought to an end and the nuns to be confined in their cells.

This appeared to have ended the nuns' hysteria and hallucinations, and for a while all was quiet. The peace was to be short-lived, however, and hysteria broke out again later that year.

Grandier had made powerful enemies in the course of his life, among these no less a person than Cardinal Richelieu. He was supposedly the author of a satire against Richelieu in 1618, and this had been brought to the Cardinal's attention. Unfortunately for Grandier, one of Richelieu's relatives was one of the Loudun nuns, and he was not best pleased to hear that the nuns had been accused of faking demonic possession.

Richelieu, in an effort to get his revenge on Grandier, appointed Jean de Laubardemont head of a commission to investigate the nuns' claims. The exorcisms were resumed, and this time they were held in public. The nuns responded with fits, ravings, a series of obscene postures and descriptions of hallucinations. Members of the public found all this very shocking, particularly because the women were in holy orders. Grandier's position was looking rather desperate and, to make matters worse, some of his former mistresses came forward with stories of Grandier's adultery and fornication, conducted in the church itself and therefore sacrilegious.

Finally Grandier himself was ordered to officiate at one of the public exorcisms. The nuns' behaviour grew more wild and their claims more extravagant. Grandier was accused of witchcraft and put in prison in the castle of Angiers in 1633. He was duly searched for evidence of the devil's mark (page 163). Such a mark was allegedly found on Grandier's body, although it was claimed that the reason why certain areas on his body seemed insensitive to pain or touch was that he had been cut or stabbed so severely elsewhere that his attention was so focused on the pain of the wound that he failed to notice being touched elsewhere. The physician who was in charge of preparing Grandier for torture denied the presence on his body of devil's marks, as did the Poitiers apothecary, but they were ignored.

The supposed presence of devil's marks simply added to the danger of Grandier's situation. He was already in a great deal of trouble, and this had been added to by the production of a piece of paper that was alleged to be a pact between Grandier and the devil, signed in blood by Grandier and countersigned by the devil and various demons. It was claimed that this piece of evidence had been taken from the devil's own files by the demon Asmodeus, one of those who had supposedly possessed the nuns.

This was clearly an extremely unlikely story, but it was accepted as evidence of Grandier's involvement with the devil and with witchcraft. The allegation was so bizarre that it had the effect of making some people think that things had gone quite far enough. Voices were raised in Grandier's defence and even some of the nuns spoke in his favour, offering to make a retraction of their allegations against him.

Given Richelieu's determination to bring about the downfall, and preferably death, of Grandier, it was clearly unwise to speak in the latter's defence. People wishing to give evidence for the defence were encouraged to remain silent lest they themselves be charged with witchcraft. As for the nuns' suggested retraction, it was treated by the prosecution as evidence that the devil was helping his servant Grandier. Even the sight of Jeanne d'Anges in court with a noose around her neck, threatening to hang herself if she were not allowed to retract the allegations of demonic possession that had brought Grandier to his present perilous situation, was to no avail. It is said that some of the nuns were offered pensions by Richelieu if they would agree to appear for the prosecution.

Grandier was duly found guilty in August 1634 and sentenced to death by hanging and then burning at the stake. Throughout the trial and post-trial proceedings, Grandier steadfastly declared his innocence of any crimes connected with witchcraft or the devil. Unlike many people accused of witchcraft, the priest refused to implicate anyone else. This refusal to suggest that he had accomplices in his alleged witchcraft further angered his accusers, and extreme torture was used in order to make him do so. They broke both his legs in such a horrible manner that it was said that marrow was seen to ooze from his broken limbs. When he prayed to God for help, they said that he was invoking the aid of his master, the devil.

Still he refused to implicate others, and his tormentors took their final revenge. He was supposed to be allowed to make a last statement before hanging, but when he began to declaim his innocence, the friars who were supervising his execution threw so much holy water on his head that he was prevented from speaking. Furthermore, he had been sentenced to be hanged before being burned, as was usually the case, but in order to subject him to as much agony as possible, the noose was so tied that it could not be tightened. Thus the rope did not strangle him and when he went to the stake he was still alive.

It was to be expected that the death of Grandier would see the end of the nuns' hysterical antics, supposedly caused by demonic possession instigated by him. However, this was not the case. The antics continued and were even more lewd than before. The language of the nuns caught up in these hysterical outbursts grew more and more crude. People were shocked to hear of this, but this did not prevent them from rushing to witness the public exorcisms for themselves to see and hear the goings-on.

Eventually, in 1637, the niece of Cardinal Richelieu, the Duchess d'Aiguillon, protested to her uncle about the lewd show the nuns were putting on. By this time he had no interest in the affair, having demonstrated his power and having got rid of a priest who might have caused him political problems, and Richelieu simply stopped paying the money to the nuns that had been awarded to them during the trial. This had the effect of dramatically lessening the activity of the nuns.

Jeanne d'Anges continued to have hysterical fits and was not seemingly cured of these until a visit to Italy to seek help from the tomb of St Francis de Sales in 1638. She died in 1665. Her role in the accusations made against Grandier are subject to debate. Some say that she was a complete fraud, wishing to harm Grandier, some say that she was an attention-seeker, some say that she probably suffered from epilepsy and others that she may have suffered from schizophrenia. Whatever the truth of the matter, she certainly succeed in drawing attention to herself and to the town of Loudun.

The history of all this was the subject of a book by Aldous Huxley, *The Devils of Loudun* (1952), and the subject of a Ken Russell film, *The Devils* (1971).

Dorothy Green

One of the Morpeth Witches, Green was accused with Mary Hunter of casting a spell over a mare belonging to a local man, John March, the spell resulting in the animal's death. March, himself, claimed that a swallow would not leave the horse alone one evening and after this harassment the mare had become ill. Four days later it was dead. Thus did people come to connect any misfortune with witchcraft.

The Morpeth trial records are not very helpful, but it seems likely that the accused witches, including Green, all of whom pleaded not guilty, were acquitted.

Rebecca Greensmith

One of the Connecticut Witches (page 72), Greensmith was accused of witchcraft in the town of Hartford in 1662 on the evidence of a girl called Ann Cole. Cole became subject to fits, and this was construed to be a result of possession by the devil or demons. In the course of these fits she is said to have made accusations in Dutch, a language that she did not speak, against a Dutch girl living locally and against Greensmith.

The Dutch girl was fortunate enough to be acquitted but Greensmith was not so lucky. When Cole made her accusations Greensmith was already being held on other charges of witchcraft. The claim that was the basis of the latter charges was that she had been seen in the company of strangely dressed demons, although it was later suggested that these might have been North American Indians wearing ceremonial headdresses.

Greensmith did her case untold harm by claiming to have had intercourse with the devil after he had appeared before her in the form of a deer. With this evidence from her own lips she could hope for nothing other than a charge of guilty and the death sentence. Her husband, Nathaniel, was also convicted and put to death with her, although he denied knowing anything about her involvement with witchcraft and protested his own innocence.

Nathaniel was not the only one to go to his death on the evidence of Greensmith. It was her contention that a coven of witches was in the habit of gathering at a spot near her house, their members regularly indulging in shape-changing and turning themselves into crows and other creatures. It is likely, as was often the case of people accused or found guilty of witchcraft, that Cole named names and informed the authorities of the identity of the people whom she had seen at the coven. Whether this was the case or not, several others, both men and women, were accused of attending the coven mentioned by Greensmith. They were arrested, tried and at least some them were executed by hanging

Isobel Grierson

Grierson was found guilty of witchcraft and first strangled and then burnt at the stake on the hill of Edinburgh Castle in 1607. She was one of many convicted witches who owed her plight to her neighbours. The wife of a labourer from Prestonpans, near Edinburgh, Grierson was much disliked and feared by those around her.

Eventually the general animosity against her resulted in one of her neighbours, Adam Clark, accusing her of harming him by means of witchcraft over a period of months. She was supposed, among other activities, to have taken the form of a cat, traditionally a favourite disguise of witches, in order to find a way of getting to the Clark cottage after dark. When there, it was alleged that she and other cats terrified the inhabitants.

As was frequently the way with charges of witchcraft, one charge led to another and other neighbours came up with allegations, glad to see harm come to someone whom they disliked so much. She was accused of making Robert Peddan sick until he eventually paid up some money that he owed her, that she had brought sickness on his wife on several occasions and that she had caused the ale that he was brewing to go bad.

Other neighbours went forward with similar allegations, and Grierson was charged. She was not allowed any defence, a situation that was by no means uncommon, although in fact a defence rarely did any good. As indicated above, she was burned at the stake, the victim of her neighbours' dislike and vengeance.

Louis van Haecke

Haecke (1828–1912) was a Belgian Catholic priest who substituted for the traditional Catholic mass a distorted version at the heart of which was a sexual theme and which included various traditional pagan rites and elements. At these masses, conducted not only in Bruges in Belgium but in Paris also, the priest officiated wearing a skullcap with horns on top of it. Rites included the desecration of the Christian host, and the orgiastic activities that took place were reminiscent of those claimed to take place at the traditional witches' sabbats.

The priest's obsession with sex and devil-worshipping was brought to light by a writer called Joris-Karl Huysmans. Having heard rumours of the priest's black magic activities, Huysmans persuaded a woman of his acquaintance, named Berthe Courriere, to become part of a coven based in Bruges and to supply him with details as to what took place. When she reported back to him he wrote a novel based on her account, and this came to the ears of the Bishop of Bruges.

The bishop initiated an inquiry into Haecke's alleged activities but the time of witch hysteria had long gone, the inquiry was not pursued with much rigour and was finally dropped.

George Hahn

The Vice-Chancellor of Bamberg at the time when there was mass torture and slaughter of people accused of being Bamberg Witches (page 60), Hahn was so horrified by the situation that he felt compelled to protest. This was a brave thing to do, given the stringent witch-hunts that were going on, and it proved to be foolhardy too. He himself was accused of witchcraft, as were his wife and daughter, and all three were executed in 1628.

The tortures that were in force during the Bamberg Witchcraft Trials (*see* Chapter 2, Witchcraft Trials, page 17) were notorious even by the usual horrific standards of witchcraft trials. As was the case with so many others, Hahn was subjected to such terrible pain that he would have confessed to anything to be free of it. He duly made a formal confession, and, again as was the case with so many others, in the course of his confession made accusations of witchcraft against others. As a result of this five burgomasters were accused and found guilty.

Isobel Haldane

Accused of being a witch, Haldane was tried in Perth in Scotland in 1623. Details of her trial are unusually well documented, and the evidence given against her largely took the form of reports that she had succeeded in curing sick people. It was claimed by her accusers that these powers of healing must have been granted to her by the devil, but Haldane, while admitting to such powers, said that she had learned the art of healing from the fairies. Various people testified to having been helped by her. Some claimed to have received herbal remedies from her and others claimed that she had saved their sick children's lives by the simple expedient of washing them, the theory being that the disease was transferred from the children to the water.

The other major charge against her was that she had the gift of prophesy and had prophesied the death of various local people, these deaths all having occurred in the way that she had foreseen. She accounted for this gift by describing an extremely unusual incident that had befallen her some ten years before.

According to Haldane, she had been lying in bed when she suddenly found herself being taken from the bed by some unidentified force and left on a hillside. The hillside opened and she entered into the opening, staying inside the hill for three days. At the end of these three days she was taken back to the outside world by a man with a grey beard who told her the names of those who were going to die in the near future.

Although there is much detail in the records of Haldane's interrogation, the documentation as to what her fate was is absent. It is likely, however, that in the spirit of the times she suffered a similar fate to those accused of witchcraft, some of them on much shakier evidence, and was found guilty, strangled and burnt at the stake.

Katherine Harrison

One of the Connecticut Witches (page 72), Harrison was fortunate enough to be tried after the first wave of witchcraft hysteria in Connecticut had passed, there being fewer trials after 1662. Although she was tried in 1669 and sentenced to death, these were slightly more clement times and the death sentence was changed to one of banishment.

Catherine Henot

One of the Cologne Witches (page 72), Henot was accused of putting a spell on some of the nuns of the order of St Clare. She was tried by the church court, but Cologne was noted as a city of tolerance and she received a much fairer trial than she would have done elsewhere in Germany. In particular she was allowed her own defence counsel.

The church court, having listened to the evidence, found her not guilty. Alas for Henot, a higher ecclesiastical power in the form of Archbishop Ferdinand of Cologne stepped in and ordered Henot to be tried by a different court. This time it was quite a different story. The second court brought in a verdict of guilty and she was sentenced to death by burning.

Mary Hunter

One of the Morpeth Witches, *see* Dorothy GREEN, page 91.

Isobel Insh

Named by John Stewart (page 116) as one of the accomplices of Margaret Barclay (page 60), Insh was arrested by the authorities who also claimed to have received evidence of her witchcraft from her eight-year-old daughter. She was confined in the belfry tower of the local church and, knowing what tortures lay ahead for an accused witch, tried to escape, from the tower. In so doing she suffered a severe fall and died from her injuries.

Mary Johnson

A native of Wethersfield, Johnson was one of the Connecticut Witches (page 72). Although there was no other evidence, she was tried and hanged after confessing to having been guilty of child murder and to having had sexual intercourse with the devil.

Ursula Kempe

The woman at the heart of the trial concerning the St Osyth Witches, Kempe was a midwife and nursemaid who was also known for her healing skills and allegedly for her skill in undoing spells placed on people by means of sorcery. She was alleged to have successfully cured the illness of a young boy and to have taken offence when the boy's mother, Grace Thurlowe, did not invite her to be nursemaid to her infant daughter. When the child fell out of her cot and broke her neck, there were rumours that Kempe was behind the incident, she having used her magic skills to bring about the death.

No explicit accusations were made and Thurlowe must have decided to ignore the rumours because she asked Kempe to treat her for an arthritic condition. After prescribing a complicated and bizarre remedy that seemed to help the condition, Kempe was enraged to find that her patient refused to pay her fee.

At this point Thurlowe's complaint began to get worse and she, remembering the previous rumours, began to suspect witchcraft. She therefore made a formal complaint to the authorities and they decided to investigate the matter. Kempe was sent for trial and her eight-year-old son, Thomas Rabbett, was called upon to give evidence against his mother and her witchlike activities. This he did, and it was then suggested to Kempe that she would be treated with leniency by the courts if she made a formal confession of guilt with regard to witchcraft.

Kempe then poured out a confession confirming her son's claim and going into detail about her four familiars, two cats, a toad and a white lamb, and of how she had fed them partly on drops of blood from her body. According to her testimony, the familiars had helped her to commit several crimes. In particular, she alleged that the lamb, unusual as a familiar since traditionally familiars were unable to take the shape of lambs, had rocked the crib in which the Thurlowe child had lain and knocked her out of the crib.

She then put herself at the mercy of the court but not before she had given the names of other women in St Osyth whom she claimed were witches. She claimed to have seen evidence of their activities by peering through their windows and to have received information about their deeds from the white lamb that was her familiar. Neither her confession nor her identification of other supposed witches did her any good. The prosecution went back on its promise to show clemency if she confessed and she was hanged, after admitting to the causing of three killings by sorcery.

Her allegations against others resulted in a considerable number of people being tried since the people accused by her made accusations against others. Fourteen women were formally charged and two of them, including Kempe, were hanged. The other was Elizabeth Bennet (page 62).

Beatrice Laing

The woman at the centre of the Pittenweem Witches, Laing was accused of witchcraft in 1704 by a young blacksmith's apprentice, Patrick Morton in the village of Pittenweem in Fife in Scotland. He claimed that she took revenge on him for being unable to find the time to forge some nails for her because he was busy with other work.

He further claimed that her revenge had taken the form of using magic to make him ill, the illness taking the form of a weakness in the limbs and a tendency to fits. He added to his claims the fact that he had been pinched by Laing and an accomplice and had the marks to prove it.

The local minister backed Morton's claims and Laing was duly tried. After being subjected to some of the tortures that were used on supposed witches to encourage them to confess, principally being forced to stay awake for five days and nights, she made a confession. Not only did she implicate herself, but she named others as her accomplices. One of these, Mrs Nicholas Lawson (page 97), had also been accused by Patrick Morton of aiding and abetting Laing but Janet Cornfoot (page 74) and Isobel Adam (page 58) were now also named.

Laing was among the more fortunate of those who were accused of witchcraft. As was quite common among people who had confessed to witchcraft under the duress of torture, she withdrew her confession after she had recovered sufficiently from the ravages of the torture. She was not executed but placed in the stocks as a warning to others and then thrown into a dungeon to endure solitary confinement for some months.

This may not seem like very benign treatment, although at least she had escaped with her life, but she was eventually released on payment of a small fine. Her suffering did not end there, because her supposed connection with witchcraft meant that her family did not want her at home with them. She had no choice but to become a wanderer and eventually died in St Andrews.

As was frequently the case with charges of witchcraft, the original accuser was found to be a deceiver. Patrick Morton was found to be an impostor, having been encouraged in his accusations by the local minister, Patrick Cowper.

Mrs Nicholas Lawson

One of the so-called Pittenweem Witches, Lawson was accused with Beatrice Laing (page 96) of making a local apprentice blacksmith ill by means of witchcraft because he, Patrick Morton, had refused to carry out work for her. She was further accused by Laing after the latter had been tortured into confessing.

Eliphas Levi

This was the pseudonym of Alphonse Louis Constant, born in 1810 in Paris, who achieved fame as an occultist. Although he developed an interest in magic at quite a young age, he decided to make the church his career and became a priest. This did not prove to be a wise decision as he had great difficulty in observing the vow of chastity and his interest in left-wing politics did not endear him to his superiors. He was jailed for his political writings and dismissed from the church.

Alphonse became more and more interested in the occult and was influenced by a man named Ganneau who claimed to be a reincarnation of Louis XVII and also claimed to have prophetic powers. Renaming himself Eliphas Levi, the Hebrew equivalent of his first and middle names, he took a trip to London in 1854 where he developed his interest in necromancy.

Levi practised magic but he appears to have been more a commentator than a skilled practitioner. He gave lessons in the occult and is best known for his influence on later generations through the medium of his writings, such as *The Dogma and Ritual of High Magic*, in which he wrote extensively about tarot cards, published in 1861, and *A History of Magic*. He had several admirers, among whom was Edward Bulwer-Lytton, an English author whom he visited in England in 1863. The latter was also greatly interested in the occult and appears to have been greatly influenced by Levi. Levi, himself, acknowledged the influence of the English occultist, Francis Barrett (page 61), author of *Magus*, published in 1801.

Temperance Lloyd

One of the Exeter Witches (page 79), Lloyd was held to be queen of the covens to which her co-accused, Susanna Edwards (page 79) and Mary Trembles (page 118), were also supposed to belong. She had already been tried on charges of witchcraft twice before the trial that led to her execution in August 1682 and, like her co-accused, openly admitted to being associated with witchcraft. Like the other two involved in the trial, she was elderly and practically destitute. She is reported to have seemed untroubled by the fact that she was found guilty and is said to have chewed nonchalantly on a piece of bread as she went to the gallows.

Effie Maclean

Properly called Euphemia Maclean, she was one of the people accused of being part of the coven known as the North Berwick Witches (page 103). A feature of the trials concerned with this group was that several of the accused were of high social standing, this being thought to be partly the reason that the king, James I of Scotland, decided to take on the role of interrogator at the trials. Like Barbara Napier (page 102), Maclean was one such person, being the daughter of Cliftonhall.

Unfortunately, neither her highborn connections nor the six lawyers whom she engaged to plead her case were instrumental in saving her life. Her links with the Earl of Bothwell were her undoing because he was rumoured to have initiated plots to kill the king in order to take his place on the throne and so he was the king's sworn enemy.

This attitude of the king influenced his feelings towards any friend or relative of Bothwell and he was determined to show Maclean no mercy despite her position in society, and she was found guilty and executed. It was common for people to be strangled before being burnt at the stake to save then the agony of being burned alive. This privilege was not accorded to Maclean and she went to the stake alive.

Magee Island Witches

The last witch trial to take place in Ireland, in 1711, concerned eight women from Magee Island near Carrickfergus in County Antrim. Tried in Carrickfergus, they were accused by a servant girl, Mary Dunbar. A servant in the house of James Haldridge, she claimed to be being tormented by the spirits of the women and was attacked by seizures or went into fits if she were near any of them. During the seizures she claimed to have vomited up a weird selection of objects, such as feathers, pins and large waistcoat buttons.

The case was further complicated by the fact that shortly before the arrival of Dunbar in Haldane's house, the household had been subjected to what appeared to be poltergeist activity and then Haldridge's mother was stricken with a pain in her back and died a few days later. Witchcraft was suspected and so it was already in the air before Mary Dunbar came on the scene with her accusations.

Seven of the women were arrested, and the women were tried solely on Dunbar's evidence and without a defence counsel. There was a lack of unanimity among the three judges, and there was sympathy for the women because they had been previously believed to be of good character and were regular attenders at church. However, the jury found them guilty. Compared with many of the sentences for witchcraft theirs were relatively light. They were not executed but subjected to a year each in prison and also had to undergo four periods each in the pillory.

Andrew Mann

By his own confession a witch, Mann, in order to save himself from trial and execution, and doubtless to obtain financial gain, as was the case with most witch-finders, turned king's evidence and was appointed by the authorities as an official witch-finder, his task involving the naming of witches and providing the initial evidence to enable the authorities to embark on the trial.

Magdalen Mattsdotter

One of the witches involved in the Mora Witch Trials in Sweden, she was accused of witchcraft by her own children and her servant girls. She was burnt at the stake but it was later found that the servant girls had invented the whole charge out of envy of their mistress. It was by no means unusual in the general hysteria that surrounded witch trials for servants to trump up charges against their mistresses.

One of the main features of these Swedish witch trials was the number of children involved. Indeed, it was children who first brought the allegations of witchcraft in the area to light. Some of these were executed along with many adults and even more were severely punished in other ways.

Alice Molland

Generally held to be the last person to be officially executed in England for supposedly practising witchcraft, her hanging taking place in Exeter in 1684. It has been suggested that two women were hanged in Northampton as late as 1705 and that, even later, in 1716, a woman and child were hanged in Huntingdon. Because of a lack of records these claims are thought to be fictitious.

Although Molland may have been the last person to be officially hanged for supposed connections with witchcraft, she was not the last to die because of charges of witchcraft. Many died when they were set about by mobs of people who were convinced they were witches and many also died in the course of being subjected to the cruel tests that were used in an attempt to establish that someone was a witch.

Nanny Morgan

Although she lived a considerable time after supposed witches had ceased to be prosecuted, Nanny Morgan (1789–1857), who lived near Much Wenlock in Shropshire, was suspected by many people in the area of being involved in witchcraft. The end of witchcraft as a legal offence did not destroy belief in witchcraft and such belief was often stronger in rural areas.

Her reputation as a witch was based partly on the fact that she told fortunes, an art she was supposed to have learnt from a gang of gypsies with whom she travelled around in her youth. It was also based on the fact that she was alleged to keep live toads in her cottage and toads were much connected with witchcraft, often supposedly acting as witches' familiars.

Some of her neighbours were convinced that Morgan had the power of the evil eye, this meaning that she could do them harm in some way simply by fixing them with a stare. Many of them were thus extremely nervous of her and would go to great lengths not to offend her.

This was manifested by the attitude of her lodger, William Davis, to her. It was his wish to give up his lodgings in her cottage and to live elsewhere but he was scared to tell her of his intended departure in case she became angry and practised her magic on him. Some of her neighbours advised him that if his landlady did indeed put some kind of spell on him he could undo the influence of this by using a technique known as scoring above the breath. This involved drawing blood from an accused witch from an area above their mouth and nose.

Shortly after this advice was given, Davis left Morgan's house. It was noticed that his clothing was stained with blood and when Morgan was found dead, killed by a series of stab wounds, Davis was immediately suspected of murder. He confessed that he had indeed committed the crime but had done so only in an attempt draw blood and to undo the effects of any spells that she had put on him.

Morpeth Witches *see* Anne FORSTER.

Maria Renata Singer von Mosau

One of the last people to be at the centre of an episode of witchcraft hysteria in Germany, which saw so many witch trials, she was put to death in 1749. She was a nun in a convent near Würzburg and had been well respected for many years when she felt moved to challenge in 1745 the acceptance of one Cecilia Pistorini to the convent. The latter suffered from seizures and hallucinations and Mosau considered that she was not a suitable candidate for the order.

Her objections were set aside and Pistorini was duly admitted to the order. Shortly after this, some of the other nuns began suffering from seizures and showing other signs popularly held to be associated with demonic possession. One of these nuns died and accused Mosau of having been the instigator of her possession by demons.

An investigation was begun, and Oswald Loschert, the Abbot of Oberzell, was disposed to believe the allegations of witchcraft against Mosau. Services of exorcism were conducted with a view to ridding the nuns of their seizures and demons, but no improvement was perceived. Meanwhile Mosau was confined to her cell. When a search was made of the cell, various herbs and potions are alleged to have been uncovered. On the basis of this and other evidence, the nun was charged and subjected to torture.

In the course of torture she made a formal confession of guilt and claimed that she had been introduced to witchcraft in Vienna by a grenadier who had then introduced her to the devil in Prague. After this meeting she turned from her faith in God and made a pact with the devil when she was a child of fourteen. According to her testimony, she had been following the devil's instructions when she had entered the convent at the age of nineteen and had thereafter received regular visits from him in her cell. She confessed also to flying on a broomstick to witches' gatherings in Würzburg. She did not implicate other people in her confessions, a common practice in witchcraft trials when hysteria surrounding sorcery was at its height.

As well as admitting to causing demonic possession in her fellow nuns, Mosau confessed to desecrating the host, clearly a terrible crime in the eyes of the church. In order to prove how she had succeeded in stealing the host, she showed to the authorities the scars of the wound that she had made in her body to conceal the host. Mosau was charged with, and found guilty of, witchcraft and heresy.

She was beheaded in Mareinberg in June 1749 and her corpse burned to ashes.

Barbara Napier

One of the people accused of being part of a coven known as the North Berwick Witches (page 103), Napier put in a plea that she was pregnant when she was called to trial and was given special dispensation and allowed to go free. An unusual feature of the trials relating to the North Berwick Witches was that some of the accused were of high birth or had aristocratic connections, this being one of the factors said to have encouraged King James I to take on the role of interrogator. Napier was such a person, being related to the Laird of Carschoggill.

Alice Nokes

Nokes was one of the Chelmsford Witches (page 69) who was tried in the second wave of witchcraft trials to hit Chelmsford. She was tried at the same time as Elizabeth

Francis (page 81), the charge being that she had caused death by means of sorcery. She confessed to being a witch and was executed by hanging.

North Berwick Witches

This refers to an alleged coven of witches operating in the region of East Lothian near Edinburgh. The methods of torture used in their trial (1590–92) were most severe, and indeed the hysteria surrounding this trial was to spread throughout Scotland and England, leading to other horrific trials.

The trials were particularly noteworthy in that they involved the king, King James VI of Scotland, later James I of England. Some of the accused claimed that they had plotted together with the help of the devil to raise a storm to sink the ship in which he sailed to Denmark to collect the woman who was to be his wife. Later confessions included suggestions that members of the coven had made a wax model of the king and melted it, preparing some kind of magic powder made from parts of a corpse and a shroud. Another confession claimed that the coven had tried unsuccessfully to get hold of an article of clothing from the royal wardrobe with a view to smearing this with poison procured from the body of a black toad that had been suspended by its feet for three days.

The king decided to officiate at some of the trials himself, and thus began his interest in witchcraft, which was to lead him to write a treatise on witchcraft, entitled *Daemonologie*, published five years after the end of the trial. There was much public interest in the trial, partly because of the involvement of the king, partly because of the high social standing of some of the accused and partly because of the sensational nature of the detail of some of the confessions.

The coven identified as the North Berwick Witches included Gilly Duncan (page 77), the first to be accused. On giving her confession after extremely painful torture, as was often the case with people accused of witchcraft, she claimed a list of people as being her accomplices. These included Agnes Sampson (page 110), whose trial was noted for the sensational detail covered by her confession forced out of her by terrible tortures. Some of these revelations involved the king. The revelations grew more and more sensational so as to be completely unbelievable but the king angrily insisted that he believed them.

Other supposed members of the coven were Barbara Napier (page 102) and Effie Maclean (page 98), who were both of high social standing. John Fian (page 79), a schoolteacher, was also accused of being involved. All of these had had the finger of suspicion pointed at them by Gilly Duncan, and Sampson, Maclean and Fian were all found guilty and put to death.

Rebecca Nurse

One of the Salem Witches (page 110), she was an extremely pious person and one of the most respected people in the community. Consequently many people were shocked by the girls' claims about her. It is widely believed that if the girls had begun their accusations with someone such as Rebecca Nurse the Salem situation would not have got as out of hand as it did because people would have viewed the girls' accusations with incredulity. Unfortunately, by the time Nurse was accused the situation had already gone too far, with most people all too ready to believe the girls' hysterical claims.

At the time of the accusations she was an invalid and aged seventy-one. Originally accused of having her spectre beat Ann Putnam and of having had her spectre try to get Mrs Thomas Putnam, Ann's mother, to sign a devil's pact, she then was accused of having brought about the painful death of Benjamin Holton after an argument over his pigs getting into her fields. Despite her upstanding reputation, her age and her frailty, she was found guilty and hanged on 19 July 1692.

Isobel Ogg

One of the supposed witches in the Aberdeen witch trials in 1596, she was accused of raising storms. This was a common accusation directed at those against whom evidence of witchcraft was being sought, the charge being that they were conspiring with the devil to bring on such storms. *See* Chapter 2, Witchcraft Trials, page 17.

Margaret Ogg

One of the supposed witches involved in the witchcraft trials in Aberdeen in 1596, she was accused of poisoning meat. *See* Aberdeen Witches, page 57.

Sarah Osborne

One of the Salem Witches (page 110), she was an easy target for the girls, being old and bedridden. Furthermore, she had been involved in local scandal, having had her servant staying in her house with her before she married him, and had been married several times. Local people did not feel moved to protest when she was accused. Tituba (page 117) claimed that she had travelled through the air with her to coven meetings and that she kept a familiar in the shape of a winged creature with a woman's head. She died in prison.

Mary Parsons

One of the Connecticut Witches (page 172), she confessed to various witchcraft activities in the town of Springfield, Massachusetts. In 1651 she was tried in Boston for the murder of her child. Although found guilty, she was later reprieved.

Pendle Witches

A coven of witches who were alleged to indulge in witchcraft in the Pendle Forest in Lancashire, the Pendle Witches were at the centre of a mass trial in 1612. The trial, which became known as one of the most notorious in England, would perhaps never have come to be if it had not been for the fierce rivalry of two local peasant families.

The two women considered to be at the head of these families were once close friends and had long been rumoured locally to dabble in witchcraft, being at the very least exponents of herbal remedies. One was Elizabeth Sowthern, known as Old Demdike, and the other was Anne Whittle, known as Old Chattox. Both women had two of the major requisites of one likely to be accused of witchcraft. They were both elderly women and they were both extremely physically unattractive, being archetypal withered hags. People were said to be scared of the very sight of them

The friendship of the two women, and consequently of that of their families, came to an abrupt end in 1601. As with many family feuds throughout history, the feud was based on a seemingly petty incident. It was begun by the granddaughter of Sowthern, Alison Device, reporting the theft of clothes linen and some meal. The following Sunday Alison claimed that she saw some of the missing items being worn by Anne Redfearne, daughter of Whittle. This was enough to set in train a series of accusations and counter-accusations that was to result in a bitter feud.

It was popularly supposed that Whittle was the more powerful of the two old crones as far as witchcraft was concerned, and Alison's father, John Device, was afraid that she would use her expertise in the black art to bring harm to his family. He thus decided to try to prevent this by promising to give Whittle an annual gift of meal in order to appease her wrath. This appears to have worked well enough as a pacifier until John's death.

Thereafter the feud started up again and was vicious enough to come to the attention of a local justice of the peace, Roger Nowell. He set about the well-nigh impossible task of investigating and of putting an end to the incessant quarrelling between the families. Once again there was a series of accusations and counter-accusations as both families sought to outdo each other in extravagant claims of wrongdoing. This proved to be their great disadvantage because claims of witchcraft emerged.

It was said that Sowthern had turned to witchcraft many years before and had sold her soul to the devil in return for him arranging for her to have anything she wanted. From then on, allegedly, the devil visited her in various forms on several occasions. Whittle, not to be outdone, was also said to have sold her soul. Various members of both families were also said to have been converted to witchcraft.

Nowell, the justice of the peace, hearing some of this, became alarmed and decided to investigate the allegations of witchcraft. Accordingly, he imprisoned in Lancaster Castle three of the women who had been allegedly associated with the black art. These were Elizabeth Sowthern, Anne Whittle and Whittle's married daughter, Anne Redfearne.

As they awaited trial they were joined in their jail by Sowthern's granddaughter, Alison Device, then aged eleven, the girl who had started the family feud by making accusations of theft. She was imprisoned on charges of having bewitched a pedlar who had refused to give her some pins, after which he became ill with pains in his side.

Alison admitted to cursing the man and to being of the opinion that she had caused his illness by doing so. Meanwhile Sowthern openly admitted to being a witch. By the time they were brought to trial they had been joined by others accused of witchcraft and many of these were from the two feuding families. More were to join them after it was reported that members of the feuding families had got together to plot to blow up Lancaster Castle in order to release the prisoners from it.

By this time there was a goodly number of people awaiting trial, the accused being charged with the deeds generally associated with witchcraft, such as causing harm to livestock, but also being charged with several killings. At the trial the son and daughter of one of the accused, Elizabeth Device, both gave evidence against her, with sensational accusations of her involvement with witchcraft. The son was simple-minded and the daughter was well under the minimum age for witnesses of fourteen, but these facts were not taken into consideration. Their mother made a full confession of witchcraft.

At the end of the trial, ten of the accused were sentenced to be hanged. Sowthern had been spared the gallows by dying in prison before the beginning of the trial but her former friend and enemy, Whittle, was hanged, as was Anne Redfearne, Whittle's daughter, Alison Device, Sowthern's granddaughter, and Elizabeth Device, among others. Partly because of the sheer numbers involved the trial became known throughout the north of England.

Joan Petersen

Known as the Wapping Witch, Petersen appears to have used such as powers as she had for the good of her fellow men, so, if she were a witch at all, was likely to have been a white witch. Because she had been helpful to many, in that she had seemed to cure illness in people and livestock, there appears to have been several people who wished to come forward to speak in her defence when she was accused of witchcraft. It is said that of these some were frightened into not testifying, doubtless being afraid that they in turn might be accused of witchcraft, and others were bribed not to give supportive evidence.

Although her supporters were discouraged from attending the trial, there were people who were hostile to her who were all too eager to attend. They accused her of some of the charges usual in witchcraft trials – that she had cast spells on people, in particular on a child, and that she had a familiar, a squirrel rather than the more usual cat or dog.

One of the judges at Petersen's trial, Sir John Danvers, a friend of Oliver Cromwell, seemed unduly set on finding her guilty. The reasons for this are unclear but the result was in no doubt. Petersen was found guilty and hanged at Tyburn in 1652.

Pittenweem Witches

A set of supposed witches located in the fishing village of Pittenweem in Fife in Scotland in the early eighteenth century. The charges of witchcraft were set in train by the allegations of an apprentice blacksmith, Patrick Morton. He accused two women, Beatrice Laing (page 96) and later Mrs Nicholas Lawson (page 97), of damaging his health by means of witchcraft because he had been too busy to forge some nails for Laing. Morton was later found to have made the whole thing up, possibly because of the ant-witchcraft teachings of the local minister, Patrick Cowper, but not before Laing had been tortured into confessing and had implicated Janet Cornfoot (page 74) and Isobel Adam (page 58) and others. *See* Pittenweem Witchcraft Trial, page 22.

Elizabeth Proctor

One of the Salem Witches (page 110), Elizabeth Proctor was the wife of John Proctor (page 108). They were the employers of one of the girls involved in the hysterical accusations, Mary Warren. The latter at one point tried to retract her accusations once the Proctors had been arrested but the other girls refused to allow this and accused her of being a witch so that she had to reaffirm the charges and say that the spectre of John Proctor had tormented and made her sign the devil's pact. Both Elizabeth and John Proctor were regarded as being upstanding citizens, but by the time they were charged the hysteria was such that no one was safe from being charged and convicted. Elizabeth Proctor was found guilty but was not executed because she was pregnant. Later she was reprieved.

John Proctor

One of the Salem Witches (page 110), husband of Elizabeth Proctor (page 107). Both of them, particularly John, annoyed the authorities by their condemnation of the proceedings and their refusal to believe in witchcraft. Mary Warren, one of the girls involved in the hysterical charges of witchcraft, was the servant of the Proctors, and when she first began having her fits, John threatened to beat her. The fits disappeared, only to come back after the threat was over. Warren bore her employers, particularly John, a grudge and it was only a matter of time before they were charged. John Proctor was found guilty and hanged on 19 August 1692.

Mother Redcap

An elderly woman who lived in a village near Cambridge in the early part of the twentieth century and claimed to be a witch. She alleged that she was endowed with her powers by a black man after she had signed her name on a pact that he gave her. This harked back to the pacts with the devil that were such a part of witchcraft lore when witchcraft hysteria was at its height, but Redcap does not appear to have made any deal by which she gave her soul to the devil in exchange for material gain.

According to Redcap the black man had promised her familiars who would do her bidding, and certainly she appears to have been regularly accompanied by a cat, rat, mouse, toad and ferret. The old woman fared much better than those associated with witchcraft in previous generations as she was allowed to go about the even tenor of her ways, although her neighbours were quite well aware of her claims. This may well have been as her supposed powers were directed at helping others, say by healing, rather than at harming them.

Not for her was the horror of hanging or burning at the stake. She died quietly in 1926.

Anne Redfearne

One of the Pendle Witches (page 105).

Helen Rogie

One of the supposed witches involved in the witch trials in Aberdeen in 1596, Rogie was accused of making waxen images of anyone she disliked with a view to bringing harm on them. This was an extremely common charge when seeking to establish evidence of witchcraft. *See* Aberdeen Witches, page 57.

St Osyth Witches

The St Osyth Witches were part of the accusations of witchcraft that plagued parts of Essex for many years. A village near Brightlingsea in Essex, St Osyth was the home of around fourteen witches who were tried for witchcraft at Chelmsford in 1582 (*see* Chelmsford Witches, page 69). In common with some other witch trials, the incident that sparked off this particular one was in the nature of a village quarrel that became exaggerated and embellished out of all proportion.

The person first accused was Ursula Kempe (page 95), a local woman of little means who tried to make a living from working as a nursemaid and midwife and from her skill as a healer. It was reputed that she could undo spells that had been placed on people and supposedly caused them harm. This was to be her undoing because she fell foul of one Grace Thurlowe who accused her of witchcraft with relevance to treatment for her arthritic condition.

The trial of the St Osyth Witches was noteworthy for its use of child witnesses who were well under the official age at which witnesses were allowed to give evidence, and this trend was to continue in future witch trials. Such a witness was Kempe's eight-year-old son. Partly because of her son's testimony, but mostly because she was assured that the court would treat her with clemency if she confessed, she duly confessed and, as was frequently the case with confessions of witchcraft, implicated several of her neighbours. They in turn implicated others, and eventually fourteen women stood accused. The charges were various, ranging from the relatively minor, such as preventing beer from brewing, to the major one of causing death by sorcery, twenty-four people being alleged to have died by such means.

When the trial came to an end, Kempe was sentenced to execution by hanging, as was Elizabeth Bennet (page 62). Of the others, Annis Herd was especially fortunate to be acquitted since she was charged with causing death by sorcery, a charge that usually resulted in execution.

The trial increased the witchcraft hysteria in the area and in the Chelmsford Witchcraft Trial of 1645 (*see* Chapter 2, page 18), instigated by the witch-finder

Matthew Hopkins (*see* page 34), were several accused witches from St Osyth.

Salem Witches

One of the best-known mass witchcraft trials occurred in Salem, Massachusetts, from 1692 until 1693. Whilst not large by European standards the number of the accused was very great in terms of the New World. Nineteen people were found guilty and executed by hanging. It is thought that over one hundred and forty people were arrested as suspects on the say-so of a group of hysterical young girls. Of those who were not executed some avoided death on the grounds of pregnancy, some confessed to witchcraft in order to save their lives, some were reprieved, some escaped, and towards the end of the hysterical period, when people were no longer taking the girls so seriously and when spectral evidence was no longer allowed, many were acquitted. For further details *see* Chapter 2, Salem Witchcraft Trials, page 23. *See* also George Burroughs (page 68); Giles Corey (page 73); Martha Corey (page 73); Sarah Good (page 85); Sarah Osborne (page 104); Elizabeth Proctor (page 107); John Proctor (page 108); Tituba (page 117); John Willard (page 124).

Agnes Sampson

An elderly midwife, Sampson was one of those supposedly involved in the alleged coven operated by the North Berwick Witches (page 103), whose members were put on trial between 1590 and 1592, North Berwick being a town down the east coast from Edinburgh. She is noted for the detailed and sensational revelations that she made at her trial, including those involving a supposed plot against the king, James VI. Although she went on to make extravagant claims with reference to her connection with witchcraft and the devil, Sampson at first declared her innocence.

She was accused of witchcraft by Gilly Duncan (page 77), accusations by whom set off the trials of the North Berwick Witches. In her formal confession, forced out of her by torture, Duncan was moved to identify Sampson as one of her accomplices. On denying any connection with witchcraft, Sampson was ordered by the authorities to be shaved so that the telltale devil's mark could be looked for, this being an imprint supposedly left by the devil somewhere on the bodies of his followers. Just about any mark was taken as such a sign and an indication of guilt.

The searches for such a mark could be embarrassing and humiliating, and in Sampson's case the search resulted in the location of a mark in her genitals, which was declared to be a devil's mark. This being taken as clear evidence of her association with witchcraft and the devil, the next step was to submit Sampson to a series of tortures. One of these was thrawing (page 52), to which Sampson's accuser, Gilly Duncan, was also subjected. This involved jerking the victim's head violently by means of a rope. The old woman was also forced to be deprived of sleep until she confessed to her supposed misdeeds and was forced to wear a witch's bridle. The latter was a fearsome device, made of iron, that was put over the supposed witch's head and held down her tongue so that she was unable to speak, the idea being to prevent the person from speaking and so from giving voice to any curses that she might bring down on her accusers or tormentors.

In the light of this severe torture, and of the fact that the authorities threatened to repeat it, it is hardly surprising that Sampson eventually formally confessed to witchcraft. Officiating at her trial and at those of her fellow-accused was none other than the king, King James VI of Scotland, later to become James I of England. It is said that one of the reasons for his taking on such a role was that some of the accused were of noble connections.

Sampson, having once confessed, went to town on the crimes that she claimed to have committed in her role of witch. She laid claim to some of the more usual activities associated with witchcraft, including keeping a dog as her familiar, using charms to harm people and livestock and attending sabbats, orgiastic meetings of witches.

When speaking of the sabbats she went into great and lurid detail, speaking of sailing from a Hallowe'en sabbat to North Berwick in a series of sieves and kissing the buttocks of the devil in a ceremony in a church there.

The accused then went on to tell of how she and other members of the coven set about trying to use their witchcraft to bring about the death of the king, once by raising a storm and throwing a cat with a dead man's limbs strapped to its paws into the sea in the hope that this would make the king's ship sink on its voyage to Denmark to collect his bride-to-be, once by melting a wax image of the king in a fire, and once by attempting to get hold of one his garments so that they could smear it with poison obtained from a black toad left suspended by its feet for three days.

Many were disposed to think that all this was a result of an old woman's fevered imagination, and, of course, it is highly possible that her mind had been deranged by the terrible tortures to which she had been subjected. Even the king claimed at one point that he felt that Sampson and some of the others were not telling the truth. However, he claimed to have been brought round to believing their stories when, according to him, Sampson was able to whisper to him the very words that he and his bride had said to each other on their wedding night. The king took this as positive proof of Sampson's association with witchcraft, although, since no one else heard her

111

whispers, it is possible that this was all invented by the king so that the accused could be found guilty and suitably punished as a warning to others never to become involved in witchcraft. Probably he was also not enamoured of anyone claiming to have tried to kill him, whether in fact these claims were true.

The claims made by Sampson and her co-accused were so unlikely that the court was inclined to disbelieve them, and at one point the members of the jury voted to have the charges dismissed. This did not please the king, however, and to appease his anger the court was assembled again and Sampson and some of her co-accused were found guilty. Sampson was executed.

Alice, John and Agnes Samuel

Known sometimes as the Warboys Witches, their supposed witchcraft practices having taken place in Warboys in Huntingdonshire, the Samuel family, Alice and her husband and daughter, were all charged with witchcraft and found guilty. However, it was originally only Alice, an elderly woman in her seventies, who was involved.

The Samuels were neighbours to a family named Throckmorton who lived in Warboys. One day when Alice went to visit them one of the Throckmortons' five daughters, ten-year-old Jane, took some kind of fit. The likelihood is that this was an epileptic seizure but, of course, not much was known about seizures in those days and the girl accused Alice of having caused the fit. Someone being accused of witchcraft on the say-so of a young girl was to prove a common element in witch trials, as was the fact that one girl's historical claims could affect others. So it was with the Throckmorton girls who were soon afflicted by the same fits as their sisters.

A Cambridge doctor was sent for to find a reason for the seizures but was unable to identify any medical reason for them. This was enough for the presence of witchcraft to be suspected. It is to the credit of the Throckmorton parents that at first they dismissed the notion of their daughters' condition being the result of witchcraft and bore no ill-will towards Alice Samuel.

The condition of their daughters worsened, however, and they became desperate. They finally decided to approach Alice with the suspicions that had been aroused. Unfortunately for her, the fits of the girls grew ever more violent, as was to be the case in several later trials. The hysteria spread and soon other members of the household claimed to be affected by seizures. Again this was to become a common feature of witch trials.

It happened that the girls took to having fits only in the absence of Alice and, in an attempt to alleviate their supposed suffering, the old woman was ordered to become a permanent resident in the Throckmorton household for the time being. This was to be her undoing because, not only did they now have fits in her presence, but they began to accuse her of other deeds associated with witchcraft.

The wife of the man who owned the land inhabited by the Throckmortons came to call to see if she could do something about the undue influence that Alice was claimed to have over the girls. This was none other than Lady Cromwell, grandmother of Oliver Cromwell, who was to become Lord Protector of England. She is said to have cut off and burned some of Alice's hair in attempt to destroy any spell that she might have put on the girls. This appeared to have no effect on the girls' fits.

Shortly afterwards Lady Cromwell was to make a claim that did Alice's case no good whatsoever. She alleged that she had had a terrible nightmare in which she was attacked by Alice Samuel and her cat, cats being commonly held to be familiars of witches. The nightmare affected her so badly that she became ill and died some fifteen months later. On her death, when suspicions against Alice were rife, it was claimed that when Lady Cromwell had cut off part of her hair the old woman had asked her why she was treating her thus when she had not done her any harm as yet. It was the 'as yet' that did it. People began to speculate that this had been a threat of future harm.

Meanwhile Alice, not knowing how else to stop the girls' fits, ordered them to stop having seizures. This they did, and this was taken as further proof of Alice's involvement in their cause. By this time Alice was extremely distressed and confused. She went to visit the local minister and confessed that she must indeed be a witch if she was making the girls' fits happen. Having taken time to think about the situation and to recover her senses a bit, she withdrew the confession, only to have the Throckmorton girls start having fits all over again.

This was now taken as proof that the elderly Samuel woman did indeed have a magical influence over the girls, and she was questioned about her activities by two local justices of the peace and the Bishop of Lincoln. Again, as was hardly surprising, given her age and the amount of stress to which she had been subjected, she was moved to confess her guilt and even gave some details of witchlike activities.

Accusations of witchcraft had a nasty habit of seeming to be infectious, and soon other members of the local community were supposedly recollecting magical things done by Alice or her husband or daughter. For example, they claimed that livestock had been harmed, and even killed, by them.

Agnes, the daughter of Alice, refused to admit to any association with witchcraft but she was found guilty with her parents and all three were hanged in April 1593. It was a terrible illustration of what the hysteria of young girls can bring about.

After the executions the seizures suffered by the Throckmorton girls mysteriously cleared up. In line with the law, the property of the condemned witches was forfeited. It became the property of Henry, Lord Cromwell, and he used the money to set up a fund to be used to finance the preaching in Huntingdon of an annual sermon against witchcraft, the last of these sermons being given as late as 1814.

Sathan

The name of the cat who was the familiar of first one of the Chelmsford Witches (page 69), Elizabeth Francis (page 81) and then another, Agnes Waterhouse (page 121).

Michael Scott

Scott was renowned for his scholarship and, although he spoke out against necromancy and magic, is reputed himself to have been particularly adept at the art of sorcery. Little is known of his early life except that he was born in the second half of the twelfth century, possible in Balweary, near Kirkcaldy in Fife, Scotland. His family are assumed to have been fairly affluent. He was sent to Oxford to study and after this travelled extensively

Mother Shipton

The name given to a woman who was born, probably around 1488, as Ursula Southeil in Knaresborough in Yorkshire to Agatha Southeil, a young pauper who died giving birth to Ursula in a cave. Agatha was credited with the power of clairvoyance, healing and the ability to cast spells on people and animals.

Ursula was said to have inherited her mother's skills and her extremely unattractive physical appearance seemed to confirm this in some people's eyes, the archetypal witch being an elderly, ugly old woman. Ursula may have been ugly but she was not old at the time she first became associated with strange happenings. From her childhood weird incidents are alleged to have occurred when she was in the vicinity, such as furniture moving around and houses being ransacked without any sign of anyone being present.

Because she was so strange looking and because of her reputation, people were afraid of Ursula, and it was said that those who made fun of her rather grotesque appearance were likely to be harmed in some way. Although she was widely assumed to have the ability to bewitch people, it was as a prophetess and clairvoyant that she was best known. Despite her unfortunate appearance, she married at quite a young age, twenty-four, a carpenter by the name of Tobias Shipton, although, apart from this basic fact, little is known of him. She thus changed her name to Shipton and became known as Mother Shipton.

Mother Shipton is credited with a whole range of prophecies. She was well known in her lifetime and even better known after various books of her prophecies were written, although it is likely that some of her supposed prophecies were the invention of these later writers, who included Richard Head who published a book of her predictions in 1667.

Her prophecies mainly took the form of rhymes and riddles that could be variously interpreted, and the events that she is alleged to have foretold include the Great Fire of London, the invention of the motor car, the California Gold Rush, the building of Crystal Palace in London, World War II and the women's liberation movement. One prophecy that she appears to have got right was the one that she made regarding her own death. She died about the age of seventy around 1560 and was buried outside York, although her supposed association with witchcraft prevented her from being buried on hallowed ground. Her fame lives on today and the cave where she was born is a tourist attraction.

It is as well for Mother Shipton that she lived when she did. Had she lived later when the country was in the grip of witchcraft hysteria she is unlikely to have lived so long. She just missed the legislation passed in England against witchcraft in 1563 in the reign of Elizabeth I.

Ellen Smith

One of the Chelmsford Witches (page 69), who was tried in the second wave of witch trials in Chelmsford, which took place in 1579. She was charged with causing the death of a child by means of sorcery, made a formal confession to using witchcraft and was hanged at the same time as Elizabeth Francis (page 81).

Elizabeth Sowthern

With Anne Whittle, Sowthern was one of the most prominent of the Pendle Witches (page 105).

Stamford Witches

In the spring of 1692, around the time of the hysteria that surrounded the infamous

Salem Witches, some women were accused of witchcraft in the town of Stamford in Connecticut. The charges were brought by a young girl, Katherine Branch, a servant girl in the employment of one Daniel Westcot. She first of all complained of fits. Such fits, which were very probably a result of epilepsy, were frequently associated with witchcraft at the time.

At the same time she complained about experiencing a pricking feeling in her chest when she was gathering herbs. She claimed to have seen a cat who had promised her good things if she would go with it, and later she alleged to have been approached by ten cats threatening to kill her for having revealed to others what had happened to her during her herb-gathering.

She continued to have fits on a regular basis for about two weeks and claimed also to be suffering from hallucinations. The wife of Daniel Westcot was a sensible woman and was not disposed to believe her servant's claims that witchcraft was involved. She sent for a midwife to see if she could diagnose or cure Branch's condition. At first the midwife thought that the girl's fits had some natural cause and subjected her to various treatments, such as bleeding. When none of these was effective the midwife came to the conclusion that there was witchcraft involved.

Then Branch began to names. These included Elizabeth Clauson (page 70), Mercy Disborough (page 76), Goody Miller, Hannah and Mary Harvey, and Mary Staples. Of these, Goody Miller panicked and fled to the colony of New York in order to avoid arrest. The two Harveys and Staples were held under suspicion of witchcraft. As was common in witchcraft trials, people were invited to come forward and provide information that would testify to their guilt. Unusually, not many did. Indeed, only two people offered testimonies against them and they were all three acquitted.

Of the other two, Disborough was tried and found not guilty and Clauson was tried, found guilty and sentenced to death but reprieved on appeal.

John Stewart

The person who was responsible for the authorities being able to arrest Margaret Barclay (page 60) for witchcraft in connection with the running aground of her brother-in-law's ship. He claimed to have powers of clairvoyance and claimed to know that the ship had been lost before evidence of this was established. It was his claim that he had been asked by Barclay for a curse with which to bring down the ship and that he had seen Barclay and accomplices making clay figures of her brother-in-law and fellow-sailors and throwing them into the sea so that the men might suffer the fate of being lost at sea.

It was sadly a common occurrence for people to try to implicate others when they were accused of witchcraft, whether or not this was part of a forced confession. The authorities had heard of Stewart's claimed clairvoyance in connection with the loss of the ship and arrested him as a witch. He in turn accused Margaret Barclay. Barclay succeed in escaping torture but not death. Fearing the torture and the terrible death he would be likely to have to endure he succeeded in somehow freeing himself from his shackles and took his own life by hanging himself in his cell.

Tituba

One of the Salem Witches (page 110), Tituba was the servant of the local minister, Samuel Parris, and one of the earliest of the women in Salem to be charged. Tituba was from the West Indies, she and her husband, John, having been taken to Salem as slaves by Parris who had been a merchant in Barbados. They were given the surname Indian but this is unlikely to have been their real name.

Tituba's duties including looking after the nine-year-old daughter of the house, Elizabeth Parris, and her eleven-year-old cousin, Abigail Williams. It is thought highly likely that Tituba regaled the girls with tales of her native country, including stories of voodoo. Apparently the girls and some of their friends then became interested in the occult and started dabbling in such activities as fortune-telling before the onset of their hysterical fits. Had it not been for the advent of Tituba to Salem, it is a distinct possibility that the Salem witchcraft hysteria would never have taken place.

It might be thought inevitable that Tituba was one of the girls' first accused. She knew too much about them and so was a likely target. In addition, being an exotic stranger and a poor one, in the community people would be unlikely to leap to her defence. Tituba was moved to confess to witchcraft, probably because, like others, she had been assured that a confession would result in a reprieve or at least save her from the gallows.

Such an assurance did not always bear fruit in witchcraft trials, but in fact Tituba's life was spared in the light of her confession and she was sent to prison for an indefinite period. However, since it was part of the ethos of witchcraft trials that the accused had to pay for the expenses of the trial, whether they lived or die, Tituba was eventually sold as a slave to recoup the trial costs.

Tituba's imagination was obviously at work in the course of her confession. She claimed to have gone to coven meetings with Sarah Good and Sarah Osborne and that there was a coven in Massachusetts led by a tall, white-haired man dressed in black, later assumed to be George Burroughs (page 68). The latter, she claimed, had forced her to sign the devil's pact, and she claimed to have seen nine other names on this. This naming of names of others was a common feature of confessions in witchcraft trials

Mary Trembles

One of the Exeter Witches (page 79), who, with her co-accused, Susanna Edwards (page 81) and Temperance Lloyd (page 98), was accused of witchcraft and executed by hanging in August 1682. She seems to have been the least strong of the three, allegedly having been recruited to the coven by Edwards and having wept on her way to the gallows after having been found guilty.

Trèves Witches

The German town of Trèves, situated in the Rhineland and now called Trier, was the centre of much witchcraft hysteria in the later part of the sixteenth century. The area had been subject to several misfortunes and was in a mood to blame these misfortunes on any available scapegoat. At the time witchcraft hysteria was affecting Luxembourg and this soon spread, becoming widespread in Trèves in 1582.

The campaign of terrible persecution (*see* Chapter 2, Witchcraft Trials, page 17) that raged resulted in the deaths of six thousand accused witches between the years of 1587 and 1594. It was remarked upon by a commentator that many of these executed Trèves Witches were extremely affluent, the implication being that their wealth had been a factor in the accusations laid against them, since those found guilty of witchcraft had their possessions confiscated.

One of the accused Trèves Witches was Dietrich Flade, originally a civil judge officiating at witchcraft trials. The original charge against him was that he was too lenient in his judgements. Found guilty of this charge, he was removed from the post. Later he himself was accused of witchcraft, found guilty and executed. Such was the hysteria of the times.

Charles Walton

Charles Walton (1871–1945) lived in the village of Lower Quinton in Warwickshire and in this area was popularly held to be a witch. He is perhaps best remembered for his murder.

This area of England had long had an association with witchcraft and belief in the art was likely to survive there longer than in other areas. The Rollright Stones, a megalithic stone circle in the locality, were long thought to be associated with witches and a gathering place for covens. Indeed there is a legend that maintains that the stones were originally a Danish king and his army who were turned to stone by a local witch.

Walton was an agricultural worker who lived with his niece, Edith, and was a recluse. He was regarded as being a skilled clairvoyant and appeared to have strange powers with regard to birds. It is said that he was able to converse with birds and to direct them to do as he wished, having the same skill with some animals, but on a latter scale. He bred large natterjack toads in his garden, which was quite likely to call witchcraft to mind since toads played quite a large part in witchcraft lore. His presumed association with witchcraft was also said to take him at night to the Rollright Stones, supposedly to watch witches performing their rituals.

It was alleged that he acquired his prophetic skills when he was a boy after encountering a black dog three nights running on nearby Meon Hill. On the third night the black dog is said to have changed into a headless woman. The next day his sister died. Walton became extremely introverted and developed powers of clairvoyance.

On 14 February 1945 Walton set out to do some work in the fields of a farmer whose land lay near Meon Hill, carrying a pitchfork and billhook for use in his work. The farmer saw him at midday but he failed to return home at his appointed time. A small search party was got up to look for the old man and its members came upon his body lying at the foot of a willow tree. His body had been cruelly mutilated, his pitchfork having been thrust so violently through his neck that it had nearly beheaded him and his billhook having been used to make a cross-shaped wound in his chest. Not surprisingly his face held a look of terror.

It was difficult to account for Walton's murder, since he was very much a man who kept himself to himself. The local people suspected that it was his supposed connection with witchcraft that had led to his death. This suspicion was heightened by the fact that a black dog had been found hanged on Meon Hill a few days after the old man's death.

The Scotland Yard detective Robert Fabian was put in charge of the investigation and probably assumed that the crime could be solved relatively quickly, given the size of the village. His investigations were hampered by the silence and lack of cooperation that he encountered among the villagers. Fabian's men took four thousand statements and around thirty samples of clothing, hair and blood but the murderer of Walton remained unidentified. It was assumed that the death was in some way connected with witchcraft but nothing was ever proved.

There was a suggestion that Walton's death might be what is now known as a copycat crime. In 1875 in a neighbouring village called Long Compton an elderly woman suspected of witchcraft, Anne Turner, was murdered by a mentally retarded man called John Haywood because he thought that she had bewitched him. The method of murder was the same in both cases. Turner, too, had been pinned to the ground with a pitchfork and had had her chest slashed in the shape of a cross.

Another theory was that Walton was the victim of an attack by someone who thought he had been bewitched by him and who was intent on removing the spell by a method known as scoring above the breath, a procedure well known around the time of the witchcraft hysteria. In order to destroy a spell by scoring the breath the bewitched person had to make the witch bleed above the nose or mouth.

A third suggested possibility was that Walton's murder was connected with a pagan ritual. The date of his death, 14 February, was the date on which the druids undertook blood rituals in order to ensure abundant crops. The crops of the previous year had been poor, and it was thought that someone might have come up with such a solution to ensure fertility. The ritual involved draining the blood of a dead man or woman into the soil.

It was suggested that perhaps Walton had been selected to have his blood used because he had been accused of using witchcraft to bring about poor crops. He was alleged to have taken some of the natterjack toads that he bred and harnessed them to toy ploughs so that they could run across the fields and blight the soil.

There may have been some more rational reason behind Walton's death. None was ever found, however, and the identity of the perpetrator of the crime was never discovered.

Wapping Witch

A name given to Joan Peterson (page 106), who was found guilty of witchcraft and hanged at Tyburn in April 1652.

Warboys Witches

A name given to three members of a family called Samuel who were accused of practising witchcraft in Warboys in Huntingdonshire and brought to trial at Huntingdon in 1593. The case had many of the elements that were to become typical of witch trials in later years when witchcraft hysteria reigned. *See* Alice, John and Agnes Samuel, page 112.

Agnes Waterhouse

One of the first of the Chelmsford Witches to be accused, Waterhouse was a peasant woman in her early sixties from Hatfield Peverel. She was to be the first of many in the area to be accused and tried. She was charged with the killing of a man name William Fynee, it being alleged that she had used sorcery to affect him with a wasting disease. She was tried by no less a person than the Attorney-General, Sir Gilbert Gerard. This indicated how seriously witchcraft was taken and was to influence the thinking of others in later trials.

Children were used to testify in court, uncorroborated statements of guilt were accepted and, fatally for Waterhouse, the devil's mark (page 165) was found upon her. Waterhouse confessed and was hanged, it not being in her favour that her cat, supposedly her familiar and accomplice in Fynee's death, was named Sathan. This cat had been given to Waterhouse by Elizabeth Francis (page 81) who was also charged with witchcraft, as was Waterhouse's daughter Joan Waterhouse (page 121).

Joan Waterhouse

It was common to assume that witchcraft ran in families, and it was quite usual for members of the same family, particularly mother and daughter, to be accused of being witches. Thus it was in the case of the Waterhouse family from Hatfield Peverel in Essex. Joan Waterhouse was the daughter of Agnes Waterhouse (page 121) and, like her mother, was one of the early Chelmsford Witches (page 69). Aged eighteen she was not accused of the same crime as her mother but was charged with having caused damage to the limbs of a twelve-year-old girl, Agnes Brown, it being very common for children to be accusers in charges of witchcraft.

The girl claimed that a black dog, allegedly Sathan, a black cat owned by Agnes Waterhouse, in an assumed shape, had been present at the time of the in juries. Fate, not to mention the authorities, was kinder to the daughter than the mother and Joan was acquitted.

Thomas Weir

A military man, who became extremely eccentric as he grew older, Weir voluntarily confessed to witchcraft at the age of seventy. He had seen distinguished service as a soldier in the Parliamentarian army in Ireland in 1641 and became commander of the Edinburgh City Guard in 1649. He was extremely religious and was a much respected senior figure in the Presbyterian church in Edinburgh. His history of extreme piety made all the more extraordinary his claims of witchcraft.

In the light of his previous character no one was inclined to believe his confession and assumed that he was mentally ill. However, doctors were duly sent for and they gave it as their professional opinion that he was sane. In the light of their findings the Provost of Edinburgh felt obliged to arrest Weir. He lived with his sister and, since his confession had also implicated her, she too was arrested.

They were both brought to trial in April 1670, but there was no mention of witchcraft in the charges, since it would have been an embarrassment to the Presbyterian church to have one of their senior figures accused of sorcery and of consorting with the devil. Weir had in fact confessed to sorcery but he had also confessed to incest, adultery and sodomy, and it was with these that he was charged – incest with his sister, adultery with his sister's servant girl and sodomy with horses and cattle. These were hardly charges befitting a man of such piety but clearly the church members thought that anything was better than witchcraft.

His sister by this time was in a mental state that was even worse than that of Weir. She confessed to having sold her soul to the devil and to having kept a familiar that enabled her to spin yarn at three or four times faster than the average woman. She also maintained that her brother did practise witchcraft and used a carved wooden staff that he carried everywhere to work his spells.

The court confined itself to finding both accused guilty of incest and bestiality and set aside the question of witchcraft. The accused were both condemned to death. Weir was strangled and burnt at the stake and his sister was hanged the following day.

Many people charged with witchcraft were elderly people and many of them were women. It is likely that many of these were in some way mentally unbalanced. Certainly it seems almost certain, despite the doctor's findings, that Weir was not entirely sane.

Jane Wenham

Wenham was the last person to be sentenced to death by an English court on charges of witchcraft, although the sentence was never in fact carried out. The sentence of execution established by the court had been passed against the wish of the judge, Sir John Powell. He was able to delay the death of the condemned woman until he was able to secure a royal pardon for her and obtain her freedom.

Nicknamed the Wise Woman of Walkerne, in recognition of the fact that she was an inhabitant of Walkerne in Hertfordshire, Wenham had long been labelled locally as a witch, although she became extremely angry if anyone accused her of having anything to do with witchcraft. Wenham was more formally accused of witchcraft in 1712 when a local servant girl, Anne Thorne, who was employed by the local minister, claimed that the woman had caused her to have fits and to vomit pins. These were standard charges in witch trials, especially when made by girls or young women. Thorne further accused Wenham of causing her to suffer from hallucinations in which she saw demons in the form of cats and of using her magic to force her to run half-a-mile, despite the fact that she was suffering from an injured leg.

It often took just one accusation of witchcraft for a whole series to follow. Soon other local people were supposedly remembering incidents that damned Wenham. She was duly arrested and formal proceedings begun. She was searched for evidence of the devil's mark (page 163), but Wenham was lucky not have any such mark identified on her body.

This did not do her much good, however, for at this point she decided to make a full confession. Admittedly, she claimed to be a white witch, practising her art only in the cause of good. She seemed fully convinced that she had magical powers that she had probably used in healing, but it was not white magic that was of concern to her accusers. It was the black art in which they were interested, and soon they charged her with conversing with the devil in the shape of a cat. Then further supposed evidence against her was brought to court. This took the form of some ointment that was found under her pillow. Bizarrely, it was judged by the prosecution to have been made from human fat.

This was enough evidence against her, and she was found guilty and sentenced to death. As has been described above, she was saved from execution by the intervention of the judge. There was such strong feeling against her in some quarters, however, that she was unable to return to her cottage and resume her normal life. She did not fare too badly because she was saved from a life of wandering when a local man who was sorry for her provided her with a cottage in Hartingfordbury. There she lived until her death in 1730.

The case attracted a great deal of public interest – and not just at local level. It resulted in much debate on the subject of witchcraft, and several pamphlets about the Wenham affair were published.

Anne Whittle

With Elizabeth Sowthern (page 115), Whittle was one of the most prominent of the Pendle Witches (page 105).

John Willard

One of the Salem Witches (page 110), Willard was a local farmer and a deputy constable. In the latter post he had been responsible for issuing the initial writs against the accused witches. He became convinced, however, that the real guilty parties were the hysterical girl accusers and made his views known. It was a foregone conclusion that the girls would take their revenge on him and, realising this, he fled. Unfortunately for him, he was captured a few days later and charged following accusations made against him by Mrs Putnam and some of the girls. He was unable to recite the Lord's Prayer faultlessly, probably because he was nervous. This was held to be clear evidence of an association with witchcraft and he was convicted and hanged on 19 August 1692.

Christine Wilson

Also known as the Dalkeith Witch, Dalkeith being a town near Edinburgh, Wilson was accused of witchcraft and sent for trial in 1661. The noteworthy thing about her trial is that the authorities used a method known as bier right as a test of witchcraft.

This test was used in cases where witchcraft was alleged to have resulted in murder and involved getting the accused witch to touch the dead body of the alleged victim. If the corpse began to bleed it was taken as absolute proof that the accused was a witch. Unfortunately for Wilson, when she laid her hand on the wound that had killed her supposed victim it is said to have begun to bleed profusely. She was therefore declared to be guilty without further ado.

The bier right test did not originate with witchcraft trials. It was originally used in murder trials, it being part of folk legend that a corpse that had been the victim of murder would begin to bleed when it was in the presence of the murderer, or at least when he or she touched it.

Janet Wishart

One of the supposed witches involved in the witchcraft trials in Aberdeen in 1596, Wishart was suspected of murdering one man by magic and causing severe illness in another. She was also charged with removing body parts from a corpse of someone who was hanged while it was still on the gallows, the said body parts supposedly being for use in her pursuit of witchcraft. *See* Aberdeen Witches, page 57.

Elizabeth Woodville

The eldest daughter of Sir Richard Woodville and Jacquetta, Duchess of Bedford, Elizabeth Woodville (c. 1437–92) married the English king, Edward IV in 1464 in a secret marriage ceremony. There were many people who were against this marriage since it was deemed to be politically unsuitable. There were attempts made to discredit it and to invalidate it.

Woodville, who had previously been married to Sir John Grey but had been widowed when he was killed in battle in 1461, first met the king in Whittlebury Forest. A rumour was started by those wishing to invalidate the marriage that she had deliberately set out to ensnare the king and that she and her mother, the Duchess of Bedford, had made use of witchcraft in the process. When the king was imprisoned by the Earl of Warwick after an uprising in 1469, the rumours grew more persistent, since the king was not there to challenge them.

A man called Thomas Wake produced a figure of a knight cast in lead that had a wire tied round it. He claimed that this had been fashioned by the duchess as part of her scheme to ensnare the king for her daughter. Another man, John Daunger, said that two more figures had been fashioned and that one had represented the king and the other the duchess's daughter.

Wake made formal charges against the duchess, and the case went to court in 1470. By that time the king was out of prison and Daunger, nervous of incurring the king's wrath, retracted his statement about the figures and denied that he had suggested that the duchess was involved in witchcraft. This left the case somewhat short on evidence and the duchess was acquitted.

However, complications arose on the death of Edward IV in 1483. The late king's son, Edward, was in line to become the next king as Edward V. If the marriage of his mother, Elizabeth Woodville, to Edward IV could be invalidated then he would not ascend the throne, being illegitimate. Instead the throne would pass to Richard of Gloucester, brother of Edward IV. It was obviously in Richard's interest to have the marriage invalidated.

It is said that Richard then turned rumours of witchcraft towards Elizabeth Woodville and towards the mistress of the late king, Jane Shore. Richard had a withered arm that had been in such a condition since birth. He chose conveniently to forget this, however, and accused Woodville and Shore of causing the damage to his arm by means of witchcraft. Many knew that this condition had been present at his birth but they were too terrified to say so.

Shore was imprisoned in the Tower of London and all her property was confiscated.

She was also compelled to do penance by walking barefoot through the streets of London wearing only a smock. Woodville, who was Richard's main target, fled for refuge to Westminster, taking with her her youngest son. Richard then crowned himself king as Richard III and later imprisoned the boy who should have been Edward V and his brother in the Tower of London, where they were to die in mysterious circumstances.

Elizabeth Woodville had tragically lost both her sons, but she did at least acquire the title of dowager queen when Henry VII ascended the throne of England in 1485. She died in Bermondsey Abbey in 1492.

Elizabeth Wright

The mother of Alice Goodridge (page 85) who was accused with her daughter of witchcraft largely because she had given her a dog, the dog being claimed to be a witch's familiar. It was very common to suppose that witchcraft ran in families and very often a mother or daughter would be charged as well as the accused. Goodridge died in jail before she could face the death sentence but history does not record what happened to Wright.

John Wrightson

Known as the Wise Man of Stokesley, he was known throughout the area south of Durham and around north Yorkshire at the beginning of the nineteenth century for his powers as a white witch. These supposed powers were used by him in various ways that were beneficial to those with whom he came in contact. For example, people sought his help in finding lost or stolen possessions and to cure sick livestock and they came from miles around so to do. It was his contention that his magical powers were effective only when he was fasting.

Alice (Alse) Young

One of the Connecticut Witches (page 72), Young was the first person to be executed after anti-witchcraft legislation was passed in the state in 1642. She was hanged in May 1647.

Chapter 4

Witchcraft Connections

There were many things traditionally associated with witchcraft, whether these were living creatures, plants, objects, or rituals. Some of the best known of these are categorised below.

Creatures and Deities

bat

Because of its dark colour and its nocturnal habits bats were often associated with evil and death. In some cultures they were seen as harbingers of death and witches were once popularly thought to be able to change themselves into bats for ease of gaining access to buildings. It was thought in some areas of Europe that a house might be protected against witchcraft if a dead bat were nailed on the outside of a house, such as a window or shed, provided that the bat had been carried three times round the outside of the house before being killed.

The blood of the bat was allegedly used in witches' potions, particularly in the potion known as flying ointment, which was an aid to the witch's ability to fly on her broomstick. Bat's blood was also sometimes used in the celebration of the rite known as black mass (page 183).

bee

The bee, more specifically the queen bee, had an unusual role in the European witchcraft trials organised by the Inquisition. The interrogators were always on the lookout for some reason for accused witches being able to withstand torture without making their confessions which were so vital to the legal system. One of these alleged, and extremely unlikely, reasons was that, if the accused witch swallowed a queen bee before being arrested by the authorities, he or she would be able to sustain the torment of torture and the rigours of the trial without confessing to involvement in witchcraft.

blackbird

The colour black from early times has been associated with death and also with evil. Thus any creature of that colour was likely to be suspect. This being the case, it was almost inevitable that a blackbird would be numbered among those creatures likely to be regarded as a witch's familiar (page 132). The fact that this was so points to the difficulty that the accused witch had in proving that he or she did not have a familiar. Even today, when chemicals in herbicides and pesticides have taken their toll of wildlife, blackbirds are by no means an uncommon sight. In the days of rampant witchcraft hysteria blackbirds would have been even more common a sight, always popping into gardens in search of food and thus condemning any old woman whose garden they chose to potential charges of witchcraft.

black cat see CAT.

black dog

As has been indicated above, black has long been regarded as the colour of death and evil. A dog of whatever colour was always a likely candidate as an alleged witch's familiar (page 132), although the dog was not so closely associated with witchcraft as its traditional enemy, the cat (page 129). An old woman, especially an unattractive one behaving strangely, who lived alone and kept a pet for company, at the height of the witchcraft hysteria, especially in England, was at grave risk of being accused of being involved in witchcraft and of keeping a familiar.

Her predicament was even worse if the dog was black in colour for that was thought to be a favourite shape of the devil. It was alleged that the devil often assumed the shape of a large black dog at witches' orgiastic gatherings or sabbats. Tradition had it that he most commonly turned himself into a dog when he adopted a suitable position for receiving an obscene kiss or a kiss on the buttocks from his devoted followers.

boar

This was one of several animal shapes alleged to be favoured by the devil, particularly if the boar was black in colour, the colour black being traditionally associated with evil as well as death. The devil in the shape of a boar, which was held to be a very virile creature, featured in many supposed confessions from accused witches.

cat

Throughout the ages the cat has been a favourite household pet, often being a companion to someone living alone. This made it practically a certainty to be identified as a familiar (page 132) of an accused witch, a demon that would help her work her magic. As was the case with other creatures suspected of being familiars, an accused witch did not actually have to own a cat for her to be accused of keeping one as a familiar. One chancing to pass her door, go into her garden, rub against her, etc, was enough.

Any cat was suspect but a black cat was exceptionally so, since black cats from earliest times were associated with the supernatural. In this respect cultures adopted ambivalent attitudes towards the black cat. Some saw it as a force for good, a symbol of good luck and healing, while others viewed it as a portent of bad luck. The ancient Egyptians regarded it as sacred.

As has been mentioned above, it was popularly thought that many witches kept cats as familiars, sometimes allegedly being rewarded with drops of their mistress's blood for their part in helping the witches to cause death, damage and injury. It was also thought that cats as familiars were handed on from generation to generation and sometimes from friend to friend.

Cats have long been valued for their companionship. However, at times of witchcraft hysteria people were nervous of being near a cat, fearing that it might be a demon in disguise. They felt that it might be a witches' familiar spying on them and listening in to their conversations with a view to causing them harm. Because of their association with witchcraft cats were often cruelly treated. It was not unusual for them to be attacked or killed and cats whose owners had been convicted as witches were particularly at risk. They were often burned alive, especially in continental Europe.

Cats were feared not only because they were suspected of being familiars of witches but because it was suspected that they might even be witches who had taken the shape of cats. Witches were traditionally thought to be able to change shape and the cat was a favourite shape. If a cat was injured in some way, whether deliberately or accidentally, and an old crone in the village appeared with a wound in the same area of the body, it was automatically assumed that she was a witch who had been injured when in the form of the cat. It was popularly held that witches could change into cats nine times in their lives. The devil also was traditionally supposed to adopt the shape of a cat from time to time, thus preventing some people from harming a cat in case it was the devil in disguise and took reprisals on his attacker.

Thus it was difficult to decide whether a cat was a simple feline companion, a familiar, a witch or a devil. One test was devised to determine which cats were entirely innocent. They were put into a bowl of holy water and observed to see if they would try to escape. It was thought that those cats that were witches in disguise would try to escape from the presence of the holy water since witches avoided all things associated with God. This was not a very reliable test as most cats hate water and would probably try to escape.

Thus, just as many innocent people died during the reign of witchcraft hysteria so did many cats.

cock

The cock in many cultures is associated with light and in some is considered to be a force for good. Because of the bird's associations with concepts that were the opposite of the concepts associated with witchcraft, darkness and evil, it was popularly believed during the periods of witchcraft hysteria that witches sacrificed cocks as an insult to God, who was also associated with light and goodness. The crowing of the cock at dawn heralded the reappearance of light after a period of darkness and was a sign to witches that they must bring an end to their orgiastic gatherings or sabbats.

Witches were also alleged to use cocks in storm-raising, a practice that they were supposed to indulge in with a view to sinking ships at sea or destroying crops on land. Supposedly they sacrificed the birds over their cauldrons as they wove the relevant spells.

crow

The crow, like several other black creatures, has through the ages often been treated with suspicion. The bird, like the raven (page 138), was often seen as an omen of disaster and often of death and so was avoided where possible. Its specific role in witchcraft was as a familiar (page 132), people imagining that it was a demon in the shape of crow that flew around carrying out its mistress's orders and helping her work her harmful magic.

demon

Originally in pre-Christian cultures and in non-Christian cultures the word demon could be applied to a spirit, whether good or evil. Christianity, however, characterised them as being evil spirits and servants of the devil. Demons thus came to be depicted as having the same kind of shape as the devil but in miniature, although they were seen as having the ability to adopt any shape they chose at will. By this means were they able to spread their evil and cause death and destruction.

The study of demonology was once a subject that occupied the attention of many scholars. According to these experts demons were divided into a complex system of hierarchies. There were thought to be many thousands of demons, most of whom belonged to the minor hierarchies.

Ashtaroth

The best known and most major of the demons included Ashtaroth. He was associated with science and secrets and was thought to be useful in rituals relating to divination. Supposedly he gave off a terrible stench. Ashtaroth was linked with witchcraft for his alleged role in demonic possession, being one of the senior demons supposedly involved in the possession of the Loudun nuns.

Asmodeus

Another well-known and major demon is Asmodeus. He was associated with rage, revenge, lust and lechery, and was regarded as the demon most likely to be at the heart of any demonic possession of a sexual nature. It was said that if witches and sorcerers successfully conjured him up he could help them attack or destroy their enemies.

Beelzebub

Another major and powerful demon was Beelzebub. He was regarded as being the prince of demons and was known as the Lord of the Flies, because he often adopted the shape of a fly when he made an appearance.

He was traditionally linked with witchcraft in that he was thought to reign over sabbats. This was appropriate since he was associated with gluttony and orgies and supposedly copulated with the witches in the course of the sabbats. His name was chanted by witches at sabbats and at black masses (page 183). Like Ashtaroth, he was said to have been involved in the demonic possession of the Loudun nuns.

Belial

Another major demon was Belial. His name is sometimes used as a synonym for Satan, but as a demon he was associated with treachery and lies and with the creation of wickedness in humankind, especially when this wickedness was associated with sexual perversion, lust or lechery. He was considered to be not only exceptionally evil but exceptionally, and deceptively, beautiful in appearance.

Demons generally were associated with witchcraft in at least two respects. They were supposedly given the role of helpers to witches after the latter had taken allegiance to their master, the devil. In order not to advertise their evil presence, the demons took the form of creatures whose presence would not cause suspicion. These commonly included cats, dogs, hares, rabbits, toads and ravens. Such demonic witches' assistants were known as familiars.

demonic possession

Many cases of supposed witchcraft during the height of the witchcraft hysteria involved what was known as demonic possession. Nowadays cases that supposedly involved this phenomenon are thought to have been the result of deception or hysteria or instances of epilepsy or schizophrenia.

Innocent people were supposedly possessed by demons at a witch's request, and under the influence of the demons they would begin to behave in a way that was not at all in keeping with their own personalities. For example, people who were renowned for their quietness, piety and chastity might start acting in an extremely noisy, wild and lewd way. Often the victim's features took on horrible, distorted expressions and their voices became rasping or guttural. It was thought that witches could transmit demons by means of potions or foods, especially those foods, such as apples, that were common and seemed harmless.

The established cure for demonic possession was exorcism. During this exercise, priests or ministers would attempt to get the demon to leave the victim's body by calling on God and the saints to release the person from the evil presence. Sometimes the victim was physically beaten in order to force out the demon.

devil

The devil, also known as Satan or Lucifer, known to Christians as the archenemy of God, became associated with witchcraft in the Middle Ages when the idea came into being that witches worshipped the devil, not God. He remained associated with witchcraft for a long time but is not linked to modern witchcraft.

In medieval times the devil was regarded as being a real being and, like demons, he was credited with the ability of changing shape at will. Consorting with the devil was a common charge laid at the door of someone accused of witchcraft. Many confessions, often extracted from accused witches by means of standard questions and in some cases by torture, referred to the devil making a physical appearance. He was said often to take the form of a dark man dressed in black but sometimes he seemed to prefer animal disguises and appeared to the witches in the form of a black dog, a wolf, a goat or toad.

Witches supposedly took an oath of allegiance to the devil, many by the signing of a devil's pact in their own blood. In return he promised them increased magical powers and a familiar (page 132), a demon in the shape of a dog, cat, hare, etc, as an assistant. He also allegedly used to mark the bodies of his initiates in some way, the mark being known as a devil's mark. Such a mark was zealously searched for by investigators on the bodies of accused witches and just about any mark could be claimed to be a devil's mark.

He allegedly frequently put in an appearance at sabbats, and many witches confessed to having sexual intercourse with him. Part of a witch's initiation supposedly involved kissing the devil's buttocks. For the purpose of such a ceremony it was said that the devil often took the shape of an animal, such as a big black dog or a boar.

dog *see* **BLACK DOG.**

familiar

The witch's familiar was a common feature of witchcraft in England and Scotland, although not in mainland Europe. In England in 1604 under the tenets of the Witchcraft Act it was made a felony 'to consult, covenant with, entertain, employ, feed or reward any evil and wicked spirit'. Familiars became extremely important in witchcraft trials when the notorious witch-finder Matthew Hopkins was zealously trying to bring charges of witchcraft against as many people as possible. In those times the possession of a cat was enough to have the owner charged with suspected witchcraft.

The familiar was regarded as being a minor demon assigned by the devil to a witch to help her or him to carry out acts of magic and generally act as an assistant in return for vowing allegiance to him. Witchcraft was essentially a secret business and questions would have been asked if the demons had appeared in their allegedly usual guise, the traditional shape of the devil but in miniature. In order not to attract attention, therefore, the familiars changed shape and became creatures that would not arouse comment.

Many familiars supposedly took the shape of household pets, black cats being an exceptional favourite but dogs were also popular, as were several wild animals, such as hares, toads, rabbits, mice, and sometimes weasels and hedgehogs. Birds, such as blackbirds, crows, ravens, and even insects, were also suspected of being demons in disguise. Some witches supposedly had several familiars and it was possible to inherit a familiar or be given one by a fellow-witch. Familiars were thought to be able to adopt more than one shape and to be able to disappear at will.

Witches were allegedly very appreciative of their familiars and their help and rewarded them by taking good care of them. A special reward was said to take the form of drops of the witch's blood, sometimes sucked either from a finger, a protuberance on the skin or even a supernumerary nipple. Familiars sucking blood were thought to leave marks on the witch's skin, and evidence of such marks was carefully searched for during examination of an accused witch. Some witches were said to baptise their familiars and to give them odd names, totally unlike usual Christian names.

The role of the familiar in a witch's household was a general one. They acted as companions and assistants and were supposedly particularly useful in helping the witch to cause death and injury to her neighbours or their livestock or property. For example, familiars were meant to be able to cause milk to go sour, to make cows unable to give milk, to render animals sterile and to make crops fail. At the height of the witchcraft hysteria if an animal or bird, or even an insect, was spotted at the scene of death or disaster it was instantly identified as a familiar and a likely owner sought.

Owners of pets, particularly if they were old women who lived alone, were particularly at risk of being accused of keeping a familiar. When witchcraft hysteria was at its peak, however, and particularly during the ultra-zealous witch-finding activities, it was enough to be seen in the company of a creature, however accidental and brief this encounter was, to merit a charge of keeping a familiar.

A curious feature of the belief in familiars is that there are no records indicating that such creatures ever came to the aid of their accused owners. Mostly they seem to have disappeared. Sometimes a close watch was kept on imprisoned witches in case familiars adopted the shapes of insects and crept in to the prison to help their owners escape. It appears that they need not have bothered because the familiars seem to have turned out to be an ungrateful lot, despite the generous treatment that had been meted out to them by their owners.

Familiars are not unknown in modern witchcraft but these are not believed to be demons in disguise. Instead they are seen as animal companions that are often sensitive to psychic powers and vibrations.

goddess

In modern neo-pagan witchcraft it is the goddess, not the devil, who is at the centre of its creed. She is regarded as being the source of magical power as well as being the major life force. Gerald Gardner did much to promote the importance of the goddess in modern witchcraft in the 1950s after the establishing of his own coven.

Modern witches have also been influenced by the feminist movement and the increased role of women in the world at large. This has added significantly to the emphasis that is laid on the role of the goddess in modern witchcraft.

In modern witchcraft there are often two beings at the head of the movement—the goddess and the horned god (page 136), a union of female and male. These are represented in covens by the high priestess and the high priest. On the other hand, there are some modern witches who regard only the goddess as the head of the movement. The goddess is frequently regarded as a trinity, known as the triple goddess, comprising the female roles of virgin, mother and crone.

goat

The goat is traditionally associated with virility and lust. In European witchcraft tradition, although rarely in England or Scotland, the goat was also frequently regarded as a shape adopted by the devil at orgiastic gatherings of witches, or sabbats. Several of the accused witches forced under torture to make supposedly voluntary confessions described the devil in the form of a goat presiding over rituals. Some also recounted how they had sexual intercourse with the devil in this shape or gave him an obscene kiss, a kiss on the buttocks.

In classical mythology the god Pan was depicted as a creature that was half-human, half-goat. A similar figure has been associated with witchcraft, although it is more associated with Satanism, the worship of the devil. The symbol of the satanic goat is known as Bahomet.

hare

The hare, like the cat, was associated with witchcraft on two counts. It was held to be a common familiar (page 132) of witches, using its famed ability for speed to help him or her carry out spells and harmful deeds. The hare was also thought to be a favourite shape adopted by witches as a disguise.

There are legends in which hunters wounded a hare only to see later an old hag in the village wounded in the same part of the body. Similar tales tell of hares being killed by hunters only to metamorphose back into human corpses.

Hecate

In Greek mythology, an ancient goddess whose powers were various. She could bestow wealth, victory and wisdom, good luck on sailors and hunters, prosperity on youth and on flocks. She was afterwards confused with other divinities and finally became especially an infernal goddess who was invoked by magicians and witches.

hedgehog

In common with the cat and the hare, the hedgehog was held to fulfil two roles in witchcraft. Although less commonly associated with witchcraft than the cat, the hedgehog was thought to be a favourite disguise of witches, able to infiltrate gardens, outhouses and even houses without attracting as much attention as a black cat or dog. So strong was this belief that many innocent hedgehogs were killed on the assumption that they might well be witches. The hedgehog was also thought to be an occasional familiar, particularly useful to witches who wished to do harm to livestock.

high priest *see* HORNED GOD; COVEN.

high priestess *see* GODDESS; COVEN.

horned god

In modern neo-pagan witchcraft the horned god is the male consort of the goddess. In covens he is represented by the high priest who sometimes wears a horned helmet or a headdress with antlers. Although the horned god in modern witchcraft is representative of sexuality, power and vitality, unlike the devil, he does not use his attributes in an evil way.

The concept of the horned god is thought to date back to Palaeolithic times. He was often depicted as being half-man and half-animal as well as wearing horns. He was traditionally associated with woodlands, the hunt and fertility.

horse

In pre-mechanical days the horse was extremely valuable to its owner, both as a form of transport and as a draught animal in agriculture. It was therefore seen as a prime target for the evil of witches who wished to bring harm to the owner. Owners feared that witches might make the horse go lame, become ill or even die. Because of this, horse-owners were wont to try to protect their animals from the spells of witches by surrounding them with things that were traditionally thought to ward off witches. They might hang a horseshoe on the stable door or hang a sprig of rowan on it. Alternatively, they might hang either on the stable door or round the animal's neck a stone with a hole in it, known as a hagstone and sometimes known as a witch-stone. It was thought that the hanging of brass bells or shining horse brasses on the horse would keep at bay any witches or familiars because they would be dazzled by the brightness of the objects.

Witches were alleged sometimes to borrow horses without permission in order to get to their orgiastic gatherings or sabbats. Supposedly, owners would be made aware of this unauthorised borrowing only in the morning, when the animals would be exhausted and sweating. Witches were also credited with the ability to stop a team of horses dead in their tracks and to keep them in that state until they chose to let them start up again. This could have a disastrous effect on farmers who were trying to plough fields, and some tried to avert this happening by having the driver of the said team of horses carry a whip made of rowan, a favourite anti-witch tree.

At the height of the witchcraft hysteria witches were alleged to adopt the shape of horses and thus probably saved themselves the bother of borrowing horses to transport them to their sabbats. The horse was also one of the shapes that the devil was thought to assume from time to time. The horse was regarded as being too big to be a familiar (page 132).

incubus

Incubus was the name given to a lustful demon that had sexual intercourse with women as they slept and made the women have erotic dreams. Such demons were thought to have associations with witchcraft in that they were alleged to have sexual intercourse with witches at sabbats, sometimes taking the forms of goats.

lizard

Lizards were thought to have at least two connections with witchcraft. The creature was widely believed to be a common ingredient in the renowned witch's brew of evil appearance and evil smell. It was also thought to be one of the shapes that a demon might adopt as a witch's familiar (page 132).

owl

The owl has had something of a mixed history in legend and mythology. To the ancient Greeks it was a symbol of wisdom, but the ancient Romans saw it as a bird of ill-omen whose presence or call often presaged death, illness or disaster. In the Middle Ages the owl was allegedly the shape sometimes adopted by a demon or familiar (page 132) when accompanying a witch on a broomstick or flying around helping her carry out her magic.

rabbit

Like the hare (page 135), the rabbit was traditionally held to be a possible disguise for a witch's familiar (page 132), which would hop around swiftly to aid her in carrying out her magic. As was also the case with the hare, the rabbit was held to be one of the common shapes that witches adopted to disguise themselves. It was bad luck for an old woman if she lived beside a field or wood containing rabbit warrens.

A rabbit's foot is traditionally associated with good luck.

raven

Because black has been traditionally associated with darkness and evil, black creatures throughout the ages have tended to be viewed with suspicion. Like the crow (page 130), but to an even greater extent, the raven was regarded as a bird of ill-omen whose presence was held to portend disaster or death. The raven was avoided as much as possible because it was a popular tradition that adopting the shape of a raven was a common pursuit of the devil.

At the time of the witchcraft hysteria it was alleged to be a favourite shape for a witch's familiar (page 132), having the ability to fly around the place helping her to carry out her black deeds against her neighbours. It was unfortunate for an old woman if she had a house near a place where ravens were liable to settle or gather, as this made her a prime target for accusations of witchcraft.

striga

The striga in classical mythology was a blood-drinking night-spirit. Striges were depicted as being women who could adopt the shape of terrible birds of prey with huge talons and misshapen heads. In such guises they were said to prey upon men and children as they lay asleep. They were alleged to have misshapen breasts full of poisonous milk that they fed to children. As far as men were concerned, the striges were alleged to turn back into women in the course of attacking them and had sexual intercourse with them.

As time went on the striges became identified with demonology, and in the Middle Ages they were regarded as female witches.

spider

The spider was associated with witchcraft in that it was alleged that witches used spiders, caught in pots, to cast spells in their practise of storm-raising. Otherwise spiders were regarded in many cultures as symbols of luck and considered to have the ability to ward off disease. It was considered unlucky to kill them.

toad

The toad is one of the creatures most commonly associated with witchcraft, and it was alleged to have several functions. It was said to act as a witch's familiar (page 132) to aid her in her acts of witchcraft, especially acts that involved the use of poison, and to accompany her to sabbats. Toads were quite common, and it was not necessary for a woman actually to possess one in order to be accused of having one as a familiar. A toad in the garden or anywhere near the house was enough to bring on the accusation. The creatures were regarded as having attributes that made them particularly suitable to be familiars in that they were allegedly easy to tame, easy to look after and were endowed with psychic powers.

The toad was also involved in shape-changing, which was a traditional feature of witchcraft. It was said to be a favourite shape for witches to adopt and it was thought that the devil himself sometimes changed into a toad.

The toad is traditionally associated with poison. Its skin contains glands that secrete a poisonous substance if the creature is alarmed in any way. This made the toad a favourite ingredient in witches' brews over which they cast their spells. Toads were also allegedly used by witches to make themselves invisible. In order to achieve this feat, witches are reputed to have mixed toad spittle and the sap of the sow thistle and then smeared the resultant potion on the skin in the shape of a crooked cross.

The toad was also supposedly useful in detecting poison as well as creating it. It was thought to carry a jewel inside its head that would become hot in the presence of poison. Such a stone was much sought after by people with enemies, and there were many stones that laid claim to be genuine toadstones but that were in fact fakes. A test of genuineness involved placing the stone in front of a toad. If the toad jumped towards the stone as if to take it, then the stone was held to be genuine.

Yet another association between witchcraft and the toad existed. Some witches were alleged to use them in a bizarre way to bring painful death to their enemies. Supposedly they avenging witches baptised toads with the names of the relevant enemies and then tortured the creatures to death under the belief that such action would bring a similar fate to the enemies.

Because of its associations with poison and witchcraft, and because it is regarded as an ugly creature, the toad has long been regarded with dislike or fear. Its reputation was not enhanced by the fact that it was thought to cause warts in anyone who handled it. On the other hand, people were reluctant to kill them, because tradition had it that killing a toad would bring on a storm of rain.

weasel

The weasel was held to be one of the animal shapes favoured by witches as disguise. This was perhaps because it is a swift, lithe animal that could slip in and out without being easily seen. As well as being associated with witchcraft, the weasel was thought to be a creature of ill-omen, bringing death or disaster by its presence or call. If one was unlucky enough to encounter or hear its call then the recommended way of supposedly warding off any ill effects was to throw three small stones or pebbles in front of one and to make the sign of the cross a total of seven times.

It was claimed that the gift of divination or prophesying would be granted to someone for a period of a year if he or she would only consume the heart of weasel while it was still beating.

wolf and werewolf

The wolf is traditionally regarded as a fierce, dangerous creature and associated with evil and the supernatural. In some European cultures the wolf was regarded as a creature of ill-omen whose appearance presaged death or disaster, and in some it was closely associated with the devil, being regarded as a favourite shape for the devil to adopt.

The wolf was also associated with witchcraft, especially at the height of witchcraft hysteria. Witches were popularly held in some areas to be able to turn themselves into wolves so that they could roam the land striking terror into people's hearts and inflicting injury and destruction. This alleged taking on of the shape of a wolf was known as lycanthropy.

When the accused witch allegedly took on the guise of a wolf, he or she was known as a werewolf, literally man-wolf, but, according to legend, there were other werewolves who were not witches. These were people who supposedly did not choose to adopt the shape of wolves but had been destined to do so, perhaps because they had been born under a curse. Such people, mostly but not always men, supposedly changed into wolves regularly, usually on nights of a full moon, and immediately took over the alleged attributes of wolves, fierceness and evil, whatever their attributes were when they were in their own shapes. Alleged signs of being a werewolf included having hair on the palms of the hands.

People

cowan

In modern neo-pagan witchcraft cowan is the term used for someone who is not a witch and so has not been initiated into witchcraft. The word is derived from a Scots word for a mason who did not serve an apprenticeship.

warlock

Warlock is a term sometimes used to describe a male witch or sorcerer. In modern witchcraft most men preferred to be known simply as witches and even historically the word witch was recognised as referring to either sex. In fact a huge proportion of accused witches were women.

white witch

White witch was the name given to someone who appeared to be endowed with magical powers but who used them for good rather than evil, black being the colour associated with those alleged witches who used their supposed gifts to cause harm. White witches, for example, might be herbalists and healers, but some were allegedly able to counteract evil spells, tell the future or mix love potions.

Unfortunately for many so-called white witches, to the investigators during the height of the witch hysteria it mattered not what the accused witch used her powers for. They regarded these as having come from the devil and so the white witch was as doomed as any other witch.

Plants

angelica

One of several plants traditionally thought to endow protection against witchcraft. It was also thought to protect against some diseases, such as the plague. This aromatic plant is sometimes called the Root of the Holy Ghost from its association with St Michael.

apple

The apple has long been associated with magic. Both the whole fruit and its peel were widely used in divination. In divination where there was a love interest it was thought that apple peel might take the form of the initial of a future love.

Witches were popularly thought to use apples in order to poison people, and this belief is reflected in the tale of Snow White, who was given a poisoned apple by her wicked stepmother that put her to sleep. Apples were also said to play a role in demonic possession since witches supposedly used the fruit to transmit the demon to the victim.

bay

The bay tree was often planted close to houses with a view to protecting its inhabitants. It was meant to be able to ward off disease, particularly the plague, as well as evil spirits and witches. The leaves of the tree were used as a means of prophesying the future. They were set alight and if they crackled as they burnt then all would be well. If, on the other hand, they burnt without making a noise then misfortune would occur. Bay leaves were also used medicinally by those who used plants in the treatment of various diseases and who were often suspected of witchcraft for so doing.

bryony

A climbing plant that is said to have acted as a substitute for mandrake in witches' potions and brews if they were unable to obtain the latter. Known for its aphrodisiac properties, bryony was also thought to increase fertility and was used in healing to reduce bruising.

deadly nightshade

This was used both as an aid to witchcraft and to ward it off. Witches were said to be able to increase their powers of divination if they consumed small amounts of the plant, the berries of which contain belladonna. If they overdid the dose, however, they could end up either dead or mad. The plant was also held to be one of the ingredients in the preparation known as flying ointment, traditionally concocted by witches to help them fly through the air.

If the plant was useful to witches, they also had cause to dislike and fear it. It was thought that a sprig of the plant either placed in a house or worn by a person had the property of warding off evil spirits, including witches, from livestock as well as people. Like other anti-evil plants, it was also thought to protect against disease.

egg tree

The egg tree was used in America to ward off witches and their magic. It was a dead bush that had its branches cropped and was then covered in a great many blown eggs and set up near a house or cabin.

elder

The elder was associated with witchcraft in that it was a favourite wood from which to fashion their wands. It was also said to be a common ingredient in witches' brews, the stems of the dwarf bush being a reddish colour in autumn and thought to look as though they contained blood. Elder trees were viewed with suspicion because they were thought to be inhabited by evil spirits and it was feared that the devil might come down the chimney if elder wood was burnt on the fire. Witches were supposed to have the ability to turn themselves into elder trees and were thought often to congregate under elder trees. There was a great fear of elder being brought indoors as it was thought that it would bring death into the house.

In common with deadly nightshade, however, the elder tree was considered to have anti-evil properties as well as evil ones. Cutting a stem from a dwarf elder bush was regarded as being a way of causing injury to any nearby witch. Furthermore, the elder could be used to identify witches and ward off any injurious actions that they might be plotting. This was supposedly done by smearing a little elder juice on the eyes, an action that was meant to result in the person so treated being able to see any witches who were in the neighbourhood and to perceive what they were up to.

Although elder was not to be taken indoors, it was regarded as being a good thing to hang a bough of it, cut on the last day of April, at the entrance to the house since this acted as a deterrent to witches and warded off their magic. Amulets of elder worn by people were meant to have the same effect.

fern

The fern was one of several plants that were associated with both witchcraft and anti-witchcraft activity. Seeds collected from the plant on Midsummer's Eve and carried around were thought to enable the carrier to become invisible. Such seeds were also thought to be an ingredient in flying ointment, a preparation allegedly made by witches to enable them to fly through the air.

An anti-witchcraft device could be made from the male fern if was gathered on Midsummer Eve's and the fronds removed until there were only five remaining, leaving the plant resembling the human hand. This was then smoked over a bonfire until it became hard. It was then thought to be ready to confer immunity from the evil of witches or evil spirits on the person who carried it. Because of its resemblance to the human hand it was known as a lucky hand.

foxglove

Originally known as folk's glove, but also known as witches' glove, the plant was thought to be poisonous and a common ingredient in witches' potions. Many people who were accused of witchcraft in England and Scotland were simply people who experimented with herbs to try to alleviate or cure injuries or disease.

The foxglove was one of the plants used by such people, and in the middle of the eighteenth century a Shropshire doctor, William Withering, discovered that the foxglove did indeed have curative properties. Having heard of the success of a supposed witch in curing dropsy, he contacted her, learned of her use of foxglove and extracted from it the unknown drug now known as digitalis. This discovery proved to be a major breakthrough in the treatment of heart disease and the drug was later synthesised.

garlic

Traditionally garlic was known for its healing and beneficial properties and indeed has become so again nowadays when there has been a renaissance in herbal medicine. It is used, for example, as an aid to the cure and prevention of colds and other infections. The ancient Romans gave it to soldiers to wear in battle in the belief that it would raise their courage levels.

However, garlic was also used traditionally as a powerful protective agent against the forces of evil. Witches, demons and vampires were all thought to be deterred by this pungent plant. Garlands of garlic were worn around the neck or hung in houses, often near windows, with such a purpose in mind. Garlic collected in the month of May was thought to be particularly effective. The Greek hero Odysseus is said to have used garlic to protect his men against the witchcraft of Circe, the sorceress who had the ability to turn people into swine.

Garlic was also used in informal trials. Someone suspected of a crime was asked to throw a clove of garlic into a fire. If the clove popped the person was considered to be guilty.

hawthorn

Hawthorn is one of several trees and plants that were credited with being used both by witches and against them. The tree was long thought to be cursed because thorns from it were thought to have formed the crown that was put on Christ's head when he was being crucified.

Witches were thought to use thorns from the hawthorn when they were jabbing effigies so as to cause pain, injury or death to the person whom the effigy represented. The thorns were also thought to feature in other black magic practices.

The hawthorn was, however, also used as a witch deterrent. A hawthorn bush planted by a house entrance was thought to ward off witches, it being thought that they might get caught in the thorns.

People seem to have been slightly ambivalent about hawthorn blossom. On one hand, it was considered to be unlucky to take hawthorn blossom indoors. On the other hand, some thought that decorating the rooms of a house with hawthorn blossom would keep witches and other evil spirits at bay.

hazel

The hazel tree was one of several trees and plants that was thought to be both advantageous and disadvantageous to witches. The wood was so prized by witches for its magical properties that they used it to make their wands. The nuts were used at Hallowe'en in a procedure that was intended to check up on the fidelity of a lover. Two nuts were placed in the fire by the person testing a lover's fidelity. If the lover was unfaithful the nuts would jump in the air.

Hazel was also used to protect against witchcraft. Sprigs of witch hazel would be tied over the entrance to houses to stop witches from going in and to ward off their magic.

hemlock

Hemlock, being a poisonous plant, was traditionally associated with the devil and with witches. It was credited with the ability to summon demons and was supposedly much used in witches' brews and potions. Hemlock was held to be one of several ingredients that went into the preparation of flying ointment with which witches allegedly smeared themselves to help them in the process of flying through the air.

henbane

Henbane is a poisonous plant and so was a natural plant to be associated with witchcraft. Witches were meant to use it in their brews over which they concocted their spells. When the plant was burnt the fumes were said to conjure up demons. The plant was also said to be a useful aid to clairvoyance, and it was used in love potions because of its supposed aphrodisiac properties.

mandrake

Mandrake is a poisonous plant that grows in the Mediterranean region. Traditionally a major ingredient of witches' brews, the root of the plant was thought to have valuable magical properties as well as being considered to be an effective soporific and aphrodisiac. The thick root of the plant is meant to resemble a human in shape – hence its name, and it was used traditionally in healing as well as a magic ingredient.

It was believed in medieval times that witches harvested their mandrake roots from the bottom of gallows trees. This was because the mandrake plant was supposed to spring up from the semen or other body droppings that fell from the decomposing corpses of those who had committed crimes and had been executed for these.

Skill was thought to be required in digging up the root of the mandrake. Digging it up with one's own hands was meant to end in agonising death or impotence. It was thought safer to use a dog in the plant's uprooting. According to one tradition, it was enough simply to get a dog to dig up the root, but according to another the procedure of uprooting involved digging around all but a very small portion of the root. A dog was then tied to this and left. On trying to follow its owner the dog would pull out the root, often strangling itself in the process. As the root parted company with the soil, it was alleged to let out a loud, terrifying shriek and sometimes to sweat blood.

It was said that witches sometimes undertook a spell to endow the mandrake root with the gift of speech, having first covered it in human blood and placed berries on it to represent eyes and mouth. If the spell worked, the mandrake root was then said to be able to communicate to witches information about what was going to happen in the future and also to advise them of the location of hidden treasure.

marigold

The marigold flowers were much used in herbal healing. For example, if it was rubbed on the skin it was thought to reduce inflammation and swelling from bites, stings and injuries. The flowers were also thought to be an aphrodisiac and so were used in love potions.

However, the marigold had a specific use in witchcraft in that it was considered to be a witch deterrent. It was often therefore planted near the entrance to a house to prevent witches from entering. Its flowers were also taken inside to ward off the evil and magic of witches.

mistletoe

Mistletoe is an evergreen shrub that from early times has been associated with the occult, having been associated with the Celtic druids who considered it sacred, like the oak tree on which it often grew. It has been used in various ways as a healing agent but it was also used as protection against witchcraft, ill-fortune and disease. It was thus hung in homes, barns and stables. A sprig of mistletoe hung from a doorway was thought to deter witches from entering the building.

mountain ash *see* ROWAN TREE.

mugwort

This plant was traditionally considered to be an effective witch deterrent. It was also thought that it could act as an antidote against several poisons and that it could be used to undo the effects of spells. The plant was also thought to protect against the plague and other diseases and to counteract the effects of fatigue

oak

The oak tree was sacred in Celtic lore and has traditionally been regarded as providing protection against evil and witchcraft. Sprigs of the tree were hung in houses or worn by people as a witch deterrent, and standing under an oak tree was thought to serve the same purpose. Trees planted at the entrance to buildings were believed to prevent witches from entering, and when the trees were planted at a crossroads their anti-evil properties were thought to be particularly effective.

oak apple

A gall formed on an oak tree, caused by a kind of wasp larva, is sometimes called an oak apple. Oak apples were traditionally used to ascertain whether or not a young child had been bewitched. For this purpose three oak apples were cut from a tree and dropped into a vessel of water. The vessel was then placed under the child's cradle amid strict silence. If the oak apples floated to the top of the water the child was deemed to be safe but if they sank to the bottom then it was deemed certain that the child had been placed under a witch's spell.

pumpkin

The pumpkin is much used to form lanterns in the festivities surrounding the American custom known as trick or treat. This takes place on Hallowe'en, and the pumpkin is now becoming increasingly commonly used for lanterns in Britain, even Scotland, where the traditional Hallowe'en lantern is made out of a turnip, a much harder vegetable to hollow out than the pumpkin.

The pumpkin is one of several plants and trees that were traditionally held to provide protection against evil in general. In order to maximise this property of the plant, it was considered best to plant them on Good Friday.

rosemary

Rosemary was associated with witchcraft in that it was thought to be able to ward off the harmful effects of the evil eye by which a person was bewitched if a witch cast a baleful glare at him or her. Sprigs of rosemary were worn by people on their persons or hung on the front door of a house to prevent witches working their magic. The plant was also regarded as being a useful aid to divination.

rowan

The rowan tree, also known as the mountain ash, was traditionally held to be a powerful protector against the power of witches. Trees were often planted in gardens or near the entrance to buildings to ensure that witches did not cross the threshold, and even the dead were protected from the evil of witchcraft by planting rowan trees in churchyards. People sometimes wore sprigs of rowan in their hats and sprigs were tied to bedsteads. Boughs of it were sometimes hung in barns, stables and cow sheds to protect livestock from witchcraft. Sometimes farm animals had twigs of rowan attached to their tails to prevent interference from witches.

The wood was sometimes used to make riding whips as a witch deterrent, and piles of it were sometimes kept inside a house with the same purpose. When new houses were being built, rowan was sometimes used in parts of their structure to keep the inhabitants witchcraft-free.

So powerful an anti-witch agent was rowan considered to be that a witch touched by a rowan branch was supposedly instantly to be taken off by the devil to Hell.

stonecrop

Stonecrop is a flowering plant the habitat of which is rocks or walls. It was often grown by doorways in the belief that it would prevent witches from entering, and sprigs of it were taken into houses for the same purpose

willow

Willow was traditionally much used in herbal medicine because of its alleged curative properties. Some varieties were used as a protection against witchcraft, although witches were alleged often to use it for making wands. It was a popular tradition that it was unlucky to bring willow catkins into a house or to burn willow wood on a fire indoors

witch hazel *see* HAZEL.

wych elm

Also known as witch elm, this tree was meant to impart luck to anyone who carried a twig of it and also to protect the carrier from witchcraft.

yarrow

Yarrow is one of several plants that were thought to deter witches and their evil doings. Consequently sprigs of it were worn on the person or taken into houses.

It was used in divination when this related to a vision of someone's future lover, the person seeking such a vision being advised to sleep with a sprig under his or her pillow.

yew

With reference to witchcraft the yew tree was considered to provide protection against witchcraft. It was also thought to protect people from ghosts and evil in general and was often planted in churchyards.

On the other hand, witches were said sometimes to use it to make wands. Some traditions indicate that it was considered unlucky to take yew into a house or to cut down a yew tree as this would bring ill-luck

Substances

amber

Amber, which is yellowish fossilized resin, was traditionally considered to protect against witchcraft or other evil. It was used in jewellery or in amulets for this purpose and to bring good luck to the wearer. Amber was also considered to have curative properties in the case of certain illnesses.

blood

Blood, which was considered to represent a person's life-force, was associated with witchcraft in various ways. Witches could get power over their enemies or over people whom they wished to harm by getting hold of a few drops of their blood. They could then make use of it in the weaving of their harmful spells and are alleged to have put samples of the blood into harmful brews or potions or else to have incorporated the blood in effigies, doll-like representations of the people whom they intended to harm.

Blood has long had associations with the making of pacts. Sometimes people cut their wrists so that their blood could mingle, this being a method of making an agreement that was totally binding. Another unbreakable pact could be achieved by signing the said pact in blood. Thus it was that the pact which witches were supposed to make with the devil as a sign of their allegiance to him was supposedly signed by them in their blood. This devil's pact was a common feature in witches' confessions, but this was because the questions put to witches to get them to confess were of such a standard nature that the confessions were bound to be similar.

The keeping of familiars (page 132) by witches allegedly often involved blood. Witches were widely believed to reward these creatures for their good work by treating them to a few drops of their own blood, sucked from their fingers, protuberances on their skin or occasionally from supernumerary nipples. Such blood marks were zealously searched for during investigations following charges of witchcraft.

Because a person's blood was meant to contain his or her life-force, it was thought that the magical powers of a witch resided in the blood. It was also thought that this power could be transmitted from generation to generation and that such power could be destroyed only by destroying a witch's blood. Thus it was that, although in England witches tended to be executed by hanging, on mainland Europe, and sometimes in Scotland, witches were routinely burnt at the stake. By burning the witches to ashes the authorities believed that they could destroy a witch's blood and her power, although as an act of great clemency convicted witches were often allowed to be strangled first, provided they had confessed.

Blood was also used in attempts at breaking the power of witches when they were still alive. In the common practice of scoring above the breath, suspected witches were attacked and cut somewhere above their mouths or noses. It was believed that if they bled from such areas then they would lose their magical powers.

In another measure believed to neutralise the power of a witch, a witch bottle was prepared. This contained some blood taken from a victim of witchcraft as well as samples of hair, nails and urine. These were then boiled together at midnight, causing much agony in the witch who had bewitched the victim and nullifying her magic. Alternatively the bottle was buried with the same result. Sometimes it was said that the witch bottle could result in the death of a witch.

bloodstone

A variety of semiprecious stone, bloodstone was much used in healing but it was also thought to be endowed with magical properties. It was thought to be an aid to the divination of natural disasters, such as storms and floods. Bloodstone was also thought to protect against evil, including witchcraft, but it was also used by witches in their magic, being thought to have the property of granting wishes.

brass

Brass was traditionally considered to be a substance that could protect against witchcraft and other forms of evil. Thus it was used in the making of amulets, worn by people to protect their persons from evil or ill-luck, and it was also used to hang on horses, in the form of horse brasses or bells, or on cows, in the form of bells to protect the livestock from the machinations of witches.

hair

Human hair was thought to be connected with witchcraft in several ways. The hair was thought to retain a strong connection with the person from whom it had been taken. This therefore meant that a witch was in a position to do more harm to an intended victim if she had some of his or her hair, even a strand or two, when putting together spells. It was also thought that people who were thought to be likely victims of witchcraft were advised to bury, or otherwise get rid of, any of their hair that was cut off to prevent a witch from getting hold of it.

It was thought that a witch could cause terrible pain to an intended victim simply by throwing a strand of his or her hair in the fire. The making of effigies, or wax images, was a favourite way for witches to harm people of their choice. If some of the relevant person's hair was incorporated into such an effigy the magic was alleged to be more powerful.

Hair was often used in the contents of a witch bottle, which was a bottle or flask filled with various ingredients, including urine and nail clippings, taken from someone who was suspected of being bewitched, the bottle being then buried or heated on a fire. The purpose of this was to counteract any spells that might have been cast by causing pain to the bewitcher. If the bottle exploded this was meant to signal the death of the witch.

Strength and power were thought in early times to reside in the hair. For example, in the biblical story Samson was deprived of his strength when Delilah cut off his hair. It was thus believed that at least some of the magical powers of witches resided in their hair. If a witch shook her head it was thought by this act of shaking her hair that she had doubled her power in strength.

When witches were arrested they were often shorn of their hair. This was partly as an act of humiliation or degradation but it was also seen as a means of depriving them of their power. Hair-shaving was also carried out to get rid of any demons or familiars that might be lurking there with a view to helping the accused witches. Another reason for the cutting of the hair of the accused witches was to allow the investigators to search particularly thoroughly for signs of the devil's mark, a mark made by the devil on a witch when he or she swore allegiance to him.

holy water *see* WATER.

iron

Although iron was traditionally used by witches, in that their cauldrons and many of their utensils were made of it, the metal was long held in folklore in many parts of the world to be a protector against evil spirits. It was commonly used to make amulets to give protection against evil, danger or ill-luck. With specific reference to witchcraft, it was believed in Europe that witches were unable to cross cold iron. With this tradition in mind, people were advised to bury a knife beneath the doorsteps of their houses so that witches would not dare to enter.

lead

According to some traditions, lead might be used in tests undertaken to determine whether or not there was witchcraft afoot. One test involved the dropping of a piece of molten lead into a vessel of water and waiting to see if the piece of lead solidified into a shape discernibly resembling something. If the piece of metal did take on a discernible shape then there was indeed witchcraft in the air and the person who was believed to be the victim of this was urged to wear the said piece of lead over his or her heart as a protection against harm by witchcraft.

Caskets containing religious relics and coffins containing corpses were formerly made of lead partly to keep away evil spirits.

nail clippings

It was thought that witches would be able to make exceptionally effective spells against someone if they had possession of something that had been part of his or her body. Thus, as was also the case with hair, a witch in possession of nail clippings could do a great deal of harm to the person from whose nails they came. It was, therefore, thought advisable for people to bury nail clippings in order to prevent a witch getting hold of these.

Nail clippings were also sometimes used along with hair (page 152) and urine in the creation of a witch bottle, which was used to counteract the effects of any evil spells that had been cast.

poison

Poison was traditionally associated with the practice of witchcraft. During the witchcraft hysteria, many people were accused of being witches because they had killed people by means of poison or made them ill by it. Before the days of specific tests it was often difficult to disprove this, especially if, as was not infrequently the case, the accused was someone who used herbs and plants to help heal people. It was thought that such people might just be using their supposed healing powers as a front while they used their knowledge of plants to poison people.

It was popularly assumed that the traditional witches' brew contained poisons. These were thought to include such poisonous plants as deadly nightshade but also poison taken from the toad.

salt

Traditionally salt was held to be anathema to evil creatures of all kinds. Its very function as a preservative made it an opposing force to the corruption of witchcraft, demons, etc. In addition it was used in Christianity to consecrate churches, and salted holy water was used in baptism. Thus salt was thought to be a deterrent to witches and their evil ways.

Witches were popularly held to be unable to eat anything salted. Salt was meant to be absolutely excluded from any of the feasts at the orgiastic sabbats, and when pressure was being applied to suspected witches to get them to confess they were sometimes force-fed extremely salty food. This was supposedly in order that they would refuse the food and confess but actually it was a form of torture in that the accused witches were force-fed such food and then deprived of water after they had developed a raging thirst.

Salt was used in various ways as a protective against witchcraft. Newborn babies might be bathed in salted water or made to eat a little salt to protect them against the evil of witchcraft. Dairymaids would sometimes put a little salt into their milk pails or butter churns so that witches would not turn the milk sour or the butter rancid.

It was thought that salt could also be used as a means of dispelling the power of a witch, even when this had taken hold. Spells were supposedly able to be broken by the action of throwing a handful of salt into the household fire every morning for nine consecutive days. Another tradition suggested that one way to break a witch's spell involved the stealing of a tile from the roof of her house. This was then to be sprinkled with a mixture of salt and urine and heated over the fire.

If a person was so unlucky as to have a witch curse him or her, it was thought that such a curse could be negated by the throwing of a handful of salt after the retreating witch. It was fortunate in such cases that some people did carry salt around with them as a deterrent against witchcraft.

spittle

Spittle was thought to have various connections with witchcraft. It was thought, for instance, that witches used their own spittle while effecting curses or harmful spells against someone. The spittle of an intended victim was also thought to be useful to witches in that it was thought to increase the power of a spell against him or her. It was thus considered unwise to spit indiscriminately.

Witches had another connection with spittle. It was believed that witches were unable to shed tears. Aware of this, the interrogators of accused witches on mainland Europe in the Middle Ages and the Renaissance accused them of having smeared spittle on their faces to emulate tears if they were found to have wet cheeks.

Spittle was thought to play a protective role in cases of the evil eye. If a witch looked at someone with a particularly baleful expression, it was thought that she was fixing him or her with the evil eye or overlooking them. By such means did she bewitch them. Spittle was thought to be able to help in reversing such bewitchment. It was thought that this might be brought about by spitting in the witch's eye.

urine

Urine was thought to have various connections with witchcraft. If a witch got hold of some of an intended victim's urine then this, like the possession of hair, nail clippings, and spittle, gave the witch more power over her victim and made her evil spell more potent. In order to prevent the witch getting hold of urine and using it for harmful purposes, likely victims were urged to spoil it in some way, for example by washing the hands in it, so that it would be rendered unsuitable for use in spells.

If a spell was put on someone then one possible counteraction involved getting hold of some of the witch's urine. This was then bottled and buried, or sometimes boiled. Such actions had the effect of making the witch ill, and often unable to urinate, and sometimes of killing her. Alternatively, a cake could be made of ingredients that included some of the bewitched's party, and perhaps some nail clippings. The cake was then tossed in a fire. Still another method of breaking a spell that involved urine was in the making of a witch bottle. This was a flask or bottle filled with such ingredients as the urine, hair and nail clippings of the victim of a witch's spells and either buried, boiled on a fire or thrown on a fire.

Urine was also said to be a useful witch-deterrent. It was suggested that families wishing to keep witches out of their houses should sprinkle the doorposts with urine. An even more drastic measure involved sprinkling the members of the family with urine.

It was alleged that at the orgiastic gatherings of witches, known as sabbats, and at black masses (page 183) blasphemous travesties of religious ceremonies were held at which urine was substituted for holy water.

water

It was a widely held belief that witches or evil spirits could not cross water. There are several tales about people saving themselves from the clutches of witches or demons by jumping over stretches of water or crossing bridges. One of the most famous of these concerns the character Tam o' Shanter in the poem of the same name by Robert Burns. After a particularly drunken session with his friends, Tam was riding home pursued by a young witch whom he had spied on dancing in a churchyard. He narrowly escaped being caught by her by riding over a river.

Water that had been consecrated in a religious ritual was anathema to witches and other evil spirits. Holy water that had been used at services conducted during Easter was thought to be a particularly powerful deterrent against witches and demons. As a witch-deterrent, holy water was sprinkled on houses, farm animals and crops to prevent interference from witches. In many places there was a man who went around delivering holy water for such purposes. Those taking part in witchcraft trials as investigators, torturers, juries or judges were often advised to keep a dish of holy water so that they might use it to ward off any manifestations of witchcraft. In the well-known film *The Wizard of Oz*, the character called the Wicked Witch of the West simply melts away when covered in water.

Water was involved in a notorious test of witchcraft. This was known as swimming (*see* Chapter 2, Witchcraft Trials and Executions, page 46). In the carrying out of the test an accused witch was bound hand and foot and thrown into a stretch of water. If he or she sank it was seen as proof of innocence, although the exercise often resulted in death. If, on the other hand, he or she floated to the surface then this was taken as a sign of guilt. It was sometimes held that the water would not accept someone who had turned his or her back on Christianity and baptism and become a heretic.

Water was used in various healing processes. In neo-pagan witchcraft salted water is used to purify tools and to anoint participants in the rites.

Objects, Places and Concepts

aiguillette

Witches were alleged to use this knotted loop of thread to induce dissatisfaction in marriage, particularly to induce impotence, or even castration, in men and sterility in women. The device was also thought to incite couples to enter into adulterous relationships. The idea was particularly popular in France in the sixteenth century, and people were so convinced by its validity that many couples got married secretly and privately rather than publicly in church where the witch might get to work with her aiguillette during the marriage ceremony.

amulet

The concept of an amulet, an object that would protect against harm, goes back to earliest times and survives to modern times. The word comes from the Latin *amuletum*, meaning 'means of defence'. Amulets were typically worn on the body, often being worn round the neck, but this was not necessarily the case.

Amulets were widely used outside witchcraft for their supposed healing properties. However, they were specifically used to protect against witchcraft when witchcraft hysteria was its height. They sometimes took the form of pieces of paper on which were written some kind of holy words, such as the Lords' Prayer, in the hope that witches would be deterred from practising their craft by the presence of something associated with God.

bell

The ringing of church bells was considered to be anathema to witches and evil spirits, and they quickly disappeared at the first sound of them. During times such as Hallowe'en when witches held their sabbats, or orgiastic gatherings, townspeople would ring the church bells so that the witches would not fly over their houses on their way to the gathering. So powerful were church bells as a witch-deterrent that witches were said to fall off their broomsticks if they heard them ring. Storms were often assumed to be the result of a witch's deliberate storm-raising. Therefore, at the first signs of a storm, townspeople sometimes rang the church bells to dispel the evil work of the witch.

Other bells were also thought to be a witch-deterrent. Bells were sometimes hung at entrances to prevent witches and evil spirits from crossing the threshold. They were also frequently hung around the necks of horses, cows or other livestock to keep them safe from witchcraft, and human beings sometimes wore them as amulets.

According to some traditions, bells could sometimes be put to use by witches and sorcerers to summon the dead. It was thought that for bells to be used in this way they had to be made from a particular combination of metals, inscribed with various symbols. Tradition had it that the bell was then wrapped in green cloth and buried in the middle of a grave in a churchyard for seven days. The bell was then thought to be suitable for the purpose of summoning the dead.

black book *see* GRIMOIRE.

bodkin

Bodkins were frequently used in the test for witchcraft known as pricking (*see* Chapter 2, Witchcraft Trials and Executions, page 45). The sharp end of a bodkin would be used to prod an accused witch all over in an attempt to find a spot that was insensitive and so thought to be a mark of the devil. If the accused person was showing no sign of having such insensitive areas then the investigators would often use a cunning ploy. They would stab one area of the body with the sharp end of a bodkin exceptionally violently and then immediately touch another area of the same body very lightly with the blunt end. The result often was that the person concerned was hurt so badly by the sharp stabbing that he or she almost failed to notice the touch of the blunt end and so was put in the supposed position of having an insensitive area of the body, a supposed mark of the devil.

book of shadows

This was a kind of guidebook to witchcraft, being a book outlining beliefs, rituals, chants, dances, spells, etc. There was no universal book of shadows for witchcraft in general. Each tradition, and even each coven, might have its own adaptations and variations. Such books are a major part of modern witchcraft, but little is known about their role in early times. There is some suggestion that spells, etc, were recorded informally and secretly in books, but witchcraft, until relatively late on, seems to have been largely an oral tradition. It may have been more of a written tradition than was generally assumed since it appears to have been traditional for a witch's book of shadows to be destroyed when she died.

However, Gerald Gardner (*see* Chapter 3, Witches and Magicians: The Accused and Self-Confessed, page 82), who is regarded as being the father of modern witchcraft, came into possession of the fragments of such a book when he was initiated into a coven of hereditary witches in 1939, but this was greatly amplified and changed by him and his assistant, Doreen Valiente, some of the non-traditional material coming from the works of Aleister Crowley. This Gardnerian book of shadows was in turn adapted by Alexander Sanders, and his work has consequently inspired other books in other traditions.

broomstick

When we think of witches we think of broomsticks. They are an essential part of the witchcraft tradition as evinced in fairy tales and have become part of the cultural stereotype of the witch. Witches were alleged to use broomsticks to transport them to coven meetings and sabbats. They also supposedly used them to fly out to sea in order to indulge in storm-raising (page 181).

Since the fifteenth century the broomstick was associated with witches as a means of transport through the air, although it was not the only means of air transport associated with witchcraft. Up until the late sixteenth century other implements, such as forks, shovels or cleft sticks, were associated with witch travel. It was also alleged that some witches used their familiars to transport them through the air to coven meetings and sabbats.

The creature most often suspected of being a witch's familiar was the cat, and so this was the creature that was most frequently thought to carry a witch through the air. According to one theory, the reason the broomstick is associated with witches can be put down to a linguistic misunderstanding involving the word 'cat'. This theory suggests that 'cat' is an old dialect word for broomstick and that it was originally not the broomstick but the animal that was connected with witch travel.

The most usual reason given for the broomstick being involved in witch travel is that the broom was regarded as a symbol of woman, since it represented her domestic role in the home. Most accused witches were women. Witches were alleged to fly up the chimney on their broomsticks prior to setting off on their journeys. This belief is thought to be based on the fact that many women were in the habit of propping their brooms by the chimney or pushing it partly up the chimney to indicate her absence from home.

Yet another theory suggests that the witches' use of the broomstick as a medium of travel is a throwback to pagan times. In order to try to make their crops grow higher, it is said that people then used to mount poles, broomsticks, pitchforks, etc, and ride them like hobbyhorses through the fields, leaping as high as they could.

Although broomsticks are now very much associated with the legends of witchcraft in medieval times and in the Renaissance time, the connection between witch travel and broomsticks was much more common in continental Europe than in England. Brooms were rarely mentioned in witchcraft trials, and English witchcraft laws did not refer specifically to flying.

Witches were alleged to smear either themselves or their brooms with a preparation known as flying ointment (page 167), which they made specially with a view to improving their flying ability. It was alleged by some that the devil gave each witch a broomstick and some flying ointment on the occasion of her initiation. Others claimed that such gifts were given only to those who were weak and infirm and that it was only witches in the latter category who used broomsticks to transport them to coven meetings and sabbats.

At first witches were depicted as flying with the business end of the broom, that made out of twigs, pointing downwards, it being suggested that by this means were the witches' tracks swept away. It this image of the flying witch that is popular today, but at the end of the seventeenth century witches were often depicted as riding broomsticks with the end containing the bundle of twigs pointing upwards, sometimes holding a candle to light the way on dark nights.

It was alleged that witches sometimes fell off their broomsticks. This supposedly happened when a novice witch was unskilled in the art of travel by broomstick. Alternatively, it was alleged to happen if the townspeople rang the church bells as witches were flying over their town on known witch festival nights such as Hallowe'en. Townspeople were alleged to lay scythes and cutting hooks on the ground in order to kill any falling witches.

The broom is sometimes used in modern witchcraft as one of the witches' tools. It is used, for example, to sweep away evil or bad fortune.

cakes and wine

In modern witchcraft an esbat (*see* COVEN, page 184) usually ends with the partaking of cakes and wine, or sometimes beer or fruit juice, as an act of thanksgiving. The refreshments are often blessed by the high priest and high priestess and a thanksgiving offering made to the deities.

Cakes and wine were also thought to be served at some sabbats.

candle

Candles were alleged to have been associated with witchcraft in several ways. Traditionally they were used at sabbats in rites that were a travesty of Christian religious ceremonies. They were supposedly lit as a mark of loyalty to the devil, who supposedly often appeared at sabbats with a lighted candle placed between his horns. The witches supposedly lit their candles from this or else the devil lit them for them.

Candles made of human fat were allegedly used at black masses (page 183) in the seventeenth century. On a more mundane level, witches were sometimes supposed to put candles on their broomsticks to light their way on dark nights.

Witches were supposed also to use candles in their efforts to harm people. They allegedly identified a particular wax candle with a particular person and then, on the analogy of sticking pins into effigies or images of people, they stuck the candle with pins and set it alight, hoping to cause great pain or even death to the person with whom the candle had been identified.

Candles were thought to be able to dispel evil in some cases. If lit by the side of a dying person they were thought to have the ability to keep away demons or other evil things.

cauldron

Like the broomstick, the cauldron is an essential part of the archetypal witch according to modern perception. The cauldron played a major part in early Celtic culture, especially in the case of the Irish Celts. It was a symbol of abundance and was thought never to run out of food at a feast. It was also seen as a symbol of regeneration, an aspect of the cauldron that was revived by the modern witch Gerald Gardner (page 82) in a celebration of the winter solstice at which the cauldron was set alight. The coven then danced with increasing speed round it and the high priest and high priestess joined hands and leapt over the burning cauldron, followed by the other members of the coven.

It was popularly thought that a witch kept a cauldron on the boil in order to weave evil spells. The cauldron was meant to contain an evil witches' brew containing such things as bat's blood, toads and their poison, lizards, various poisonous plants and even human flesh or fat. Over this brew the witch was meant to mutter incantations and cast spells to harm people or animals. Witches were thought to be able to cause storms at sea by throwing the contents of their cauldrons into the sea. They traditionally concocted their flying ointment (page 167) in their cauldrons.

The cauldron supposedly played an important part at sabbats, but this time its role was that of a cooking pot. The devil, or his representative, if he was not present, would preside over the cauldron that provided the feast of which all the witches partook. Individual witches allegedly took their cauldrons to sabbats where, it was said, they sometimes boiled up babies or small children for the sabbat feast.

charm wand

A charm wand was a glass stick, often formed like a walking stick, that was filled with tiny seeds or beads or else decorated with countless hairlines in the glass. It was kept in a house, and its supposed purpose was to prevent demons or other evil beings such as witches from carrying out any evil deeds. Apparently the belief was that evil beings would be diverted from their evil purposes by a desire to count the seed, beads or hairlines.

cross

It was widely believed that witches, demons and other evil beings were unable to withstand the power of the cross, the powerful Christian symbol. Thus people either wore crosses or made the sign of the cross to ward off the evil power of witches.

crossroads

The point where roads intersect has long been associated with magic and evil. Hecate, the Greek goddess of witchcraft, was also goddess of crossroads and animals were sacrificed to her there. Witches were alleged to gather at crossroads in order to conjure up the devil and his demons, and some spells were considered to be more effective if they were cast at a cross roads.

The evil reputation of crossroads was enhanced by the fact that it was often the site of the local gallows. The bodies of suicides, criminals and convicted vampires were often buried near a crossroads, supposedly because the ghost of the deceased would be unable decide which road take to get back home.

devil's mark

This was a mark supposedly put by the devil on initiates to witchcraft. This mark was allegedly made in several ways. The devil might simply touch the skin of the initiates with his finger, place a kiss on it, rake it with his claw or brand it with a hot iron. Such marks if found on the body of an accused witch were taken as proof positive of involvement with witchcraft.

The marks were routinely searched for during the investigation of an accused witch. The search was often extremely humiliating to the people involved, usually women. The devil supposedly often chose to leave his mark on a place on the body where it was most likely to remain hidden, under the eyelids, under the armpits, in the genitalia area or body cavities. Fortunately for the investigators, the exact nature of a devil's mark was ill-defined. Some such marks might be of a particular shape, such as cloven hoof, a hare, a spider or other creature. It is extremely easy to imagine that marks bear a resemblance to something and, in any case, the shape was not always held to be important.

Despite the nebulous nature of the alleged devil's mark, it was widely believed that it was extremely easy to differentiate between the devil's mark and other innocent marks on the skin. Given the circumstances, this would clearly not have been the case, especially where the investigator was intent on finding a devil's mark where at all possible. Nevertheless, this belief made the doctors who advised on the searches reluctant to raise the point that ordinary marks, such as birthmarks, looked much the same as supposed devil's marks.

The absence of an obvious mark did not save an accused witch, because it was alleged that sometimes the devil was so cunning as to leave an invisible mark. Patches of insensitive skin that did not bleed were thought to be particularly connected with the devil. In order to identify such areas of the body, accused witches were subject to the painful act of pricking (page 45). This involved being jabbed all over by a sharp object such as a bodkin (page 159).

The concept of a devil's mark seems to us now unbelievable, but many thousands of people, especially in continental Europe, were executed on the strength of this supposed backup evidence to the original, often baseless, accusation.

devil's pact

The devil's pact was a pact entered into by someone being initiated into witchcraft by the devil. This played a great part in many witchcraft trials and was mentioned in the *Malleus Maleficarum* (page 171), a guide to witchcraft and to the prosecution of accused witches. The concept of the devil's pact was enthusiastically embraced by the Inquisition, as this was held to show that witchcraft was simply an extension of heresy, witches being clearly seen to be turning to the devil and away from God. Getting accused witches to confess to having signed a pact with the devil was a major part of the investigation, and torturing of accused witches and references to this were an essential part of the standard catalogue of questions in investigations.

The pact with the devil could be an oral one, according to tradition, but more usually it was written down on a blank piece of parchment and signed in blood, the initiate being required to use blood taken from the left hand. The absence of such supposedly written documentation was put down to the fact that the devil usually kept the actual pacts, although a piece of paper purporting to be such a document was produced at the trial of Urbain Grandier in relation to the Loudun nuns (*see* Chapter 3, Witches and Magicians: The Accused and Self-Confessed, page 88).

Signing such a pact with the devil supposedly ensured the devil's help with the working of magic, whether this was for personal gain or otherwise, and the provision of a demon, known as a familiar (page 132), to act as an assistant. In turn, the initiate witch is alleged to have pledged allegiance to the devil and his or her soul. Pacts were often signed in public at a sabbat, but they could also be signed in a private ceremony or through the auspices of another witch.

The signing of the pact allegedly was sometimes accompanied by other rituals. These included the common one of the devil making some kind of mark, known as the devil's mark, somewhere on the body of the initiate, the mark being made in several ways, such as by the devil touching or kissing part of the body, raking his claws on it or branding it with a hot iron. Other suggested accompanying rituals included the initiate having sexual intercourse with the devil or giving him an obscene kiss (page 172), a kiss on the buttocks under his tail.

Accused witches very often confessed to having signed a pact with the devil, questions relating to this being very much a part of the standard investigation, because they had been tortured out of their minds or because they had been misled into believing that confession would save them from execution.

effigy

The use of effigies formed in the likeness of people whom witches wished to harm was allegedly common in witchcraft, and the practice can be traced back to ancient Egypt. Effigies were often made of wax, but other materials, such as clay, stuffed cloth or wood, were also used. They were sometimes called poppets, as they were in the Salem witchcraft incident.

It was thought that if a witch inflicted some damage to the effigy, a similar fate, in the form of pain, injury or even death, would affect the person whom the effigy represented. The harmful magic brought about by the creation of an effigy was supposedly made more potent by the incorporation in the effigy of some traces of the person. Thus hair, nail clippings, blood, saliva, sweat, sexual fluids, excrement, dust taken from footprints or a piece of clothing might be used in the creation of an effigy. It was because of people's fear of effigies that they were particularly careful about where they disposed of hair (page 158), nail clippings and so on.

Once the effigy had been fashioned, the witch might stick it with pins, thorns or nails to cause pain or injury in the corresponding part of the person's body. A nail through the heart, for example, was meant to cause death to the person within a short time.

Alternatively, the effigy might be slowly melted or burned, sunk in water or buried. In the latter case the victims were thought to be doomed to suffer a wasting disease.

Such was the fear inspired by effigies that it was not unknown for someone to become ill at the very suggestion that one had been made of him or her. Once an image had been made, there was little a victim could do unless the witch changed her mind about inflicting harm, although it was thought that harm could sometimes be averted if the victim got hold of the effigy and buried it. The conviction that witches caused harm to their enemies by means of effigies was so strong that the possession of something that vaguely resembled an effigy was enough to bring an accusation, and even a conviction, of witchcraft.

egg

The egg was associated with witchcraft in various ways. It was popularly believed that witches could sail on the stormiest of seas by means of whole eggshells. Another popular belief was that witches could bring death to people by boiling eggs in a bucket. Eating eggs was thought to put one at risk from being influenced by witches unless the shells were thoroughly broken up after the contents had been consumed

elements

The four natural elements of earth, air, water and fire are central to modern witchcraft. They are associated with the cardinal points of the magic circle (page 171). The influence of the four elements plays an important role in the modern initiation ceremony in which the person being initiated lies on the floor within the magic circle with each of the four limbs stretched towards one of the elements.

elf-arrows

Elf-arrows were thought to be used by medieval witches to harm or kill their enemies or their enemies' livestock. These were then said to be elf-shot. This belief was particularly strong in Scotland, Ireland and Celtic parts of England, and it was thought that the skill of firing elf-arrows had been taught to witches by elves and fairies. Any unexplained decline in health could be ascribed to the victim having been elf-shot. The arrows were thought to be often invisible, but sometimes it was claimed that actual arrows had been found in the vicinity of an ill person or animal. The likeliest explanation of this is that these arrows were prehistoric arrow-shaped flints.

evil eye

This was the name given to a baleful look from a witch by which a victim might be bewitched and consequently suffer some kind of harm, injury or even death. This was associated with witchcraft but by no means restricted to it, since the concept dates back to early times and is found in cultures worldwide.

People with particularly piercing eyes were especially suspect in this respect, as were people with anything unusual about their eyes, such as having a squint or having eyes of different colours. Small children and animals were said to be at greatest risk from the evil eye. Children were often given amulets, such as red ribbons attached to their underwear or a piece of coral to wear about their persons, to protect them against this evil influence. Animals often had bells tied round their necks to protect them from the evil eye.

If amulets failed and a witch happened to cast an evil eye on (or overlooked, as this action was called) someone then some kind of counteraction had to be taken. Various incantations could be used, preferably by a white witch, but spitting, preferably spitting in the eye of the overlooker, was considered to be effective. Making a clenched fist with the thumb pushed between the index and middle fingers, known as making a fig sign, supposedly reminiscent of the devil's horns, and directing this at the suspected overlooker was also meant to counteract the evil eye.

five-fold kiss

This is a ritual of modern witchcraft involving kisses bestowed on five parts of the body, usually the feet, knees, the area above the pubic hair, the breasts and the lips. The kissing is carried out within a magic circle to the accompaniment of blessings and on a man-to-woman or woman-to-man basis.

flying ointment

This was the name given to a preparation concocted by witches to facilitate their flying on their broomsticks. They were alleged to smear it on themselves and/or on their broomsticks. The ointment was supposedly prepared according to instructions given by the devil and was alleged either to be black or dark green in colour. The ointment was said to contain, among other things, the fat of human babies who had been killed before baptism, various plants, such as belladonna and hemlock, and bat's blood.

garter

Garters were considered in traditional witch lore to be associated with the devil. Also known as pointes, garters were alleged to form part of the devil's dress.

Garters are associated with modern witchcraft but with a different purpose. They are worn in various rites as badges of rank. The garter is considered to be the ancient emblem of the high priestess.

grimoire

Also called black books, grimoires were handbooks of magic that were popular in the Middle Ages and were particularly common from the seventeenth to the early nineteenth centuries. Such handbooks gave such details as what to wear, what tools to use, what incantations to recite, descriptions on how to create magic circles, and what recipes and spells to use in the practice of magic. The purpose of them was partly to help witches improve their magic techniques, but grimoires are traditionally thought to go back to ancient times and were thought originally to have been designed with the purpose of conjuring up and controlling demons and spirits.

Much of the material for later grimoires is said to have come from the Key of Solomon, attributed to King Solomon, the biblical king who was known for his wisdom and who is said to have commanded a host of demons. *See* book of shadows, page 159.

grove

A grove is the meeting place of a group of modern witches, usually in an outdoor setting. The name can also be used of the group itself.

hagstone

In witch lore a hagstone was a small stone with a hole in it that was hung in houses or on stable or cowshed doors or worn about the person or on animal's necks to keep witches away. Hagstones were used particularly to keep witches from borrowing horses at night to ride to sabbats and returning them in the morning exhausted and soaking with sweat. They were hung on bedsteads to keep away demons that caused nightmares.

hand of glory

This was the name given to the severed right hand of a hanged man, usually a murderer, this being supposedly rich in magic properties and therefore much valued by witches. It was thought to be at its most effective if it was cut from the corpse before it had been cut down from the gallows. Then it was wrapped in a piece of shroud, squeezed dry of blood and fluid, and pickled in an earthenware vessel with salt, long peppers and saltpetre. After two weeks it was removed from the pickling substance and laid out to dry in the sun in the so-called dog days of August or dried in an oven with vervain.

The blood and fluids that had been extracted from the hand were mixed with salt and other ingredients, reduced to a dry powder and stuffed back into the hand. Candles were then made from the fat of the murderer, the wicks of the candles often supposedly being made from the hanged man's hair. These candles were then fitted to the hand between the fingers. Another method of curing and lighting the hand involved bleeding the hand, drying it and dipping it in wax so that the fingers themselves could be lit and act as candles. Yet another method involved simply drying and pickling the hand and setting the fingers alight.

The hand of glory was reputed to be able to immobilise people and render them speechless. People breaking into houses at night supposedly used hands of glory to make sure that the occupants did not stir. It was believed that witches' brews would be particularly lethal if there was a hand of glory alight as they boiled.

horseshoe

The horseshoe is a common symbol of good luck. However, it was also regarded as providing protection against witches and other evil beings. To be used as a witch-deterrent it was hung with the ends pointed downwards, as opposed to upwards as in its use as a good luck symbol. The horseshoes were made of iron, which was regarded as a powerful witch-deterrent, and were hung on stable doors to prevent witches from borrowing horses to transport them to sabbats. If placed on the door to a house or other building the horseshoe was thought to prevent witches from crossing the threshold. If it was placed at the entrance to a chimney it was thought to prevent a witch from flying down the chimney on her broom. Tied to a bedstead it was thought to prevent the sleepers from having nightmares thought to be caused by demons. It was a condition of the anti-witch powers of horseshoes that they were never removed from the place where they had been installed. *See* horse, page 137.

image *see* EFFIGY.

knot

Witches were alleged to make use of knots in the course of their magic to aid them in the casting of effective spells. They were also said to conduct a ritual involving the tying of a knot in a length of cord, this ritual having the effect of rendering impotent the male partner in a marriage. A favourite time for witches to conduct such a ritual was on the occasion of the marriage of a man whom they particularly disliked. To counteract the spell of impotence, the bridegroom was advised to leave the shoelace in one of his shoes untied [?] as he walked up the aisle during the wedding ceremony.

If a witch wished a dying person particular harm, she supposedly tied knots on the bedclothes on the deathbed. This act reputedly prolonged the death throes of the person.

Witches were said to be able to control the winds at sea by means of cords with three knots tied in them. The untying of one knot was meant to result in a gentle southwesterly wind, the untying of the second in a strong north wind and the untying of the third in a veritable tempest. Sailors often bought these supposed wind-controllers.

Knots were also supposedly used by witches to cause death to their enemies. A string with nine knots tied in it and hidden away was meant to have the power to bring a lingering death to the intended victim. This was known as a witch's ladder.

kiss of shame *see* OBSCENE KISS.

left hand

Since Christ is traditionally depicted as sitting at God's right hand, this hand became associated with good and righteousness. Witches were popularly supposed to use their left hands more than their right hands to stir their brews and work their evil magic. They were also thought to do as many things as possible in an anticlockwise or widdershins direction, the opposite direction to which the sun passes through the heavens. When witches made their pacts with the devil as indications of their oaths of allegiance, they supposedly signed the pact in blood taken from their left hands.

All this was unfortunate for people who had more dexterity with their left hands than with their right hands. They were at risk of being accused of witchcraft or some other evil.

ligature

Ligature was the use of magic to make a man impotent. This could be done by witches by tying a knot or knots in a length of cord and keeping this hidden. The spell could not be broken unless the cord was located and the knots untied.

Another method of ligature involved the giving of potions to the hapless male. *See* knot.

magic circle

Such a circle was associated with witchcraft and was regarded as being an area within which magic could be conducted without danger of the person or people involved in the magic bringing harm to themselves. For example, it was traditionally held that witches could call up demons from within the safety of the circle. The circle, traditionally nine feet in diameter, was regarded as having the ability to enhance the magical power of the witch. Witches were strongly advised against leaving the magic circle until their magic ritual was complete on pain of possible death.

The magic circle is also used in modern witchcraft to establish a field of energy, and the altar and any tools to be used in a ritual, such as the wand, cauldron, etc, are placed within the confines of the circle. Candles are placed on the floor or ground at the four cardinal points, or quarters, and consecrated with the four elements – earth, water, air and fire.

A magic circle can sometimes also be formed as a protective force. Formerly circles might be drawn around the beds of sick people to keep away demons. Later, magic circles have been used to ward off psychic forces.

Malleus Maleficarum

Regarded as one of the most comprehensive guides to witchcraft ever published, this was more a guide to the prosecution of witches than to witchcraft itself. First published in Germany in 1486, it was compiled by Heinrich Kramer and James Sprenger with the approval of Pope Innocent VIII. They were greatly feared as part of the Inquisition, the role of which was to stamp out heresy using extremely cruel methods. At that time, particularly in Europe, witchcraft was seen as a form of heresy, so it was considered necessary to stamp it out in the same way.

The publication consisted of three parts. The first part was concerned with how the devil and his witch followers carried out a variety of evil deeds against both humans and animals. The second part was concerned with how witches cast spells and bewitched people and animals, and what could be done to prevent or undo this, and it made specific reference to witches making pacts with the devil. The third part was concerned with the legal process of trying accused witches, mentioning torture as an incentive to confession and the right of judges to make false promises of clemency to the accused to prompt confession, and it gave instructions on death sentences.

The book became phenomenally successful in Europe within a remarkably short time and became a bible for investigators and judges. Later writers used it as a basis for their own writings. It was not until 1584 that there was an English edition and the influence of the book was much more muted in England than on the continent.

obscene kiss

This was one of the names given to the kiss that witches bestowed on their master, the devil, on his buttocks underneath his tail. Also known as the kiss of shame, or *osculum infame*, such a kiss was part of the ritual at sabbats, and it is alleged that all initiates had to bestow such a kiss at their first sabbat. It was claimed that the devil often adopted an animal shape when he was receiving this particular from of allegiance.

osculum infame see OBSCENE KISS.

pentacle

The pentacle, which is a five-pointed star with a single point upright, has long been regarded as a powerful symbol in magic. It is extremely important in modern witchcraft. The pentacle is most often known as a pentagram, particularly when it is written or drawn. It is the witch's symbol of positive force and is also a symbol associated with protection.

The pentacle, in the form of a clay, earthenware or wax disc inscribed with a pentagram and other symbols, is used to consecrate the magic circle.

Traditionally the pentacle, as well as increasing the magic powers of magicians, witches, etc, was thought to be a protector against witchcraft and other forms of evil.

Pentagrams were, therefore, frequently drawn on doors in order to prevent witches or evil spirits from entering.

pentagram *see* PENTACLE.

pin

Pins were alleged to play various roles in witchcraft. Witches supposedly used them in the pursuit of their magic, and people were advised always to pick up any dropped pins to prevent witches from using these in the casting of their spells. Pins were also used by anyone who had fashioned an effigy of an enemy and wished to harm that person, the pins being stuck into various parts of the effigy's anatomy in the hope that this would cause pain in a corresponding part of the person and might even lead to death.

Witches were also accused of using pins to make various curses. One of these involved the taking of a lemon, uttering various incantations over this and sticking it with various pins, including several black ones.

Pins were used in witchcraft trials in the search for any trace of the devil's mark (page 163), the finding of which was held to represent evidence of witchcraft. In the test for witchcraft known as pricking (page 45) pins, bodkins or other sharp objects were jabbed into the skin of witches in the hope of locating an insensitive area or an area that did not bleed and so supposedly proving an association with the devil.

People who were supposedly in the grips of demonic possession (page 177) often supposedly vomited up pins along with other objects.

poppet *see* EFFIGY.

scissors

Scissors were thought to offer protection against witches and other evil beings. It was advised that if a pair of scissors was left under the threshold of a house or under a doormat then no witch would dare seek entrance, particularly if the scissors were left in an open position, thereby making a shape approximating that of the cross.

tears

According to tradition witches could not shed tears, which were meant to be an offence to the devil. If an accused witch did not weep in the course of the pain caused by testing and torturing, it was assumed by the investigators that she could not weep and therefore must be a witch. No recognition was given to the fact that the accused witch might be in too much shock to cry and that in any case tears are more often a response to emotional trauma than to physical pain.

If an accused witch was found weeping privately in her cell this was not an advantage to her. It was simply assumed that this was a deception inspired by the devil. It was also alleged that witches smeared their faces with spittle in order to fake tears on their cheeks.

wand

The wand, the concept of which goes back to prehistoric times, was the allegedly magic stick that witches used in the casting of their spells and in the invocation of spirits. It was alleged that witches were given wands by the devil at the time of their initiation. The wand could be made of various materials. Most usual was the wood from the hazel tree but wood from the willow was also common, it being considered best to cut the wood when the moon was full or waxing.

wart

The archetypal witch is depicted as being an ugly old woman, and in England especially it is the case that many people who were accused of witchcraft were in fact simply unattractive, eccentric old women. The stereotypical image of the witch often involves a wart, which adds to the ugliness. In fact if a person was accused of being a witch it was particularly if she had a wart somewhere on her body, especially one on a hidden part of the body. It was highly likely that a zealous investigator searching for supposed evidence of witchcraft would designate such a wart as a witch's mark (page 176).

It was important for people to avoid getting warts and to get rid of them if they had them. One way to avoid getting warts was supposedly to avoid handling toads. There were various traditional ways of getting rid of warts. One of these also involved toads, but it was most unfortunate for the toad concerned. The sufferer from warts was urged to carry a toad around in a bag worn around the neck until the creature died. Other less dramatic ways included tying a piece of silk around the offending wart or spitting on it every morning. These are only a few suggested remedies because getting rid of warts seems once to have been a major preoccupation.

witch ball

A glass ball, originally about seven inches in diameter, once hung in windows as a witch-deterrent and was then used as a decoration. Many were mainly blue or green in colour, and some were made of reflective glass to act as convex mirrors. Witch balls were popular in England from the eighteenth century onwards.

witch bottle

A witch bottle was used to counteract any evil spells that might have been cast by witches. It consisted of a glass, iron or bellarmine bottle or flask into which went some of the victim's urine and often also a piece of hair and some nail clippings. There are various traditions as to what happened to the bottle after that.

One indicates that the witch bottle was buried, causing the spell to be lifted and also causing the witch who had cast the spell to suffer great pain or discomfort. Another suggests that the witch bottle was put on the hearth at midnight and left to boil. This supposedly resulted in great pain being inflicted on the caster of the spell, causing her to lift the spell. Alternatively, the witch might be drawn to the scene of the boiling and thus cause herself to be identified. Yet another tradition has it that the bottle of urine was thrown on the fire and when it exploded the spell was broken and the witch killed.

Some suggest that there was originally quite a ceremony associated with the witch bottle when the idea first came into being. According to this suggestion, the heating of the bottle was accompanied by the saying of the Lord's Prayer backwards. Such a recitation was traditionally associated with witchcraft, and it was supposedly the case that the combination of the urine-boiling and the recitation would remove the spell from the victim and also make it applicable to the person who had cast it.

The custom of making witch bottles is said to have been introduced to England from Holland. It became popular in parts of England, particularly in East Anglia where there was a strong belief in witchcraft and where the custom is said to have survived for some considerable time.

witch box

A witch box contained things that were meant to protect the inhabitants of a house from the evils of witchcraft. Witch boxes were common in England in the sixteenth and seventeenth centuries and consisted of small wooden boxes with glass fronts.

They might contain, for example, a sprig of rowan, or of any other tree or plant that was thought to act as a protection against witchcraft, a paper with some holy words written on it, a cross and anything else that was regarded as being a witch-deterrent. Sometimes a magic spell of protection was cast over the box. Selling such boxes was one of the ways in which witch-finders made money when zealously going from town to town seeking out witches to accuse and charge.

witch's hat

In modern depictions of traditional witches they are almost always wearing tall, pointed hats with broad brims. These are as an essential part of the witch stereotype as a broomstick and yet early descriptions of witches do not indicate any special headwear for them. In medieval woodcuts witches do not appear wearing pointed hats but either have flowing hair or are wearing whatever form of headwear was popular at the time.

There are various theories as to why the wide-brimmed pointed hat has become associated with witchcraft. The most popular one is that such a hat is an adaptation of the hat commonly worn by Puritan women in England in the early seventeenth century. These were blunt-topped but otherwise bore a resemblance to the stereotypical witch's hat.

It was during this period that witchcraft hysteria in England was at its worst. It has been suggested that the move from the blunt top to the pointed top as far as witches were concerned was because the top of the pointed hat was thought to represent one of the devil's horns.

Another suggested reason for the witch's hat is that it is an adaptation of the brimless, conical cap. The theory is that perhaps an artist at some point added a broad brim to this in the belief that this addition made the cap more suitable for women.

The pointed hats play no part in the rituals of modern witches. Most wear nothing on their heads, although some wear headbands decorated with a crescent moon or other symbol placed on the forehead.

witch's ladder *see* KNOT.

witch's mark

This took the form of a protuberance on the skin, or occasionally an extra nipple. In fact such a mark was probably a wart, mole, a birthmark or simply a raised spot or bump. To the witch investigator such a protuberance was evidence of witchcraft as it was taken to be the site where a witch suckled her familiar (page 132), it being a popular belief that a witch rewarded her familiar by letting it suck a few drops of her blood. Protuberances that secreted either blood or other fluid, or even those that were red in colour, were thought to be particularly suspect.

As with the search for the devil's mark (page 163), the investigators searching for a witch's mark were exceptionally zealous. Exceptional attention was made to the hidden areas of the body, such as under the tongue or in the folds of the vagina. Almost anything could be judged to be such a mark, and many an innocent person was convicted on the grounds of bearing what were undoubtedly innocent marks. The search for a witch's mark was a major part of witchcraft trials in England and Scotland and later in New England.

Acts and Actions

dancing

Dancing played a large part in the festivities enjoyed by witches at their sabbats. Much of the dancing was said to be of an indecent or obscene nature, and it is claimed that the witch dancers were often naked. It is said that it was traditional for the dancing of the witches to get faster and faster until the dancers went into a frenzy and committed all manner of sexual acts. The devil allegedly was often present on such occasions and at least some of the dancing witches supposedly had sexual intercourse with him.

Modern witchcraft also has a dancing element as part of its rituals, but this is totally unlike that allegedly present in sabbats. A circle dance known as the Dance of the Wheel is performed in celebration of the winter solstice.

demonic possession

The idea of people being taken over by demons is an ancient one and by no means restricted to its association with witchcraft. With reference to witchcraft it was believed that witches could introduce demons into people so that they were completely taken over and began behaving and speaking very strangely. Witches allegedly often introduced demons into their victims by means of innocent-looking food, such as apples.

Allegedly, once the demon was introduced the victim might be affected in a number of different ways. Some would go into fits, faint regularly or seem to be attacked by bouts of severe pain, and some would behave wildly, very loudly and often obscenely. Alterations were supposedly often spotted, and some supposed victims allegedly seemed to undergo physical changes and even change their shape radically. It was claimed that some had gross distended bellies and would from time to time vomit up strange objects such as pins. Others, it was claimed, seemed to suffer from a wasting disease. Voices allegedly often changed completely, often becoming much deeper and gruffer than was usually the case.

There are almost certainly several rational explanations of the supposed demonic possessions that were so widespread at the height of the witchcraft trials. Some of the people who were supposedly possessed by demons were very likely suffering from a variety of mental illnesses while those who simply had seizures may well have been suffering from epilepsy. Others very probably decided to act in the way in which they had heard possessed people acted in order to draw attention to themselves, and in this they usually succeeded. They could add to this attention by naming a particular witch or witches.

One person faking the antics of the possessed in order to draw attention to himself or herself often had a knock-on effect. Others would also indulge in such behaviour, perhaps in what would be known today as a copycat exercise and perhaps as a hysterical reaction. There seems little doubt that in the relatively closed communities, such as nunneries or small towns, that were affected by supposed demonic possession, there was at least an element of hysteria. One person would start behaving wildly and others would follow suit, carried away by the whole thing and perhaps wanting to share in the attention. It is possible that some people faked demonic possession and named a specific person as the cause simply out of vengeance for some supposed ill. Where nuns or young women were involved it is thought that repressed sexual desire might have been a factor.

It must often have been obvious that there was something decidedly suspect going on when demonic possession, especially mass demonic possession, was claimed. However, at the height of the witchcraft hysteria the investigators were more intent on proving accused witches guilty than on finding them innocent. Therefore many cases of supposed demonic possession were not looked into very carefully.

The most popular cure for demonic possession was exorcism. This involved a priest ordering the demons to depart and sometimes the use of holy water and prayer. Often the exorcist tried to identify the demon or demons by name, supposedly indulged in arguments with him or them and issued threats. Exorcism, often conducted publicly, was repeated until the demons were gone. In cases where the supposed demonic possession was the result of a desire for attention or a need for revenge, the public exorcism often effected a cure since there was once again attention on them.

drawing down the moon

This is a ritual of modern witchcraft. In this ceremony the high priestess of a coven goes into a trance, reciting a poetic address that is sometimes spontaneous. By this process she becomes the goddess, symbolised by the moon.

elf-shooting *see* ELF-ARROW.

exorcism *see* DEMONIC POSSESSION.

flying *see* BROOMSTICK.

grave-robbing

According to tradition, witches often used human remains in the casting of their spells and in the making of their brews. Thus they were accused of desecrating graves and removing parts of the corpses. They allegedly were particularly anxious to obtain parts of the corpses of those who died young in a violent way, and people who had met their deaths on the gallows were of especial interest to them. Supposedly witches sometimes bribed executioners into parting with the corpses or parts of the corpses of those whom they had put to death. Of even more interest than the corpses of the hanged, it was claimed, were the corpses of babies who had died before the ceremony of baptism could take place.

hand-fasting

In modern witchcraft the rite corresponding to marriage is known as hand-fasting. The ceremony takes place within a magic circle and is officiated over by the high priest and high priestess of the relevant coven. The union effected by hand-fasting is not designated to be lifelong but to last as long as love lasts. In some ceremonies the couple taking part in the ceremony leap over a broomstick in the expectation that this will bring them luck.

initiation

Certain traditions are associated with the initiation of witches, although these varied from period to period, place to place and tradition to tradition. Some of the alleged rituals associated with initiation included the signing of the devil's pact (page 164), the marking by the Devil of the initiate in some way, thereby imposing what was known as the devil's mark (page 163), and the bestowing by the initiate of an obscene kiss (page 172) on the devil's buttocks.

The new witch, it was alleged, sometimes underwent a travesty of the Christian baptismal ceremony and was given a new name. Sometimes the initiate was rewarded with a familiar (page 132) and some of the tools of her new trade, such as a broomstick and some flying ointment (page 167). In some cases it was claimed that the new witch was required to have sexual intercourse with her master, the devil.

lycanthropy

This refers to the supposed transformation of a human being into a wolf. *See* werewolf, page 140.

maleficia

This referred to the evil or harmful deeds that witches supposedly carried out. There were a whole range of these, and they included injuring or killing people or livestock by bewitching them, the making of an effigy (page 165), again with the purpose of injuring or killing someone, or overlooking someone, that is, using the evil eye (page 167). Turning milk sour, turning butter rancid, spoiling beer as it brewed, making hens cease to lay or cows cease to give milk or damaging crops were among the least of their supposed bad deeds. Storm-raising (page 183) was another deed of which witches were often accused.

metamorphosis *see* SHAPE-CHANGING.

overlooking *see* EVIL EYE.

possession *see* DEMONIC POSSESSION.

scrying

Witches were credited with the ability to divine the future by concentrating on something with a shiny, reflective surface, such as a mirror or a crystal ball. This was sometimes known as scrying.

sending

This referred to the sending of creatures, such as animals or birds, to effect a piece of magic or to carry out a curse rather than the person behind the magic or curse going in person and being identified. In the case of witchcraft the creature involved was alleged to be her familiar (page 132).

shape-shifting, shape-changing

It was widely believed that witches were capable of changing their physical form. This they supposedly did so that they could perform their evil deeds without being spotted. The transformation or metamorphosis was allegedly often brought about by the smearing on the body of a magic ointment, sometimes given by the devil and sometimes made by themselves, and the performing of a magic ritual.

When witches changed shape they allegedly often adopted the shape of an animal, especially cats, dogs or hares, but there was a wide choice. The belief that they could change shape was often not to the advantage of witches. This was because any cat, dog, hare or other creature seen around the village or town at some scene of disaster could very easily be claimed to be an accused witch in disguise and indeed this could be the sole basis of a charge of witchcraft.

storm-raising

Among the activities most popularly associated with witchcraft was storm-raising, an activity that might be indulged in both by witches who lived by the sea and those who lived inland. The coastal witches were wont to raise tempests in order to cause wrecks at sea while their inland equivalents were more inclined to raise storms in order to destroy crops and buildings and to injure or kill people.

Allegedly there were several ways in which witches could storm-raise. For example, they were thought to throw the contents of their cauldrons into the sea after a sabbat (page 185) to work up a fierce storm. They were credited with the ability to throw bolts of lightning as they flew on their broomsticks whether over sea or land. It was alleged that they could raise rain storms by sacrificing cocks in cauldrons or by digging holes and either pouring water into these or urinating in them.

At the time of the witchcraft hysteria people were much more reliant on weather than was the case in later times. Communities were very much agriculture-based, and if anything happened to the crops it was a disaster for the whole community. Often scapegoats were sought in the face of such natural disaster and at the times of the witchcraft trials villagers looked around for a likely person to accuse of witchcraft and storm-raising. *See* knot, page 170.

transvection

This refers to the alleged transportation through the air of witches, usually on broomsticks. *See* broomstick, page 160.

Words

charm

We are more used nowadays to regarding charms as objects that bring luck. Originally, however, they were words, phrases or chants spoken in connection with magic. With reference to witchcraft, charms were used both by witches and by those wishing to protect themselves against witchcraft.

Witches allegedly chanted charms over their brews or over their tools to make these more effective and also chanted them over effigies for the same purpose. Others might recite a charm before they retired for the night or chant one over someone who was ill in order to keep witchcraft at bay. Certain charms were thought to be effective in curing ailments.

Some charms were written down on parchment, paper or wood and carried about the person. These were the forerunners of charms as we know them. Modern witchcraft uses the concept of the spoken charm but modern witches do not refer to the word as such, preferring such terms as chanting or incantation.

hex

A hex, meaning a curse or malevolent spell, is a term that ultimately derives from the German *Hexe*, a witch. Hex was a common term in the American colonies and was brought there by the Pennsylvanian Dutch who had borrowed the term from German. People who wished to harm other people or get revenge on them for some reason would consult someone thought to be a witch in order to get hexes placed on their enemies. There were also people who claimed to specialise in removing such hexes, and these might be consulted by those who were experiencing a period of particular misfortune and were of the opinion that a hex might be at the root of this

night spell

This was not a spell cast by a witch but a set recitation said at night before going to sleep that was intended to keep the sleeper free from the activities of witches or other evil beings while he or she was asleep.

Gatherings and Groups

black mass

The black mass is depicted as being a travesty of the holy mass held in Catholic churches. In fact the black mass is more a feature of Satanism than witchcraft, and modern witches do not indulge in this, since they do not worship the devil. There is little evidence that old-style witchcraft was associated with black masses and few confessions of witchcraft are thought to refer to them. Some confessions might include some details connected with the concept of the black mass, such as desecration of the host, the defilement of the cross or saying the Lord's Prayer backwards, but there is no evidence that there was a single established rite. The connection between witchcraft and the black mass, however, is one that appealed to writers of novels and film scripts and so the two are now linked in people's minds.

coven

Coven was the name traditionally given to a group of witches who allegedly met together on a regular basis, the word being probably linked to the verb 'convene'. The concept of witches' covens dates back to the twelfth century but the concept did not come into its own until the witchcraft trials of the Renaissance period.

It suited those who were convinced that witches existed and who were determined to get rid of them to think of them as meeting in subversive groups to plot harm. This increased people's fear of witchcraft and also gave great scope for witches who had confessed to have supposed evidence for naming names of others. It was one of the features of witchcraft trials that those who were accused and either voluntarily or involuntarily confessed identified others whom they claimed were also involved in witchcraft. Claiming that one had attended a coven with several others made such claims appear more plausible.

Whether there existed such an organisation as a coven is at best open to debate. In England at least the archetypal witch was a solitary old woman of unattractive appearance and eccentric habits who laid claim to healing powers and a supposed gift of clairvoyance. Such a person seems very unlikely to have belonged to an organised coven. The British anthropologist Margaret Murray (*see* page 5) did much to foster the idea that covens were prevalent and also the idea that they consisted of thirteen people, this probably based on the idea of Christ and the twelve apostles, in the case of witchcraft the devil substituting for Christ. This has been much disputed, however, and there is little evidence to support the theory.

The British popular concept of a witch was of a strange old woman living alone except for a cat or other pet, taken to be her familiar (page 132). It seems unlikely that such a person would belong to a structured group but it often suited the authorities to believe this.

The coven is part of the organisation of modern witchcraft, each coven being an independent unit. There are few statistics relating to these as many prefer to practise witchcraft without drawing attention either to themselves or to the groups to which they belong. It would be difficult to keep count as practically any professed witch can start a coven. Each coven screens anyone who expresses a desire to join and each is thought to have its own book of shadows (page 159).

The coven meets regularly, such a meeting being known as an esbat. Such meetings may take place either outdoors or inside and usually take place thirteen times a year on the occasion of the full moon. However, it depends on the individual coven how often they choose to meet and some meet much more frequently.

Members of a coven are known as coveners and are led by the high priestess, representing the goddess (page 135), sometimes sharing the leadership with a high priest, representing the horned god (page 136). The traditional number in a modern coven is thirteen, but this is far from being rigid and the number can vary from around three to twenty.

grove *see* GROVE.

Hallowe'en

Hallowe'en, celebrated on 31 October, occurs on the eve of All Soul's Day and is the equivalent of the Celtic festival of Samhain, associated with fire and death. Hallowe'en is the festival most associated with witchcraft, it being an occasion when ghosts and demons are said to walk the earth, and allegedly it was the occasion of one of the major sabbats.

The festival is celebrated by children, and often now by grownups, by attending fancy-dress parties dressed as witches, ghosts, etc, and by making lanterns out of turnips or pumpkins. In Scotland the children go 'guising', that is, they disguise themselves in fancy-dress costumes and go around local houses performing some kind of act of entertainment and receiving in return small gifts, such as apples or sweets, and various traditional games are played. These customs are now being confused with the American custom of trick or treat, when children go round the houses asking for sweets or other treats in exchange for not doing any harm to the householders.

sabbat

A sabbat allegedly was a celebratory gathering of witches involving feasting, drinking, wild naked dancing and abandoned sexual activity reminiscent of old pagan rites. The word was first mentioned in relation to a witchcraft trial in Toulouse in France in 1335 but it was not commonly used until the middle of the fifteenth century. In England the term was much later, around 1620.

The sabbat was essentially a tribute to the master of the witches, the devil, who was usually present, and it was alleged that he would have sexual intercourse with at least some of the witches present. Sabbats were supposed to take place at infrequent but regular intervals and to attract a large attendance. Witches traditionally flew to them on their broomsticks. Sabbats were thought to be night-time occasions, breaking up when the cock crew and signalled dawn.

Various activities, other than the feasting, drinking, wild dancing and lewd sexual behaviour, allegedly took place at sabbats. Particularly in Europe it was thought that sabbats were occasions when the black mass (page 183) was held, this being a heretical parody of the Catholic mass. The sabbat was allegedly a favourite occasion for initiation (page 180) ceremonies, with much signing of the devil's pact (page 164), etc. It was also supposedly one of the few occasions on which the devil met his followers en masse and the latter indulged in the practice of bestowing on him the obscene kiss (page 172), a kiss on his buttocks. Sabbat activities, it was claimed, might involve the witches reciting to the devil catalogues of the evil deeds that they had carried out since the previous sabbat. A particularly macabre aspect of the sabbat is that it was associated with the sacrifice, cooking and eating of unbaptised infants.

It suited witch-finders very well to spread belief in sabbats. Questions about them were part of the standard inquisition of accused witches to elicit confessions. A confession that included attendance at a sabbat, at which hundreds or even thousands or other witches, might allegedly have been present, gave immense scope for other people being named. It was a feature of witchcraft trials that when people confessed, often after considerable pressure and torture, the self-confessed witches named other people as witches also.

Modern witchcraft retains the concept of the sabbat but such gatherings have nothing to do with the devil, involving feasting and dancing without the lewd diabolical rites. They are held regularly, often at times of old pagan seasonal festivals held to celebrate the changing of the seasons.

Walpurgisnacht

According to the German witchcraft tradition, Walpurgisnacht, celebrated on 30 April and the occasion of the Celtic celebration of Beltane Eve, was the occasion of one of the major witch sabbats. Witches throughout Germany, Holland and Scandinavia supposedly held such a sabbat on mountain tops and indulged in the usual rituals and orgies thought to be a regular part of sabbats.

Modern witches tend to celebrate this date also with feasting, dancing and rituals but there is no connection between such celebration and the devil or demons. It is more a recognition and celebration of the changing seasons.

Chapter 5

A–Z of the Occult and Supernatural

A.A. *see* ARGENTUM ASTRUM.

ABADDON The Hebrew name for the DEMON ruler of the creatures emerging from the bottomless pit, in the Bible, Revelation, 9: 1–11, known in Greek as Apollyon.

ABOMINABLE SNOWMAN or YETI A gigantic creature, vaguely human in form, but covered in reddish hair, which is believed by many people to dwell in the Himalayas. There have been numerous reports of alleged sightings of this creature since the early nineteenth century, none of which can be confirmed. In 1951, Eric Shipton, a member of the Everest Reconnaissance Mission, took a photograph of a giant footprint which he had found in the snow. This gave some credence to claims that the creature existed.

ABRACADABRA A magical word, which is thought to have been originally used by Gnostics (*see* GNOSTICISM) as a CHARM. Recital of the word was believed to bring protection against disease, and it was a popular charm against the plague in Europe in the Middle Ages. It has now been adopted by modern conjurers and illusionists as a meaningless conjuring word.

ABRAMELIN THE MAGE *see* MATHERS, SAMUEL

ABRAXAS A magical word, thought to have been originally used by the Basilidian Gnostrics as a CHARM, and engraved on amulets, many of which were decorated with the figure of a half-human, half-animal deity, the personification of the word.

The word abraxas is composed of the seven Greek letters which, when taken as numerical values and added together, make 365, the number of days in a year.

ACHATES *see* AGATE.

ADEPT A term used to denote any person who has acquired a high degree of knowledge and skill in occult lore and practice, for example in MAGIC or ALCHEMY.

ADJURATION A command, frequently formulaic, used in such rituals as the summoning of ANGELS or DEMONS, or the EXORCISM of malign spirits.

ADONAI *see* TETRAGRAMMATON.

ADYTUM The most sacred part of a temple or holy place, in orthodox religion or occultism.

AEROMANCY The ancient art of foretelling the future through observation of the weather and atmospheric phenomena. Cloud formations, thunder, lightning and comets were thought to be particularly significant.

AETHER *see* ETHER.

AETITES A precious stone, which was believed to have magical properties. It was allegedly formed in the oesophagus or stomach of an eagle and was believed to have particular powers to prevent miscarriage or premature childbirth, if worn as an AMULET by a pregnant woman. It was also recognized as a cure for epilepsy.

AFRIT In Arabic mythology, a kind of evil DEMON, of enormous size and great power.

AGARES A DEMON, named in the LEMEGETON and described as an elderly man riding on a crocodile, carrying a goshawk. One of the powers attributed to Agares was that of causing earthquakes.

AGATE Also known as Achates, a semi-precious gemstone which was believed in ancient times to have various magical properties, such as offering protection against scorpions and snakes, driving away thunder and lightning, and ensuring victory in battle to the wearer.

AGATHODEMON A good spirit or DEMON worshipped in Ancient Egypt. The agathodemon took the form of a serpent with a human head.

AGE OF AQUARIUS The name for a time predicted by astrologers, when the Earth will move out of the zodiac sign of PISCES into AQUARIUS, and which will be characterised by spiritual enlightenment, harmony and world peace. The dawning of this new age has been predicted to occur at various times, including the start of the third millennium A.D.

AGRIPPA [von NETTESHEIM], CORNELIUS [HENRY], (1486–1535) A German soldier, physician, theologian, astrologer and alchemist, born in Cologne. Agrippa taught for some time at the University of Dole, but after being charged with heresy, he left Germany and moved to England. He travelled widely thereafter, residing in Italy, the Netherlands, Switzerland and France at different times in his life. He finally died in Brussels. Agrippa published a number of books, the most famous of which is De Occulta Philosophia, and he acquired a legendary reputation, in part self-cultivated, as a powerful magician and gifted seer. His reputation earned him the patronage of various wealthy and prominent people, but also brought him into considerable conflict with religious authorities and gave rise to several wild stories about him. Agrippa was said to have been accompanied on his travels round Europe by a familiar in the shape of a large black dog, which drowned itself when its master died.

AHAZU-DEMON A Semitic DEMON, which was thought to be responsible for inflicting disease.

AHRIMAN The name of the principal DEMON or spirit of supreme Evil in ZOROASTRIANISM. Ahriman is the opposing force to AHURA MAZDA.

AHURA MAZDA or ORMUZD The supreme Good and source of all creation in ZOROASTRIANISM. He is opposed by AHRIMAN, with whom he is continually in conflict.

AIM or AYM A DEMON named in the LEMEGETON, appearing as a man with three heads; one human, one feline and the third, that of a snake. He was said to have the power of setting cities and fortifications ablaze.

AIR SIGNS In ASTROLOGY, the signs of the ZODIAC that are associated with the ELEMENT of air: GEMINI, LIBRA and AQUARIUS. They are also known as the Air Triplicity. People who are born under any of these signs are likely to be organized and rational rather than intuitive. *See* TRIPLICITIES.

AKASHA or AKASA The first and most important of the five elementary principles of the universe according to Hindu teachings. The other four principles are all derived from Akasha, which is limitless, all-pervading and all-encompassing. It is sometimes referred to as the Soniferous ETHER. The concept of the Akasha has also been introduced to Western occultism and has been absorbed by Wicca, Theosophy and other belief systems. Everything that happens on Earth, from the smallest passing thought to the biggest world event, is said to make its mark on the Akasha, where it is chronicled for posterity. Those who have a high enough degree of knowledge and understanding are believed to be able to consult the Akashic Chronicles, or Akashic Records.

ALASTOR According to Roman legend, a kind of avenging DEMON or evil genius, tormenting the living with the grudges of the dead. Alastor was also said by some writers to be a surname of Zeus, the king of the ancient Greek gods, who was sometimes known as the avenger.

ALBERTUS MAGNUS (c.1200–80) A theologian, philosopher, scientist and alchemist, born in Lauingen, Germany. It is said that as young man, he saw a vision of the virgin Mary and following this experience took holy orders. Undoubtedly a man of great intelligence and learning, he was the author of many works on a variety of subjects, notably Summa Theologiae. He was for a short time bishop of Ratisbon (Regensburg) and was a gifted teacher, having among his students Thomas of Aquinas. His breadth of knowledge and interest in ASTROLOGY and ALCHEMY earned him a reputation as a magician, but in reality he led a life that was inspired by an unquestioning faith in God. He was canonised in 1931.

ALCHEMY The name given to an ancient and secretive art, forebear of the science of chemistry. The aims of alchemy were threefold; to turn base metals into gold, to find the elixir of life and to find a cure for all diseases. The key to achieving these three aims was believed to be the **PHILOSOPHER'S STONE**, a hypothetical substance which alchemists constantly strived to discover in their investigations. It is known that alchemy was practised in China before the birth of Christ. It was said to have been passed on by the spirit of a sage named Lao Tzu, to Chang Tao-Ling in the first century AD. In Egypt, the history of alchemy is traced back to **HERMES TRISMEGISTUS**, in the twelfth century BC. Several works written by Hermes Trismegistus were allegedly destroyed, leaving only three main documents; the Asclepian Dialogues, the Divine Pymander and the **EMERALD TABLET**, the last of which is regarded as the first major work on alchemy. From Egypt, the study of alchemy spread to Greece and then to Arabia and from there, during the time of the Crusades, to Europe.

There were two aspects to alchemical study. The first aspect was practical; scientific research and experimentation. This was driven by the simpler notion that firstly, 'corrupted' base metals could be physically transformed through certain chemical processes into pure metal, i.e., gold, and secondly, that through similar processes, a substance could be produced to make men immortal. The second aspect of alchemy was philosophical and spiritual, driven by the idea that through esoteric study and meditation, the alchemist could take himself onto a higher plane of consciousness, thereby unlocking the mysteries of life. The Magnum Opus (Great Work), the ultimate goal of the alchemist, was therefore similarly ambiguous. The language of alchemy was rich in symbolism and the knowledge of its secrets always jealously guarded by the privileged few who had access to it. Consequently, it is hard to distinguish between the two aspects of the study and much of it remains a mystery.

There was a strong alliance between alchemy, and **MAGIC** and **ASTROLOGY**. In the Middle Ages, it was believed that certain demons could be raised who would reveal the secrets of transmutation to the sorcerer who summoned them. Alchemists took note of planetary influences when determining the most auspicious time to carry out certain procedures.

A number of people allegedly achieved the Great Work in their lifetime. These include **ALBERTUS MAGNUS** and a Scotsman named Alexander Seton, who is said to have demonstrated his knowledge to scientists around Europe in the seventeenth century. But their achievements were never successfully passed on to others. St Thomas of Aquinas, a pupil of Albertus Magnus, is said to have destroyed his master's work after his death. Seton never disclosed the secret of the powder with which he effected his magical transmutation of lead into gold.

The practical aspect of alchemy led to a number of useful scientific discoveries, including the art of distillation, and as the practice of alchemy gradually fell into disrepute and declined in the seventeenth century, a new science, chemistry, was enjoying its infancy, feeding on the knowledge the alchemists had left behind.

ALECTROMANCY An ancient form of **DIVINATION** using a cock. Piles of grain are placed inside a circular arrangement of letters of the alphabet, one pile by each letter. The cock is placed in the centre of the circle and is allowed to feed at will from any of the piles. Observers take note of the corresponding letters. These are then put together to form words or names, which indicate the answers to specific questions.

ALEMBIC An apparatus for distillation, used by Medieval alchemists. *See* **ALCHEMY**.

ALEUROMANCY A method of **DIVINATION** using flour. Slips of paper on which certain words or sentences are written are rolled into tiny balls and coated in flour. The balls are then mixed, then those who are participating in the ritual share them out and read them to determine what lies ahead.

ALIEN ABDUCTION Belief in alien abduction is very much a phenomenon of the twentieth and twenty-first centuries, particularly of the last fifty years. It is based on the alleged experiences of a significant number of people, and the accounts they have given of these experiences. These people believe that they have been given the opportunity to experience life on another planet, or to meet extraterrestrial beings, after having been 'taken', either physically or in a **PSYCHIC** sense, to an alien environment. Most commonly abductees believe they have been selected as subjects for research and experiment by extraterrestrials, or as channels of communication. Some alien abductions are believed to be abductions of the physical body, which, after being sedated, is removed to an extraterrestrial environment, either a spacecraft or another planet. Subjects feel that their abduction resembles a military manoeuvre and commonly report moving into what seems to be an enormous tunnel of light before finding themselves, almost instantly, in an alien environment, where biological experiments are conducted–primarily, genetic testing. Other abductions are believed to be either dreams, or a form of **OUT-OF-BODY EXPERIENCE**, which has external causes, i.e. has been generated by extraterrestrial intelligence. Both of these are associated with the abductee reporting seeing a large beam of extraordinarily bright light. In the case of dreams, the beam is seen on waking. In the case of OBEs, it is seen at the beginning of the experience, as if it is a force extracting the soul from the body. Alternatively, rather than facilitating a full OBE, the beam may be a channel for telepathic communication. (*See* **TELEPATHY**.) A third kind of perceived alien abduction presents different possibilities. It presents itself as what appears to be **PAST LIFE RECALL**. Abductees give an account of memories which they have of being in alien environments, most commonly in what appear to be military facilities, either on another planet or in a spacecraft. Opinion is divided regarding these cases. On the one hand, they may be alien 'souls' in human bodies (and thus, not strictly speaking, abductees). On the other hand, the subjects may simply be recounting, as personal 'memories', information that has been transferred by telepathy on some previous occasion.

Sceptics will always argue that tales of alien abduction spring from overactive imaginations, or, in some extreme cases, psychosis. But the possibility that communication with extraterrestrial beings may be possible, even if it is involuntary, continues to excite a sizeable body of people.

ALL HALLOWS' EVE *see* **SAMHAIN**.

ALLOCES A **DEMON** named in the **LEMEGETON**, said to appear as a lion-faced soldier, mounted on a horse.

ALOMANCY A method of **DIVINATION** using salt. Little is known about the practice, but it is thought to consist of interpreting the patterns made by spilled grains of salt.

ALPHA The first letter of the Greek alphabet. In **OCCULTISM**, it is used to symbolise a beginning, either the beginning of all things or, of a particular event or ritual.

ALPHITOMANCY An ancient method of ascertaining the guilt or innocence of a person suspected of having committed a crime. A loaf of unleavened barley bread would be prepared for the suspects to eat in front of witnesses. If the suspects were seen to suffer indigestion afterwards, their guilt was thereby considered proven.

AMDUSCIAS A **DEMON** named in the **LEMEGETON**, said to appear first as a unicorn and then as a man. At the command of the sorcerer, he was said to create the sound of loud music and to be able to bend trees.

AMON A **DEMON** named in the **LEMEGETON**, and described as having the appearance of a fire-breathing wolf with a serpent's tail.

AMORC The Ancient Mystical Order Rosae Crucis. An organization based in the United States which claims to have Rosicrucian origins. *See* **ROSICRUCIANS**.

AMULET An object, either natural or man-made, which is carried or worn as a charm to bring good luck, ward off ill or deflect the **EVIL EYE**. Natural objects used as amulets are often unusual in appearance (e.g. strangely shaped stones or bits of wood), or rare (e.g. a four-leaved clover). Certain specific objects or plants became almost universally accepted as amulets in different cultures worldwide and while some were believed to protect their owner from bad luck or evil in a general sense, others were thought to be effective against particular problems, such as diseases, or identifiable enemies. **GARLIC** was believed to offer protection from a number of things but in particular, vampires. In the Highlands of Scotland it was believed for a long time that the rowan tree offered protection against witchcraft. Sprigs of rowan would be carried as amulets by people who feared they might be in danger from witches and rowan trees were planted at the gates of churchyards. The ancient Egyptians, who used a wide variety of amulets, frequently wore pieces of jewellery with the **EYE OF HORUS** on them as protection against the **EVIL EYE**. Man-made amulets might have occult symbols inscribed upon them. Amulets are similar to **TALISMANS**, but are not believed to give the wearer specific powers, as talismans do.

AMY A **DEMON** named in the **LEMEGETON**, said to appear first as a blazing fire and then as a man.

ANATHEMA A form of **CURSE**, in particular one made which is made within an ecclesiastical context against something or someone considered heretical or diabolical.

ANDRAS A **DEMON** named in the **LEMEGETON**, taking the form of a raven-headed angel, mounted on a jet-black wolf. He was said to have the power to provoke discord and conflict.

ANDREALPHUS A **DEMON** named in the **LEMEGETON**, said to appear first as a screaming peacock and then as a man. Skilled in mathematics and astronomy, he also had the power to make men cunning and could transform them into birds.

ANDROMALIUS A **DEMON** named in the **LEMEGETON**, said to appear as a man holding a serpent and to have the power to solve crimes of theft, identify and punish the thieves and find treasure and stolen goods.

ANGELS Messengers of God, intermediary spirits between God and man. Belief in the existence of angels is shared by several cultures worldwide and angels feature in Judaism, Christianity, Islam and **ZOROASTRIANISM**. They are generally represented as winged creatures, most commonly winged humans. Although they are supposedly servants of God, angels are not necessarily good spirits. Some doctrines link angels closely with **DEMONS**, regarding the latter as angels who have rebelled against or fallen out of favour with God.

The Jewish and Christian religions view the angelic host much like an army, consisting of different ranks, each with a particular sphere of influence. A fifth century work by the Greek churchman, Dionysius the Areopagite, De Hierarchia Celesti, described a ranking system of angels consisting of nine orders, arranged in three triads. The first triad consisted of Seraphim, Cherubim and Thrones. In the second triad were the Dominions, Virtues and Powers and in the third, the Principalities, Archangels and Angels. Popular beliefs tend to relate to only two of these orders; angels and their higher order counterparts, archangels. Angels and archangels have played an important role in magical tradition. Like **DEMONS**, it was believed that angels could be summoned in magical rituals. Their powers were invoked for benevolent purposes, for protection, healing, etc.

The belief that angels interact with mortals persists, not only collectively in orthodox religion and **OCCULTISM** but also on an individual level. Angels are believed to communicate with humans in a number of different ways. They may be seen (eg as a bright light, a radiant being, or a ghostly figure), or heard. They may also make their presence felt without auditory or visual signs, and can intervene to alter some course of events in a person's life. The Bible and the Koran both give accounts of several incidents involving angelic visions and interaction between humans and angels. The most familiar one in the Bible is the appearance of the angel Gabriel to the Virgin Mary. Many occult adepts claim to communicate directly with, or to be inspired by, one or more angels. Angelic visions have allegedly been experienced by a significant number of people, some religious, some not. These visions seem to be particularly liable to occur when the subject is near death. And there is still widespread belief in something akin to a guardian angel, although not always identified as such; some sort of counterpart to the cruel hand of fate or forces of evil, who intervenes unexpectedly to avert personal disaster. Reports of narrow escapes from death, for example, frequently make reference to the survivor having sensed a presence, a voice, or a more vague 'something', giving them a feeling that they were being protected, guiding them out of trouble or warning them of impending danger. In many cases, the person involved has been moved to reassess his or her beliefs regarding the existence of supernatural forces.

ANGELICAL STONE A **CRYSTAL**, allegedly a gift from the **ANGEL** Uriel, which was owned by the astrologer John **DEE**. Dee's assistant used it for communicating with the spirit world.

ANIMAL ESP Psychic ability possessed by animals. Dogs and cats in particular have long been believed to possess psychic powers. Their behaviour in certain circumstances, therefore, might be taken to be portentous. The belief that cats can sense the presence of ghosts is quite widely held and there are numerous stories of cats behaving strangely in places which appear to be haunted. Dogs are said to be uncannily sensitive to approaching danger and death, which may involve either themselves, or their owners. Sometimes a normally friendly dog seems to know when someone is not to be trusted and reacts aggressively to their presence near its owner. There are also many documented cases of dogs behaving in a manner that is disturbingly out of character immediately before a disaster. Claims regarding the telepathic powers of dogs range from simple displays of apparent empathy on the part of the animal ('he knows how I am feeling'), to reports of dogs responding to telepathic distress signals sent by an owner far out of sight and earshot. There have been several well-known incidences of both cats and dogs travelling tremendous distances through unfamiliar territory to places unknown to them, in order to find owners who have moved and left them behind.

ANIMAL MAGNETISM *see* **MESMER**.

ANIMA MUNDI The spirit, or soul of the World. Ancient philosophers believed this to be the universal life force, and perceived it as essentially female.

ANIMISM The attribution of spirit, or immaterial life force, to all natural things, whether animate or inanimate.

ANKH An Egyptian cross with a looped top, symbolic of life and regeneration. In ancient Egyptian art and artefacts, deities are frequently represented carrying an ankh in one hand. Ankhs made from a variety of materials have been used as charms since ancient times.

ANTHROPOMANCY An ancient method of **DIVINATION** whereby the entrails of dead people were examined to determine the answers to questions about the future. Human sacrifice was involved in order to obtain a corpse to examine. It is thought that not all victims were dead before the process of examination was carried out.

ANTHROPOSOPHY The name of the spiritual doctrine developed by Rudolf **STEINER**.

ANTICHRIST The great enemy of Christ who is destroyed at the time of his second coming, referred to by the apostles and identified with the great seven-headed beast, whose number is 666, in the Book of Revelation in the New Testament. The Antichrist has been identified both with false doctrine, and with individual enemies of Christianity. The Lutherans and other Protestant groups named the pope the Antichrist. *See* **CROWLEY**.

ANUBIS In Egyptian mythology, the god of the dead, who led the dead into the other world. He is either represented as a jackal-headed man or as a crouching jackal. After the death of Osiris, Anubis embalmed and mummified his body to preserve it, thus inventing the Egyptian funeral rites. He was also responsible for weighing the souls of the dead.

APOLLONIUS OF TYANA A Greek Pythagorean philosopher and mystic of the first century A.D. He was born in Tyana, Cappadocia, and opted for a life of austerity in his quest for spiritual enlightenment. Apollonius travelled widely, visiting India, Italy, Spain and Greece, and earned a reputation as a great thinker, clairvoyant and magician. He spent the last part of his life in Ephesus, where he devoted much of his time to teaching. He is believed to have lived to a very old age. Following his death, a shrine was erected to him at Tyana. A highly romanticized version of his life story was written in the second century A.D. by Philostratus. *See* **LEVI**.

APOLLYON *see* **ABBADON**.

APPARITION A phantom sight, sound, smell or presence that appears unbidden. Ghosts and disembodied voices are forms of apparition. Apparitions usually manifest themselves spontaneously, but are commonly associated with death, dying and warnings of danger.

APPORT A term used for any object or creature appearing, or materializing, as if from thin air, during a **SEANCE**. The appearance of such things at meetings with mediums was quite common during the nineteenth century when seances were fashionable and popular events. The famous spiritualist Madame **BLAVATSKY** was among those who claimed to have the power to bring apports from the spirit world into material presence. It is now generally thought that in the majority of cases at least, the appearance of apports was little more than a conjuring trick on the part of the **MEDIUM**.

AQUARIAN AGE *see* **AGE OF AQUARIUS**.

AQUARIUS (21 January–18 February) In **ASTROLOGY**, the eleventh sign of the **ZODIAC**, represented by the sign of the water-carrier. Aquarius is a **FIXED** sign, a **CARDINAL** sign and feminine. Its **RULING PLANET** is Uranus.

Character: Aquarians are caring and idealistic, sensitive to the natures and needs of others, but very independent and individualistic. They have high moral ideals and seek after beauty, both aesthetic and spiritual. They are great advocates for progress, providing they can see that it is for the better, especially if it is likely to benefit others and consequently, the typical Aquarian takes a lively interest in science, technology and politics. Aquarians do not go out of their way to conform; many might be seen as slightly eccentric. Nonetheless, their non-conformity will not be such that it hurts or offends others. It might be expressed in dress, eating habits or interior decoration at home, but it is not likely to be outrageous. Beneath the eccentricity will often lie a streak of true genius; Aquarians have a great capacity for surprise. Laziness, however, is a fault of many who are born under this sign, and this can mean that some Aquarians fail to fulfil their true potential. A desire for freedom of expression and action can also lead to clashes with authority.

Aquarian children are generally quite friendly and co-operative with their peers, but some may struggle to conform in a formal school setting. They may also have a tendency to be dreamy and forgetful.

Personal relationships: Aquarians make staunch, empathetic and caring friends. They are great romantics and in partnerships and marriage they are likely to remain faithful, although it might take them some time to make the initial moves towards commitment. They are frequently reluctant to reveal the depth of their feelings.

Aquarians are generally understanding and committed to their children's needs, but may, at times, seem rather emotionally distant.

Career and business: Aquarian curiosity, inventiveness and love of progress make a career in science or technology a viable option. Their natural interest in other people leads many Aquarians to opt for careers in teaching or social work, but others opt for the independence of working alone. Many Aquarians dream of greatness but fail to achieve it because of lack of commitment.

Health: Aquarians tend to suffer from problems with their legs, either through injury or disease. They may also suffer from circulatory problems. Aquarians are likely to take an active interest in promoting their own health and wellbeing and may be interested in alternative medicine.

Colour: Blue.

Gemstones: Aquamarine, sapphire, turquoise, moonstone.

Animals: Dog.

Flowers: Orchid, snowdrop, foxglove.

ARADIA In modern **WITCHCRAFT**, the daughter of the great Goddess **DIANA**, who is invoked in a number of rituals. The legend of Aradia was published by an American, Charles Leland, in 1889, as Aradia, or Gospel of the Witches, and was allegedly passed down to him orally by a Tuscan witch. According to the legend, Aradia was sent to earth by Diana to teach the art of witchcraft, both good and bad. Although the authenticity of Leland's version of the legend is doubted, the rituals recorded in the document form at least the basis for many of the rituals of modern **WICCA**.

ARCANA *see* **TAROT.**

ARCANUM A secret, or something hidden. In **ALCHEMY**, the Great Arcanum is the elixir of life, or the secret of its discovery.

AREA 51 An area of government-owned land, approximately sixty square miles in size, which is situated just over 90 miles north of Las Vegas in the United States of America and contains within it the dry bed of Lake Groom. Within the area is an air force base, a strictly controlled zone where civilians are denied access, and which is believed to be used as a testing site for new, secret, military aircraft. Area 51 has been for a number of years the focus of a great amount of speculation and controversy, fuelled by alleged sightings of **MYSTERY HELICOPTERS, UFOS** and alien beings in the vicinity. A number of UFO investigators claim that crashed alien spacecraft are taken to Area 51 for investigation and that using a process known as 'reverse engineering', scientists are using their findings to construct new craft. Area 51 has also been linked with strange and unexplained **CATTLE MUTILATIONS** which have been occurring in various parts of the world, but particularly in the United States, since the 1960's.

ARGENTUM ASTRUM (A.A.) An esoteric magical society founded by Aleister **CROWLEY** in England in the early 1900's. The society was formed following Crowley's acrimonious departure from the **ORDER OF THE GOLDEN DAWN.**

ARIANROD In Welsh mythology, the name of a goddess who bore twin sons; Dylan Eil Ton, who became a sea god, and Lleu Llaw Gyffes, who had magical gifts in arts and crafts. In **WICCA**, Arianrod is one of the names used for the **GODDESS**.

ARIES In **ASTROLOGY**, the first sign of the **ZODIAC**, represented by the figure of the ram. Aries is a **CARDINAL SIGN**, a **FIRE** sign, and masculine. Its **RULING PLANET** is Mars.

Character: People who are born under the sign of Aries are typically energetic, assertive, competitive, enthusiastic and courageous. They are potentially good leaders and good at taking the initiative in any enterprise., but their enthusiasm needs to be tempered with caution as they can be impulsive and rash, and may exhibit a tendency to be domineering. They enjoy a challenge and make eager competitors, but can be guilty of disregarding the needs or feelings of others in their efforts to attain their goals. Aries children require firm but encouraging guidance and benefit from the opportunity to use their energy constructively in sport and other challenging activities. Their tendency to be impatient may manifest itself in a lack of attention to detail or loss of interest in some activities, particularly in schoolwork, but if they can be kept focused on the final outcome of a task, their natural competitiveness will help them to achieve it.

Personal relationships: Aries men and women will both benefit from having strong partners, who are able to resist the Arian tendency to dominate. Arians make passionate and warm lovers and are generally faithful, but in some cases, if any partnership in which they are involved loses its vitality and excitement, they may be tempted to move on. Aries men and women will be loving parents, eager for their children flourish and do well. They will encourage their children to participate fully in any activity in which they show an interest, but they should always make the effort to be sensitive to their children's individual needs, to resist any tendency to be overbearing and to be realistic in their expectations.

Career and business: A large variety of careers offer the kind of challenges upon which a typical Arian thrives, and Arians are particularly suited to positions which give them the opportunity to show initiative and leadership.

Health: Arians generally enjoy good health, but the sign rules the head and face, so subjects may be prone to conditions such as migraine, sinusitis and acne.

Colour: Red

Gemstones: Ruby, amethyst, jasper.

Animals: Ram, tiger, leopard.

Flowers: Thistle, gorse, honeysuckle, wild rose.

ARIGO, JOSE A famous Brazilian practitioner of **PSYCHIC SURGERY** who operated on several hundred patients during the nineteen sixties. His activities aroused considerable scepticism and criticism from members of the orthodox medical profession, and he was accused of being a fraud. Nevertheless, in spite of rigorous investigation, nobody could successfully prove that Josés crude 'operations', which he carried out in a state of trance, with the most basic of tools, were hoaxes.

ARITHMOMANCY An ancient form of DIVINATION using numbers. *See* NUMEROLOGY.

ARK OF THE COVENANT The wooden chest, encased in gold and surmounted by two golden cherubim, which was constructed by the people of Israel to contain the stone tablets on which the ten commandments were inscribed. The Ark was sacred and could be touched by none but the Levites (priests). It had the power to kill any others who touched it. It was placed in Solomon's Temple at Jerusalem and it is said to have been lost when the temple was destroyed in the 6th century BC. The Ark has become the subject of a number of occult legends. There are several theories as to where it is now located; in Israel, Egypt or Ethiopia, for example. There have been some outlandish theories put forward regarding the nature of its lethal powers, including the claim that it was a form of communications device for contact between Earth and extraterrestrial intelligence.

ASCENDANT In ASTROLOGY, the name given to the sign of the ZODIAC that is appearing over the eastern horizon at the time of a person's birth, in the place where he or she is born. It is also known as the Rising Sign. The ascendant is an important element in the interpretation of a natal HOROSCOPE, as it marks the beginning of the first house, and determines much about a person's personality. If someone is born at dawn, their SUN SIGN and ascendant will be the same.

ASCETICISM The denial of bodily comforts and pleasure in order to achieve greater holiness, or alter one's state of consciousness. Asceticism is practised in some forms of YOGA, and by some branches of the Christian religion, Islam, Hinduism and Buddhism. It is also used in some forms of magical practice as a means for preparing for ritual.

ASGARD In Norse mythology, the world above MIDGARD, where the gods dwelt in their palaces. *See* YGGDRASIL

ASHTAROTH, ASHTORETH, or ASTAROTH 1) The name of the Semitic goddess of love and fertility. Identified with the Phoenician goddess ASTARTE and ISHTAR, the Babylonian goddess. 2) A DEMON named in the LEMEGETON, said to appear as a hideous, angel mounted on a hellish dragon and to have very foul breath. He had the power to know all secrets and to make men wise in all things.

ASMODAY A DEMON named in the LEMEGETON, said to have webbed feet, a serpent's tail and three heads; the first, that of a bull, the second, that of a man and the third, that of a ram. He appeared mounted on a dragon and breathing fire. He had the power to endow men with great wisdom in science, philosophy and astronomy, and to make them invisible. Along with **BELETH, BELIAL** and **GAAP**, Asmoday ruled over all the legions of demons.

ASPECTS In **ASTROLOGY**, a term for the angular relationships between the **PLANETS** themselves, and between the planets and the **ASCENDANT** and midheaven, at the time of drawing up a **HOROSCOPE**. These relationships affect the way in which planetary influences work on personality, relationships, etc.. The major planetary aspects are conjunction (close together), opposition (at opposite ends of the chart), trine (120 degrees apart), square (90 degrees apart) and sextile (60 degrees apart). When the planets are in conjunction and fall within the same sign, their influences merge and are strengthened, indicating a powerful personality. Opposition is a negative aspect and can mean areas of conflict. Trine and sextile are positive, and the planets work well together in these aspects, but square is negative, with the influence of one planet impeded by that of the other.

Aspects between the planets and the ascendent and midheaven will have influence on individual personality and the way in which a person presents himself to others.

ASPORT The disappearance of an object which apparently cannot be explained and which appears to defy the laws of science. The phenomenon is commonly associated with **SEANCES** and is the reverse of an **APPORT**, the unexplained appearance of an object.

ASSIMILATION A term used to describe a method of **PSYCHIC** healing whereby the healer removes illness from his patient via his own body. The procedure entails a certain amount of risk to the healer, who may bring the illness upon himself. However, if the healing is successfully carried out, the healer will display symptoms of the illness only briefly, and to a lesser degree.

ASTARTE The name of the Phoenician goddess of love and fertility. *See* **ASHTORETH**.

ASTRAGALOMANCY A method of **DIVINATION** using astragali, knucklebones, which are cast in order to answer questions about the future. Astragalomancy is still practised in some parts of Africa. Similar divinatory practices exist which involve the use of pebbles or pieces of wood.

ASTRAL An adjective used in **OCCULTISM** to describe that which exists around and throughout the physical world, yet lies beyond the reach of the senses.

ASTRAL BODY The spiritual manifestation of the physical body, separable from the physical body in sleep, unconscious states and in **OUT-OF-BODY EXPERIENCE**. The soul.

ASTRAL PLANE An invisible, all-pervading level of reality, which is believed to be reachable through altered states of consciousness or **OUT-OF-BODY EXPERIENCE**. The spiritual realm.

ASTRAL PROJECTION *see* OUT-OF-BODY EXPERIENCE.

ASTRAL TRAVEL *see* OUT-OF-BODY EXPERIENCE.

ASTROLOGY The study of the relationship of cause and effect between the movements of the stars and planets in the heavens, and people and events on earth. Popular astrology concerns itself for the most part with celestial influences on people, their personalities and their destiny, but astrologers can also apply their skills to other areas of human activity, such as agriculture, animal husbandry, meteorology and medicine.

The study of astrology dates back to ancient times. It is thought to have originated in Babylonia several hundred years BC, but archeological and documentary evidence shows that for several centuries, it has played an important part in the lives of people in many different cultures worldwide, and has featured prominently in a variety of religious and esoteric traditions.

Natal astrology, which is the most popular branch of astrology, involves the drawing up of a **HOROSCOPE** for the time and date of a person's birth, noting the positions of the Sun, Moon, planets and signs of the **ZODIAC** in the heavens at that time. A natal horoscope, accurately drawn up and interpreted by a skilled astrologer, presents a picture of an individual that is as unique as the individual him or herself. Several factors are considered to have an influence upon a person's personality and fate.

The constellation through which the sun is travelling on the day of a person's birth dictates a person's sun sign. Both a person's **SUN SIGN** and **ASCENDANT**, or rising sign, are important in determining character and personality. The position of the planets in the heavens at the time of a person's birth, the **HOUSES** in which they are positioned and their **ASPECTS**, both above and below the horizon, are also considered to be influential upon that person's nature and destiny. *See also* **ELECTIONAL ASTROLOGY, HORARY ASTROLOGY, PLANETS, RULING PLANET, ZODIAC.**

ATHAME A knife with a black hilt which is used as a ritual, symbolic tool by witches. It represents the masculine aspect. In modern **NEO-PAGAN** practice, its use is strictly confined to symbolic acts.

ATLANTIS A mythical vast island, said to have been sunk beneath the ocean thousands of years ago after a cataclysmic earthquake and tidal wave. The people of Atlantis were, according to legend, a powerful, proud and sophisticated race who ruled several countries. The earliest writing concerning Atlantis is that of Plato, who placed the island opposite the Pillars of Hercules in the Atlantic ocean and described it as being larger than Asia and Libya combined. The Atlanteans led a utopian existence and acquired great wisdom, wealth and power. But corruption crept into their society, undermining their strength and inviting the wrath of the gods. The Atlanteans suffered defeat in battle at the hands of the Greeks and shortly afterwards, within the space of a twenty-four-hour period, the island had sunk and the race was lost for ever.

It is unlikely that there ever was such a place, but the possibility has intrigued scientists and occultists for many centuries. Rudolf **STEINER** claimed that he had been able to consult the Akashic Records (*see* **AKASHA**) and had found out information about the origins of the island. Both he and Theosophist Madame **BLAVATSKY** believed the Atlanteans to be the fourth Root Race, descended from the people of another mythical lost land, **LEMURIA**.

AUGUR A title used by the ancient Romans to refer to a person who practised **DIVINATION** by observing the song and behaviour of birds. The term later came to be used in a general sense to refer to anyone who practised divination or prediction.

AURA An invisible body of energy believed to surround all living things, emanating from within. Belief in the existence of such an entity dates back to ancient times. Although not perceivable by the naked eye, it is believed that a person's aura can be seen psychically, using **CLAIRVOYANCE**, as a multilayered, multicoloured halo of light which varies in appearance according to the individual's state of physical and mental health. Attempts to analyse the phenomenon, or render it visible, have been met with scientific scepticism. In the early twentieth century, Dr Walter Kilner, a London physician, experimented with methods of diagnosis of illness through observation of (what he alleged to be) a patient's aura, using a viewing apparatus which he had invented. **KIRLIAN PHOTOGRAPHY**, invented in 1939, is another controversial technique whereby, it has been claimed, auras can be studied. **NEW AGE** therapists frequently conclude a session of treatment by sweeping, or cleansing a patient's aura with their hands.

AURIC HEALING A method of psychic healing. Initially, auric healing involves **CLAIRVOYANCE**, to visualise the patient's **AURA** and diagnose the problem. The healer, placing hands on the patient's aura close to the source of pain, will then use willpower to draw out negativity and increase the flow of **PRANA** through the patient's body. In order to avoid the danger of absorbing any of the harmful negativity from the patient, the healer shakes it away from himself periodically during the treatment.

AUSTROMANCY A method of **DIVINATION** through observation of the winds and cloud movement. It is similar to **ALEUROMANCY**.

AUTOMATIC WRITING Writing which is produced in a state of trance, in which the writer appears to be the channel through which another intelligence is working. (*See* **CHANNELING**.) The writer has no control over what is written and most commonly has no awareness of its content until after the event. Whilst sometimes what is produced is apparently meaningless, there are records of people having written music, having written backwards, in mirror writing, or in a foreign language previously unknown to them. In many cases, the writer will say that what has been written has been dictated by a spirit whose voice they heard during the trance state.

Automatic writing is one of the means by which it is believed the spirits of the dead can communicate to the living through a **MEDIUM** during a **SEANCE**. Hyde Lees, the wife of W.B. **YEATS**, experimented extensively with automatic writing. The **GLASTONBURY SCRIPTS** are a particularly well-known example of automatic writing.

AVATAR In Hinduism, a visible manifestation of a deity, or its incarnation in animal form.

AVEBURY A village in Wiltshire in the south of England, built on the site of the largest and most ancient prehistoric stone circle in Europe. A wide outer bank, some fifteen feet high, encloses a deep circular ditch within which a circle of one hundred stones of monumental size once stood. Many of the stones remain. Inside this circle are the remains of two smaller circles. The circles are thought to have been built around 2000 BC by the Beaker People and the site may have been used as a burial ground or religious centre.

Avebury stands on the conjunction of **LEY LINES**, by which it is connected to **GLASTONBURY** and other major sites. Like some other sites of this sort, Avebury is associated with paranormal activity, including reports of **UFOS**, and it is believed to be a place of great psychic energy.

AVESTA The holy scriptures of **ZOROASTRIANISM**, said to be the teachings of **ZOROASTER**, founder of the religion.

AXINOMANCY An ancient method of **DIVINATION** whereby the movements of an axe, balanced on a stake, were observed, in order to determine the answers to questions. Alternatively, similar observations could be made from a piece of **AGATE**, placed on a white-hot axe head.

AZAZEL In Semitic and Mohammedan demonology, the name of a **DEMON**, who fell from grace and was renamed **EBLIS**..

BAAL *see* **BAEL**.

BAALZEBUB *see* **BEELZEBUB**.

BABA YOGA The name of a witch in Russian folklore, who was said to prey on young children, cooking them and eating them.

BACKWARD BLESSING The recital of the Lord's Prayer backwards, which was believed in the sixteenth and seventeenth centuries to have played a part in witches' Devil worship.

BACON, ROGER (1214–1292) Born in Somerset and educated at Oxford and Paris, Bacon entered the Franciscan brotherhood in the late 1240's as a man of considerable learning, skilled in philosophy, mathematics, science and alchemy. He wrote a number of works on various subjects, including his Opus Majus , published in 1267. His superior knowledge made him the object of both envy and suspicion within the church and his life became the subject of many legends which were largely based on ignorance. According to one of the legends, Bacon constructed a magical brazen head, a bronze statue which was capable of speech. In 1277, the content of some of Bacon's philosophical writings brought the wrath of the church authorities down upon his head and he was imprisoned. He remained in captivity until shortly before his death in 1292.

BAEL A DEMON named in the LEMEGETON, said to appear as a king, who had command over 66 legions of spirits. He was said to be able to change his appearance at will.

BALAM A DEMON named in the LEMEGETON, said to take the form of a three-headed monster with a serpent's tail and fiery eyes. One head was a ram's head, the second, a man's and the third, that of a bull. He appeared mounted on a bear and had the power to make men invisible.

BALNEUM MARIAE The medieval precursor of the modern cooking utensil, the bain-marie. It was a double cooking pan, the outer one of which was filled with water and placed on the flame, providing controlled and gentle heat to warm the contents of the inner pan. It was used in alchemical experimentation. The name means 'Mary's bath' and may have its origins in the legend that Mary, sister of Moses, knew the secrets of ALCHEMY.

BANSHEE In Celtic folklore, a form of female APPARITION. Although it was believed that the banshee was not necessarily invisible, she kept herself well hidden and only made her presence known either by singing mournfully, or by wailing. The sound of a banshee was believed to warn of imminent death. In 1692, in Glencoe, Scotland, more than forty members of the Clan Macdonald were surprised as they slept and killed by members of Clan Campbell, but it is said that shortly before the massacre, some members of the doomed clan heard the sound of a banshee wailing and took flight, thereby saving themselves from death.

BAPHOMET The name of a DEMON allegedly worshipped by the ORDER OF THE KNIGHTS TEMPLAR, said to take the form of a goat, with human hands and a scaled body. A figure of Baphomet has also featured in the rituals of some satanic cults. Baphomet is sometimes erroneously identified with the HORNED GOD of NEO-PAGAN religions.

BARBATOS A DEMON named in the LEMEGETON, said to appear as a hunter with an enormous retinue. He had the power to understand the language of birds and animals.

BARQU A **DEMON** named in some medieval texts, who was said to have knowledge of all the secrets of **ALCHEMY**.

BASILIDIANS The name of a sect of Gnostics. *See* **GNOSTICISM**.

BASILISK In Greek mythology, a terrible serpent that had the power to kill by looking at, or breathing upon its victim.

BATHIN or BATHYM A **DEMON** named in the **LEMEGETON**, said to appear as a man with a serpent's tail, mounted on a horse. He had the power to transport men from one place to another.

BEALTAINE or BELTANE The name for the ancient Celtic fire festival, and one of the eight sabbats in the calendar of **WICCA**, which takes place between sunset on April 30th and sunset on May 2nd. The name of the festival means 'Bel-fire', Bel being the Celtic god of light. The Druids celebrated Beltane by lighting fires on hilltops on the night of April 30th. The ancient Druid ceremony of burning a giant **WICKER MAN**– reputedly filled with sacrificial humans or animals–is also associated with Bealtaine. The festival is traditionally a celebration of the return of summer, flowering and fertility. Maypole dances, which are still a feature of Mayday celebrations, were originally conceived as fertility dances, performed around the symbolic phallus of the Maypole. See **SABBAT**.

BEELZEBUB or BAALZEBUB 1) A god worshipped by the Philistines, identified with the Phoenician god Baal. 2) A high-order demon, said to appear as a monstrous fly, sometimes equated with **SATAN**.

BEL *see* **BEALTAINE**.

BELETH A **DEMON** named in the **LEMEGETON**, said to be a king of demons of terrifying appearance, mounted on a horse. Along with **BELIAL**, **ASMODAY** and **GAAP**, the Lemegeton names him as a ruler among the demons.

BELIAL A **DEMON** named in the **LEMEGETON**, said to be of the highest order of demons, appearing as a sweet-voiced angel in a fiery chariot. He was said to be unwilling to obey the commands of any sorcerer who summoned him unless he was bribed with gifts and sacrificial offerings. Along with **BILETH**, **ASMODAY** and **GAAP**, Belial ruled over all the legions of demons.

BELL, BOOK AND CANDLE An phrase associated with an important part of the Roman Catholic rite of excommunication (expulsion from the communion of the church), in which the priest rings a bell, closes the bible and extinguishes a candle. It is symbolic of the excommunicated person's separation from God, spiritual death and condemnation to eternal darkness.

BELLS Bells have played an important role in the religious and magical practices of many cultures since ancient times. The sound of a bell is widely believed to have the power of warding off evil spirits and for this reason, bells have become an integral part of many magical rites and also feature in the Christian church and Eastern religions. In religious prayer and meditation, the repetitive ringing of small bells may be used, like **CHANTING**, as a means of focusing the mind and achieving a higher level of consciousness. Bells are also associated with **NECROMANCY**, as tools to be used in summoning the spirits of the dead. *See also* **PASSING-BELL.**

BELOMANCY An ancient method of **DIVINATION** using arrows, in which the answers to questions were determined by the speed, direction and distance of an arrow's flight.

BELPHEGOR In Medieval demonology, the name of a **DEMON**, who was supposed to have the power to bestow great wealth on those whom he favoured.

BELTANE *see* **BEALTAINE.**

BENANDANTI In Italy, the name given to a group of people from the Friuli region of Italy who were believed to have supernatural powers and who came to be associated in the sixteenth and seventeenth centuries with **WITCHCRAFT** and **SATANISM.** The benandanti were people who were born with a caul over their head at birth, a sign that they were in possession of inborn powers of **CLAIRVOYANCE** and **HEALING.** Like shamans (*see* **SHAMAN**), they were believed to be able separate their spirits from their bodies in dream or trance states, and take on the forms of animals and fly. Their magical powers were used primarily for benevolent purposes, such as protecting the fertility of the fields from witches, against whom they did battle, and curing those who had been bewitched. During the period of the Inquisition, the benandanti fell under the scrutiny of the church authorities, who equated their activities with those of witches and other evil-doers.

BERITH, BEAL or BOLFRY A **DEMON** named in the **LEMEGETON**, said to have the power to change metals into gold. *See* **ALCHEMY.**

BERMUDA TRIANGLE An area in the Atlantic ocean, situated within a hypothetical triangle drawn between the points of Florida, Puerto Rico and Bermuda, that has become associated with a number of unexplained events, including the disappearance of several ships and aeroplanes and reports of **UFOS.** The history of such events allegedly dates back to the fifteenth century, and investigators of the paranormal have taken a lively interest in the area since the 1940's, when a number of American military planes disappeared without trace, in what appeared to be favourable flying conditions, having given no radio signals beforehand to indicate that they might be in distress. In addition to the great number of vessels and aircraft that have disappeared, there have been a number of incidents where flight crews operating in the area have reported unexplained failure, or erratic operation of navigational instruments. It has been suggested that this indicates a concentration of electro-magnetic forces in the area. Given that the area is extremely large and prone to extreme weather conditions, scientists argue that the number of lost craft is not excessive. Nevertheless, the Bermuda Triangle continues to fascinate many investigators and remains a focus for myth, speculation and controversy. The Bermuda Triangle is also referred to as The Limbo of the Lost, The Devil's Triangle, the Hoodoo Sea and the Twilight Zone.

BESANT, ANNIE née WOOD (1847–1933) English Theosphist and social activist, born in London. She married an Anglican cleric, the Reverend Frank Besant in 1867, but separated from him in 1873. She joined the National Secular Society and in 1874, became vice-president. She published one of her most important works, The Gospel of Atheism, in 1877. Besant became an ardent socialist and campaigned vigorously for birth control, working closely with socialist politician Charles Bradlaugh, and was prosecuted for obscenity following the publication of a pamphlet on family planning. She also joined the Fabian Society. In 1888-9, Besant became interested in **THEOSOPHY** and following a meeting with Madame **BLAVATSKY**, became immersed in the Theosophical movement. She travelled to India a few years after that and became involved in politics there. She was appointed President of the Theosophical Society in 1907, and held the post until her death. Along with her colleague Charles Leadbetter, Besant took the child **KIRSHNAMUTRI** under her wing, and travelled to Great Britain and the United States with him, declaring him as the world's new great teacher and attracting thousands of followers. This caused a split in the Theosophical movement and in later years, Kirshnamutri himself renounced all claims that had been made about his status. While continuing her interest in Theosophy and writing widely on the subject, Besant courted further controversy by campaigning vigorously for home rule in India. She was elected president of the Indian National Congress in 1917.

BIBLIOMANCY A term for a number of methods of **DIVINATION** using books, in particular the Bible. One form of bibliomancy involves drawing inferences from passages selected at random. *See* also **RHAPSODOMANCY**.

BIFRONS A **DEMON** named in the **LEMEGETON**, said to appear either as a monster or as a human and to have the power of teaching wisdom in all branches of the arts and sciences.

BIGFOOT *see* **SASQUATCH**.

BILOCATION The appearance of one person in more than one place simultaneously. Whilst the real, bodily person will appear normal, the phantom, or spectral double is likely to be unresponsive to attempts to engage him or her in conversation and may act automatically.

Reports of apparent bilocation are frequently associated with imminent death, such as when a close acquaintance has 'seen' someone at or around the time they have died, some distance away from their actual place of death. It has also been claimed that some holy people and occult adepts were able to perform such feats at will. *See* DOUBLE.

BIRDS OF OMEN A term for certain birds whose appearance was believed in ancient times to presage certain future events, either good or ill. Augurs could read meanings into the appearance of such birds, the numbers in which they were seen and their activities. Although traditional beliefs regarding birds and ominous associations differ from country to country, ravens are almost universally associated with divination and MAGIC. The traditional rhyme, 'One for sorrow, two for joy,' reflects some popular Western beliefs about magpies as birds of omen.

BIRTH SIGN In ASTROLOGY, the name of the sign of the zodiac under which someone is born. Also known as a SUN SIGN.

BIRTH STONES In ASTROLOGY, precious or semi-precious stones that are associated with signs of the ZODIAC. Birth stones are believed to be lucky for those who are born under the sign with which they are associated. Opinions differ widely as to which stones are related to which signs.

BLACK ARTS The practice of BLACK MAGIC.

BLACK MAGIC MAGIC practised for evil purposes, frequently involving the INVOCATION of evil spirits, or the Devil.

BLACK MASS A parody or perversion of the Roman Catholic rite of mass, allegedly conducted in SATANISM. In the sixteenth and seventeenth centuries, when prevailing beliefs in Church and governments throughout Europe linked WITCHCRAFT inextricably with Devil worship, witches were commonly accused of having taken part in a form of black mass. A number of obscene and blasphemous practices were alleged to take place on these occasions, including sexual orgies, animal sacrifice and the disinterring of corpses. In the more recent past, damage to church buildings and animal remains found in and around churches on occasion have led to claims that black masses are still conducted.

BLAVATSKY, HELENA PETROVNA (1831–91) Born Helena Hahn in Russia, the co-founder of the Theosophical Society led a colourful and nomadic life from her late teens. In 1848, she married General Blavatsky, a much older man, but separated from him after only two years and took to travelling, mainly in the East. Blavatsky apparently discovered she had psychic ability in childhood, and her interest in the occult grew as she moved into adulthood. She was a larger-than-life character with a forceful personality and experienced no difficulty in attracting an audience for her theories concerning science, religion and the occult, convincing others around her that she was a gifted clairvoyant and **MEDIUM**. She arrived in America in 1873 and met Henry Steel Olcott, a spiritualist, in New York. The two paired up and in 1875, formed the Theosophical Society. The aims of the society were to unite all mankind in brotherhood, to investigate and disseminate knowledge about ancient religions, philosophies and mysteries and to investigate the unexplained laws of nature and develop the latent psychic powers of humans. The society came under attack from critics, most notably the medium D.D. **HOME**, and around 1880, Blavatsky and Olcott moved to India, where they established a new centre for the society. In 1877, Blavatsky published Isis Unveiled, and in 1888 another work, entitled The Secret Doctrine. These works laid out Blavatsky's theories about creation, science and religion and the mysteries of the universe. But it was largely Blavatsky's personality and apparent ability to perform a number of feats of mediumship, including **LEVITATION** and **CLAIRVOYANCE**, that attracted numerous new members to the Theosophical Society. Blavatsky's psychic powers did not stand up under investigation, and the Society of Psychical research denounced her as a fraud, but in spite of this, the Theosophical Society continued to flourish and attracted a number of prominent converts, including Annie **BESANT**, and Rudolf **STEINER**, who subsequently abandoned the movement to pursue his own doctrine of **ANTHROPOSOPHY**. *See* also **THEOSOPHY**.

BLOODSTONE A term applied to a number of different stones with red markings, including haematite and chalcedony. Bloodstones are widely believed to have healing powers and to provide protection from the **EVIL EYE**.

BOAZ AND JACHIN The names of the twin bronze pillars in Solomon's Temple, which, according to Kabbalistic doctrine, are symbolic of polaristic forces, between which balance is found.

BODIN, JEAN (1529–1596) A monk, political philosopher, writer and campaigner against **WITCHCRAFT**, born in Angers, France. One of his published works, De La Demonomanie des Sorciers (1580), fuelled witch-hatred in France and influenced contemporary witch-belief in much the same way as **MALLEUS MALEFICARUM** had done a century earlier.

BOGY or BOGEY A traditional term for a hobgoblin or demon, sometimes referred to as the 'Bogey-man'. The term is sometimes used to refer to the Devil.

BOOK OF CHANGES *see* **I CHING**

BOOK OF THE DEAD An ancient Egyptian funerary work, of which several versions (none complete) have been found on papyrus or in stone inscriptions. It contains instructions for the preparation of the mummy and for rituals and magical spells to allow the dead person to pass safely from this world into the next.

BOOK OF THE SACRED MAGIC OF ABRAMELIN THE MAGE *see* **MATHERS**.

BOOK OF SHADOWS The name given to a (traditionally hand-written) book of ethics, laws, rituals and spells, used by practitioners of **WICCA** and passed on in sections to be copied by initiates as they progress through the degrees of initiation. There is no standardized version of this text, as each **COVEN** will have their own individual methods of practice, adapted over time to suit their own requirements and preferences, but the principles underlying the content of the book will be the same. The book of shadows of Gerald **GARDNER**, which has sections written by Doreen **VALIENTE**, has been particularly influential in the practice of Wicca nowadays, and the rituals of many covens closely follow the content of Gardner and Valiente's work.

BOOK OF THOTH A name for the **TAROT** pack. *See* **THOTH**.

BORLEY RECTORY A house that earned the reputation in the 1930's as the most haunted place in England. The rectory was built on the site of an older house in 1863, and in 1929, it came to the attention of Harry Price, a psychic and investigator into the paranormal, when it was reported that an alarming amount of **POLTERGEIST** activity was taking place there. The occupants of the house were also hearing footsteps and seeing ghostly figures. Price carried out rigorous investigations over a period of some years, eventually leasing the property for a number of months and monitoring and recording supernatural occurrences there twenty-four hours a day. In spite of claims that Price was a fraud, and had manufactured 'evidence' of paranormal activity, a great many people continued to believe that the rectory was haunted. The rectory was burned to the ground by accident in 1939 and over the next few years, the strange occurrences associated with the house apparently decreased in frequency and finally stopped altogether.

BOTIS A **DEMON** named in the **LEMEGETON**, said to appear as a hideous viper, but with the ability to transform into human shape.

BRAHAN SEER A legendary Scottish seer, many of whose prophecies have been fulfilled. Although the exact identity of the Brahan Seer is unknown, he is said to have been a man called Coinneach Odhar, or Kenneth Mackenzie, and to have been born on the Island of Lewis early in the seventeenth century. He is then said to have moved to the mainland, where he worked as a labourer on the lands of the Earl of Seaforth. Odhar had the gift of **SECOND SIGHT**, and with the aid of a magical white stone was able to see far into the future. The Countess of Seaforth consulted Odhar on a number of matters. One day, Odhar informed her that her husband, who was away, was committing adultery. Infuriated by the news, the countess ordered Odhar to be put to death for sorcery, and he was burnt in a tar barrel. Before he died, Odhar put a terrible curse on the countess's family, the Mackenzies of Seaforth. The curse was fulfilled over two generations, during which the family was struck by a series of tragedies after which left no surviving members. Other prophecies attributed to the Brahan Seer include the building of the Caledonian Canal and the Highland Clearances.

BRAZEN HEAD *see* **BACON, ROGER**

BROCKEN A mountainous peak in the Harz mountains in Germany, for many years associated with **WITCHCRAFT**. The summit of the mountain is said to be a hexentanzplatz, or witches' dancing place, where witches assemble for wild revelries to celebrate Saint **WALPURGIS** Night. The mountain is popular with hill-walkers, and there have been several reports over the years of climbers being frightened by a large and mysterious figure appearing out of the mist. This phenomenon is not unique to Brocken. Similar apparitions have been reported by climbers on a number of mountains around the world. *See* **GREY MAN**.

BROOMSTICK According to many fairy-stories, the broomstick is the traditional method of transport favoured by most witches, but according to witch-beliefs in Europe in the Middle Ages, the broomstick was by no means a necessity. Witches could fly from place to place in the form of animals, or mounted upon animals. They could use magical potions to enable them to take off into the night sky. Isobel Gowdie, tried for witchcraft in Scotland in 1622, confessed that some straw and a few well-chosen words were enough to provide her with a magical mount upon which she could travel to her meetings with the Devil.

Broomsticks are used in some rituals of modern **WICCA**, such as handfasting, the Wiccan wedding ceremony.

BROTHERS OF THE SHADOW A term sometimes used to denote those who practise **BLACK MAGIC**.

BUCKLAND, RAYMOND (1934–) Born in England, Buckland emigrated to the United States in the 1960's. His interest in witchcraft brought him into contact with Gerald Gardner and following Buckland's initiation into the Craft, he formed his own coven with his wife, Rosemary, in America. He followed the Gardnerian tradition for some years, but in the 1970's founded his own tradition, which he named Seax-Wicca. Buckland founded and ran the American Museum of Witchcraft and Magic and has written and published a number of books and articles on witchcraft and related subjects.

BUER A **DEMON** named in the **LEMEGETON**, said to be healer and a master of philosophy and logic.

BULWER-LYTTON, SIR EDWARD GEORGE EARLE (1803–73) A popular Victorian novelist, born in London and educated at Cambridge University, Bulwer-Lytton had a great interest in the occult which inspired much of his fiction. He also wrote two nonfictional works on occult themes, a life of **PARACELSUS** and a study of **ROSICRUCIANISM**, and formed his own magical society. One of his novels, The Coming Race, introduced the idea of Vril, an energy with terrible destructive potential, controlled by a race of underground beings. Although fictional, the book was interpreted as a work of prophecy by some people and inspired the formation of a number of occult groups with racist leanings.

BUNE A **DEMON** named in the **LEMEGETON** and said to take the form of a three-headed dragon, one head being that of a man, the second that of a dog and the third, that of a griffin. He had the power to endow man with great wealth and wisdom.

CABALA *see* **KABBALAH**

CACODAEMON A general term for a devil or evil spirit, derived from the Greek kakos, 'bad' and daemon, 'spirit'. The opposite in nature to an **AGATHODAEMON**.

CADER IDRIS A mountain in Gwynnedd, Wales, which has legendary associations.

CADUCEUS In Classical mythology the rod of Hermes (Greek) or Mercury (Roman), the messenger of the Gods. The rod is generally pictured with intertwined serpents round it and wings at the top. The symbol of the intertwined serpents round the rod has been adopted by the medical profession, but also features in the symbolism of Eastern religions and occultism. It can be seen in some representations of **BAPHOMET**.

CAGLIOSTRO, COUNT ALESSANDRO [Guiseppe Balsamo] (1743–95) Born in Sicily as Guiseppe Balsamo, the man who was to become Count Alessandro Cagliostro, adventurer, magician and alchemist, sought greater things than the humble life of his parents. Educated at the local monastery by Benedictine monks, Cagliostro learned some of the rudiments of chemistry and medicine, which fuelled a thirst for more. The details of his early adulthood are unclear for much of it is embellished by legend, but it is thought that he spent a number of years travelling around Europe and in Egypt, accompanied for much of the time by a man called Althotas, who claimed to be an alchemist. Together they moved into high society, convincing those whom they met that they held the secrets of eternal youth. During a visit to Malta, Althotas died and Cagliostro then married a beautiful young woman named Lorenza Feliciani. He continued his travels with her, peddling a variety of 'cures'. In the mid 1770's, Cagliostro settled in London for a while, and there he was initiated into the Freemasons. (*See* **FREEMASONRY**.)He used the knowledge he gained within the order to advance his career further and increase his wealth, travelling with his wife round Europe, performing miraculous cures and feats of **CLAIRVOYANCE** and mixing freely with royalty and nobility. He also sought initiates into Egyptian Freemasonry, his own invention, which he claimed was founded on the true Egyptian origins of Freemasonry.

In 1785, already under suspicion of fraudulent activities, Cagliostro became caught up in the 'Queen's Necklace Affair', was accused of theft and fraud and imprisoned in the Bastille for a year. He resumed his travels on his release, continuing to promote Egyptian Freemasonry, but his popularity was waning and his reputation as a worker of wonders dwindling. His activities incurred the wrath of the church authorities and he was finally imprisoned in Italy, where he died. A colourful and charismatic character, Cagliostro left a legacy of doubt behind him. Whether or not his 'Egyptian Freemasonry' was an invention purely for his own gain, whether or not his reputation as a healer, clairvoyant and magician was based entirely, or partly on fraud, will never be known.

CAIM A **DEMON** named in the **LEMEGETON**, said to take the form either of a thrush or of a sword-bearer. He was attributed with the power to enable men to understand the language of birds and animals.

CAMBION A term used by **BODIN** and others to denote the offspring of an **INCUBUS** or **SUCCUBUS**. It was believed that the cambion was not necessarily evil.

CANCER (22 June–22 July) Cancer is the fourth sign of the **ZODIAC**, represented by the sign of the crab. It is a **CARDINAL** sign, a **WATER** sign and feminine. Its **RULING PLANET** is the Moon.

Character: Cancerians are protective both of themselves and others. They are often sensitive and may be easily hurt, although appearing tougher than they really are. Cancerians are frequently anxious and prone to brooding on minor worries., but will generally resist help or counselling from others, seeing this as interference. Typically, their feelings, hopes and dreams will go much deeper and further than they will ever be prepared to admit to others. Both their tendency to worry and their protective nature can lead them to exhibit a certain frugality–sometimes meanness. This tends to be a symptom of their anxiety about what the future might hold rather than an unwillingness to share. Once they have set their hearts on achieving a goal, Cancerians will pursue it doggedly, in spite of any personal sacrifices required of them, or obstacles in their way. Cancerians will also be able demonstrate remarkable intuition and sound judgement. Cancerian children will benefit from praise and acknowledgement of their efforts and achievements. They may be slow, initially, to make new friends and may take time to adapt to changes in environment, particularly when facing hurdles such as starting school, but they will be loyal and thoughtful towards those with whom they form a bond.

Personal relationships: Cancerians will make exceptionally caring partners, husbands or wives, but their partners will need to make certain allowances for their tendency to be moody and take offence easily. Cancerian parents will demonstrate great sensitivity to their children's emotional needs and will be naturally very protective of them, but must guard against over-protectiveness which might clash with a growing child's need for increasing independence.

Business and career: Cancerians will be conscientious and industrious in any sphere of work they choose, but are particularly suited to the caring professions, social services, service industries and governmental posts. They may have a tendency to suffer from work-related stress.

Health: Cancerians may be prone to diseases of the respiratory system, or stomach problems. They may overindulge in food and alcohol, to the detriment of their health.

Colour: silver.

Gemstones: Emeralds, moonstones, pearls.

Animals: Otter, seal

Flowers: Poppy, white lilies and roses.

CANDLEMAS *see* **IMBOLG**

CANDLES Candles have held an important place in magic and religion for many centuries. In religious worship and beneficial **MAGIC**, their light is symbolic of life and enlightenment, the banishment of the dark and hence, of the forces of evil. Candles can be used in **DIVINATION**, for ritual purification of an area, and in a wide variety of magical spells. In **BLACK MAGIC**, they have traditionally been used in rituals for summoning demons and the spirits of the dead, and in black masses. Candles made from the fat of dead humans were supposed to have particular powers, protecting robbers as they plundered people's homes, and showing the way to hidden stores of wealth. (*See* **HAND OF GLORY**). In modern witchcraft, candles play an important role in ritual. One is placed at each of the four compass points around the **MAGIC CIRCLE**, to represent the four **ELEMENTS**. In recent years, there has been a revival of popular interest in candle magic. Candle magic involves the selection of coloured candles for use in spells, according to the magical attributes associated with each particular colour (blue–dreaming, psychic awareness, red–power, sexual prowess, etc). Black candles are never used in modern witchcraft or in popular candle magic. Black is the colour of evil and disharmony and the use of black candles is associated only with black magic and **SATANISM**.

CAPRICORN (22 December–20 January) In **ASTROLOGY**, the tenth sign of the **ZODIAC**, represented by the sign of the goat. Capricorn is a **CARDINAL** sign, an **EARTH** sign and feminine. Its **RULING PLANET** is **SATURN**.

Character: Capricorn subjects are generally very practical people, hard-working and focused, but they also tend to be quite reticent and secretive characters. When in pursuit of any goal, they never shrink from self-sacrifice or difficulty and never lose sight of their ambitions. Some of the noblest and most courageous figures in history have been born under the sign of Capricorn. Capricornians have no desire to lead others except in cases where their knowledge and experience dictates that they have a right to do so, in which case they will expect their authority to be accepted unquestioningly. They take pleasure in the learning process and may be very knowledgeable on a variety of subjects. The downside of this is that they do not suffer fools gladly. Capricornians can be very pessimistic and morose and are likely to be fearful of risk-taking. They are generally quite slow to anger, and avoid situations of conflict where possible, but when they are hurt or badly upset by someone, their displeasure will be clearly expressed. They make formidable enemies, for they can be quite cruel and can harbour long-term grudges. A common Capricornian failing is a tendency to be suspicious and untrusting, sometimes to the point of paranoia. Miserliness is another fault of some Capricorn subjects.

Capricorn children will generally be quite self-contained, and often be as happy in the company of adults as they are with their peers. They typically have quite a serious approach to life and are diligent pupils in school. They are rarely lazy or disorganized.

Personal relationships: Capricorn subjects are more likely to have a small group of close friends than a crowd of acquaintances. They are very loyal to home and family and when they find a partner, will demonstrate the same consistency with him or her. When a partnership or marriage becomes difficult, the Capricornian will do his best to persevere and work through the problems rather than run away. Capricornians are likely to make devoted parents, but should guard against being over-strict and serious.

Career and business: Capricorn subjects have a great capacity for hard work and will generally contribute maximum effort to their chosen career. They may become workaholics. Their enjoyment of learning might lead them to become academics, lecturers or teachers. Their methodical approach makes them suitable for careers such as librarianship, computer work, research and cataloguing. A variety of careers involving practical knowledge and manual work might also appeal to a Capricorn subject.

Health: Capricornians may suffer from a string of minor ailments in childhood. In adulthood, they may have problems with their knees or teeth. Many Capricornians are prone to depressive illness.

Colours: Black or dark brown.

Gemstones: Amethyst, onyx, jet.

Animals: Dog, elephant.

Flowers: Pansy, ivy, nightshade.

CAPUT MORTUUM 'Dead head', a term used in chemistry and originally in ALCHEMY to denote that which is left over to be discarded after certain chemical processes, such as distillation, have been carried out.

CARDINAL SIGNS In ASTROLOGY, the four signs of the ZODIAC that mark the beginnings of seasons: ARIES (spring), CANCER (summer), LIBRA (autumn) and CAPRICORN (winter). They are also known as the Cardinal Quadruplicity. A shared characteristic of people who are born under any of these signs is a potential for leadership. *See* QUADRUPLICITIES.

CARTOMANCY A term for a number of divinatory practices using cards, including the TAROT, derived from the Greek manteia, 'DIVINATION' and the Latin carta, a card.

CATALEPSY A state of complete inaction and unconsciousness, which can be caused by epilepsy, but may also be deliberately induced by hypnosis or meditation. Cataleptic seizures were once thought by some to be a sign of demonic POSSESSION. Cataleptic states are sometimes self-induced by eastern mystics to alter their state of consciousness.

CATTLE MUTILATIONS A bizarre phenomenon, involving the deaths of several thousand cattle, which has perplexed farmers and investigators around the world since the 1960's. Whilst it is accepted that all farm livestock, particularly in areas where large wild animals hunt, is vulnerable to predators, these cattle mutilations display none of the signs of typical predatory attack. There are no signs of struggle, nor any ground disturbance (tyre tracks etc) in the fields where the animals are found. The cattle are found dead, with wounds that appear to have been inflicted with surgical precision. Although organs and parts of the body–frequently the reproductive organs–may have been removed, there is no sign of the tearing of flesh associated with animal attack. In many cases, the wounds appear to have been cauterised. Frequently, bones have been broken, but the breaks are clean, without bone splintering. It is commonly found that the animals have been drained of blood, although there is no blood staining on the corpses or on the ground.

Several theories, most of which are outlandish, have been put forward to explain this phenomenon. One of the most recent, put forward by investigators of the paranormal in the United States, is that there is a link between the cattle mutilations and sightings of MYSTERY HELICOPTERS. According to this theory, the cattle may have been lifted by these machines and taken elsewhere to be killed and examined for research purposes. The theory offers no explanation for the cattle being carefully replaced in the field afterwards.

CAULDRON An iron cooking pot, associated in folklore and fairytales with WITCHCRAFT, particularly with the preparation of poisons and magical potions. The cauldron also has associations with ALCHEMY, where such vessels were used for experimentation.

Numerous very large cauldrons have been unearthed in archeological sites around Great Britain, and it is thought that these may have served a variety of purposes; as communal cooking-pots for feast days, as modes of conveyance for bodies to burial sites and as ceremonial symbols of prosperity, plenty and regeneration. In modern NEO-PAGAN practice, the cauldron is a tool, used in ritual as a symbol of the feminine aspect. It may be used to hold ritual fires, or as a container for burning INCENSE.

CELESTIAL BODIES The Sun, the Moon and the planets. In ancient times, only five planets were known to exist; Mercury, Mars, Jupiter, Saturn and Venus and ASTROLOGY for many centuries was concerned only with the effects of these five, along with the Sun and Moon, on earth and its inhabitants. The discovery of Pluto and Uranus subsequently altered the study of astrology considerably. Each planet has certain qualities and influences different spheres of human activity. *See* PLANETS.

CENSER A container in which INCENSE is burned, used in religious ceremonies and occult rituals.

CENTURIES *see* NOSTRADAMUS.

CERNE ABBAS GIANT A giant figure, cut into the chalk on a hillside in Dorset close to the village of Cerne Abbas. The figure, which has an enormous erect phallus, is thought to be a representation of a fertility god of ancient times, possibly CERNUNNOS, and to have been worshipped at another ancient site nearby, an earthwork called the Trendle. It is believed that women who wish to become pregnant should walk around the figure of the giant seven times.

CEROMANCY A term for a form of DIVINATION using wax. The term is derived from the Greek keros, 'wax' and manteia, 'divination', and the practice involves dropping melted wax into water and interpreting the shapes it makes when it sets.

CERNUNNOS A Celtic pagan god of hunting and fertility. He is generally represented with a man's torso but may have the head of a bull, a ram, or a man with deer antlers. In WICCA, Cernunnos is one of the names given to the HORNED GOD who is worshipped in ritual practice as the male counterpart to the GODDESS.

CHAIN A term used in SPIRITUALISM for the common practice of a number of people linking hands, or making some similar physical connection one to the next in a circle, in order to gather and strengthen the PSYCHIC energy which has been created through individual effort.

CHAKRAS In YOGA, Buddhism and THEOSPOHY, a term for a number of focal points of spiritual energy or life force in humans, that are invisible to all except clairvoyants, and described as swirling vortices. They act as receivers, transformers and transmitters of PRANA within the person. Most traditions locate seven principal chakras in a vertical line from the head to the ankles, each associated with different aspects of physical and spiritual wellbeing, affecting different parts of the body and different aspects of temperament, feelings and attitudes. Blockage of a chakra is thought not only to affect adversely the parts of the body which it controls, but also to alter the aspects of mood and psychological wellbeing with which it is linked.

CHALICE In WICCA, a cup or goblet that is used as a ceremonial tool, representing the ELEMENT of water. The chalice and ATHAME used in ritual together are also symbolic of the feminine and masculine aspects respectively.

CHANGELING A fairy child, usually ugly or deformed, left in the place of a human child who has been taken away to the fairy kingdom. It was once believed that all unbaptized children were at risk of being stolen by the fairies and people took careful precautions to prevent such an occurrence.

CHANNELLING The passing of information from non-physical beings to living humans through a human MEDIUM. The most widely known form of channelling in the West occurs in SPIRITUALISM, where mediums enter a state of trance voluntarily, to receive communications from the spirits of the dead. These communications may be passed on in a variety of ways, such as AUTOMATIC WRITING or speaking through the voice of the medium. The reputation of Spiritualism has suffered from periods of overexposure and profiteering, which encouraged fraudulent practices, but channelling is a process that has been used by several different cultures for many centuries and retains its credibility for many people. In the ancient tradition of shamanism, the SHAMAN alters his or her state of consciousness in order to receive messages from spirit guides. Channelling was also involved in some of the ORACLES of ancient Greece and Rome, where the priests or priestesses acted as mediums between the Gods and men. In some cases, the people through whom the channelling takes place do not voluntarily take part in the process, but find messages coming to them unbidden, or feel themselves being taken over by the spirit who wishes to communicate through them. Demonic POSSESSION is closely related to channelling. In more recent times, a number of people claim to have been used as channels of communication between extraterrestrial intelligence and humans. *See* ALIEN ABDUCTION.

CHANTING The intonation and repetition of words, verses or phrases, which may be used as an aid to meditation, a means of concentrating thought in devotion or a method of altering one's consciousness, leading to a trance state. The efficacy of chanting has been recognized for hundreds of years in religious, shamistic and magical practice worldwide. *See* INCANTATION.

CHARM Derived from the Latin carmen, 'song', a charm is a spell, or formulaic recitation used for magical purposes. In sixteenth and seventeenth century Britain, many of the charms allegedly used by witches for healing or other purposes were corrupted forms of Christian prayers, or parts of the Roman Catholic liturgy.

'Charm' is also used as a term for an **AMULET** or **TALISMAN**.

CHEIROMANCY or **CHIROMANCY** *see* **PALMISTRY**.

CHEIROGNOMY or **CHEIROGNOMY** *see* **PALMISTRY**.

CIMEIES A **DEMON** named in the **LEMEGETON**, appearing as a mounted soldier and said to have command over the continent of Africa.

CIRCE In Greek mythology, a sorceress who lived in exile on the island of Aegea and had the power to turn men into beasts. When Odysseus visited the island, Circe turned all his men into pigs.

CIRCLE A term sometimes used for a **SEANCE**. The circle holds an important place in the symbolism of occult traditions, representing the cycle of life/death/rebirth, and also the sphere of protection which magical adepts cast around themselves before they perform rituals. *See* **MAGIC CIRCLE**.

CLAIRAUDIENCE A term, meaning 'clear hearing', for a form of **ESP**; the perception of sounds that are inaudible to normal hearing. These sounds include the voices of deities, demons, spirit guides or dead people, sounds coming from events in the past or the future, and the sounds of earthly events (such as flowers growing) that are normally impossible to hear. The faculty of clairaudience may be inborn, or it may be developed with practice. Some people's clairaudient faculties can only function in a state of trance, but to others, clairaudient sounds come unbidden. *See* **CHANNELLING**.

CLAIRSENTIENCE A term, meaning 'clear sensing' for a form of **ESP**; a supranormal ability to experience, through the senses, that which cannot be perceived under normal circumstances. The term can be used to apply to **CLAIRAUDIENCE** and **CLAIRVOYANCE**, or supranormal perception involving any of the three other senses.

CLAIRVOYANCE A term, meaning 'clear sight', for a form of **ESP**; the ability to see that which is invisible to the eye under normal circumstances. The clairvoyant may have sight of events past, future or elsewhere, or may be able to see things from the spiritual world. Skilled clairvoyants are also thought to be able to see a person's **CHAKRAS** and **AURA**.

CLEIDOMANCY or CLIDOMANCY A term derived from the Greek kleis meaning 'key' and manteia, 'divination', applied to any method of **DIVINATION** involving the use of a key. One common method was using a key as a pendulum, and determining the answers to questions from the direction in which it swung.

CLEROMANCY Divination using small objects such as coloured pebbles or dice.

CLOUD DISSOLVING The ability to make clouds disappear by **PSYCHIC** means. It is one of a number of weather changes that **SHAMANS** claim to be able to effect by effort of will.

CONAN DOYLE, SIR ARTHUR *See* **COTTINGLEY FAIRIES**.

CONE OF POWER A mass of collective psychic energy, formed by witches working in a MAGIC CIRCLE, focusing their psychic powers together towards a common goal.

CONJURATION In magical traditions, a term used in a general sense for the casting of spells to achieve certain ends, and in particular, in ceremonial magic, for the ritual summoning of demons.

CONTROL A term sometimes used to denote a spirit through which a MEDIUM or SHAMAN communicates with the spirit world. Controls may also be referred to as 'spirit guides'.

CORDS Cords are used as a tool in modern WITCHCRAFT, for binding initiates in ceremonies of initiation and in other rituals. Each member of a coven will have their own set of cords, which usually consist of three, thin, nine-foot lengths of cord, each of a different colour, most commonly red, white and blue.

COTTINGLEY FAIRIES In 1917, photographs which had been taken by two girls, Elsie Wright and Frances Griffiths, caused a sensation. The girls claimed that the pictures, which showed small winged people, were of fairies, and vehemently denied having used any trickery in taking the photographs. Instead, they stated that they were on quite friendly terms with the tiny creatures. Several people, including the author Sir Arthur Conan Doyle, who was fascinated by the occult, became convinced that the photographs were genuine. The photographs are now generally acknowledged to have been fakes, although Elsie and Frances never actually admitted to having tampered with them.

COVEN An organized group of witches who meet together for ritual and celebration. Although covens were popularly believed from the Middle Ages onwards to consist of thirteen members, there is little evidence to suggest that this ever was the general rule in the past. Witchcraft in history, and in particular in the Middle Ages, has been more associated with women than men, but the modern NEO-PAGAN coven is likely to contain a balance between male and female members, working in partnerships. In Gardnerian WICCA, the number thirteen is favoured—six men and seven women, one of the women being the high priestess—but it is not a rule. Many Wiccans prefer working in smaller groups. Covens are self-governing, and free to develop their own customised rituals and traditions, providing they adhere to the WICCAN REDE.

CRAFT NAME The name adopted by a NEO-PAGAN witch upon entry into the Craft. Although society nowadays has a much more liberal attitude to the practice of witchcraft, most covens are still secret organizations, and the use of pseudonyms helps to preserve anonymity. The adoption of names to be used by fellow witches is not new. During the sixteenth and seventeenth centuries, many of the men and women who were brought to trial accused of practising witchcraft confessed to having another name within the coven. These names were said to have been given to the women by the Devil when they renounced their Christian baptism and gave themselves over into his service. *See also* **WITCHMARK**.

CROP CIRCLES Mysterious circular and geometric patterns that appear suddenly and without explanation in ripening grain fields, flattening the crop. The lack of paths or tracks leading into the circles from the edges of the fields has caused many people to believe that they are unlikely to have been man-made, although many have been exposed as the work of hoaxers. Many of the patterns which have been found in crop circles are extremely intricate and some appear to have symbolic significance. A number of people have speculated that they have been made by UFOs. The phenomenon first came to light in the nineteen eighties in England, but has also occurred in a number of other countries. 'Crop-watching' has attracted a large number of enthusiasts, who travel to sites in various locations, observing and recording details of each new pattern that emerges.

CROWLEY, ALEISTER [Edward Alexander] (1875–1947) The son of strict Plymouth Brethren parents, Crowley was born in Leamington Spa in England. Following the death of his father when he was eleven years old, Crowley rebelled against his repressive background and became increasingly fascinated by the occult. He studied at Cambridge University, where he proved himself to be both a capable student and an excellent mountaineer, but did not complete his degree. His quest for further knowledge of practical **MAGIC** led him to seek membership of the Hermetic Order of the Golden Dawn, a magic sect which was based in London, and of which the poet W B **YEATS** was a prominent member. Crowley advanced rapidly within the order but his arrogance and the obvious threat he posed to the leadership led to his expulsion, and he left London. A sizeable legacy gave him the freedom to pursue his interests full-time and also to travel extensively, exploring the beliefs of other cultures. While living at Boleskine House, a property on the shores of Loch Ness in Scotland which he bought for the purpose of taking his practice to a higher level, Crowley's reputation for extreme living and bizarre behaviour grew, with his own encouragement. He actively sought notoriety throughout his life, revelling in the name of The Beast, a title originally given to him by his exasperated mother when he was young.

Crowley founded his own sect, the Argentinum Astrum, or Silver Star, before joining the Ordo Templi Orientis (*see* **ORDER OF THE ORIENTAL TEMPLARS**), and ultimately taking over leadership. Throughout adulthood, he wrote prodigiously, and many of his works, although indicative of his considerable knowledge of matters occult, were undoubtedly self-aggrandising.

In the 1920's, Crowley moved to Sicily, where he founded the Abbey of Thelema, there to live according to the formula for life he had created for himself and his followers, which he called the Law of Thelema; 'Do what thou wilt shall be the whole of the Law.' The community he set up there soon earned a reputation for drugs and sexual depravity, and after the suspicious death of one of the members there, Crowley and his followers were told to leave Italy. Crowley eventually died bankrupt, addicted to heroin, but unrepentant, in second-rate lodgings in Hastings.

Crowley's life was without doubt a colourful and excessive one, and his influence on those who surrounded him was powerful. Indeed, it seems as if association with Crowley was more than some people could take. Alcoholism, mental disturbance and even suicide blighted the lives of several people who knew him well. Nonetheless, Crowley's magical studies and writings have had considerable influence on students of the occult over the years and continue to do so today. *See* also **TAROT**.

CRYPTOZOOLOGY The study of mysterious creatures which allegedly can be found on earth, but the existence of which is denied by scientists. If reports of alleged sightings of such creatures are to believed, they are increasing constantly in number and variety. Many of them are believed to be **EBE**s.

CRYSTALS The clarity of crystals has for a very long time been associated symbolically with clear-sightedness and crystals have been and still are widely used as aids to meditation and tools for **SCRYING**. Crystals are also believed by some to have certain occult powers and in recent years there has been a great rise in interest in crystal healing, a **NEW AGE** therapy which has its origins in ancient practices. Crystals and gemstones, both precious and semi-precious, have been believed for hundreds of years to have certain healing powers, either of a general nature or in relation to particular kinds of disease.

CRYSTAL GAZING *see* **SCRYING**

CTHULHU MYTHOS The imaginary creation of Howard Phillips Lovecraft (1890–1937), an American science fiction writer, whose books attracted considerable cult following. In Lovecraft's writing, Cthulu was a demonic object of devotion for strange aquatic creatures who lived on earth before human civilization. Lovecraft's work was inspired by his own preoccupation with the occult and belief in magic as a greater source of knowledge about the world than science.

CURSE DOLL A human image, constructed for use as a tool in a form of malevolent **SYMPATHETIC MAGIC**. Curse dolls, or similar objects, are common to many cultures worldwide. Whatever is done to the doll is believed to be replicated in the form of harm done to the intended victim. Curse dolls are also known as poppets.

CURSE The act of wishing or invoking harm upon another. Curses have been used since ancient times by people of all cultures and in particular by religious leaders and occult adepts. In Christianity, the rite of excommunication acts as a form of curse, condemning the excommunicant to eternal damnation. The voicing aloud of a curse, in particular within the intended victim's earshot or with their knowledge, was widely believed to be more effective than a curse made in secrecy or silence, although sceptics might argue that victim's knowledge and consequent fear were more likely to be detrimental to his wellbeing than the supposed power of the curse. Additional power was afforded to a curse if the person making it had in his or her possession an item belonging to the person cursed. Curses could also be formulaic; stock phrases or spells adopted into local or national tradition. The object of a curse need not be specific; thus, it was believed possible for a curse to be laid upon anyone who transgressed certain rules; in this respect, the curse is closely linked to the TABOO.

CURSE OF THE PHARAOHS A curse allegedly affecting those who participated in archeological investigation of the tombs of the Pharaohs in the Valley of the Kings in Egypt. The premature deaths of several Egyptologists who had been involved in different projects in the area since the early 1900's, led to speculation that a general curse had somehow been put into effect following the opening up and disturbance of sacred royal burial chambers. More specifically, the Curse of the Pharaohs is associated with the tomb of the young King Tutankhamun, which was discovered by Howard Carter and Lord Caernarvon in 1922. It is said that inside the burial chamber was an inscription in hieroglyphics, warning that the penalty for disturbing the tomb was death. Shortly after his first entry into the tomb, Lord Caernarvon died suddenly.and inexplicably. Caernarvon's death was followed over the course of the next eight years by twenty-one more deaths. All the people who died had either visited the tomb, been involved in the removal and study of Tutankhamun's mummified body, or had taken part in the collection, cataloguing and study of the artefacts within the tomb.

CRYSTALOMANCY A form of SCRYING, using a crystal or crystal ball as a speculum. It is also known as Crystal-gazing.

DACTYLIOMANCY A method of DIVINATION using a finger ring, most commonly by observing its movements in response to questions of the 'yes/no' variety, when it is suspended from a thread. Dactyliomancy has been popular for many years as a method of finding out the sex of a baby in the womb.

DAEDALUS In Greek mythology, the architect of the great LABYRINTH in which the Minotaur was kept on the island of Crete. After having helped Ariadne to rescue Theseus from the labyrinth, Daedalus was imprisoned by King Minos. In order to escape from the island, he constructed wings for himself and his son Icarus, which were made from birds' feathers and wax. Daedalus escaped, but Icarus flew too close to the sun and the wax melted. He fell from the sky and was drowned in the sea. Daedalus is a popular figure in occult lore because of his associations with secret knowledge (i.e. the construction of the labyrinth) and also his legendary ability to transcend the human condition through flight.

DAEMON or DAIMON In Greek mythology, an intermediary (generally benevolent) spirit between humans and gods, a source of assistance, advice or inspiration to humans. After the advent of Christianity, daimons became associated with DEMONS, essentially evil spirits.

DAGHDA In Irish mythology, the name of the father of the gods, and leader of the TUATHA DE DANANN (The children of Danu), who were believed to be a magical race who inhabited Ireland before the Celts. Daghda was associated with fertility and abundance and with war. He was said to possess a magical cauldron which overflowed with food and drink.

DANTALION A DEMON named in the LEMEGETON, said to appear as a man of many faces, both male and female. He had the power to read the thoughts of men and women and to alter them at will.

DEAD SEA SCROLLS *see* GNOSTICISM.

DEASIL or DEOSIL Clockwise, or sunwise. Deosil movement is traditionally associated with witch dances and rituals in 'white', or benevolent magic. *See* WIDDERSHINS.

DEATH PRAYER In BLACK MAGIC, a prayer to a DEMON or spirit to cause the death of an enemy.

DECARABIA A DEMON named in the LEMEGETON, taking the form of a pentacle, and said to be able to cause flocks of singing birds to appear.

DEE, JOHN (1527–1608) An astrologer, mathematician, philosopher and alchemist, born in London and educated in London and Cambridge. Dee acted as royal astrologer to Queen Mary I of England, but fell under suspicion of conspiracy to kill her by magic and was imprisoned for a while. After the death of Mary, Dee served in the Admiralty under Elizabeth I, working in naval intelligence, exploration and map-making. Although it appears that he did not possess great psychic powers, he was deeply interested in the occult. He employed the services of a man called Edward Kelley, who worked for him as a MEDIUM, communicating with spirits by CRYSTAL–GAZING. Dee acted as transcriber for the messages which Kelley received from the spirit world. *See* ANGELICAL STONE.

DEMETER In Greek mythology, the goddess of fertility and agriculture, identified in WICCA with an aspect of the GODDESS.

DEMIURGE In **GNOSTICISM**, the term used to refer to the creative force responsible for making and ruling the world and all within it. The demiurge was an inferior being to God, who ruled supreme in the spiritual realm.

DEMOGORGON The name of a monstrous power of hell. The name is derived from the Greek daimon, 'demon' and gorgo, 'monster'. Demogorgon was once considered to be a **NAME OF POWER**, and the very mention of it was believed to invite the most dreadful misfortune.

DEMON A term for an intermediary spirit between gods and men, derived from the Greek daimon, Latin daemon. Spirit beings, that are similar in nature to demons and able to interact with or influence the fate of humans, feature in the belief systems of several different cultures worldwide. In the Old Testament, the term was used synonymously with 'devil', to denote a fallen **ANGEL**, working against God on earth. Although the Greek daimon was most commonly a benevolent spirit, the demon of Christian times in the Western World became essentially evil. The Middle Ages saw an increasing preoccupation with demons. Theologians and demonologists of the period sought to arrange demons into hierarchies, similar to those of **ANGELS**, with Lucifer at the head and a large number of works were published on the subject, particularly with regard to demons and **MAGIC**. Many of the demons named in the Medieval Grimoires were originally pagan deities, given a new identity and terrible attributes. Thus Beelzebub, originally a god of the Philistines, became a demon of the highest order appearing as a gigantic fly, and **ASHTORETH**, the Phoenician goddess, became a male, foul-breathed, soothsaying demon. Seven demons were popularly believed to be associated with and have power over the seven deadly sins of man. Lucifer was the demon of pride; Beelzebub, gluttony; Asmodeus, lust; Satan, anger; Leviathan, envy; Belphegor, sloth and Mammon, greed. Many and varied catastrophes and ills were ascribed to the work of demons and it was believed that it was within the powers of skilled magicians and sorcerers to summon them and harness their powers for their own ends. This belief persists in Western **BLACK MAGIC**. The appearance of demons was believed to vary considerably, from almost human to truly monstrous, and it was believed that they could change their appearance–or sex–for the purposes of their interaction with mortals. The Medieval fear of demons gave rise to the idea that sexual intercourse was possible between these terrible spirits and humans. The demons could change themselves into human form for the purpose of satisfying their sexual appetites by preying upon sleeping humans. *See* **GRIMOIRE, INCUBUS, SUCCUBUS**.

DEMONIC SEAL In the **LEMEGETON**, each of the seventy-two named demons was ascribed a symbolic sign, which the sorcerer had to wear as a **LAMEN**, or talisman, to protect him when summoning the demon to his service.

DEMONOMANCY A method of **DIVINATION**, involving the summoning of **DEMONS** and interpretation of the signs given by them in response to questions.

DEUTOROSOPHIA The Greek term for **SECOND SIGHT**.

DEVA Originally a Sanskrit word meaning 'shining one' or 'god', the term broadly refers to a spiritual being, but has different connotations in different cultures. In Hinduism and Buddhism, a deva is a benevolent, superior spiritual being, whereas in **ZOROASTRIANISM**, it is an evil entity, a demon of **AHRIMAN**. According to Theosophical belief, devas are knowledgeable, powerful and benevolent spirits in the Divine ruling hierarchy. Some occultists nowadays use the term 'devas' to refer to **NATURE SPIRITS**. *See* **FINDHORN**.

DEVIL Derived from the Greek diabolus, Latin diabolus, the term may used to denote any evil spirit or **DEMON**, but is used in particular as the title of **SATAN**, the supreme spirit of evil and enemy of God, the most powerful of the demons who were created by God as angels, but rebelled against him and became evil of their own volition. Unlike dualistic religions such as **ZOROASTRIANISM**, where the forces of good and evil are equally balanced in opposition, Christianity does not see the Devil as an equal power to God, the supreme being of all. The Devil is known by several names, including **SATAN**, **LUCIFER** and **BEELZEBUB**.

DEVIL'S MARK *see* **WITCHMARK**

DEVIL'S TRIANGLE *see* **BERMUDA TRIANGLE**

DIANA Roman goddess if the Moon and of hunting, identified with the Greek deity Artemis, sister of Apollo. In modern **WITCHCRAFT**, Diana is one of the names by which the **GODDESS** is known.

DIRECT WRITING Writing produced by a spiritual entity without the use of a human **MEDIUM**. Direct writing has allegedly been witnessed in seances, where words or hieroglyphics have appeared on slates, or pieces of paper, which have been made available for that purpose. It may also occur as a sign of **POLTERGEIST** activity. In some cases, direct writing has appeared without any apparent means for making such marks having been in the vicinity.

DIVINATION The art of foretelling the future or discovering things about the unknown, using divine, or spiritual inspiration or assistance. Some forms of divination, including **AUGURY**, **ASTROLOGY** and **AUSTROMANCY**, involve the systematic interpretation of signs or omens from natural phenomena. Divination may also be practised using tools, such as bones, cards or **RUNES**, which are cast or selected apparently at random and interpreted according to the patterns or combinations that they make. Other forms of divination involve more direct contact with the spirit world through someone such as a priest, **SHAMAN, ORACLE** or psychic, who is acknowledged to have supernatural powers and is able to receive information from the spirit world through dreams, trances, clairvoyance, etc. *See* **AEROMANCY, ALECTROMANCY, ALEUROMANCY, ALOMANCY, ALPHITOMANCY, ANTHROPOMANCY, ARITHMOMANCY, ASTRAGALOMANCY, ASTROLOGY, AUSTROMANCY, AXINOMANCY, BELOMANCY, BIBLIOMANCY, CEROMANCY, CLEIDOMANCY, CLEROMANCY, CRYSTALOMANCY, DACTYLOMANCY, DEMONOMANCY, DOWSING, EXTISPICY, FENG-SHUI, FORTUNE-TELLING, GEOMANCY, HYDROMANCY, I CHING, NECROMANCY, NUMEROLOGY, OGAM, ONEIROMANCY, ORACLE, PALMISTRY, RHAPSODOMANCY, RUNES, SCRYING, SECOND SIGHT, TAROT.**

DJINN In Moslem and Arab mythology and religion, a form of spirit or **DEMON**. Djinn could assume a variety of shapes, including human form. They had considerable powers. They were not necessarily evil spirits, but many were. They could be harnessed by magical adepts and their powers used for their masters' ends.

DOUBLE or DOPPELGANGER A ghostly appearance of a person at some distance from where his or her physical body actually is. The phenomenon of the doppelgänger is well documented in several countries worldwide and is commonly associated with the imminent death, or severe illness of the person whose double is seen. Doubles may appear disengaged with their surroundings and move silently and strangely mechanically. The phenomenon can be interpreted as **ESP** on the part of the viewer, or the double may be a projection of the **ETHERIC BODY** of the person seen. *See* **BILOCATION, WRAITH.**

DOWSING A method of **DIVINATION** using rods or pendulums, to locate a variety of things that are hidden underground. Dowsing may be used to find water or mineral deposits, or to locate ley lines, underground pipes and cables, archeological sites, buried artefacts, unexploded bombs or bodies. Documentary evidence exists to show that the art of dowsing was practised in Ancient Egypt and China many centuries ago. Although it was perceived as a form of devilish magic and condemned by the church in Europe during the Middle Ages, the practice continued and nowadays is flourishing in several countries throughout the World, where it is used in a variety of spheres of activity, including industry, archeology and crime detection. The traditional tool of the dowser is a forked stick, in particular one made of hazel or apple, but a variety of metal, wire or wooden rods may be used, or a pendulum. Dowsing may be done on site, or at a distance, using a map of the area to be searched. On site, the dowser will walk over the area holding his dowsing implement in his hand, concentrating on a mental image of the object of the search. A violent jerk or twitch of the dowsing implement indicates the spot beneath which the hidden thing is lying. In spite of the fact that the art of dowsing continues to defy scientific explanation, it is widely accepted as an effective means of detecting a variety of things. The services of expert dowsers are particularly in demand in the fields of mineral excavation and water sourcing, where their success rate has frequently been found to be greater than scientific methods of detection. Experiments have shown that a larger proportion of children than adults are successful when they try dowsing for the first time. Many people believe that this is because children are less likely to be sceptical about the process, and this theory has led to the suggestion that dowsing ability may be something which is latent in all of us, but requires an element of open-mindedness, or even faith, in order to be discovered.

DRACULA The name of a fictional **VAMPIRE**, creation of nineteenth century author, Bram Stoker. Bram Stoker's hugely popular work was based on his knowledge of Slavic vampire legends, and the image of Dracula had considerable influence upon modern Western belief about vampires.

DRAGON PATHS (lung-mei) The name given by the Chinese to a network of hypothetical lines across the landscape, marking out the flight-paths of dragons from place to place. These lines are, like **LEY LINES**, associated with fields of concentrated energy emanating from the earth. *See also* **FENG-SHUI**.

DRUIDS The name given to a group of priestly intellectual elite in ancient Celtic cultures, who comprised poets, philosophers, healers, diviners, shamans and magicians. There is little information surviving about the ancient Druids apart from the writings of some Roman authors, including Julius Caesar in his Gallic Wars. The Druids were said to believe in reincarnation and to worship nature gods. The oak tree was sacred to them, as was **MISTLETOE**, which they harvested from oak trees with a golden knife or sickle. It is thought that they practised ritual human and animal sacrifice (*see* **WICKER MAN**), and they were also said to be well-versed in **ASTROLOGY** and **MAGIC**. There is no connection between the Druids of ancient times and the proliferation in the twentieth century of **NEO-PAGAN** groups who call themselves Druids and celebrate the pagan seasonal festivals at **STONEHENGE** and other ancient sites.

DYBBUK In Jewish folkloric tradition, a form of evil spirit from the realms of the dead, who can possess and take control of human beings.

EARTH SIGNS In astrology, the signs of the **ZODIAC** associated with the **ELEMENT** of earth: **TAURUS, VIRGO** and **CAPRICORN**. They are also known as the Earth Triplicity. People who are born under any of these signs tend to be practical and dependable. *See* **TRIPLICITIES**.

EBE Extraterrestrial Biological Entity. The term is used for any form of creature believed to be dwelling in, or coming from, another planet. Speculation that extraterrestrials have visited, and continue to visit, this planet has been fuelled by numerous alleged sightings of alien creatures at different locations around the world, particularly in the last five decades. Some of these alleged sightings correspond with reports of **UFO**s in the same area.

EBLIS In Islamic mythology, the name of the ruler of the fallen **ANGELS**. Before the fall, he was known as **AZAZEL**.

ECTOPLASM The name of a viscous substance appearing in the course of a **SEANCE**, frequently through the mouth of the medium, which is said to be a physical manifestation of spirit activity. It is allegedly white and semi-transparent in appearance and is said to have a distinctive smell. Sceptics refuse to believe that such a substance exists and declaim reports and photographs of its appearance as fraud.

EL CHUPACABRAS or THE GOAT-SUCKER A monstrous creature, sightings of which have been reported in Puerto Rico and more recently, in Brazil, New Mexico, Texas and Florida. It has allegedly been responsible for the deaths of large numbers of goats, sheep and other farm animals. Sightings of El Chupacabras were first reported in the 1990's, in a part of Puerto Rico that has been linked with a number of other **FORTEAN PHENOMENA**, including the **MOCA VAMPIRE**, which may be the same creature. El Chupacabras has been described as being not unlike a gargoyle, between one and a half and two metres in height, with bat-like wings, red eyes, and fangs protruding from a lipless mouth. It stands on two muscular legs, which resemble those of a kangaroo, and its 'arms' appear skeletally thin, with clawed hands. Spiny protuberances run the length of its back. Those who have allegedly seen El Chupacabras most commonly believe that it is a creature from an alien civilization. Although several people claim to have seen the creature, there is no photographic or other substantial evidence to prove its existence. The animals which have allegedly been killed by it are typically found to have a single, piercing wound somewhere about their bodies, frequently on the head. There are no bloodstains to be found on or around the dead animals, but all blood has been drained from their bodies.

ELECTIONAL ASTROLOGY The drawing up of a **HOROSCOPE** for the purpose of working out the most favourable time to undertake a particular activity or to stage a particular event. In recent years, electional astrology has seen a resurgence in popularity in the Western World, and been used by a number of prominent people, including celebrities and politicians, to help them to plan major events of their personal and public calendar around the most favourable dates. Electional astrology also plays a part in the practice of **FENG-SHUI**.

ELEMENTALS Invisible **NATURE SPIRITS** which, according to medieval belief, lived in and ruled over the four **ELEMENTS**. **GNOMES** ruled over Earth, **SALAMANDERS**, Fire, **SYLPHS**, Air and **UNDINES**, Water.

ELEMENTS The four elements of earth, fire, air and water play a central role in all occult practice, both as physical essentials for the sustainability of life and as spiritual principles, symbolising aspects, or qualities of the universe. In astrology, each of the signs of the **ZODIAC** is associated with one of the elements, giving people born under that sign certain characteristics. It was from the four elements that early alchemists believed everything on earth was made. In modern **WITCHCRAFT**, the four compass points are linked to the four elements; North to Earth, South to Fire, East to Air and West to Water. 'Elemental' candles are burned at these points round the **MAGIC CIRCLE** throughout the performance of all rituals. The magic circle and witches' tools are also consecrated with the four elements; the **PENTACLE** representing Earth, incense representing Air, candle flame representing Fire, and salted Water.

In Chinese culture, five elements are recognised; earth, fire, wood, water and metal. *See* **FIVE ELEMENTS**.

ELEUSIAN MYSTERIES *see* **MYSTERIES**.

ELIGOR A **DEMON** named in the **LEMEGETON**, said to be a knight who possessed the power of prediction, particularly with regard to military matters.

ELIXIR In **ALCHEMY**, a substance supposed by some to be a liquid, by others, a powder, which was believed to guarantee freedom from sickness and eternal life. It was sometimes equated with the **PHILOSOPHER'S STONE**, which was believed to be the key to transmuting base metals into gold.

ELOHIM *see* **TETRAGRAMMATON**.

ELONGATION The apparent growth, or stretching, of the body of a **MEDIUM**; a phenomenon which has allegedly been witnessed in **SEANCE**, where it has been perceived as evidence of spirit activity controlling the medium.

EMERALD TABLET A legendary tablet, said to have been discovered in Alexandria, which was inscribed in Arabic with alchemical secrets and was allegedly the work of **HERMES TRISMEGISTUS**. The contents of the Emerald Tablet first became publicly available in the second century A.D., in Latin translation. The opening sentence is Quod superius est sicut quod inferius et quod inferius est sicut quod superius ad perpetranda miracula rei unis. This saying may be roughly translated and reduced to 'as above, so below', meaning that everything in the spiritual world is mirrored on earth, and it is a principle that underlies all occult philosophy and practice in the Western World.

ESBAT A meeting of a **COVEN** for discussion, worship, initiations and magical purposes. Esbats may take place at regular intervals, or at the discretion of coven members. In modern **NEO-PAGAN WITCHCRAFT**, the ordinary esbat is distinguished from the **SABBAT**, which only takes place on one of the eight festivals of the pagan year.

ESP (EXTRASENSORY PERCEPTION) A general term for the PSYCHIC discovery of certain information by any person; impressions, feelings or thoughts which a person can have, giving them knowledge of something (in the past or in the future, or happening some distance away) about which they would otherwise not know. CLAIRAUDIENCE, CLAIRVOYANCE and TELEPATHY are forms of ESP.

ETHER or AETHER A term in OCCULTISM for the all-pervading essence, which is intangible and invisible to all except clairvoyants. *See* AKASHA, QUINTESSENCE.

ETHERIC BODY The etheric body is viewed as an individual's 'other' body, essentially different from the physical body, hidden and intangible to the physical senses, yet pervading the physical body and surrounding the consciousness, or soul. Some people view the etheric body as different from the ASTRAL BODY, while others equate the two. It is believed that in ASTRAL PROJECTION, the etheric body leaves the physical body and travels with the person's spirit.

EVIL EYE The causing of ill-fortune by one person to another through a glance. Belief in the phenomenon of the Evil Eye dates back to ancient times. There is evidence that the concept has existed in many countries worldwide and it is still prevalent in certain cultures. It is generally associated with malice, or jealousy, but in spite of this is commonly thought to work subconsciously. All manner of misfortunes have been blamed on the effects of the Evil Eye and in every culture where belief in it has existed, there is a wealth of practices, charms and incantations that have been used as means of protection against or removal of the Eye.

EXORCISM The action of expelling an evil spirit by the performance of certain rites. Exorcisms are practised in many cultures where it is believed that harmful spirits can disrupt the lives of human beings, and where there is a belief in the concept of demonic POSSESSION. Exorcisms can be performed either to rid particular places of evil spirits, or to expel a spirit from a person whom it has possessed. In most cultures where it is practised, exorcism is considered to place the person performing the rites at considerable risk, and it is generally performed only by those who have appropriate skills, knowledge and strength of character. Along with prayers or spoken charms and the use of strong odours and sacred or magical substances, most exorcisms involve the INVOCATION of a higher power; a deity or a supreme spirit. In Judaism, exorcism was performed by invoking the names of one or more angels, superior in power to the spirit which was being exorcised. In the Christian religion, exorcisms are performed in the name of Jesus Christ. The Roman Catholic rites of exorcism are based on guidelines laid down in the Rituale Romanum, written in 1614. Exorcisms commonly involve considerable disturbance in the place where they are being performed, as the spirit struggles against the force trying to expel it.

The victim can suffer great physical distress during the procedure, exhibiting violent symptoms such as vomiting, muscle spasms and fits.

EXTISPICY A method of DIVINATION using animal entrails (most commonly, lamb or goat), which was practised in a number of places in ancient times, including Greece and Rome. The liver and intestines were removed from a freshly slaughtered animal and laid out for inspection. The organs were studied for auspicious abnormalities in appearance and for signs of disease which might indicate future events. There might have been real benefits in the practice for nomadic peoples. Signs of disease in the organs of one of their animals, taken as a bad omen and making them reach a decision to move to another place, may have been a real indicator of inadequate or unsuitable grazing or some other environmental hazard in the present location.

EXTRASENSORY PERCEPTION *see* **ESP.**

EYE OF HORUS A stylised form of decoration, frequently found on tombs and amulets dating from ancient times in Egypt, depicting the eye, or eyes of the Egyptian sun-god Horus. It was believed to offer protection against evil. Amulets bearing the eye of Horus were commonly made from gold, silver or precious stones.

According to Egyptian legend, Horus had one black eye and one white. The black eye (the left) represented the Moon and the white eye (the right) represented the Sun. Horus had his left eye torn out by his uncle Seth, who had also murdered his father Osiris. THOTH repaired the eye and Horus gave it to Osiris who reigned in the Underworld.

FAIRY A general term which is applied to a wide variety of supernatural beings, believed both to act upon and to interact with the human world. Evidence of belief in such beings can be found in the folklore of many countries, and is particularly widespread in northern European traditions. Fairies have been traditionally viewed with a mixture of respect and fear, and were believed to be capable of causing either harm or good. They could use their magical powers to help humans in farming, housework, husbandry or love, but they were also capable of acts of considerable cruelty. They could whisk a human child away to their fairy kingdom, and leave an ugly and fractious CHANGELING in its place. They could take on human form and bewitch a hapless human into falling in love with them. Fairyland, or the fairy kingdom, was commonly imagined as a place accessible from the human world but hidden from normal sight. It was also believed to be a place where time seemed to bear no relation to real time in the human world; those who gained entry to the land of the fairies and re-entered the human world would find that in what had seemed to be a short time in fairyland, many years had passed on earth. Fairies were believed by some people to be the spirits of the unbaptised dead, by others, intermediary spirits between God and man, or **NATURE SPIRITS**. A fourth belief regarding fairies views them as pagan races of small people who lived in Europe before the time of the Celts, who were driven into obscurity and in time came to be attributed magical powers, including invisibility.

Beliefs about the appearance of fairies varied widely: they could resemble tiny, winged humans, giants, or elf-like creatures. They were generally believed to be invisible to most people, save a privileged few with powers of **CLAIRVOYANCE**.

Neo-pagans nowadays view fairies as nature spirits, and call upon their assistance in rituals.

FAKIR A mendicant holy man, in particular a Moslem who has chosen a life of poverty and self-denial for religious reasons. Traditionally, fakirs are workers of wonder and can perform spectacular feats, some of which appear to involve techniques of meditation or self-induced trance which enable the fakir to overcome pain and physical discomfort.

FAMILIAR A **DEMON** assistant of a witch or magician. Familiars were believed to have been given to witches by the Devil and frequently took animal form, for example cats, mice, toads and flies, but could also, it was said, appear as monstrous creatures. They could be summoned to assist in magical operations and acted as intermediaries between the witch and the Devil. The Medieval Grimoires name a large number of demons who may be magically summoned using prescribed rituals to serve as familiars for specific purposes. *See* **GRIMOIRE**.

FASCINATION A term used in magical tradition for bewitchment.

FAUST or FAUSTUS, DR JOHANN A legendary figure of sixteenth century Germany, who was said to be a magician and astrologer, who made a pact with the Devil in order to achieve his earthly desires of great knowledge and physical pleasure. In return for the Devil's assistance, Faust traded his soul, which the Devil duly claimed after an agreed period of time. The legend of Doctor Faust was popularised by the plays written by Christopher Marlowe and Goethe. Throughout history, many similar legends have evolved around the lives of a number of prominent people from various countries.

FENG-SHUI Meaning 'wind and water' in Chinese, Feng-shui is an ancient and complex Chinese philosophy concerning the forces that work within the Universe. The practice of Feng-shui involves the search for the optimum balance between the five elements which the Chinese pervade every aspect of life in varying proportions; wind, water, earth, fire and metal. It is also concerned with selecting or adapting man's environment, both manufactured and natural, to facilitate the flow of Ch'i, the universal life-force, in order to promote health, harmony and success in life, work, one's wider surroundings and local living space. Every aspect of life and death may be affected positively or negatively by Feng-shui. It is as important for a burial site to be planned with regard to Feng-shui as it is for a new office block, school or home. There are two traditional forms, or 'schools' of Feng-shui; the Form school, which places emphasis on the visually perceptible aspects of landscapes, buildings and all that they contain, and the Compass school, which concerns itself with complex calculations relating to the **FIVE ELEMENTS**, the four cardinal points of the compass, **ASTROLOGY**, **DRAGON LINES** and the calendar. The calculating instrument of the Compass school is the lo-p'an, which is based on a traditional compass but has an additional, intricate web of lines, circles, numbers and figures which enable relative calculations regarding astrological, directional and calendrical influences to be made for any place that is being assessed. In practice, the two schools of feng-shui are interdependent, and most feng-shui experts will use a combination of visual assessment and calculation when asked for a consultation.

FERN SEED The microscopic seeds of some ferns were believed to have the power of making a person invisible and were much sought after by alchemists.

FETISH An object, sometimes man-made, that is believed to have a spirit residing within it, which man can summon to serve him for a particular purpose. The spirit has been persuaded to take up residence within the object by one person or a group of people and thereafter will remain there. Fetishes can be worn as personal charms for particular reasons (protection, success in hunting, the acquisition of wealth, etc.,) or can belong to a group or tribe of people and be kept in a communal place, for example a fetish temple, ready to be called upon in appropriate situations. Fetishes may be natural objects, particularly unusual or strangely-shaped ones, or may be sculptures, or carved figurines. Fetishism is central to many ancient African tribal cultures.

FETISHISHM *see* **FETISH.**

FINDHORN An experimental community and garden, founded by Peter and Eileen Caddy and Dorothy Maclean in the north-east of Scotland. In spite of inclement prevailing weather conditions and poor quality, sandy soil on an exposed site, the newly-established garden quickly produced crops of vegetables and a variety of other plants that were outstanding in size and quality. The founders believed that the garden's success was attributable to the assistance of 'devas', spirits of nature with whom they communicated and consulted for guidance on nurturing their crops. The community attracted considerable publicity, grew in size and became a focus of interest in the 1970's for **NEW AGE** thinkers globally.

FIRE SIGNS In **ASTROLOGY**, the signs of the **ZODIAC** that are associated with the **ELEMENT** of fire: **ARIES**, **LEO**, **SAGITTARIUS**. They are also known as the Fire Triplicity. People who are born under any of these signs are likely to have a passionate nature, tending towards impatience and impulsiveness. *See* **TRIPLICITIES**.

FIREWALKING A supranormal feat involving walking over burning, white-hot coals, without sustaining injury. Firewalking is performed by fakirs and other occult adepts. *See* **FAKIR**.

FISHER KING In several Medieval romances, the keeper of the **HOLY GRAIL**. In Le Roman de Percival, a twelfth century romance, the Fisher King is the uncle of Percival, one of the knights of the Round Table.

FIVE ELEMENTS In Chinese culture, five essential elements are recognised; earth, fire, wood, water and metal. Each has particular associations. Earth is associated with security, the centre of things, flat shapes and 'earthy' colours. Fire is associated with joy, the South, the summer, and the colour red. Wood is associated with newness, health, the East, the spring and the colour green. Water is associated with mystery, the North, the winter and the colour black. Metal is associated with strength, the West, the autumn and the colour white. These five elements have to be balanced in order to promote harmony and well-being in one's activities and environment. *See* **FENG-SHUI**.

FIVEFOLD KISS A ceremonial salute between a man and a woman which is made up of eight kisses on five areas of the body; feet (2), knees (2), lower abdomen, breasts (2) and knees. The fivefold kiss is an integral part of many Wiccan rituals. *See* **WICCA**.

FIXED SIGNS In **ASTROLOGY**, those signs that mark the middle of seasons; **TAURUS** (mid-spring), **LEO** (mid-summer), **SCORPIO** (mid-autumn) and **AQUARIUS** (mid-winter). They are also known as the Fixed Quadruplicity. A shared characteristic of people born under any of these signs is stability. *See* **QUADRUPLICITIES**.

FLYING The belief that witches could fly from place to place was central to popular witch-belief in the Middle Ages in Europe. Confessions made by numerous women brought to trial on charges of **WITCHCRAFT** gave details of how this magical feat was achieved. Some witches claimed to use a magical ointment or lotion, which, when rubbed on their bodies, allowed them to travel through the air. Some mounted magical animal steeds, while others used their powers of **SHAPE-SHIFTING** to transform themselves into birds. Others still mounted bundles of straw, pitchforks, or **BROOMSTICKS**. It may be the case that the use of hallucinogenic substances can account for some of these beliefs.

FOCALOR A **DEMON** named in the **LEMEGETON**, said to appear as a man with griffin's wings and to possess the power to change the weather and sink ships.

FORAS A **DEMON** named in the **LEMEGETON**, said to appear in human form and to have the powers of teaching men great wisdom and making them invisible.

FORNEUS A DEMON named in the LEMEGETON, said to take the form of a sea monster, and to have the power to make men skilled in rhetoric and loved by their enemies.

FORT, CHARLES HOY (1874–1932) Born in Albany and trained as a journalist, Fort gave up his career whilst living in New York and devoted all his time to researching, cataloguing, and writing about reported phenomena for which there appeared to be no rational, scientific explanation. Deeply scornful of the scientific community, Fort maintained that the absence of scientific proof that strange phenomena (such as frogs raining from the sky, SPONTANEOUS HUMAN COMBUSTION or UFOS) could exist, was not enough to prove that they did not. Fort published four books featuring his research; the Book of the Damned (1919), New Lands (1923), Lo! (1931) and Wild Talents (1932). He proposed a number of outlandish theories, without argument or attempt at proof, to offer some form of explanation for various marvellous occurrences, but there was little consistency in these. His main purpose was to document a wide variety of phenomena and present them as a challenge to the dogmatic approach of the scientific world. Although largely ignored by the scientific community, Fort's work became increasingly popular with a wider readership and his interest in the apparently inexplicable has become a preoccupation of many like-minded people around the world today.

FORTEAN PHENOMENA A term for a wide variety of supernatural or bizarre phenomena that defy rational explanation within scientific or natural laws. They are named after the America journalist Charles FORT, who devoted his life to researching and writing about them. In the 1930's, the Fortean Society was founded in Fort's name by Theodore Dreiser, an American novelist. Fortean phenomena feature in several publications and film and television productions around the world and continue to be a source of popular fascination.

FORTUNE, DION [Violet Mary Firth] (1891–1946) Dion Fortune was the name adopted by Violet Firth, who became a prominent figure in occult circles in Great Britain in the first half of the twentieth century. She became interested in the occult at a young age, when she discovered that she had PSYCHIC abilities. Her studies of JUNG and her own work as a psychotherapist deepened her interest. She was initiated into the ORDER OF THE GOLDEN DAWN, but eventually became disillusioned with both the workings of the organization and its leadership, and left to found her own society, the Community of the Inner Light. Fortune wrote a number of books on the occult, including *Sane Occultism* (1929), *Psychic Self-Defence* (1930) and *The Mystical Qabalah* (1935). She also published several fictional works on occult themes. Her written works, both fiction and non-fiction, have had a profound influence on modern Westen OCCULTISM. The magical society which she formed, now known as the Society of the Inner Light, is still in existence.

FORTUNE-TELLING A general term for a number of methods of **DIVINATION** which are practised largely for the purposes of entertainment at fairgrounds, etc. Popular methods of fortune-telling include **PALMISTRY, TASSEOMANCY** and **CRYSTAL-GAZING**.

FREEMASONRY A secret brotherhood with some five million members worldwide, the aims of which purport to be God-fearing, harmonious, mutually beneficial and charitable. Although no-one can be sure exactly where or how the fraternity came into being, Freemasonry is generally believed to have its origins in the British guilds of stonemasons, in Medieval times. Stonemasonry was a craft the masters of which held considerable status and the secrets of their trade were closely guarded. Secret handshakes and passwords, both still used in Freemasonry today, were commonly used between members of the guilds. There have been claims that Freemasonry in Great Britain began in Scotland and there have also been attempts to link the Freemasons with older secret orders from other countries, in particular the **ORDER OF THE KNIGHTS TEMPLAR**.

The organization existed in a somewhat fragmentary form, with individual lodges functioning autonomously, until the eighteenth century. In 1717, several lodges in England combined under the title of the Grand Lodge, which functioned as a central administrative body. Over the next three decades, Ireland and Scotland followed suit.

Membership of the Freemasons is exclusively male and embraces a wide range of occupations, thus offering members useful social contacts and valuable networking opportunities in business and career.

Much of the ritual and practice of the Freemasons remains shrouded in secrecy, giving rise to speculation that there is a more sinister aspect to the order. Throughout the history of Freemasonry, this secrecy has been at the root of varying degrees of opposition to the brotherhood from religious and political authorities.

Those who become members of the Freemasons progress through three degrees; Entered Apprentice, Fellow Craft and Master Mason. Higher degrees may be also be achieved, and these are conferred by bodies of more advanced Freemasons.

FRIAR BUNGAY An English magician of the fourteenth century, who is said to have helped King Edward IV in battle, by raising mists using magic, to confuse the enemy.

FURCAS A **DEMON** named in the **LEMEGETON**, said to appear as a hairy, bearded old man, mounted on a horse and carrying a sword. He was said to be adept in various methods of **DIVINATION**.

FURTUR A **DEMON** named in the **LEMEGETON**, said always to lie unless commanded to speak the truth. He could control the weather and give answers to all manner of questions regarding esoteric matters. He appeared as a hart with a flaming tail.

FUTHARC or FUTHORC The name given to the 24 Germanic **RUNES**, derived from the first six letters of the runic alphabet; Fehu (f), Uruz (u), Thurisaz (th), Ansuz (a), Raido (r) and Kaunaz (k).

GAAP A **DEMON** named in the **LEMEGETON**, said to take the form of a human. He had the power to teach great wisdom and to make men invisible. Along with **BLETH**, **BELIAL** and **ASMODAY**, Gaap was of the highest order of demons and a ruler among them.

GABRIEL The name of an **ARCHANGEL** in Judaism and Christianity, identified with Jibril in Islam. Gabriel is associated with revelation (in Christianity, with visiting the virgin Mary and telling her she will give birth to the Saviour of mankind), with intellect and with spiritual awareness.

GAIA In Greek mythology, the Earth goddess, wife of Uranus and mother of the Titans and the Cyclops. The name Gaia is now widely used to refer to the Earth. In 1969, the scientist James Lovelock put forward a controversial theory known as the Gaia Hypothesis, which suggested that the Earth and all within it functioned as one whole, a sophisticated organism capable of regulating its own environment in order to sustain the life within it. The concept of Gaia, the Earth-organism, and the responsibility of humans to play their part in maintaining equilibrium within it, is central to **NEW AGE** thinking in general and, more specifically, to the practice of **WICCA**.

GALGAL A modern form of **DIVINATION**, derived from the teachings of the **KABBALAH**.

GAMIGIN A **DEMON** named in the **LEMEGETON**, described as alternating between equine and human form.

GANZFELD STIMULATION The practice of using sensory deprivation to facilitate **ESP**, which has been used for a number of years in **PARAPSYCHOLOGY** experiments . One subject, who has been selected as receiver, is placed in a comfortable sitting or lying position in a soundproof room, wearing headphones to blank out extraneous noise, and cup-shaped eyepieces which allow the eyes to remain open but block out vision. A second subject, the sender, is placed in a separate room, and focuses on an image or object which the receiver is later asked to identify. The removal of sensory and auditory distractions, which can induce a trance-like state in the receiver, is believed to increase receptivity to telepathic signals and research has shown that successful identification of the images projected increases noticeably in frequency under these conditions.

GARDNER, GERALD B[ROUSSEAU] (1884–1964) Born in Liverpool, England, Gerald Gardner is recognised as the man who revived witchcraft in the twentieth century in the West. He was born into a well-to do family and had a somewhat unconventional upbringing, spending a great deal of time travelling round Europe with his nurse for the benefit of his health. As a young adult, he travelled to the Far East and worked in rubber and tea plantations in Malaya for a number of years. He returned to England in the 1930's. Garner had a fascination with the occult from quite an early age and his family claimed descent from Grissel Gairdner, a Scotswoman who was burned as a witch in 1610. On his return to England, Gardner joined an order called the Co-Masons. He was then introduced to a witch **COVEN** which met in the New Forest, and he was initiated into this coven in 1939. At that time, the practice of **WITCHCRAFT** was still illegal in Great Britain, and initiates made every attempt to maintain secrecy regarding their practices. Gardner published a book entitled High Magic's Aid in 1949, giving away many of the secrets of the coven to which he belonged. This led to him breaking away and forming his own coven. After 1951, when the last of the laws against witchcraft were repealed, Gardner did a great deal to publicise further the continuing practice of witchcraft in Great Britain. His book Witchcraft Today, published in 1954, stated his belief in the link between modern witchcraft and ancient pagan religion. Gardner's work, although not universally popular among the ranks of practising witches, proved enormously influential. Several covens were set up, practising the Craft in what was later to be coined The Garderian Tradition. Modern practitioners of **WICCA** generally acknowledge a considerable debt to Gardner and a large amount of Wiccan ritual practice closely follows the guidelines set down in Gardner's **BOOK OF SHADOWS**, which he developed over a number of years with the assistance of Doreen **VALIENTE**.

GARLIC A strongly aromatic plant of the onion family, with edible bulbs. Garlic has anti-viral and anti-hypertensive properties. In **OCCULTISM**, it has a long history as an **AMULET** against the **EVIL EYE** and vampires.

GELLER, URI (1946–) An Israeli psychic who became famous in the 1970's for his telepathic powers and his ability to bend metal and stop or start watches and clocks using the power of his mind. (*See* **PSYCHOKINESIS**.) Geller discovered his **PSYCHIC** powers by accident when he was a child and experimented at home with mind-reading, metal bending etc. for a number of years before becoming a full-time performer. He rapidly rose to fame, performing astonishing feats on television. He could replicate drawings that had been made previously by members of the audience and sealed in envelopes. He could also repeat number sequences which other people had written down, or were thinking of. His psychokinetic powers seemed to be effective not only within his immediate surroundings, but over a distance of several hundred miles. When Geller performed on television, bending cutlery and fixing clocks by power of thought, the television studios would be flooded with calls from viewers reporting that similar things were happening in their own homes.

Geller's success worked against him in the end. Although experiments conducted at the Stanford Research Institute in California seemed to prove that he did in fact possess remarkable powers of **ESP**, he was plagued with criticism and claims of fraud and within a few years was forced to retire from public life. He has made rare appearances on television since then and has made his living as a very successful mineral dowser, working for oil and mining companies.

GEMATRIA A numerological system of word interpretation, which is thought to have originated in Babylon or ancient Greece, and which has been used by Kabbalists since the early Middle Ages or before to find hidden meanings in the Scriptures, particularly the Pentateuch. The Kabbalist gematria is based on the twenty-two letters of the Hebrew alphabet, each of which is accorded a numerical value from 1 to 9. The numbers for the letters in words can then be combined in a number of different ways, according to certain prescribed systems, to give words their own numerical value. Different words or names which have the same numerical value can thereby be linked, or interchanged. Some words will have the same numerical value as certain numbers that have particular mystical significance, which will add a new dimension to their meaning. *See also* **NAMES OF POWER**.

GEMINI In **ASTROLOGY**, the third sign of the **ZODIAC**, represented by the sign of the twins. Gemini is a **MUTABLE** sign, an **AIR** sign, and masculine. Its **RULING PLANET** is Mercury.

Character: Gemini subjects are typically lively, bright and intelligent. They are versatile and not afraid of change, but can also be restless and nervy, subject to sudden changes of mood. They can be notoriously unreliable. There is a distinct duality in the Geminian character. Geminians are generally quick to learn and can be remarkably perceptive, analytical and logical in their approach to study, but their interest in any one field of activity or learning will not necessarily be long-lived. They are easily distracted and drawn to new challenges and this may be reflected in a string of interests and hobbies being pursued avidly for a short period and then dropped. In situations of conflict, or when confronted with a decision, Gemini subjects will be able to see the problem from both sides and will often be able to make accurate and fair judgements. They are not only good at adapting to new situations; they relish them. Communication is a strong point. Geminians typically love to travel and experience constantly changing scenery, cultures and atmospheres. Gemini children will be both rewarding and challenging. They will benefit greatly from intellectual stimulation and will pick up new skills quickly and enthusiastically. However, their restlessness may prove trying at times, and they will need firm guidance and encouragement to keep them focused on any task in hand, particularly in a classroom situation.

Personal relationships: Geminians make lively and interesting partners and friends, but they can be flirtatious and fickle and are not always reliable or faithful. Their frequent changes of mood may be hard for some partners or understand or accept. Geminians are most likely to settle with someone who is at least their intellectual equal. Gemini parents are likely to be lively, creative and fun, but may not always be as patient as is necessary and in some cases, may be preoccupied with their own interests to the detriment of their children's needs.

Career and business: Fast-paced occupations in media, public relations and advertising will suit the Geminian's energetic approach and skill in communications. Their judgement and intelligence might also suit them for a career in law, particularly in the courtroom setting. Geminians generally demonstrate good financial judgement and a career dealing on the stockmarket could well be attractive. Many prominent literary figures have been Geminians.

Health: Gemini subjects may be prone to mental stress and disorders of the nervous system.

Colour: Yellow or light grey.

Gemstones: Agate, diamond, jade.

Animals: Dog, squirrel.

Flowers: Lavender, lily of the valley.

GEMORY A DEMON named in the LEMEGETON, appearing as a beautiful woman and said to have the power to procure the love of women for any man.

GENIUS (pl. GENII) A spiritual being who has influence, either good or bad, over worldly things and human activity.

GEOMANCY DIVINATION, either from interpreting the patterns made by earth scattered on the ground, or by pebbles, seeds, etc. The term is also used to apply to the selection of favourable sites for buildings according to the physical characteristics of the landscape (*see* FENG-SHUI).

GHOST A form of APPARITION, which, if visible, most commonly resembles a human being (or part of one), but may also resemble an animal. Ghosts are thought to be manifestations of the spirits of the dead.

GHOUL In Eastern traditions, a DEMON who preyed on the dead and fed on corpses.

GIFT OF TONGUES *see* GLOSSOLALIA.

GLASTONBURY Situated in Somerset, in SW England, the market town of Glastonbury and its surroundings, including Glastonbury Tor and the abbey ruins, have long been acknowledged as England's most magical site. Glastonbury is said to lie at the crossing of several LEY LINES, linking it to STONEHENGE and AVEBURY, and supposedly causing it to be rich in spiritual energy. It has long been a place of pilgrimage for both Christians and occultists because of its religious, mythological and magical associations, and it is a favoured site for the celebration of ancient seasonal festivals. Archeological research has found evidence of habitation at the site dating from the Iron Age, at which time Glastonbury was virtually an island surrounded by marsh. It is believed that the site was sacred to the **DRUIDS**.

According to legend, Joseph of Arimathea brought the **HOLY GRAIL** to Glastonbury and concealed it in the Chalice Well, which is situated at the foot of the Tor. The well is said to have been sunk by the Druids and is reputed to have magical powers. The Glastonbury Thorn, which still flowers every year at Christmas among the ruins of the abbey, is said to have been planted by Joseph of Arimathea. Accordingly, Glastonbury is recognised as the earliest Christian site in Great Britain.

The ruins of St Michael's chapel stand on top of the Tor. The chapel was built on the site of an earlier Medieval church. Before that, according to legend, King Arthur held sway in his fortress. Arthur and the lady Guinevere are said to lie hidden safely in secret graves within the grounds of the abbey below. The abbey, long in ruins, dates from around the thirteenth century, and is the last of a series of buildings that occupied the site after the original abbey was founded in the fifth century, allegedly by St Patrick. It was one of several destroyed in England on the orders of Henry VIII, in 1539. In the early thirteenth century, some monks claimed to have found Arthur's grave, disinterred his remains and reburied them, but the destruction of the abbey some three hundred years later meant that all trace of their discovery was lost.

In the early years of the twentieth century, an archeologist named Frederick Bligh Bond began excavations on the site of the abbey. His work, he claimed, was made considerably easier thanks to a number of ghostly advisers, the spirits of dead monks from the abbey who guided him to many of his discoveries there.

In 1929, Katherine Smallwood, a sculptress, claimed to have discovered, in an area including Glastonbury Tor and some land to the south of it, a circle of signs corresponding to those of the **ZODIAC**, identifiable in the contours of various natural formations, earthworks and other features of the landscape. Her claims led to understandable controversy. While some said that the 'Glastonbury Zodiac' was little more than imaginative perception on Ms Smallwood's part, others gave credence to her views, referring to the work of Dr **JOHN DEE**, astrologer to Elizabeth I, who also claimed to have discovered similar features in the same area. *See* **GLASTONBURY SCRIPTS, AUTOMATIC WRITING.**

GLASTONBURY SCRIPTS A series of documents produced by the **AUTOMATIC WRITING** of John Bartlett and used by Frederick Bligh Bond to assist him in the excavations of the abbey site at **GLASTONBURY** between 1907 and 1912. The spirits guiding the writing were allegedly those of monks who had once lived in the abbey. The documents included a detailed ground plan of the abbey and information about the history of the abbey before its destruction in the sixteenth century. Bligh's revelations regarding his spirit guides provoked outrage within church circles.

GLASTONBURY ZODIAC *see* **GLASTONBURY.**

GLASYA LABOLAS A **DEMON** named in the **LEMEGETON** and said to take the form of a dog with griffin's wings. Among his powers was that of making men invisible.

GLOSSOLALIA Speaking in tongues. Glossolalia is typically characterised by unintelligible utterances which are believed by some to be words of some unknown or ancient language, or to contain messages from God. It is a phenomenon associated with the Christian religion. According to the New Testament, the apostles of Christ spoke in tongues when they received the Holy Spirit. Glossolalia is demonstrated in many branches of the Christian religion, for example, among Pentecostalists, Methodists, Quakers and members of the Church of the Latter-day Saints, where it is taken as a sign of baptism with the Holy Spirit.

GLYPH A sculpted or carved symbol or figure. In **ASTROLOGY**, the term is used to denote the graphic symbols which represent the signs of the **ZODIAC**.

GNOMES NATURE SPIRITS, or fairies (*see* **FAIRY**), which were believed to resemble small humans. The name of one of the four categories of **ELEMENTALS**. Gnomes were associated with the **ELEMENT** of earth.

GNOSTICISM Derived from the Greek gnosis, meaning knowledge, Gnosticism is the name of a philosophical and religious movement that originated in the area surrounding the Mediterranean around the time of the dawning of Christianity. The doctrines of the movement contained elements of Egyptian religious belief, Indian mysticism, Judaism, the Greek **MYSTERIES, MAGIC** and Christianity. Although the movement embraced sects that were manifestly diverse in individual rites and practices, Gnosticism was founded on the common underlying principle that salvation was to be found only through secret spiritual knowledge available to none but its devotees. Central to all Gnostic belief was also a dualistic view of reality; good and evil were opposed and equated with spiritual and physical being and thus, the material world was perceived as evil. The world had been made and was ruled, not by the true God, but by the **DEMIURGE**, a false creator. Physical existence was a prison from which the soul, a particle of Divine essence, had to be liberated. Salvation was only to be found through secret knowledge which would be revealed to initiates, and through renunciation of physical comforts and desires. Christian Gnostics viewed Christ as a messenger from the spiritual world, who had been sent by God to pass on secret knowledge that would free trapped souls from the physical realm. Gnosticism, unlike orthodox Christianity, gave equal status to women and men. Gnostic sects flourished in various parts of the Mediterranean in the early centuries A.D., but gradually the power of orthodox Christianity prevailed and Gnosticism declined. Gnostics, or those belonging to sects founded on Gnostic beliefs, for example the Manichaeans and the Cathars, were persecuted as heretics.

The discovery in the 1940's of a collection of Gnostic manuscripts (The Dead Sea Scrolls), near the town of Nag Hammadi in Egypt, have revealed much to historians about the diversity of Gnostic beliefs.

GOAT-SUCKER *see* **EL CHUPACABRAS**.

GODDESS, THE In **WICCA**, the undying, female side of the Divine principle, also known as the Great Mother, and called by many names which acknowledge her many different aspects, for example **ARADIA**, **ARIANROD**, **DIANA**, **HECATE**, **DEMETER**. The Goddess is lunar, presiding over the cycle of life and death and the changing seasons, and living on while the solar **HORNED GOD** weakens with the onset of the winter and dies and is reborn at **YULE**.

GOETIA The title of the first part of the **LEMEGETON**, naming seventy-two **DEMONS**. Another name for **GOETY**.

GOETY or GOETIC MAGIC Black ceremonial magic. The Grimoires are Goetic books. *See* **GRIMOIRE**.

GOG AND MAGOG In the book of Revelation in the Bible, the names of the two nations summoned by **SATAN** but overcome and devoured by God's fire at the time of the final judgement.

GRAIL, HOLY *see* **HOLY GRAIL**.

GRAND GRIMOIRE, THE Also known as the Great Grimoire, the Grand Grimoire is a work allegedly edited by a man called Antonia del Rabina from transcriptions of the writings of King Solomon. It is by reputation the most diabolic of the Grimoires, but its antiquity and source are both questionable. *See* **GRIMOIRE**.

GREAT RITE In Wicca the name for the rite performed as part of third degree initiation, and on other occasions by third-degree initiates. The Great Rite culminates in the sexual act, performed either symbolically or actually. If the latter is the case, the act will generally be performed in private. In symbolic performance of the Great Rite, the high priest takes his **ATHAME**, symbol of the masculine, and plunges it into the wine-filled **CHALICE**, symbol of the feminine, which is held by the high priestess. The Great Rite symbolises fertility and the male-female polarity that is central to **NEO-PAGAN** witchcraft, manifest in the God/**GODDESS** aspects of the Divine Force.

GREAT WHITE BROTHERHOOD According to Theosophical belief (*see* **THEOSPHY**), a number of people who have absolute knowledge of the divine, who live separately in different parts of the world and communicate telepathically with each other.

GREY A term used for a form of **EBE**, which has allegedly been sighted in **UFOS** and on Earth in various locations, particularly in the United States. It is said to be vaguely human in shape, around five feet tall, with a large head and large, black, slanting eyes which have been described as resembling sunglasses. It is dark grey in colour, with non-porous skin, like that of a dolphin or whale. A number of people claim to have communicated with Greys, either through **TELEPATHY** or during an abduction experience. *See* **ALIEN ABDUCTION**.

GREY MAN A form of **APPARITION** that has been reportedly been seen by climbers on certain mountains, most famously Ben Macdhui in Scotland. Witnesses commonly report first sensing an ominous presence in the vicinity, before seeing a large grey form, bigger than that of a human being, bearing down upon them. Although the apparition has caused no harm, those who have witnessed it have been very frightened.

GRIMOIRE A text book of black **MAGIC**, containing the names and characteristics of various demons and instructions for summoning them to the service of the magician, along with other magical secrets, spells, recipes and rituals. There are several such works still in existence, in spite of efforts by the Church in the Middle Ages to have them all destroyed. These include the **GRAND GRIMOIRE**, the **KEY OF SOLOMON, LEMEGETON, THE HEPTAMERON, GRIMORIUM VERUM** and others.

GRIMORIUM VERUM A **GRIMOIRE**, allegedly translated by a Dominican Jesuit and published in the sixteenth century in Egypt, but likely to date from much later, possibly the eighteenth century.

GROUPINGS Divisions of the signs of the **ZODIAC** into sets with shared characteristics. One grouping divides the signs according to the **ELEMENTS** with which they are associated (**WATER SIGNS, FIRE SIGNS, AIR SIGNS** and **EARTH SIGNS**) These are known as the **TRIPLICITIES**. Another grouping, the **QUADRUPLICITIES**, divides the signs into **CARDINAL, FIXED** and **MUTABLE**, according to whether they mark the beginning, middle or end of a season. The third grouping separates the signs of the zodiac into masculine and feminine.

GROUP MIND A term used to describe collective **PSYCHIC** energy, or the telepathic links formed between people participating in magical ritual. *See also* **CHAIN, CONE OF POWER**.

GURDJIEFF, GEORGE IVANOVITCH (1373–1949) A native Russian born of Greek parents, Gurdjieff rose to prominence in Europe and the United States as a spiritual teacher and leader. After spending many years travelling in Europe and Asia, meeting and conversing with people from widely different cultures, he formulated his basic philosophy of man's condition; that we live as if in a state of sleep, like automatons controlled by external forces. In order to emerge from this state, or 'wake up' and become truly conscious and self-aware, Gurdjieff claimed it was necessary to embark upon a punishing regime of self-discipline, physical exercise, close introspection and study, which he devised himself. He established a centre for his teachings, the Institute for the Harmonious Development of Man, in Paris. His doctrines were spread further afield by a number of teachers, each of whom, as Gurdjieff had done, demanded absolute obedience from their pupils. Although he had more than his fair share of critics, who dismissed him as a fraud, Gurdjieff, who clearly had a charismatic, persuasive and controlling personality, exercised considerable influence over many people, several of whom were respected intellectuals. One of his followers was a Russian journalist named P.D. Ouspensky, whose written work on the subject helped both to publicise and clarify Gurdjieff's teachings.

GUSOIN A DEMON named in the LEMEGETON, having the rank of duke and possessing the power of interpreting oracles.

GWYN APP NUDD In Welsh mythology, the ruler of Annwn, land of the dead.

GYROMANCY A divinatory practice whereby a person seeks to determine the answers to questions by spinning. Most commonly, the inquirer stands in the middle of a circle of letters and spins round until too dizzy to stand. The first card against which he or she stumbles is noted and the process is repeated as many times as is necessary to form some suggestion of a response. The dizziness of the inquirer ensures that the 'choice' of letters thus made is entirely out of his or her control.

HAAGENTI A DEMON named in the LEMEGETON, taking the form of a bull with griffon's wings but also able to appear as a human. He was said to have the power to turn water into wine and base metals into gold. *See* ALCHEMY.

HALLOWE'EN *see* SAMHAIN.

HALPHAS A DEMON named in the LEMEGETON, said to appear as a dove and to serve the function of providing the means and manpower for starting conflicts.

HANDFASTING In WICCA, a ritual joining two people together in marriage, which is performed within the MAGIC CIRCLE. It is followed by the GREAT RITE, a ritual of sexual union which may be actual or symbolic.

HAND OF GLORY A magical lamp, made from the severed hand of a hanged man. The hand was drained of blood, pickled, then dried. Candles made from the fat of the hanged corpse were then attached to the fingers. The Hand of Glory was used by house burglars, who believed that lighting it ensured that the occupants of the house being burgled would sleep deeply while their possessions were being carried away.

HARUSPEX An Etruscan term for a person who practised DIVINATION by looking at animal entrails. The term came to be used in a more general sense, to denote anyone who practised **DIVINATION**.

HAUNTING Repeated vistitations by, or the continual presence of, a spiritual entity, which may be manifested in various ways; noises, smells, changes in temperature, apparitions, etc. Hauntings are particularly associated with places where tragic or violent deaths have occurred. In many cases, the identity of the spirit responsible for the haunting is unknown, but in others, the spirit may be identified as a particular person, now dead, who once lived in or frequented the place where paranormal phenomena are being witnessed.

HECATE In Greek mythology, a deity associated with both the moon and the underworld. She was also recognised as the goddess of **MAGIC** and enchantments. She was said to visit earth to torment the living, and to haunt crossroads and burial places. In modern **WITCHCRAFT**, Hecate is recognised as an aspect of the **GODDESS**, and associated with the period of the waning moon.

HEDGE WITCH In **WICCA**, a term for a witch who practises alone and is not associated with any coven.

HELLFIRE CLUB A secret society, properly named The Knights of St Francis of Wycombe, which was founded by the English MP Sir Francis Dashwood (1708–81) and caused outrage in the more respectable ranks of society at the time. Members of the society met in the ruins of Medmenham Abbey. The society's activities contained an element of occultism, but it was more for the orgiastic nature of its meetings that the Hellfire Club earned its scandalous reputation. The group were known locally as the Mad Monks of Medmenham.

HEPTAMERON, THE A textbook of **MAGIC**, which was once attributed to Peter of Abano, a thirteenth century Italian magician, but is most likely to date from the fifteenth century or later. *See* **GRIMOIRE**.

HERBA SACRA Meaning 'sacred weed' in Latin, a name for the herb verbena, which was believed to have magical curative and protective powers.

HEREDITARY WITCH In modern **WITCHCRAFT**, a term used to denote a witch who claims to be descended from a family line of witches, and to have learned her craft from her predecessors.

HERMES The Greek name for Mercury, the messenger of the gods. In **ALCHEMY**, mercury, or quicksilver, was commonly referred to as Hermes.

HERMES TRISMEGISTUS A mythical figure, named after Hermes, the Greek deity identified with the Egyptian god **THOTH**. Hermes Trismegistus ('Trismegistus' meaning 'Thrice Great') was believed to be an Egyptian scholar and philosopher, who lived around the time of Moses, and was allegedly the author of **HERMETICA**.

HERMETICA A body of philosophical, magical and scientific writings attributed to **HERMES TRISMEGISTUS**, upon which much of Western occult philosophy is based. According to legend, the surviving literature is a small part of a much larger body of work, most of which was destroyed by fire. The real age and origins of the work—which may have had multiple authors—are unlikely ever to be known, but its influence on European alchemists, magicians and mystics has been considerable since the Middle Ages. *See* **ALCHEMY, EMERALD TABLET.**

HERNE THE HUNTER The ghostly wild huntsman of English folk tales. Herne is identified in modern **WITCHCRAFT** with the **HORNED GOD.**

HEXAGRAM *see* **I CHING.**

HOLY GRAIL A symbolic chalice featuring in Christian and Arthurian legends since Medieval times. It is believed to be the cup used at the Last Supper by Christ, and was said to have been taken by Joseph of Arimathea and filled with the blood of Christ after the crucifixion. Joseph of Arimathea was also said to have brought the Grail to Great Britain, to **GLASTONBURY**, where he founded a Christian community. The quest for the Holy Grail was the subject of several Medieval romances, including Le Roman de Perceval, written in the late twelfth century by Chrétien de Troyes, and Morte d'Arthur, written in the fifteenth century by Sir Thomas Malory. In some of these tales the Grail features as a physical object, whilst in others it is identified with the spiritual and esoteric; magical visions, hidden knowledge and human perfection.

The origins of the legends of the Holy Grail may not have been in Christian belief, but in Celtic pagan tradition, in the concept of the vessel of plenty, regeneration and rebirth; the womb of the Mother **GODDESS.**

HOME, DANIEL DUNGLAS (1883–86) A Scottish-born spiritualist and medium, who lived in America for most of his childhood and early adulthood. He displayed an astonishing repertoire of paranormal feats, including **LEVITATION** of himself and a variety of objects, producing unexplained sounds in the vicinity, causing temperature changes, **TELEKINESIS**, **APPORTATION**, and **ELONGATION**. Unlike so many other self-professed mediums, he was never exposed as a fraud.

HOODOO SEA *see* **BERMUDA TRIANGLE.**

HORARY ASTROLOGY The drawing up of an astrological chart for a particular time, in order to answer a question asked at that time.

HORNED GOD, THE In modern **NEO-PAGAN WITCHCRAFT**, the male counterpart to the **GODDESS**. Unlike the Goddess, who never dies, the Horned God, a solar deity, is believed to die each year and be reborn at the winter solstice. His peak of power is midsummer. He is identified with a number of ancient deities, including **HERNE**, **CERUNNOS**, and Pan.

The Horned God is sometimes, erroneously, associated with the demon **BAPHOMET**, or with the Devil.

HOROSCOPE An astrological chart which is drawn up to show the positions of the signs of the **ZODIAC** in the celestial sphere at a particular point in time, in relation to the **PLANETS** and the twelve **HOUSES**. *See* **ASTROLOGY**.

HOSPITALLERS, KNIGHTS (Knights of St John of Jerusalem) A religious order founded around 1070 which ran a pilgrim's resting place and hospital in Jerusalem and was then involved in the fighting of the Crusades. Like the **ORDER OF THE KNIGHTS TEMPLAR**, the hospitallers became wealthy and powerful. By the thirteenth century the order had spread its influence to Rhodes and Malta. Many of the activities of the brotherhood were conducted in secret and it is thought that they had considerable knowledge of Eastern medicine.

HOUSES In **ASTROLOGY**, twelve divisions of the sky above and below the horizon, numbered in an anti-clockwise direction from the eastern horizon, or **ASCENDANT**. Each house relates to a different aspect of a person's life, as follows:

First House: Self, a person's personality as seen by others.

Second House: Possessions, earning, income and assets, personal values.

Third House: Communication, intellectual thought and expression, education.

Fourth House: Home, a person's environment and family.

Fifth House: Pleasure, creativity and artistic ability.

Sixth House: Health, mental and physical wellbeing, duties and responsibilities.

Seventh House: Partnership, marriage, personal and business ties, conflicts and separations.

Eighth House: Sex, death, regeneration.

Ninth House: Philosophy, religion, foreign travel and new experiences, intellectual development.

Tenth House: Social status, ambitions and achievements, career.

Eleventh House: Friends, group relationships, aspirations, philanthropy.

Twelfth House: The unconscious, dreams, secrets, hidden fears, fate or **KARMA**.

HYDROMANCY A general term applied to several methods of **DIVINATION** using water, including **SCRYING**.

HYPNOSIS A sleep-like state, or trance, which may be produced in one person by another or, in some circumstances, self-induced. The technique of hypnotism was discovered by Anton **MESMER** in the eighteenth century. Mesmer called it animal magnetism and used it as a therapeutic tool in his medical practice. The technique was re-named hypnotism by a Scottish surgeon, James Braid, who carried out extensive experiments on subjects under hypnosis, and developed simpler techniques for inducing the hypnotic state. During hypnosis the subject will typically respond in an automatic manner to suggestion, and will appear to act with no regard to the external environment. Subjects under hypnosis may, at the suggestion of the hypnotist, perceive aspects of the external world differently from normal; rejecting favourite food, or seeing an old person as a young one, for example. They may also, at the hypnotist's request, conduct themselves in an uncharacteristic manner, such as reverting to childish behaviour. It has also been observed that subjects under hypnosis do not respond appropriately to pain. Stranger phenomena associated with the hypnotic state include CLAIRVOYANCE, TELEPATHY and REMOTE VIEWING.

As the study of hypnosis developed in the nineteenth century, researchers came to see the hypnotic state as one of suspension of the subject's will. A theory was developed that whilst in a hypnotic trance, the subject's repressed or unconscious thoughts and desires could be revealed and consequently, a number of psychiatrists, including Freud, began to use hypnosis in the treatment of patients with psychiatric disorders, particularly those that were of a hysterical nature. It was also discovered that hypnosis could be used to trigger Past life regression, a state in which subjects in a hypnotic trance appeared to return to, and describe previous incarnations, displaying surprising knowledge of historical detail of the time at which they 'lived'. Alongside the serious study of hypnosis in its early years, however, a new form of entertainment came into being; that of the stage hypnotist. The unethical nature of many of the popular stage acts was responsible, to a great extent, for hypnotism acquiring a disreputable image. Further doubt about the practice was raised by sceptics who denied the possibility of past-life regression and claimed that its use by mediums, who allegedly hypnotised themselves in order to contact the spirit world, was elaborate fraud.

Hypnotism is still used as a form of entertainment, but the conditions under which it is practised are more strictly controlled. As a therapeutic tool, it has regained its respectability and, when carried out by qualified practitioners, is generally accepted as a moderately effective form of treatment for some addictions and phobias. In dentistry and in medicine, it has also proved its usefulness in inducing a state of relaxation and calm, and in helping with pain relief.

There is much that still defies explanation about hypnosis. There are those that argue that it is an entirely physiological state, a form of very deep relaxation, but their arguments take no account of the fact that some hypnotised subjects have been able to 'see' things hidden from their view, to demonstrate telepathic powers, or to have knowledge of times and events about which, allegedly, they would not otherwise have known. Although it is generally acknowledged that hypnotism can be put to uses that can benefit many people, its practice is still regarded, quite justifiably, with a measure of caution. For in subjecting one person to the will of another, there will always be the potential to do as much harm as good. *See* **PAST LIFE RECALL**.

I CHING The Book of Changes, a commentary on an ancient Chinese method of **DIVINATION**, which has been used since ancient times to give users an understanding of the external forces in operation in their world at any one time. Underlying the I Ching is the concept of Yin and Yang, the two complimentary opposites at the core of all existence. Yin is female, darkness, passivity, negativity, earth, and Yang is male, light, activity, positivity, heaven, etc. The sign for Yin is a broken line and for Yang, it is an unbroken line. The I Ching was originally based a system of eight symbols known as Trigrams, formed from all possible combinations of three lines, either Yin or Yang. Each of the trigrams represents an aspect of the world and they form complimentary pairs; Heaven and Earth, Fire and Water, Thunder and Wind and Mountain and Lake. Each trigram has associations with colour, seasons, parts of the human body, family, emotions, nature, etc. The trigrams were used for predicting changes in nature. In the twelfth century BC, a man named Wen, a feudal lord, is said to have been imprisoned by the emperor and during his incarceration, to have developed the I Ching further, creating sixty-four hexagrams from all possible pairings of the eight trigrams, each of which had its own qualities and divinatory significance. Additional text was added to the I Ching by Wen's son, regarding the interpretation of the sixty-four hexagrams. The hexagrams are formed by the casting of stones, coins, or yarrow stalks. Interpretation of a hexagram that has been cast in response to a particular question may be made partly with reference to the text of the I Ching and partly through intuitive meditation on the combination of images which are evoked by the elements represented by the hexagram.

ILLUMINATI The name used, from the fifteenth century onwards, by a number of European occultists who believed that, through a mysterious process known as Illuminism, they had become the recipients of directly communicated divine wisdom, or enlightenment. Members of several different sects, including **ROSICRUCIANS** and Freemasons (*see* **FREEMASONRY**), claimed to be Illuminati. In 1776, Adam Weishaupt, a German professor of law, formed the Order of Illuminati in Bavaria. The order was run along similar lines to the Freemasons, and claimed to lead its initiates to true knowledge of Divine Reason. It attracted a number of prominent intellectuals and became quite powerful, but was suppressed by the Bavarian government ten years later.

ILLUMINISM *see* **ILLUMINATI**

IMBOLG or CANDLEMAS, ST BRIGID'S DAY, ST BRIDGET'S DAY An ancient Celtic fire-festival, celebrated on the 2nd February, to mark the turning point between Winter and Spring, and the imminent return of light and fertility to the earth. Brigid was a Celtic goddess of fertility. With the advent of Christianity, the festival was renamed Candlemas, or St Bridget's day. Imbolg is celebrated as one of the eight Wiccan sabbats. *See* **SABBAT**.

INCANTATION A phrase or verse recited or sung in magical ritual, for example as part of a spell, or when invoking spirits. The term is applied to repetitive, rhythmic chants, which are used to alter a person's state of consciousness.

INCENSE Powders or solids made with fragrant essential plant oils and tree resins, which, when burned, give off a sweet-smelling smoke. Incense has been used in religion and magic for hundreds of years. It is associated with purification and with repelling evil. It is used in modern **WITCHCRAFT** to represent the **ELEMENT** of air.

INCUBUS The term used to denote a devil or demon which could transform itself into a man in order to have sexual intercourse with women as they slept. *See* **SUCCUBUS, NIGHT DEMON**.

INVOCATION The ritual summoning of a spirit, such as an **ANGEL** or **DEMON**, or the spirit of a dead person. The medieval Grimoires (*see* **GRIMOIRE**) contain instructions for the invocations of a large number of demons, each with particular powers, who may be summoned for different purposes.

The invocation of demons was considered a dangerous process, which placed the magician at risk of **POSSESSION**. The magician had to undertake a lengthy period of preparation, which generally involved fasting and ritual cleansing. In a suitably secluded spot at a chosen time, the magician, either dressed in white or naked, would draw out a magic circle and with ritual phrases and incantations, call out the demon's name and command it to appear. Not all demons were willing to submit themselves to the will of a mortal, and the magician needed to focus all his psychic energy and strength of will in order to be sure of getting it under his control. *See also* **NECROMANCY**.

In **WICCA**, the **GODDESS**, the **HORNED GOD** and **NATURE SPIRITS** are frequently invoked in coven rituals. In Gardnerian Wicca, for example, in the ceremony of Drawing Down the Moon, which is a central element in the opening ritual at every **SABBAT**, the spirit of the Goddess is invoked by the high priest, and called upon to enter the body of the high priestess, so that it may work through her.

ISHTAR The Babylonian goddess of love and war. *See* **ASHTORETH**.

JUDGE, WILLIAM *see* **THEOSOPHY**

JUNG, CARL GUSTAV (1875–1961) Psychiatrist, born in Kesswil, Switzerland. Jung was an introspective child, who from a relatively early age, took a keen interest in the workings of the human mind. After completing his studies in medicine, he took up a post in the Burghölzi psychiatric hospital in Zurich. Jung spent some time working in collaboration with Sigmund Freud, but the two men fell into disagreement over Freud's insistence that mental disorders were rooted in unconscious sexual desires, and Jung's studies in psychoanalysis took him in a different direction. He developed the theory of the 'collective unconscious', a store of common human predispositions, or 'archetypes' (Shadow, Anima/Animus, Syzigy, Child, Self, etc.), which are made manifest in the symbols of dreams, myths and religion. His work has been highly influential in the field of psychiatry, and has also influenced the thinking of many occultists, in particular, the Theosophists. *See* **THEOSOPHY**.

KABBALAH Mystical Jewish philosophical doctrine, which was believed to have been passed from God to man, via the angels, who taught it to Adam. The teachings of the Kabbalah were then said to have been passed on by word of mouth to chosen initiates among the Jewish people, including Abraham and Moses. Much of the wisdom of the Kabbalah is derived from interpretation of information encoded in the Pentateuch. The first written texts of Kabbalistic doctrine are Sefer Yezirah, the Book of Creation, which is thought to date from the eighth or ninth century A.D., and Zepher ha Zohar, the Book of Splendour, which dates from the thirteenth century. Kabbalistic doctrine places man and God in a multi-layered cosmos and demonstrates the means by which, through knowledge, man can ascend through various levels from the material world to the divine. A major element of Kabbalistic doctrine is the belief that everything in the universe is ultimately expressed in number, and that the secrets of all existence can be unlocked through numbers. The letters of the Hebrew alphabet each have a numerical value, and by systematic reduction of words to the combined numerical value of the letters within, connections can be made between different words which are found to have the same value, and different concepts can be linked one to another. By substituting some words with others of the same value, hidden meanings can be discovered in the writings of the Old Testament which reveal more about the nature of Creation and man's place within it.. (*See* **GEMATRIA, NUMEROLOGY, TETRAGRAMMATON**). The symbolic representation of the cosmos is known as the Tree of Life, a diagram showing ten sepiroth, or aspects of God, who is limitless and all-pervading. Nine of the sepiroth are arranged in three triangles and the tenth lies at the foot. The sepiroth in the top triangle are: 1) Kether, The Crown, 2) Chokmah, Wisdom and 3) Binah, Understanding. The second (inverted triangle contains: 4) Chesed, Mercy, 5) Geburah, Severity and 6) Tipareth, Beauty. The third (inverted) triangle contains: 7) Netzach, Victory, 8) Hod, Glory and 9) Yesod, Foundation. At the foot of the tree, 10) Malkuth, Kingdom, or the Material world, stands alone. The division of the tree in this manner represents four worlds; Atziluth, the realm of the uncreated spirit, Briah, the realm of creation, Yetzirah, the realm of formation, and Assiah, the realm of the physical. The sepiroth are interconnected by twenty-two pathways. The path from the divine to the earthly leads downwards from the first sepiroth, Kether , through successive sepiroth, to the tenth, Malkuth . The sepiroth are also so arranged that they each lie on one of three pillars; the left-hand pillar is the pillar of Severity (female, passive), the middle is Mildness (balance) and the right is Mercy (male, active). Binah, Geburah and Hod stand on the left-hand pillar. Chokmah, Chesed and Netzach stand on the right. Kether, Tipareth, Yesod and Malkuth are on the central pillar. The path to knowledge of the Divine thus involves the embracing and balancing of extremes and discovering a middle way, leading towards Kether, which stands on the central pillar.

Although Kabbalistic doctrines originated in the Jewish religion, elements of it have been absorbed into other religions and the Kabbalah has had a major influence on Western **MAGIC**, **ALCHEMY** and **MYSTICISM**. In the final years of the twentieth century, interest in the Kabbalah has grown considerably, particularly in the United States, and increasing numbers of people, including several prominent figures in the world of fashion and entertainment, have been turning to the teachings of the Kabbalah in a personal search for enlightenment. *See also* **TETRAGRAMMATON, NAMES OF POWER**.

KARMA In Hinduism and Buddhism, the concept of a link of cause and effect between deeds and destiny through successive incarnations. The doctrine of Karma asserts that the quality of one's thoughts and actions throughout one's life will affect the course of the next. Karma, whether good or bad, is unavoidable in the present, i.e. one cannot change the consequences of what one has done in a past life. Equally, one's conduct in the present is of prime importance in determining the quality of future incarnations, where the consequences will inevitably be felt.

KEY OF SOLOMON, THE A **GRIMOIRE**, containing instructions for magical rituals and practices, which was particularly popular in Medieval times. The oldest surviving manuscript is thought to date from the thirteenth century, although the original writings are thought to predate this by several hundred years.

KING'S EVIL An old name for scrofula, tuberculosis of the lymph glands which was believed to be cured if the sufferer was touched by the hand of a king.

KIRK, ROBERT (c. 1644–1692) A Scottish minister from Aberfoyle, who is remembered chiefly for writing The Secret Commonwealth of Fairies, which he published in 1691. The book contained a wealth of detail about the fairy world, supposedly gleaned from Kirk's own experiences, and also included some information about witches, notably on the means of identifying a **WITCHMARK**.

KIRLIAN PHOTOGRAPHY A technique for taking photographs of objects placed on a photographic plate positioned within an electric field. The photographs show a multicoloured halo of light surrounding the objects. The process was discovered by chance in 1939 by Semyan Kirlian, a Russian electrician. The first photograph he took in this way was of his own hand, and he and his wife then experimented with a variety of natural objects. They found that only living tissue, whether animal or vegetable, showed the light effect, and that the colour and intensity of the light surrounding the object varied under certain conditions. Newly picked plant stems showed a particularly bright area of light emanating from the place where the stem had been broken. Tearing a small piece off a leaf immediately before taking a picture, Kirlian was surprised to see the resultant photograph showed a halo of light outlining the shape of the whole leaf. Subsequent research has shown that the glow emanating from parts of the human body change when the mood of the subject being photographed alters, and similar changes are noted when people are under physical stress, or unwell.

Many researchers believe that Kirlian photography shows nothing more than a simple electrical discharge, but others believe that the technique demonstrates the existence of the **ETHERIC BODY** which surrounds and pervades all animate things, and that Kirlian photography may be a useful tool of diagnosis in traditional medicine or in **PSYCHIC HEALING**. This claim is given further weight by the fact that more recent research has shown that acupuncture points around the human body show up as bright flashes of light on Kirlian photographs.

KNIGHTS TEMPLAR *see* **ORDER OF THE KNIGHTS TEMPLAR.**

KNIGHTS HOSPITALLERS (Knights of St John of Jerusalem) *see* **HOSPITALLERS, KNIGHTS.**

KIRSHNAMUTRI, JIDDU (1895–1986) Born in Madras and adopted by the Theosphist Annie **BESANT**, Kirshnamutri was taken to England to be educated and proclaimed as a Messiah and guru by Besant. The Order of the Star of the East was formed in his honour and he attracted a huge number of followers. He turned away from his position in 1929, denying his right to be a spiritual leader and disbanding the Order. He took to travelling the world, advocating self discovery and self responsibility, which he believed were only achieveable after the rejection of formalised religions and belief systems.

KUNDALINI A source of tremendous physical and spiritual energy, described as a coiled serpent, which is said to lie dormant at the base of the spine until awakened through devotion or self-sacrifice, or through spiritual and physical discipline, in particular Tantric and Kundalini **YOGA**. The controlled awakening of kundalini is said to be characterised by an overwhelmingly pleasurable experience spreading through the body from the base of the spine, a state of bliss and an alteration of consciousness and sublimation of the ego. But when kundalini is awakened forcibly, in an uncontrolled fashion or without guidance, the energy may manifest itself in a variety of unpleasant ways. Subjects may experience tremor, physical pain, cramps and mental disturbance which can vary in severity from mild anxiety to psychosis.

LABYRINTH An intricate pathway, leading from a single outer entrance to an inner core via a tortuous route. Some labyrinths, or mazes, may incorporate several false pathways. Labyrinths may be constructed above ground, with boulders, hedges or mounds outlining the pathways, or underground, as a maze of tunnels. Labyrinthine patterns have been found in ancient stone carvings and artefacts in various places around the world and have also been incorporated into the design on the floors of a number of Medieval ecclesiastical buildings. The most famous labyrinth is the mythical subterranean construction designed by **DAEDALUS** on the island of Crete, to house the Minotaur. Some researchers believe that the early representations of labyrinths may have been representations of the human mind, or of the world, with the centre as the source from which life sprang. It is possible that some labyrinths were constructed, much like the Cretan labyrinth, as traps, but to contain malign spirits rather than monsters. Labyrinths have long had associations with secret knowledge, mystery and revelation, along with an ever-present element of danger; the idea of embarking upon a spiritual journey from which one may never be able to return, or the potential of discovering hidden evil forces which may overpower the seeker of wisdom.

LAMEN A talisman or magical protective symbol. *See* **DEMONIC SEAL**.

LAMIA In Greek and Roman mythology, a demon who could change back and forth from human to serpent form and who was believed to feed on human flesh and blood. The term eventually became used as a synonym for 'witch'.

LEMEGETON Also known as the Lesser Key of Solomon, the Lemegeton is a **GRIMOIRE** in four parts, describing the hierarchies of demons and angels, and instructing the reader how they may be summoned and for what purpose. The four parts are named Goetia, Theurgia Goetia, The Pauline Art and the Almadel. Earliest examples of the Lemegeton in existence date from the seventeenth century, but the original may have been written much earlier.

LEMURIA A mythical lost continent which the Theosophist Madame **BLAVTSKY** and others claimed once existed, extending over the Pacific ocean and part of the Atlantic. Believers claimed that Lemuria existed before the age of **ATLANTIS** and was covered by water shortly after Atlantis rose. Blavatsky stated that Lemuria was the home of the third Root Race of mankind. *See* **THEOSOPHY**.

LEO (23 July–23 August) In **ASTROLOGY**, the fifth sign of the **ZODIAC**, represented by the sign of the lion. It is a **FIXED** sign, a **FIRE** sign and masculine.

Character: Leo subjects are typically proud, confident, creative and generous. They are born organisers, but may have a tendency to be bossy and overbearing. Their enthusiasm can spill over into impatience at times and they can benefit from a calming (and restraining) presence by their side. Leos are characteristically big in presence and action; they are loyal and demonstrative friends, staunch defenders of the weak, passionate fighters for their chosen cause, masters of the sweeping gesture. Most Leos are straightforward in their dealings with all whom they meet and will not suffer deceit in others. Their direct manner can, however, result in tactlessness. They love flattery and can, quite often, be quite vain, but will usually be generous with their time, energy and money when called upon to be so. Leos appreciate their physical comforts and may be rather extravagant and self-indulgent. They make good leaders but may be ungracious when others try to lead them. Whilst they benefit from having the courage of their convictions, they may be somewhat intransigent. Leo children are generally outgoing, friendly and popular, but may be resented by their peers if they constantly seek the starring or commanding role. They may particularly enjoy physically challenging or dangerous sports, facing danger with apparent nonchalance, but they will be vulnerable to teasing or criticism. Wounded pride is worse than physical injury to a Leo.

Personal relationships: Leos are easily seduced by flattery and will throw themselves wholeheartedly into romance, but they may irritate their partners by constantly needing to be the centre of attention and displaying a tendency to be moody. Having made a successful partnership, however, most Leos will be loyal, affectionate and demonstrative. As parents, Leos will protect their children's interests fiercely and be generous with their time and energy. They must, however, ensure that as their children grow up, they are allowed to follow their own chosen path in life, rather than one that has been mapped out for them a by well-meaning but domineering parent.

Career and business: Leos will flourish when they reach the top in their chosen profession. Many will seek prominence in public life, either as politicians, leaders of industry or as performers on stage or screen. They love the trappings of success and enjoy taking charge of people. If they have a long climb to the top of their career, they are likely to find it hard. They are better managing than managed. The Leonine love of luxury may lead some to follow a career in the manufacture or trade of luxury goods.

Health: Leos typically enjoy good health and love fresh air and exercise, but may be vulnerable to problems of the heart or spine.

Colour: Gold or orange.

Gemstones: Ruby, amber, topaz.

Animals: Lion.

Flowers: Sunflower, marigold.

LEPRECHAUN In Irish folklore, a kind of **FAIRY**, who is generally perceived as a helpful but mischievous spirit, and who resembles a very small human.

LERAJE or LERAYE A **DEMON** named in the **LEMEGETON**, said to appear as an archer, clad in green, and to have the power to start conflicts.

LEVI, ELIPHAS [Pseudonym of Adolphe-Louis Constant] (1810–1875) Born and educated in Paris, the French occultist Eliphas Levi entered the priesthood as a young man, but his political leanings and esoteric interests led to his expulsion from the church. Thereafter, Levi turned to a career in journalism, pursuing his interest in the occult through study, teaching and writing. His numerous books on the occult, the most important of which was The Dogma and Ritual of High Magic, published in 1861, were significant factors in the revival of interest in magic in the early 20th century and were influential upon the practices of several occult groups, in particular, the **ORDER OF THE GOLDEN DAWN**. Aleister **CROWLEY**, a former member of the Order of the Golden Dawn, claimed that he was the reincarnation of Levi, who died in the year of his birth. Levi was, for the most part, more concerned with the theoretical rather than the practical aspect of magic, but his fascination with **NECROMANCY** led him to experiment in this field. In 1845, he took part in an attempt to conjure the spirit of Appolonius of Tyana, a magician from the first century. An account of his experiences is given in his writing.

LEVIATHAN In the Bible, a huge monster of the sea, possibly a crocodile or a whale. Leviathan has also been used as a name of **SATAN**.

LEVITATION The rising up and floating in the air of heavy objects or human bodies, without visible physical means and in defiance of the laws of nature. Levitation is a form of **PSYCHOKINESIS**. Human levitation may be involuntary or involuntary. Involuntary levitation has been reported in cases of bewitchment, demonic **POSSESSION** and **POLTERGEIST** activity. Voluntary levitation is a feat performed by mediums and other occult adepts, sometimes in a state of trance. The levitation of objects may be caused either through the exercise of **PSYCHIC** power, or by a spiritual being, who may or may not be acting through a human **MEDIUM**. Like human levitation, object levitation is a commonly reported phenomenon in seances and cases of poltergeist activity, hauntings and possession. It is also a skill which some occult adepts can allegedly demonstrate. *See* **MEDIUM, SEANCE, TELEKINESIS, YOGIC FLYING**.

LEY LINES Lines along which a number of ancient sacred sites have been built in direct alignment, and which are widely believed to be paths of magnetic energy running through the earth. The energy is believed to be greatest at points where ley lines intersect. The discovery that straight lines could be drawn between a significant number of ancient sites in a number of places in England was first made by Alfred Watkins in 1921. Since that time a complex grid of such lines has been mapped out by various researchers, joining megalithic monuments, ancient burial sites, castles, earthworks, places of worship etc. Archeologists, initially sceptical about the matter, have been forced to agree that there appears to have been a deliberate and systematic way of thinking behind the siting of so many ancient monuments in such careful alignment. Interest has spread and in several other places around the world, including Continental Europe, China and South America, similar patterns of lines have been found. Although there is still a great deal of scepticism about the theory that there is some kind of force running through the lines, those who believe it to be true continue to research the possibility with enthusiasm.

LIBRA In **ASTROLOGY**, the seventh sign of the **ZODIAC**, represented by the sign of the scales. Libra is a **CARDINAL** sign, an **AIR** sign and masculine. Its **RULING PLANET** is Venus.

Character: The typical Libran desire for equilibrium in all aspects of life manifests itself in two very different ways; Librans can be notoriously indecisive, but on the other hand, can be skilful and diplomatic mediators. They generally seek to keep the peace in any situation in which they find themselves, and are happiest in tranquil, harmonious surroundings. Unless they believe their sense of balance is being placed under threat, they are generally easy-going, tolerant and liberal in attitude, but they have a strong sense of justice and will not put up with unfair treatment of any sort being handed out to others. In their dealings with other people they are likely to be thoughtful, courteous and kind. The typical Libran attitude to life is relatively laid-back, but Librans are not necessarily work-shy. They will put as much effort as is required into the task at hand, but they will apply themselves to leisure equally keenly. They are very sociable and will happily play their part in any congenial gathering. In an argument, they are more likely to see the merits of both points of view than take one side over the other. Librans are generally imaginative and intuitive–they may have a tendency to daydream–and frequently take an interest in history or philosophy. Their imagination allows them to place themselves in other people's shoes, making them empathetic friends. Libran children will usually be friendly and easy-going. Their laid-back approach to life may frustrate those who set higher goals than they do, and they may show some signs of laziness, but their charm and tact will win them many friends.

Personal relationships: Librans are loyal and unselfish friends, and their great capacity for accepting compromise makes them good partners in love and marriage, but this can be to their own disadvantage if they find themselves with a partner whose needs seem to outweigh theirs. They are likely to be thoughtful, faithful and considerate and will impress their partners with their efforts to promote harmony and contentment within the home.

Career and business: Librans make good mediators and are skilled in the art of sensitive communication. Some sort of job requiring counselling skills would suit many Librans very well. The Libran love of harmony, aesthetic and spiritual, means that many choose an artistic or musical profession, or opt for social work, psychology or even the ministry. Their keen sense of justice and fair play might lead some to pursue a career in law, particularly in defence.

Health: Librans may be liable to suffer from bouts of depression and nervous anxiety. They should also guard against kidney disease and problems of the lower back.

Colour: Blue or purple.

Gemstones: Sapphire, opal, lapis lazuli.

Animals: Hart, bear.

Flowers: Bluebell, violet, rose.

LILITH A fierce female DEMON, who figures in the folklore of several cultures. In Jewish tradition, Lilith was the first wife of Adam, who rebelled against his authority. Lilith was believed to prey on children, particularly newborn infants. It was also thought that she seduced men as they slept in order that she might become pregnant with demon children.

LIMBO In Christianity, the name for the place on the outskirts of Hell, where the unbaptized who have not sinned are condemned to go when they die.

LIMBO OF THE LOST *see* BERMUDA TRIANGLE.

LOA *see* VOODOO.

LOCH NESS MONSTER *see* WATER MONSTERS.

LUCIFER The light-bringer. In the Bible, in the book of Isaiah, a waning luminary, possibly a crescent moon in early dawn. Sometimes used as a name for SATAN.

LUGH The name of the Celtic god of light.

LUGHNASADH or LAMMAS One of the major festivals in the Celtic year, which was held in honour of LUGH, and marked the coming harvest. With the advent of Christianity, the festival was renamed Lammas. Lughnasadh is celebrated as one of the eight sabbats of WICCA. *See* SABBAT.

LYCANTHROPY Derived from the Greek, lykos, meaning wolf and anthropos, man, the transformation of a human into a wolf. This particular form of SHAPE-SHIFTING occurs commonly in the mythology of many cultures, in a large variety of WEREWOLF legends. The ability to change into a wolf, which was believed be either inborn or achieved through magical study and practice, might be used by sorcerers to attack their enemies. Once transformed, they could move swiftly and silently to seek out their victims, killing them and eating them or feasting on their blood. Alternatively, the transformation might be involuntary, a terrible change that took place in an unwilling victim of some blight or curse, particularly at the time of the full moon, with equally disastrous consequences for the werewolf's victims. Belief in werewolves was particularly strong in Medieval Europe and a number of people were brought to trial accused of violent crimes allegedly carried out under metamorphosis.

There have been many documented cases of lycanthropy as a form of mania, in which the sufferer believes that he is a wolf and lusts after the taste of blood.

MAGIC The art of effecting change by harnessing supernatural forces, using ritual and/ or willpower. Magic has been practised throughout the world since prehistoric times as a means of bringing about changes in the external world, either for the benefit of a community or for personal gain. Practitioners of magic communicate with the spiritual realm, tapping into forces, named or unknown, that are imperceptible to the average person, in order to gain knowledge or power to enable them to perform acts or cause things to happen in defiance of natural laws. In goetic magic, demons are summoned to the service of the magician; in theurgy, benevolent spirits or deities are invoked. Other forms of magic harness the spirits in nature, or the spirits of the dead. Since time began, magic has been used for selfish and altruistic purposes alike; to bring much-needed rain, or to destroy a harvest; to ensure victory for one's people, or to bring defeat upon the enemy; to kill or to cure. Occultists argue that any differentiation between 'white' magic (benevolent, good) and 'black' magic (harmful, bad) is misleading; magic in itself is morally neutral, but it may be used (or abused) for either good or evil purposes, according to the motivations and intentions of the people who practise it. Following this reasoning, practitioners of WICCA are aware that some of their practices have as much potential to do harm as to benefit others, and adhere strictly to the WICCAN REDE, to refrain from causing harm to anyone.

Magic has had a close relationship with religion throughout history. In ancient Greece and Rome, for example, magic and religion were intertwined. In Egypt also, the two were hardly distinguishable, and priests were magicians as much as intermediaries between the gods and man. The Hebrew prophets and the Christian saints were also workers of wonders. The notion that knowledge is empowering, beyond normal human limitations, is shared by religious and magical tradition. Whether that knowledge is of one supreme God, or of a hidden spiritual realm peopled by any combination of diverse deities, demons, dead people and nature spirits, depends on personal belief. It may even be viewed, in a sense, as knowledge of self; a greater awareness of oneself as body, mind and spirit together.

With regard to magic, it is commonly believed that only certain people, with inborn psychic abilities or gifts, will find it possible to acquire knowledge of the spiritual realm and to access and exercise the power which is available to them, but this belief is not universal. Many people believe that anyone, whether psychically gifted or otherwise, has the potential to become a magical ADEPT.

Some magical practices, such as SYMPATHETIC MAGIC and some forms of protective magic and healing magic, involve little more than the use of magical incantations, amulets and talismans. But other forms of magic, in particular 'high' or 'ceremonial' magic require the practitioner to alter his or her state of consciousness, thereby blocking out distractions from the physical realm and building up psychic energy. This state may be sought in a variety of ways; through rigorous discipline and self-denial, meditation, drugs, sexual ecstasy, chanting, drumming etc. In this state, the practitioner is able to harness and direct the forces of the spiritual realm (however they may be perceived) to work within the physical realm in accordance with his or her will.

MAGIC CIRCLE The space within which rituals and ceremonies of MAGIC and WITCHCRAFT are conducted. The circle offers protection from external, malign influences, and provides a contained, concentrated area of power. The protection offered by the circle was considered essential in goetic magic and NECROMANCY, both of which were believed to place the magician at considerable personal risk. Magic circles have also been used since ancient times to offer protection against harmful magic, or the EVIL EYE, and can be cast around buildings, infants' cradles, etc.

In modern witchcraft, the circle is generally cast by the high priestess, who draws it out symbolically on the floor with an ATHAME. It can also be marked out with rope. Although it is marked out as a flat shape, the circle is perceived as a three-dimensional space. The circle has a 'gateway' in the north-east, which is symbolically opened and closed when members of the COVEN are entering or leaving. The altar is sited to the north. The four points of the circle correspond to the four ELEMENTS; North to Earth, South to Fire, East to Air and West to Water. The circle must be consecrated before other rituals may begin and when the gathering is over, the circle is 'banished'.

MAGIC SQUARE A square comprising of lines of numbers, which when added together either vertically, horizontally or diagonally, will come to the same total. Magic squares have interested mathematicians since ancient times and in some cultures, were believed to be rich in magical symbolism and a source of magical power.

MAGUS A priest in ancient Persia. The word is now used as a general term for a magician, or **ADEPT** in occultism.

MAHATMA A term derived from a Sanskrit word meaning 'one with a high soul', which is used in **OCCULTISM** to refer to a person who has a high degree of spiritual knowledge and has reached an exalted state of being.

MALEFICIA Evil deeds performed with the intent of causing harm to others; a term which was applied in the Middle Ages to the practice of sorcery and witchcraft.

MALPHAS A **DEMON** named in the **LEMEGETON**, said to take the form of a crow and to have the power to influence enemies.

MALLEUS MALEFICARUM A work produced in Germany in 1486 and written by two inquisitors, which gathered together current beliefs about witches and **WITCHCRAFT**, in the form of a manual which could be used in the seeking out and eradication of practitioners of the evil art. Originally a work written by Catholics against witches as heretics, Malleus Maleficarum also proved influential in other countries in the sixteenth and seventeenth centuries, particularly in Calvinist Germany and Presbyterian Scotland. Amongst other characteristic features of witchcraft with which it dealt in detail, the work introduced the concept of the Demonic pact (renouncing Christian baptism and entering into the Devil's service). It was thus responsible, to a great degree, for a change in most popular theories about witches, which had previously not necessarily made any connection between witchcraft and the Devil.

MANDRAKE A herbaceous plant belonging to the Solanaceae family which is native to Europe, and was once believed to have magical properties. The thick roots of the mandrake plant have a vaguely human shape and according to legend were supposed to squeal, as if in pain, when taken from the ground. The plant contains a powerful narcotic agent and was also thought to have curative and aphrodisiac properties. Mandrake roots were often worn or carried about the person as amulets. *See* **AMULET**.

MANTRA In Hinduism and Buddhism, a word or phrase, commonly taken from Vedic scripture, that is repeated again and again, either aloud or silently, in order to calm and focus the mind, aid meditation and increase spiritual power. *See also* **INCANTATION**.

MARBAS A **DEMON** named in the **LEMEGETON** and said to appear either in human form or as a lion. One of the powers attributed to him was that of causing or curing disease.

MARCHOSIAS A **DEMON** named in the **LEMEGETON**, said to appear as a fire-breathing wolf with griffin's wings and a serpent's tail.

MARIAN APPARITION A vision of the Virgin Mary. Marian Apparitions are a relatively common phenomenon and have been reported in many parts of the world over several hundred years. At some sites, repeated visions have occurred to one or more people and also with associated supernatural events. These places have subsequently become sites of worship and religious pilgrimage. In 1858, at Lourdes, Bernadette Soubrois experienced the first of several visions of the Virgin Mary, which appeared to send her into an ecstatic trance. The grotto there, by the River Gave, became a centre of pilgrimage and healing for Roman Catholics everywhere.

MATERIALISATION The summoning of something, or someone, from the spirit world, and giving it form in the physical world. The phenomenon is most commonly associated with **SEANCE** meetings. Claims of materialisation or its opposite, dematerialisation, were commonly made by mediums (*see* **MEDIUM**), and apparently witnessed by others, during the late nineteenth century, the period when seances were at their most popular. However, many of these cases were denounced as fraud on the part of the medium, who would be using conditions of semi-darkness in the meeting room to conceal sleight-of-hand or personal disguise. *See also* **APPORT, ECTOPLASM.**

MATHERS, SAMUEL LIDDELL (1854–1918) Occultist and leader of the Golden Dawn. An academic with a reputation for eccentricity, Mathers (or 'Macgregor' as he chose to call himself) had a lifelong interest in the occult and was a Freemason. (*See* **FREEMASONRY**.) In 1887, with fellow Freemasons Dr Wynn Westcott and William Woodman, Mather became a founder member of the esoteric magical society, the **ORDER OF THE GOLDEN DAWN**. Assuming leadership of the society, Mathers developed an eclectic system of magic and devised many of the rituals in which members participated as they rose through the ranks of the Order. The Order attracted a number of learned members, including the poet W.B.**YEATS**, and flourished for several years. Gradually, however, Mathers' imperious style of leadership began to alienate other members in the Order. In 1900, disagreements and personality clashes flared into rebellion and the organization began to fragment. One former member who played a large part in the rebellion, Aleister **CROWLEY**, who left the Order to found his own organization, the A.A. (**ARGENTUM ASTRUM**), claimed to have felt the effects of a **CURSE** laid upon him by Mather for a period of many months after his departure. Mathers' intellectual abilities were considerable, and he translated a number of ancient mystical literary works, one of which was The Book of the Sacred Magic of Abramelin the Mage, a text of magical knowledge supposedly handed down by Abramelin, an Egyptian philosopher, to Abraham the Jew, a fifteenth century magician. Amongst other things, the text contained instructions for a variety of magical rituals, including the summoning of **DEMONS**.

Following the break-up of the Order of the Golden Dawn, Mathers moved to Paris, where he spent the rest of his life.

MAYPOLE *see* **BELTAINE.**

MAZES *see* **LABYRINTHS.**

MEDEA In Greek mythology, the name of a sorceress who fell in love with Jason and helped him to win the Golden Fleece from her father, the king of Colchis.

MEDICINE MAN A term for a **SHAMAN** of the North American Indian peoples, who could commune with the spirit world on behalf of his tribe. The medicine man could use his magical powers as a healer and benefactor, but was also believed to be capable of causing harm by magical means.

MEDIUM A term for a person who claims or seeks to act as a channel or route of communication between the living and the dead. Some mediums claim to have one particular contact in the other world, a spirit guide, who passes on information about the spirits of the dead for those who are still living. Others claim to receive information from a number of spirits. Historically, the medium has always been a controversial figure. For every incidence of genuine or well-intended mediumship, there has been more than one incidence of fraud. Opinion is divided three ways. There are those who believe that a bona fide medium is a person with **PSYCHIC** powers which enable her to tune into the non-physical realm, and to communicate with, or act as a channel for communications from, the beings that inhabit that realm. There are those who believe that the medium's words or actions are prompted not by the spirit world, but from within her own psyche. The third group are the sceptics who believe that all so-called mediums are either seriously misguided or tricksters. *See also* **APPORT, AUTOMATIC WRITING, CHANNELING, CLAIRAUDIENCE, CLAIRSENTIENCE, CLAIRVOYANCE, ECTOPLASM, MATERIALISATION, SEANCE.**

MEN IN BLACK Mysterious figures whose appearance has been reported after certain **UFO** sightings, or alleged **ALIEN ABDUCTIONS**, mostly in the USA. The men in black have allegedly visited those who have undergone such experiences, confiscating camera films and photographs and urging the people to keep silent about what they have witnessed.

MERLIN A mythical magician and wise man, whose character may have been based on a Welsh deity, Myrddin. The first written works in which the figure of Merlin appears, The Prophecies of Merlin, The History of the Kings of Britain, and The Life of Merlin by Geoffrey of Monmouth, date from the early twelfth century. These books were the foundation upon which the character of Merlin, son of an **INCUBUS** and a virgin, adviser of King Uther Pendragon, was built. In them the figure of Merlin, who was present in the court of King Uther Pendragon before the birth of Arthur, emerged as a sage and enchanter. Merlin featured in a number of other works of Arthurian romance in the years following, and by the time Le Morte D'Arthur had been published in the fifteenth century by Sir Thomas Mallory, his character had developed into the archetypal prophet, sorcerer, seer and keeper of wisdom.

MESMER, FRANZ ANTON (1734–1815) Austrian-born physician, discoverer of Mesmerism. Mesmer studied medicine at the university of Vienna. His reputation as a successful physician grew rapidly and the methods by which he claimed that he was able to cure so many of his patients attracted great publicity. Mesmer believed that humans and animals were linked to the earth by an invisible magnetic force, which he called animal magnetism. Seeing illness as an interruption of the flow of this force, Mesmer developed a method of treatment using magnetized rods which his patients grasped while he sent them into a trance. He performed many of his cures in public and his audiences were astonished to see how his patients behaved while in a trance. Sometimes their reactions were quite violent and they seemed to have fallen into a fit. At other times, what they said while in a state of trance seemed to indicate that they were able to see through closed eyes. Most confounding of all was the fact that so many of Mesmer's patients emerged from their trance free of the symptoms that had sent them to him. Mesmer's activities became the subject of heated scientific debate. Eventually, however, his theory regarding animal magnetism was dismissed and in 1785 he was forced to move out of the spotlight of publicity to Switzerland, where he spent the rest of his life. Mesmerism, as it had become known, had fallen out of favour. But the induction of trance states in medical treatment continued to interest many physicians around Europe and experimentation continued. In modern times, **HYPNOSIS** is now widely accepted as an effective form of treatment for a variety of disorders, including chronic pain and nicotine addiction.

METAMORPHOSIS *see* **SHAPE-SHIFTING, LYCANTHROPY**

MIB *see* **MEN IN BLACK**

MICHAEL The name of an archangel in Judaism and Christianity, identified with Mikal in Islam. Michael is associated with light and is regarded as a warrior against the forces of evil and darkness.

MIDGARD In Nordic mythology, the middle world in the cosmos, where man dwelt. It was believed to be encircled by a great ocean, in which dwelt an enormous serpent, coiled round the earth. *See* **YGGDRASIL**.

MIRRORS Mirrors and other reflective surfaces have been used for many centuries as tools for **SCRYING**. Gazing into the reflective surface is believed to reveal visions to clairvoyants. In traditional beliefs of many different cultures, mirrors have been viewed with a mixture of fear and respect. The belief that what one sees in a mirror is a reflection of the soul, which still persists in some societies, gave rise to the idea that vampires and those who have sold their soul to the Devil have no reflection.

The belief that mirrors could steal one's soul, particularly in sickness or after death, was common to many cultures around the world. Mirrors were banished from sick rooms and removed, or turned to face the wall, when someone died. But it was also widely believed that mirrors could also be used to ward off evil, reflecting the **EVIL EYE** and warding off harmful spirits. Mirrors are used in the practice of **FENG-SHUI** to reflect negative energy.

MISTLETOE A parasitic plant which grows on a number of trees, including the oak, sacred tree of the **DRUIDS**. Mistletoe was also considered sacred, its berries symbolising drops of semen, a promise of the return of fertility to the earth after winter. It was used as an **AMULET** against evil and disease. It is said to have been cut from the tree with a golden scythe during Druid celebration of the winter solstice.

MITHRAIC MYSTERIES *see* **MYSTERIES**.

MOCA VAMPIRE A strange creature which was allegedly sighted a number of times in Puerto Rico in the 1970's, and which is claimed to have killed large numbers of farm animals by draining them of blood. First reports of this creature came from the towns of Orocovis and Morovis, which are in an area where a large number of **UFO** sightings have also allegedly taken place. Reports of the Moca Vampire bear a strong resemblance to another, later phenomenon, known as **EL CHUPACABRAS**, a strange creature which is said to have similar vampiric tendencies, and which has been seen in the same region.

MOON The Moon has been associated with **MAGIC** since ancient times, and the phases of the moon have been observed by alchemists, magicians, witches and sorcerers with a view to determining the most propitious times for carrying out certain activities. Inextricably linked with notions of fecundity and fertility, the Moon is also associated with all aspects of womanhood - menstruation, pregnancy and birth, and in modern **WITCHCRAFT**, the **GODDESS** is perceived as a lunar deity and invoked in ritual to inspire witches with her power. Witches' meetings are timed according to the phases of the moon, and certain kinds of magic are believed to be most effective according to whether the moon is waxing, waning or full.

Ancient beliefs regarding the powers of the moon are reflected in the superstitions and folklore of many countries.

MORAX A **DEMON** named in the **LEMEGETON**, said to have the appearance of a bull with a man's face and to possess great knowledge of science and astronomy.

MOTHMAN A strange flying creature, said to have the appearance of a winged human with bright red eyes and something resembling a beak, which has been reported at various times in different parts of the United States since the late nineteenth century.

MURMUR A DEMON named in the LEMEGETON, said to take the form of a soldier with a griffin's head, on top of which is a crown. He had the power to control the souls of the dead.

MURRAY, MARGARET ALICE (1863–1963) A British Egyptologist, archeologist and anthropologist, whose theories regarding the origins of WITCHCRAFT have influenced the practice of the Craft in modern times. Murray studied Egyptology in London, and remained there as a lecturer and professor for some years. She also took part in a number of archeological excavations in England, Continental Europe and the Middle East. She published three books on the subject of witchcraft; The Witch-Cult in Western Europe (1921), The God of the Witches (1933) and The Divine King of England (1954), which became the subject of heated controversy among scholars. Murray's principal theory was that the practice of witchcraft as an organized pagan religion, involving worship of the GODDESS and the HORNED GOD, could be traced back to the Stone Age, and that it had survived, through the period of witch persecution in Europe, to continue into the twentieth century. In spite of the fact that many of her claims were rejected outright by other anthropologists who specialised in the study of witchcraft, Murray's work had a profound influence on Gerald GARDNER, the man who is acknowledged as the founder of WICCA.

MUTABLE SIGNS In ASTROLOGY, those signs that mark an imminent change of season: GEMINI (spring–summer), VIRGO (summer–autumn), SAGITTARIUS (autumn–winter), PISCES (winter–spring). They are also known as the Mutable Quadruplicity. A shared characteristic of people born under any of these signs is adaptability. *See* QUADRUPLICITIES.

MYSTERIES The name given number of secret cults which operated in the area around the Mediterranean in ancient times, and centred round the worship certain deities which included DEMETER, Persephone and Dionysus in Greece, and Isis in Egypt. Initiation into any of the cults, which was believed to guarantee those who took part eternal life after death in this world, is thought to have been a lengthy process and involved participants taking an oath to preserve the secrecy of its rites. The rites involved re-enactment of myths related to the deity, or deities worshipped. The Eleusian Mysteries, which were particularly influential in ancient Greece, centred round worship of Persephone and Demeter and involved rituals linked to the fertility cycle of the earth. Similarly, the Dionysian Mysteries centred round worship of Dionysus (Bacchus), the god of wine, and involved initiates participating in orgiastic rites of feasting, drinking and sex. The cult of Mithras, the god of Light, which spread from Persia to Rome, promised initiates (men of all ranks of society) protection from the powers of darkness in life and, more importantly, after death. Initiation was a long and complex process, with initiates having to pass through several levels of initiation which challenged them both mentally and physically. Bread and wine were ritually consumed, symbolising the flesh and blood of the divine bull slain by Mithras.

The rites of Judaism and Christianity (for example, Christian baptism and communion) have certain similarities to these ancient mysteries.

MYSTERY HELICOPTERS Black flying objects, similar in appearance to helicopters, whose presence in the sky has caused consternation in several different locations around the world for a number of years. The first reports of these objects were made in the 1930's, before the helicopter had been invented, but sightings have increased in frequency since the 1960's especially in the United States. Typically, these machines are seen, but not heard. A number of theories have been put forward to explain this phenomenon, including the possibility that they may be alien craft. In more recent times, some people have speculated that they may have been manufactured by the government of the United States, from the recovered remains of crashed alien craft. Mystery helicopters have also been linked with CATTLE MUTILATIONS. *See also* AREA 51.

MYSTICISM A term to denote the philosophy and practices, or way of life, chosen by those who believe it is possible to experience ultimate knowledge of, or spiritual union with, the divine. Although it is particularly associated with Eastern religions, mysticism is not confined to any one doctrine; it is an element in many different religions worldwide, including Christianity. The state to which mystics aspire is generally believed to be characterised by supreme bliss; an ecstatic state on a level beyond that of normal human experience. The achievement of such a state is generally sought through rigorous self-denial and self-discipline. In the history of Christianity, mystical practice has been characterized by withdrawal from society, celibacy, fasting, contemplation, prayer and acts of charity. The Sufis of Islam seek spiritual union with God through poverty, austerity and fervent worship. In Hinduism, mystical ascetic and contemplative practices, in particular YOGA, are followed with the aim of reaching the state of nirvana, where the soul is freed from further reincarnation and united with the divine.

NABERIUS A DEMON named in the LEMEGETON, said to appear as a black crow with a hoarse voice and to have, among his powers, that of making men skilled in rhetoric.

NAMES OF POWER Certain words, particularly the secret names of spirits, which, when uttered, are believed to unleash the power symbolised by the words. The meaning of many of these words is obscure, and frequently encoded in gematric formulae. (*See* GEMATRIA.) In magical theory and practice since ancient times, names have always had a significance beyond that of a mere label. The true names of spirits, supposedly only known by adepts, were believed to contain the essence of these spirits. To know the true name of a **DEMON** or other spirit was to have the potential to access its power, and invoking the demon by calling out its name, unleashed that power. Sometimes the power was considered too terrible to unleash, and other names, which hinted at the nature of the spirit, or ones which had the same numerological value, were used in place of the true name. The **TETRAGRAMMATON**, the true name of God, is a name of power.

NATAL ASTROLOGY *see* **ASTROLOGY**

NATURE SPIRITS A variety of spirit beings, which are believed to be invisible to all humans except those who possess powers of **CLAIRVOYANCE**, and which are said to dwell in, or to be attached to, certain aspects of the natural world, for example, water, trees, rocks, hills, etc. Although not all groups of nature spirits have specific names, it is believed that everything in nature is animated by such beings. Nature spirits include **ELEMENTALS**, elves, sprites and goblins, and also, according to some people, fairies. (*See* **FAIRY**.) They may appear as diminutive humans, winged humans, animals and in other guises, to those who claim to be able to see them. It is believed that they are capable of both harm and good, but that their influence is generally benevolent with regard to those who show respect for the natural world.

NECROMANCY Conjuring of the spirits of the dead for the purpose of **DIVINATION**. Necromancy is an ancient practice, based on the belief that the spirits of the dead have access to information about the future which living mortals are denied. Although it was condemned by the Church as a particularly despicable form of magical practice and outlawed by the State, necromancy was believed to be prevalent in England, Scotland and many other European countries in the Middle Ages. Many individuals who were tried on charges of **WITCHCRAFT** in the sixteenth and seventeenth centuries were also accused of taking part in necromantic rituals. Necromancy is generally associated only with **BLACK MAGIC**. Some of the medieval Grimoires (*see* **GRIMOIRE**) gave details of the lengthy ritual preparations, most commonly nine days, but sometimes more, which were thought to be necessary before attempting to raise the spirits of the dead. The process was believed to be fraught with danger for the magician, who risked becoming possessed. When all preparations were complete, the magician, who had to be dressed in grave-clothes stolen from other dead people, would visit the selected grave at night, draw a **MAGIC CIRCLE** around it, and disinter the corpse. Then, using prescribed magical rituals, he would summon the dead person's spirit to inhabit its body once more and answer the questions that were put to it. The corpse was then supposed to rise up and speak. Once the corpse had served its purpose and the spirit had departed, the body had then to be destroyed, most commonly by fire.

NEO-PAGAN A term used to describe a variety of religious beliefs and practices of the modern age that are said to have their origins in popular religions from pre-Christian times. The term is also used to denote a follower of these beliefs and practices. The term is derived from the Latin word paganus, which means 'rustic', or 'peasant'. Neo-paganism is characterised by polytheism, pantheism and animism. Most neo-pagans celebrate the eight festivals of the Celtic pagan year (*see* **SABBAT**), but their practices tend to be syncretistic, borrowing elements from a number of different cultures and philosophies.

NEW AGE A term coined in the 1980's to describe a wide variety of beliefs and practices, therapies and interests that rose in popularity from the 1960's onwards, when in Europe and in the United States, there was a resurgence of interest in spirituality and the environment, in seeking alternatives to 'orthodox' medicine and religion and in stepping back from the materialism and heavy dependency on technology that pervaded modern living. This trend was in part due to the hippy movement and an awareness of the forthcoming **AGE OF AQUARIUS**. Many so-called 'New Age' interests are far from new. These include **TAROT**, **FENG-SHUI**, **I CHING**, **YOGA**, acupuncture, meditation, shamanism (*see* **SHAMAN**) and **SPIRITUALISM**. A growing fascination with mysticism and the occult meant that a large number of people in the West became interested in the Eastern religions, in **MAGIC** and in neo-paganism. (*See* **NEO-PAGAN**.) Side by side with the renewal of interest in the spiritual world came a growing eco-awareness, a realisation of the need for man to find a way to live more harmoniously with nature in order to preserve the planet. The term 'New Age' is used to describe a very broad spectrum of interests, but most of them can be said to pursue the same sorts of goals; a holistic approach to physical, mental and spiritual wellbeing and a re-attunement of man with the natural and spiritual worlds and the forces at work within them. New Age interests have continued to be popular. Some forms of therapy, such as acupuncture and aromatherapy, have overcome initial hostility and scepticism and have become widely accepted as effective forms of complementary medicine. New Age ideas have also proved influential in behavioural therapy, and in sport and business psychology.

NIFLHEIM or NIFLHEL In Nordic mythology, the Underworld, ruled over by the goddess Hel. It was perceived as a place of terrible coldness, populated by giants and dwarves. The entrance to Niflheim was guarded by a fearsome dog, Garm. *See* **YGGDRASIL**.

NIGHT DEMON A term for a terrifying phenomenon occurring during sleep, suffered by a small number of people. The term 'nightmare', now commonly used to describe any unpleasant dream, originally referred to this phenomenon. People who have experienced it typically describe having had a feeling that something, or someone, was sitting on top of their chest, squeezing the life out of them.

Subjects may report that they felt as if they were being strangled, whilst others say they felt that they were being struck with considerable force, but were unable to escape because of the weight on top of them. Some may feel as if they have been paralysed during the experience. Subjects may also claim to have seen some indistinct form looming over them. Some people have this experience only once, or a small number of times, but others may find that their nights are frequently disturbed in this manner, to such an extent that some dread gong to sleep. People who have been troubled by the phenomenon typically wake up in terror, with bedclothes in disarray. Experiments carried out in sleep laboratories show that subjects undergoing such an experience will open their eyes with a look of terror on their faces, while still asleep. They often struggle violently, as if with an unseen assailant, before waking up. The exact cause of this phenomenon is unknown, but it is thought that it may have contributed to people's beliefs in Incubi and succubi. *See* **INCUBUS, SUCCUBUS**.

NINE-KNOTTED STRING A form of **SYMPATHETIC MAGIC** once used by witches to cause the death of their enemies. A piece of string would be knotted nine times, with a **CURSE** being repeated as each knot was made. The string would then be concealed in the victim's home. The victim would then allegedly feel the life being choked out of him.

NOSTRADAMUS, MICHAEL (1533–66) A French doctor and astrologer, who is best known for the prophetic verses which he wrote. Nostradamus was born in Provence and studied medicine in Montpelier. He acquired a considerable reputation as a physician during the time of the plague, but turned from the practice of medicine to pursue his interests in philosophy and astrology. In 1555, after eight years of writing, he published Centuries , a book of several hundred predictions, which was finally expanded, by 1558, into two volumes arranged in sections of 100 rhymed quatrains. The predictions were obscure and cryptic, with some words written in Latin, Greek and Hebrew, and were not written in chronological sequence, but, according to Nostradamus, they extended to the year 3797. Nostradamus became quite a celebrity following the publication of the work, which continues to be a source of fascination to many people today. Because of the obscure manner in which the predictions were written, their interpretation has been the subject of much debate. Some who have studied them claim that they cannot be applied to specific times, places or occurrences, whilst others claim that Nostradamus successfully predicted many major events in world history since his lifetime, including The Great Fire of London, the rise of Hitler and World War II.

NUMBER OF THE BEAST Here is wisdom. Let him that have understanding count the number of the beast: for it is the number of a man; and his number is six hundred three-score and six. Revelations, 13, v. 8. The 'beast', or the ANTICHRIST, whose coming is foretold in the apocalyptic prophecies of the book of Revelation, has been associated with several historical figures, including Nero and Napoleon, and is also believed by many to be a figure who is yet to come. The beast is the enemy of the Christian church, a false prophet, posing as the Messiah, performing miracles and placing his mark upon the hands or foreheads of his disciples. Aleister CROWLEY, who claimed to have been called 'The Beast' by his mother when he was a child, adopted the name and the number as his own, fuelling speculation that he was a black magician.

NUMEROLOGY A term for various methods of DIVINATION and prediction using numbers. The practice of numerology dates back to ancient times and is based on the principle that everything in the Universe, material or spiritual, can be expressed in the universal language of number. Pythagoras, Greek mathematician and mystic of the sixth century BC, believed that numbers held the key to understanding everything, and much of the symbolism which is attributed to numbers is thought to be derived from his teachings. Archeological and historical evidence shows that number, and number associations, have played a significant part for many centuries in religious belief and occult lore of a number of different countries around the world, including China, Egypt, Babylon, India and Greece. Kabbalists (*see* KABBALAH) used numbers and their meanings both in Scriptural interpretation and in magic. (*See* GEMATRIA, NAMES OF POWER.) Numbers were also widely used in DIVINATION, and a variety of systems evolved in different cultures in both the Eastern and Western worlds.

Kabbalistic number lore was based on the 20 letters of the Hebrew alphabet, but modern numerology is more commonly based on the Roman alphabet, with the letters given number values in the following manner:

A–1, B–2, C–3, D–4, E–5, F–6, G–7, H–8, I–9, J–1, K–2, L–3, M–4, N–5, O–6, P–7, Q–8, R–9, S–1, T–2, U–3, V–4, W–5, X–6, Y–7, Z–8. Modern numerology revolves principally around names and birth-dates which, when reduced to single numbers (1–9) indicate certain traits of a person's character and may also be used to find correspondences with other dates, or with other names of places, people or things, which may help to plan significant events in that person's life, choose a career, etc. There are different ways of determining a person's name number; adding all the letters in the full name, using the letters of the Christian name, or the name by which that person is most commonly addressed, using the consonants in the name, or using the vowels. A person's birth number is most commonly calculated by adding the numbers of the day, month and year and reducing them to a single digit. For example, the 12th June, 1954, can be reduced as follows:

1+2+6+1+9+5+4 = 28

2+8 = 10

1+0 = 1

The characteristics and values attached to different numbers, can vary considerably, but generally odd numbers are viewed as masculine and positive (yang), while even numbers are feminine, and passive, or negative (yin). Some of the other correspondences and associated personal characteristics are outlined below.

One: Creation, God, Unity, the Sun, the Ego. Personal characteristics: optimism, leadership, single-mindedness, selfishness.

Two: Duality, the Devil, Opposites, Yin and Yang. Personal characteristics: equanimity, fair-mindedness, deceitfulness, indecision.

Three: The Trinity, Body, mind and spirit, Procreation, Heaven. Personal characteristics: boldness, innovation, versatility, charm.

Four: The four elements, the four compass points, Earth and the physical world, solidity. Personal characteristics: Dependability, domesticity, dullness, melancholy.

Five: The five-pointed star, the human figure (head, arms and legs), the individual. Personal characteristics: Individuality, adventure, risk-taking, unreliability.

Six: Resolution, wholeness, harmony. Personal characteristics: Loyalty, tranquillity, domesticity.

Seven: Mysticism and magic, spiritual/physical union. Personal characteristics: Withdrawal, dreaminess, intellectual curiosity, aloofness.

Eight: Money, material gain or loss, Justice. Acquisitiveness, industry, strength of will, unscrupulousness.

Nine: Mental and spiritual greatness: Passion, idealism, vision, impulsiveness.

OAK A deciduous tree growing in temperate regions, which was held sacred to the **DRUIDS**. It is thought that many Druid ceremonies were carried out in oak groves, which served as temples. In modern **WITCHCRAFT**, oak is a symbol of the waxing year and personified in the figure of the Oak King, an aspect of the **HORNED GOD**.

OBE *see* **OUT-OF-BODY EXPERIENCE**

OCCULTISM The study of that which is secret, hidden, or beyond the realm of observation and scientific understanding. Occultism embraces a wide range of doctrines and practices, including eastern philosophy, ancient religions, paganism, **MAGIC** and **MYSTICISM**, and may be pursued either as an interest or more seriously, as a means of gaining insight into the secrets of creation and man's place within it, or in the search for some hidden, universal truth. In spite of all the knowledge that has been gained through scientific and technological advances over the years, a great number of people remain fascinated with the unknown, the realm beyond the physical, and turn to some form of occultism in the quest for a different, higher form of knowledge.

The latter years of the twentieth century have seen a great resurgence of interest in the occult, particularly in matters relating to physical and mental health, and many of the **NEW AGE** therapies that have become increasingly popular combine a practical approach with a spiritual aspect, seeking to harness forces outwith the physical realm to work in combination with physical treatment towards the promotion of wellbeing. Occultism does have a darker side, and in some cases people may engage in occult practices in an attempt to gain power, to exert control over their environment and other people for selfish purposes, or to harm. There are no laws to bind people to one set of beliefs or practices, and from the vast store of occult lore passed down through the ages people are free to pick and choose elements to suit their own individual interests, requirements and beliefs. Practitioners of **WICCA**, for example, perceive their craft as rooted in ancient Celtic pagan religion, but may also use elements from other cultures, such as **TAROT**, and embrace certain aspects of Eastern religions, classical mythology and the **KABBALAH**. This flexibility and eclecticism typifies occultism in the twentieth century.

OCCULT POWERS Abilities, such as the gift of **SECOND SIGHT**, or the ability to communicate with the spirit world, which are allegedly possessed by a proportion of the human population and which, if they are aware of them, enable the possessors to perceive and to understand better the non-physical realm. It is believed that only those who possess such powers are able to become effective occult adepts. *See* **ADEPT**.

OGAM or OGHAM An ancient language of Celitic origin, which is frequently found on Pictish stone monuments. It consists of twenty letters which are formed from straight, parallel lines, crossing, or finishing at, a single line through the middle of the figure. It is thought that the letters of ogam may have been used, like **RUNES**, for divinatory purposes.

OLCOTT, HENRY STEEL *see* **THEOSOPHY, BLAVATSKY.**

OMEGA The last letter of the Greek alphabet; a symbol of the end of all things.

OMEN An event or observation that is understood or interpreted as a sign of things to come, whether good or bad. The augurs (*see* **AUGUR**) of ancient Rome observed the flight of birds to find omens, and in different cultures worldwide, various natural phenomena, either common or unusual, (the appearance of certain birds, the barking of dogs, freak weather conditions, eclipses, etc.) have traditionally been understood to have ominous significance.

ONEIROMANCY A term for DIVINATION through the interpretation of dreams, derived from the Greek oneiros., meaning 'dream'. Dream interpretation is a form of divination which dates back to ancient times and is common to many cultures worldwide. In the Old Testament of the Bible, we read that Joseph, while captive in Egypt, interpreted the dreams of his fellow-prisoners and the pharaoh. Dreams can either be interpreted as precognitive, i.e. foretelling or hinting at some future event, or symbolic, i.e., containing elements which, when re-interpreted, give insight into the dreamer's mind.

ORACLE An ancient method of determining the answers to questions about future events by consulting the gods through a human MEDIUM, generally a priest or priestess. The word is also used to denote the sacred place, most commonly a shrine to a deity, where such a consultation might be made. Oracles were consulted in ancient Egypt, Greece and Rome. At the Oracle at Dodona in Epirus, a shrine to Zeus which is believed to have been the earliest oracle, the priests interpreted the sounds made by the leaves of sacred oak trees as they moved in the wind. At the Oracle of Apollo at Delphi, the sibyl, a Pythian priestess, would go through a ritual of cleansing and preparation before taking her seat on a brass tripod in the shrine to answer questions. In a state of trance, she would give her response in the form of unintelligible pronouncements which were then interpreted by priests. Answers from oracles, rather than providing a definite solution to any dilemma about the future, were often ambiguous or hard to understand.

ORDER OF TEUTONS A racist occult society, organized with different levels of initiation in similar fashion to the Freemasons (*see* FREEMASONRY), which was founded in Germany in 1912 by Theodor Fritsch, Philipp Stauff and Hermann Pohl. Hermann Pohl went on to form an alliance with Rudolf Blauer, who formed the THULE SOCIETY, which had similar doctrines.

ORDER OF THE GOLDEN DAWN A magical society founded in London the 1880's by Dr Wynn Westcott, a Freemason, in collaboration with Samuel MATHERS, who took the role of leader. The doctrines and practices of the Order, most of which were devised by Mather, contained elements from the KABBALAH, Egyptian MAGIC and Eastern OCCULTISM. Initiates progressed through a number of grades, combining study, meditation and ritual to work towards progressively higher states of consciousness and levels of psychic power. The Order attracted several intellectuals to its ranks, including the poet W.B. YEATS, and temples were founded in a number of towns in England and Scotland. Power struggles between Mathers and Aleister CROWLEY led to the gradual disintegration of the Order in the early 1900's.

ORDER OF THE KNIGHTS TEMPLAR Originally founded in Jerusalem in 1119 by two knights, Hugues de Paynes and Godeffroi de St Omer, the Order Of the Knights Templar was formed as a military and religious order whose task it was to guard the roads to Jerusalem for pilgrims and keep the Holy Sepulchre safe. Their first headquarters were at the Temple of Solomon and their organization, which grew swiftly, was divided into craftsmen, sergeants, chaplains, knights and commanders, led by a Grand Master and presided over by a ruling council. They appointed their own clergy and their meetings and worship were conducted in great secrecy. The knights wore white mantles with a red cross and were said to live a life of strict discipline and considerable self-denial. Over the course of a century, the Order spread throughout Christendom and established itself not only as a force against the pagan world, but also as a powerful commercial and trading organization. Eventually the commercial interests of the Order appeared to overtake its crusading activities and perhaps inevitably, its growing power and the secrecy of its religious rites aroused the hostility and suspicion of other secular and religious powers in Europe. Rumours began to circulate in the upper ranks of society and the church that the apparent religious piety of the Knights Templar was little more than a sham; that they had resorted to demon-worship and that their secret meetings were the scene of bizarre demonic rituals and other ungodly activities. Events reached crisis point when Philip IV of France charged them with heresy in 1307. This heralded the downfall of the Order. Similar actions were taken against the Templars in Spain, Italy and Great Britain. The French knights were arrested en masse and brought to trial. They were subjected to torture and forced to confess that they renounced Christ, worshipped a demon called **BAPHOMET** and took part in obscene and blasphemous rituals. Over a number of years and a prolonged series of trials, the movement was effectively wiped out in France. Those who did not confess, and many of those who did, were put to death. Members of the Order in Italy also found themselves facing trial, although their treatment was not universally so brutal as it had been in France. In Spain and England too, measures military or legal were taken against the Order with varying degrees of severity. Finally, in 1312, Pope Clement V issued a papal bull suppressing the Order. Conjecture at the time, and in years since, about what went on in the Order of the Knights Templar behind its veil of secrecy, may not all be unfounded. Some of the rites of the organization may have bordered on the profane, or worse. The truth behind the secrecy is unlikely ever to be known. One of the theories relating to the Order of the Knights Templar is that some of its members, escaping from France during the period of suppression, founded the Freemasons. *See* **FREEMASONRY**.

ORDER OF THE ORIENTAL TEMPLARS (ORDO TEMPLI ORIENTALIS) An occult order founded by a German named Karl Kellner in 1902. The rituals of the order revolved around sexual magic, based on some of the principles of Tantric **YOGA**.

ORDER OF THE ROSY CROSS *see* **ROSICRUCIANS**

ORIAS A **DEMON** named in the **LEMEGETON**, taking the form of a serpent-tailed lion mounted on a horse and holding two hissing snakes. He was said to be skilled in astronomy.

ORMUZD *see* **AHURA MAZDA**

OROBAS A **DEMON** named in the **LEMEGETON**, said to appear either as a horse or as a man and to possess great divinatory powers.

OSE A **DEMON** named in the **LEMEGETON**, appearing first as a leopard, and then as a human. He was said to have the power to change men into any other thing, either animate or inanimate.

OUIJA A board which derives its name from oui and ja, the French and German words for 'yes', and is which used by groups of people for communicating with the spirit world. The words 'yes' and 'no', the letters of the alphabet and the numbers one to nine are arranged in a circle round a board in the centre of which is a pointer, on which participants place their hands lightly. The pointer is supposed to move in response to questions from the group. Various forms of the ouija board have been commercially produced, but home-made ouija boards may be made from any smooth surface on which an upturned glass can slide easily. Questions are answered by reading the movements of the glass towards 'yes', 'no', or particular letters or numbers. The ouija board was once fashionable as a party game, but has also been widely used over the years by people who wish to contact loved ones whom they have lost. Its usefulness as a tool for contacting the dead is doubtful, for the pointer may be manipulated, either consciously or subconsciously, by those who place their hands on it. Reports of disturbing phenomena that have been noticed during sessions using the board have led some people to believe that there may be a real element of danger in the practice and that participants may be risking their own psychological wellbeing by tampering with forces which they do not understand.

OUT-OF-BODY EXPERIENCE (OBE) Also known as astral projection, or astral travel, out-of-body experiences have been most commonly reported as occurring spontaneously during sleep, under anaesthetic, or in periods of severe illness, particularly in coma or near death. Accounts of such experiences typically refer to a feeling of separating from one's physical body, frequently being able to look down upon it from above. Out-of-body experience can involve travel both in time and space. People from several different cultures and beliefs worldwide interpret the phenomenon as a separation of the soul, or mind, from the body, freeing it to travel on another, i.e.

ASTRAL PLANE. They claim that an out-of-body experience can be entered into and controlled, through meditation, or self-induced trance.

PAIMON A DEMON named in the LEMEGETON and described as a man sitting on a camel, knowledgeable in the secrets of arts and sciences.

PALMISTRY A method of DIVINATION consisting of reading the shape, contours and lines of the hand to find out information about character, health, past and future. The predictive aspect of palmistry is sometimes called CHEIROMANCY, and the interpretative aspect involving character analysis, CHEIROGNOMY, but the two aspects are rarely separated in practice. The major lines on the palm of the hand are named and associated with factors in an individual's life as follows: the Head Line (intelligence and practical skill); the Heart Line (love and friendship); the Life Line (longevity, health crises); the Line of Destiny (fate or external circumstance). The bumps on the palm of the hand are associated with aspects of an individual's character, interests, skills and interaction with other people. Named after the PLANETS, the bumps relate to the same qualities that are associated with the planets in ASTROLOGY. The shape and size of the individual's palms and fingers, their general appearance, the comparison of left and right hands and other details will all be taken into account by the skilled palmist to build up a complete picture.

PARACELSUS [adopted name of Philippus Aureolus Theophrastus Bombastus von Hohenheim] (1493–1541) An alchemist and physician, who was born in Einsieden, Switzerland. Paracelsus studied in Austria and Vienna and then travelled for some years around Europe broadening his knowledge of medicine. He settled for a number of years in Basle, but spent most of his life thereafter moving from place to place, teaching and practising medicine. His approach to the science of medicine, although highly controversial at the time, marked a major move forward in the treatment of disease. Paracelsus rejected the traditional theory that disease came from within the body, and instead, looked to external causes. His studies gave him insight into the disease process of a number of life-threatening illnesses, including tuberculosis, and he emphasised the value of ALCHEMY as a practical rather than a spiritual pursuit. Nonetheless, he maintained the belief that medicine was inextricably linked with MAGIC. His alchemical experiments led to the discovery of a number of laboratory techniques still in practice today, and the emphasis he placed on method and precision in the preparation of solutions or substances, whether for experimentation or for prescription, helped to lay the foundations of modern chemistry and pharmacology. Paracelsus was arrogant and outspoken, and during his life may have gained more enemies and followers, but his studies have been recognized in retrospect for their contribution to scientific and medical progress.

PARAPSYCHOLOGY The study of a variety of phenomena involving the use of supernatural mental powers, including ESP (CLAIRAUDIENCE, CLAIRVOYANCE, SECOND SIGHT, TELEPATHY) and PSYCHOKINESIS. Scientific study into these phenomena began in the late nineteenth century, when there was an upsurge in public interest in SPIRITUALISM. Societies for Psychical Research were founded in both Great Britain and America in the late 1880's, with the aim of finding hard evidence which would either back up or refute claims from scientific circles that the alleged possession and demonstration of psychic ability by numerous people was either fraudulent or imaginary. Initial experiments were set up with the aim of testing the abilities of self-professed clairvoyants or mediums under controlled conditions, but these experiments were not considered scientifically rigorous enough to either prove or disprove the claims of either side beyond doubt.

PASSING-BELL The ringing of a church bell at time of death, or after a death. The passing bell was used as a means of spreading the news that someone had died, and to invite people to pray for the soul of the departed. It was also believed to ward off evil spirits who might try to steal the soul of the dead person before a Christian burial could take place. *See* BELLS.

PAST LIFE RECALL The apparent recollection of events and/or personal identity in a previous incarnation. Past life recall can occur spontaneously, but can also be induced through hypnotic regression, a process whereby a subject is guided, under HYPNOSIS, into his or her past. On occasion, the subject will describe memories of experiences, places, people and events that apparently can not be accounted for in any way by their present life experience and are consequently attributed to a past life.

Past life recall has also become associated, in more recent years, with the idea of ALIEN ABDUCTION. Accounts given by a significant number of people of experiences in extraterrestrial environments have given rise to speculation that they may be extraterrestrial souls transferred to an earthly environment.

PENTACLE A five-pointed star (PENTAGRAM), or an amulet on which a pentagram or other figure of magical symbolism is inscribed. In modern NEO-PAGAN practice, the term is most commonly used to refer to a circular plate on which a pentagram and other magical symbols have been inscribed, which is used as a ritual tool symbolising the ELEMENT of earth, and is placed in the centre of the altar.

PENTAGRAM A five-pointed star shape, a common symbol in many occult traditions, used in both black and white magical ritual. In the upright position, i.e. with a single point uppermost, it symbolises the four ELEMENTS of air, fire, earth and water with the AETHER at the top. It can also represent a human being. In black MAGIC, the pentagram may be inverted, with two points at the top and a single point at the foot. The pentagram is used in the ritual summoning of DEMONS.

PHILOSOPHER'S STONE In ALCHEMY, the name of a hypothetical substance or secret, that was believed to provide the cure for all ills and the elixir of life and to enable the alchemist to transmute metal into gold.

PHOENIX A DEMON named in the LEMEGETON, said to resemble a phoenix and to possess a sweet singing voice. When requested to change into human form, he was said to show great obedience to any sorcerer who summoned him.

PISCES (19 February–20 March) In ASTROLOGY, the twelfth sign of the ZODIAC, represented by the sign of the two fishes. Pisces is a MUTABLE sign, a WATER sign and feminine. Its RULING PLANET is Neptune.

Character: Pisceans are typically imaginative, emotional, sensitive and caring individuals, easily hurt by criticism and prone to great swings in mood, but with a great capacity for sympathising with the misfortunes of others. Their intentions are generally good in their relationships with other people, but all too often their lack of conviction and self-confidence, combined with a tendency towards indecisiveness, can work against them. They can be quite impressionable and easily swung towards the opinions of others; their judgement can be influenced by the ideas of other, stronger characters. They need to guard against this by making important decisions alone and holding on to their own convictions. Pisceans have a natural affinity for those who are weaker than they are; many are great animal lovers, and most are very fond of children. Many Pisceans are psychically gifted and fascinated by the occult. Piscean children will be blessed with a great imagination, which means that they will quite often be happily occupied alone in their own invented world. They may suffer agonies from teasing or bullying from bolder children, but their kindness will be greatly appreciated by those who choose them as friends.

Personal relationships: Pisceans make good friends, who are sympathetic in times of trouble. In partnerships and relationships Pisceans may find it hard to cope with a strong-willed or dominant character; they may become downtrodden. They may have a tendency to put their partner on a pedestal in the early stages of love, and become sadly disillusioned at a later point in time. Piscean parents will nurture their children with a great amount of love, but must be careful to remain strong when their authority is called into question.

Career and business: Artistic or musical occupations can offer the Piscean imagination plenty of scope. Teaching and health work are also professions to which Pisceans might be drawn. Travel, particularly overseas, appeals to a great many Pisceans and any job that involves this is likely to attract them. Lack of self-confidence can lead some Pisceans to opt for work in a field where their potential is not fully realised.

Health: Pisceans often tend towards obesity, and may suffer associated health problems. They may also be prone to gout or liver problems, or have poor resistance to infection.

Colours: White or aquamarine.

Gemstones: Moonstone, sapphire, coral.

Animals: Sheep, ox.

Flowers: Heliotrope, water lily, carnation.

PK *see* **PSYCHOKINESIS**

PLANCHETTE An invention to facilitate **AUTOMATIC WRITING**, consisting of a board, on which the hand could rest, mounted on castors. A pencil point was attached to the underside of the board. Planchettes were used in **SEANCES** in the nineteenth and early twentieth centuries.

PLANETS In **ASTROLOGY**, the sun, moon and seven planets in our solar system, which exert influence over life on earth in varying degrees, according to their positions in the **ZODIAC**. Each is attributed certain qualities and associations and rules one or two signs of the zodiac.

The Sun (rules **LEO**)

Power, energy, creativity, authority.

The Moon (rules **CANCER**)

Emotion, instinct, the subconscious.

Mercury (rules **VIRGO, GEMINI**)

Communication, technology, analytical skill.

Venus (rules **LIBRA, TAURUS**)

Love, friendship, beauty, earthly treasures.

Mars (rules **ARIES**)

Independence, courage, initiative, competitiveness.

Jupiter (rules **SAGITTARIUS**)

Wisdom, generosity, success, good fortune.

Saturn (rules **CAPRICORN**)

Limitations, impediments, inflexibility, challenge.

Uranus (rules **AQUARIUS**)

Genius, invention, revolution, breakthrough.

Neptune (rules **PISCES**)

Sensitivity, intuition, compassion, spiritualism, idealism.

Pluto (rules **SCORPIO**)

Endings, destruction, regeneration, hidden power, unconscious faculty.

POLTERGEIST A ghostly, unseen spirit phenomenon, which is characterised by disturbing, noisy, unpleasant and sometimes violent activity. Poltergeist activity is generally limited to one place, but it may also centre round one particular person, leaving others in close proximity unaffected. Typical manifestations of poltergeist activity include loud noises (banging, crashing, shouting), strange smells, moving objects, which sometimes appear to be being thrown at people, apparently spontaneous fire-starting and in some cases, actual bodily violence to people in the place where the poltergeist is active. In contrast to other forms of haunting, which can continue for many years, poltergeist activity is generally relatively short-lived, lasting for a finite period of weeks or months before ceasing altogether. There have been several well-documented cases of poltergeist activity throughout the world. Some poltergeists have been identified as the spirits of particular people, whilst others are anonymous. Poltergeist activity has been particularly associated with homes in which an adolescent, usually a girl, has been living at the time. When the child is removed from the home, more often than not the poltergeist activity ceases. This has led to conjectures that either the child, at a particularly vulnerable stage in her life, has become the unwitting channel for the poltergeist's activities, or that the bizarre occurrences are a manifestation of her own inner turmoil and have been caused by her, either subconsciously or consciously. Some so-called cases of poltergeists have been exposed as fraud, but others have succeeded in defying scientific explanation.

POPPET A **CURSE DOLL**.

POSSESSION The taking over or domination of a person by a spirit or deity, either good or evil. The concept of possession is common to many cultures and religions, for example Judaism, Christianity and **VOODOO**. There are several references to divine possession in the Bible, relating to the prophets of the Old Testament and the disciples of Jesus in the New Testament. In the book of Samuel, Saul is told how he will receive the Holy Spirit in the following manner; And the Spirit of the Lord will come upon thee, and thou shalt prophecy with them, and shall be turned into another man. Similarly, the book of Acts tells how, after the ascent of Jesus into heaven, the twelve disciples are filled the Holy Spirit: And they were all filled with the Holy Ghost, and began to speak with other tongues, as the Spirit gave them utterance. Once filled, or possessed, by the Holy Spirit, the disciples became channels for God's word, and had the powers of prophecy and healing in God's name. The Bible also contains several references to demonic possession. A belief in physically manifest possession, either demonic or divine, persists within many branches of the Christian church today. The remedy for demonic possession is **EXORCISM**.

In Voodoo and some other religions, possession by deities or beneficial spirits is actively sought, commonly through self-induced trance states.

In the Middle Ages in Western Europe it was commonly believed that a variety of physical and mental disorders were manifestations of demonic possession and in some cultures around the world similar beliefs are still held. Possession, either divine or demonic, allegedly manifests itself in profound change taking place within the person who is possessed. Physical disturbances, such as convulsions, writhing and twitching are a common feature. Foaming at the mouth and vomiting foul-smelling fluid can be symptoms of demonic possession. Personality changes are also notable; accounts of demonic possession frequently refer to aggressive, highly sexualised behaviour, foul language, etc. In both divine and demonic possession, the subject may demonstrate hitherto unseen powers.

PRANA A term originating in Hinduism, but now also used in neo-paganism and a variety of **NEW AGE** health therapies, for the positive spiritual life-force that flows through all things. In human beings, both physical disease and emotional and mental disturbance are attributed to interruptions in the flow of prana through the body.

PRECOGNITION *see* **ESP**

PREMONITION A feeling of foreboding, or a growing sense of conviction, which gives a person warning of impending disaster, in some cases quite specific. There are many documented cases of people having had premonitions immediately before major disasters in various parts of the world. Some premonitions come to people when they are asleep, in the form of disturbing dreams. Some premonitions may relate to events and places about which the person having the premonition has had no previous knowledge. Many unsettling 'premonitions' will be seen, in retrospect, to be attributable to anxiety and imagination; many hundreds of others have not come true. Nonetheless, the startling accuracy with which some major events have been predicted by people's premonitions has led scientists to carry out serious investigation into the phenomenon, in Great Britain, the United States and other countries.

PRICKING The practice of piercing a suspected witch with metal pins, to determine the existence of a **WITCHMARK,** which was supposedly insensitive to pain and which, according to prevalent beliefs at the time, would not bleed when pierced. Witch-pricking became a profitable occupation in sixteenth and seventeenth century Europe, and the services of some well-known witch-prickers were widely sought, but the practice was open to fraud. Witch-pricking persisted throughout most of the period of the witch-hunts, in spite of doubts about its use as a justifiable or reliable method of witch-detection.

PROCEL A **DEMON** named in the **LEMEGETON**, said to appear as an angel and to have the power of water **DIVINATION.**

PROJECTION *see* **OUT-OF-BODY EXPERIENCE.**

PROPHECY A spiritually or divinely inspired message, either interpreting scriptures or revealing the words of a deity, in particular with reference to future, momentous events. In Christianity, Judaism and Islam, the prophets were those men who were chosen by God to deliver his word to the people. The term 'prophecy' is sometimes also used to refer to the visions of seers, such as **NOSTRADAMUS**.

PSI A term used by parapsychologists (*see* **PARAPSYCHOLOGY**) to cover those psychic powers and phenomena which fall within their field of study, including **ESP**, **TELEPORTATION**, **LEVITATION**, **PSYCHOKINESIS** and **PYROKINESIS**.

PSYCHIC An adjective to describe that which is spiritual, beyond the realm of the physical. It is particularly used to describe abilities apparently possessed by some people, which cannot be explained by physical science, for example **SECOND SIGHT** and **TELEPATHY**. Used as a noun, the word is a term for someone who demonstrates psychic abilities, for example a **MEDIUM**, or a person who has powers of **ESP**.

PSYCHIC ARCHAEOLOGY The acquiring of information about ancient sites through **PSYCHIC** means. A variety of psychic skills can be, and have been, applied in this field, including **PSYCHOMETRY**, **DOWSING**, **AUTOMATIC WRITING** and **CLAIRAUDIENCE**.

PSYCHIC CRIMINOLOGY The acquiring of information, through **PSYCHIC** means, about crimes that have been committed. Although not always known as such, psychic criminology has been practised for many centuries. In the past, many people who had powers of healing and **CLAIRVOYANCE** were also sought out for their ability to locate stolen objects. The **LEMEGETON** and other Grimoires name **DEMONS** who may be conjured to enable magicians to do this. (*See* **GRIMOIRE**.) Although modern detective work, greatly assisted by advances in forensic science and communications technology, has become increasingly sophisticated in recent years, there are still cases in which police forces feel compelled to follow lines of enquiry that are not provided by logical induction, but instead by intuition or psychic sense. Nowadays the services of a psychic may be called upon to assist in more serious cases, such as finding missing persons or concealed bodies of murder victims. The most common method used by psychics who are called upon for such tasks is **PSYCHOMETRY**.

PSYCHIC READING A term for the provision of information about the unknown by a psychic or medium using his or her **PSYCHIC** abilities in the service of another person. A psychic reading may consist of character analysis and/or the making of predictions for the future, and/or the provision of information about the spirits of the dead or missing. The information may be discovered through a variety of methods of **DIVINATION**; **ASTROLOGY**, **CLAIRVOYANCE**, **PALMISTRY**, **SCRYING**, **TAROT**, etc.

PSYCHIC SURGERY The performance of operations using supernatural powers. Psychic surgeons typically perform on their patients without the use of anaesthesia or surgical equipment, and the operation leaves no scar. The phenomenon received a great amount of publicity in the 1960's, when investigations were made into the practices of a number of psychic surgeons in Brazil and the Philippines. Although many alleged psychic surgeons have been exposed as frauds, for example using sleight of hand to produce 'growths' from their patients' bodies, and convincing their patients through the power of suggestion that a cure had been effected, it appears that there have been some patients who have inexplicably recovered from serious conditions following psychic surgery, and some practitioners continue to baffle the sceptics. *See* **ARIGO**.

PSYCHIC VAMPIRISM A term for a form of **PSYCHIC** attack, in which the attacker weakens the victim by draining his life force or spirit, using psychic means.

PSYCHOKINESIS, PK or TELEKINESIS The demonstration of the apparent power of mind over matter, involving the moving of objects through **PSYCHIC** power alone, without any physical means to do so. The phenomenon may be demonstrated in a number of ways, including movement of objects from place to place, **LEVITATION**, **MATERIALISATION** and affecting the appearance of objects or functioning of mechanical instruments (*see* **GELLER**). It is thought that psychokinesis may not only be performed voluntarily by people who have well-developed psychic powers, but may also be brought about involuntarily, or unconsciously, by people who are suffering emotional or mental disturbance. In cases of **POLTERGEIST** activity, where objects are commonly reported as being levitated, moved or thrown around by an unseen force, it is unclear whether the events are brought about by an external spirit force, or by the mind of the person around whom the poltergeist activity appears to be centred.

PSYCHOMETRY The ability to find out information about a person, thing, place or past event, or to predict future events in a person's life, by holding an object belonging to the person, or connected to the thing, place or event. Psychometry is used in **PSYCHIC ARCHEOLOGY**, **PSYCHIC CRIMINOLOGY** and other spheres of activity in which information is sought through the services of a **PSYCHIC** or **MEDIUM**.

PURSON A **DEMON** named in the **LEMEGETON** and said to appear as a man with the face of a lion, riding a bear and carrying a viper in his hand. He was said to have the power of prediction and interpreting oracles.

PYRAMIDS Ancient monumental stone structures with square bases and triangular sides which meet at an apex. The remains of pyramids have been found in Egypt and in Mexico and are thought to have been constructed as places of ceremony and burial. The skill and precision with which the building of these massive structures was carried out has amazed archeologists, mathematicians and architects. The largest of the Egyptian pyramids, the Great Pyramid at Giza, continues to fascinate researchers regarding the thinking that lay behind its planning. Externally, the siting of the Great Pyramid, its alignment and proportions, its height, base circumference and the slope of its sides, all appear to have been worked out carefully to correspond to a number of sophisticated calculations regarding astronomy and the solar calendar, the Earth's meridians and land mass, the points of the compass and measurements of sacred geometry. The intricate mathematics and geometry involved in the measurements of dimensions, angles and areas in the internal layout display further complex correspondences with astronomical and geophysical measurements. Many researchers have concluded that the pyramid did not only fulfil a practical ceremonial purpose, but was constructed as a metaphor, a symbol of man's place in the physical and spiritual universe. Other believe that the structure may contain some prophetic message to be discovered through interpretation of its internal measurements. As research continues, the Great Pyramid may yet reveal more about the depth of knowledge possessed by those responsible for its construction, and to provoke further speculation on the wealth of secret lore it may still conceal, encoded within the geometry of its construction.

Research also continues into a strange phenomenon associated with the shape of the pyramid. It is believed that the shape and proportions of the pyramids enclose a space that is in some way charged with supernatural energy. Experiments have allegedly shown that food can successfully be preserved if stored within a pyramidal container made according to the correct proportions; knives and razor blades, stored in a pyramid, do not only stay sharp, but become sharper. Some people believe that the pyramid also has curative powers, and that sleeping inside a pyramid will prolong life.

PYROKINESIS The starting, controlling or extinguishing of fires by means which are not physical. Pyrokinesis can be a manifestation of **POLTERGEIST** activity or the demonstration of an ability possessed by someone who is psychically gifted.

PYTHAGORAS (6th century B.C.) Greek philosopher and mathematician. He is believed to have been born on the island of Samos. Details of his life are unclear, but it is thought that he travelled for some time before settling in Crotona, a Greek colony in Italy. There, he established a self-governing community of his followers. They lived a life of abstinence, self-denial and study, which was believed to purify the soul and release it from the body in which it was imprisoned, ready for the next incarnation. Pythagoras, who made a number of significant discoveries in mathematics, including the geometrical theorem named after him, believed that everything in the universe could be ultimately be expressed in terms of number. His teachings had a profound influence on **OCCULTISM**.

QABBALA *see* **KABBALAH**

QUADRUPLICITIES The division of the twelve signs of the **ZODIAC** into three groups of four, according to whether they mark the onset, middle or end of a season. *See* **CARDINAL SIGNS, FIXED SIGNS, MUTABLE SIGNS.**

QUINTESSENCE In **OCCULTISM**, a term which is used to denote a fifth, unseen **ELEMENT**, which pervades and links everything. *See* **AKASHA, ETHER, ELEMENTS.**

RAPPINGS The knocking or tapping sounds with which spirits allegedly have made their presence known at seances. *See* **SEANCE.**

RASPUTIN, GRIGORI YEFIMOVICH (1871–1916) Russian peasant, mystic, healer and prophet. Rasputin was born in rural Siberia. In early adulthood, he turned to religion, after seeing a vision of the Virgin Mary, and he soon gained a reputation as a faith healer. Throughout his life, his apparent religious zeal was at odds with his lifestyle; he was a very heavy drinker and a notorious womaniser. Nonetheless, his strangely magnetic personality had a profound effect on many who met him.

News of his healing powers reached the Russian royal family and the Tsarina Alexandra called him to court to attend to her son Alexei, who suffered from haemophilia. On several occasions, Rasputin appeared to stem Alexei's bleeding by willpower alone. In spite of his scandalous behaviour, Rasputin became a favourite of the Tsarina, but his influence at court was deeply resented, increasingly so as the royal family's popularity declined. In December 1916, enraged by Rasputin's growing political power, a group of Russian aristocrats, led by Prince Yusupov, plotted to assassinate him. The almost superhuman effort that it took to kill Rasputin confirmed many people's beliefs that he possessed incredible powers. He was given food and drink laced with more than enough cyanide to kill any normal man but astonishingly, the deadly poison appeared to have little effect on him. The conspirators then shot him several times, and beat him severely, but he still would not die. Finally, they bound him and threw him in the River Neva, where he drowned.

Rasputin had predicted his own death, in a letter written shortly before the event. He had also stated in the same document that the Russian royal family and the aristocracy would be wiped out. It was a chilling prediction of the turmoil of the revolution to come.

RAUM A **DEMON** named in the **LEMEGETON**, appearing either as a crow or as a man and having the power to bring peace between enemies.

REGRESSION *see* **PAST LIFE RECALL**

REINCARNATION The rebirth of the soul, in another body, after death. Belief in reincarnation has been a fundamental part of religions and philosophies in various parts of the world since ancient times. Hindus and Buddhists believe that several successive earthly incarnations are necessary before the soul can eventually be freed to be united with the divine. Followers of Jainism, an offshoot of Hinduism, have similar beliefs. PYTHAGORAS and his followers believed that a life of asceticism was necessary in order to liberate the soul and prepare it for future incarnations. Reincarnation also featured in the teachings of Plato and Plotinus and it is central to doctrines of more recent times, such as THEOSPOPHY and ANTHROPOSOPHY, but it is denied by the doctrines of Christianity. Many people believe that it is possible to return to, or remember previous incarnations and there have been several cases of apparent PAST LIFE RECALL documented in different countries around the world.

REMOTE VIEWING Seeing objects, places, people, events, which are outwith the range of physical perception. Things said by subjects under HYPNOSIS have led many people to believe that remote viewing is possible under such conditions, but other people, particularly those with PSYCHIC abilities, can also apparently 'see' distant places and things in this manner. The phenomenon is closely linked to the idea of astral travel, or OUT-OF-BODY EXPERIENCE. It is also known as 'clairvoyant travelling'.

RETROCOGNITION Knowledge about places and events in the past, which cannot be explained by historical study or current personal knowledge and experience. Retrocognition is a feature of PAST LIFE RECALL and is also demonstrated by people who have powers of CLAIRVOYANCE.

RHAPSODOMANCY A method of DIVINATION in which inferences are drawn from verses or lines of poetry selected at random.

RISING SIGN *see* ASCENDANT

RONOVE A DEMON named in the LEMEGETON and said to have the power to enable men to speak in foreign tongues.

ROOT RACES *see* THEOSOPHY.

ROSICRUCIANS An esoteric fraternity, the existence of which first became public knowledge following the publication in Germany between 1614 and 1616 of three pamphlets; Fama Fraternatis, Confessio Fraternatis and The Chemical Marriage of Christian Rosycross. The pamphlets told, in allegorical form, of the origins of the Order of the Rosy Cross. They recounted the story of the travels and discoveries of a man (most likely a mythical character) called Christian Rosencreutz, of his founding of the Order and of the initiation of Christian and his followers into the secrets of ALCHEMY and true spiritual knowledge. The aims of the Order were primarily to heal the sick, help the needy and spread knowledge, thereby changing things for the better for mankind. The pamphlets drew a picture of an organization that was founded upon Christian beliefs, but was anti-Roman Catholic, and also embraced ASTROLOGY, alchemy and MAGIC. Although no members of the mysterious

Order of the Rosy Cross could be identified, and it now seems likely that the Order was an elaborate intellectual fiction, the publication of the pamphlets sparked great controversy. On the one hand, the idea that such a secret and potentially powerful society might exist was regarded with a certain degree of fear and suspicion. On the other hand, the possibility of achieving the degree of spiritual wisdom that was alluded to in the pamphlets intrigued and excited many scholars of the time. Many scholars sought to join the Order; none were successful. Gradually, interest turned to scorn; the pamphlets must have been a hoax. No more was heard of the Order and interest died down for a period, but from the eighteenth century onwards several organizations sprang up around Europe claiming to be affiliated to the Order of the Rosy Cross, or to have been founded upon its principles. Links with the Freemasons (*see* **FREEMASONRY**) were drawn; one of the higher degrees in Freemasonry is the 'Rose Crois'. Interest in the Rosicrucians has persisted into the twenty-first century.

RULING PLANET In **ASTROLOGY**, a planet which is considered to influence a particular sign of the **ZODIAC**. Each sign has a ruling planet, either one of the seven planets in the galaxy, the Moon or the Sun. The signs of the Zodiac and their corresponding ruling planet are as follows:

Aries – Mars
Taurus – Venus
Gemini – Mercury
Cancer – Moon
Leo – Sun
Virgo – Mercury
Libra – Venus
Scorpio – Pluto
Sagittarius – Jupiter
Capricorn – Saturn
Aquarius – Uranus
Pisces– Neptune.

See also **PLANETS**.

RUNES A term applied to a system of symbols, of Germanic origin, which have letter values as an alphabet and also have esoteric meanings and magical properties ascribed to them. They are thought to have been used mainly for magical purposes and for **DIVINATION** rather than for writing. According to legend, runes originated with an ancient tribe called the Volsungr, around the time of the end of the Ice Age. The Volsungr passed their knowledge onto other tribes who spread it through northern Europe. Stones and artefacts bearing the inscriptions of runes have been found all over Europe and in America. The earliest examples of runic inscriptions have been found in Scandinavia and date from around the third century A.D. There are a number of different runic systems, each closely related to the other, but with variations in the number, appearance and significance of the symbols used. The Elder, or Germanic **FUTHARC** is thought to be the oldest of these. It consists of twenty-four symbols, and was widely used in Scandinavia and other parts of Europe. The Anglo-Saxon futharc, which dates from a later period, originally had twenty-four symbols, to which another three were added. Divination with runes was done using stones or sticks on which the symbols had been marked. Runes were also inscribed on monuments, amulets and talismans to give them magical properties. Divination with runes has become popular once more in recent years.

SABBAT or WITCHES' SABBATH A meeting of witches. The term has been applied to any gathering of witches, but is properly used to describe meetings which take place to mark eight festivals of the pagan year which have been traditionally celebrated since ancient times:

IMBOLG, or Candlemas (2nd February)

The Spring Equinox (21st March)

BEALTAINE, or Beltane, (30th April)

Midsummer (22nd June)

LUGHNASADH, or Lammas (Around the 31st July)

The Autumn Equinox (21st September)

SAMHAIN, or Hallowe'en (31st October)

Yule, the Winter Solstice (22nd December).

Modern witches, or practitioners of **WICCA**, adhere to this tradition. In the sixteenth and seventeenth centuries, when witch persecution reached a peak in Europe, it was widely believed that sabbats were occasions of great depravity, involving devil worship, black magic, drinking, dancing and lewd behaviour, including intercourse with the Devil. The Wiccan sabbat, in contrast to this, is a **NEO-PAGAN** celebration of the natural world, fertility, the cycle of life and the changing seasons, marked with a combination of solemn ritual and festivity.

SABNACH A **DEMON** named in the **LEMEGETON**, said to take the form of a soldier with a lion's head, mounted on a horse. He constructed great armed citadels.

SAGITTARIUS (23 November–21 December) In **ASTROLOGY**, the ninth sign of the **ZODIAC**. Sagittarius is a **MUTABLE** sign, a **FIRE** sign and masculine. Its **RULING PLANET** is Jupiter.

Character: Sagittarians are generally sociable, optimistic, enthusiastic and versatile. They love physical activity and many Sagittarians participate in potentially dangerous sports. They enjoy good company and make lively, warm-hearted and generous friends, but can be unwittingly hurtful when their natural frankness causes them to be tactless. Sometimes, they can be moody, but black moods never last for long. Sagittarians are rarely deceitful and are typically very generous with help and advice when called upon. Their enthusiasm, however, can cause them to go a little too far in some circumstances. Some might see the Sagittarian's efforts on their behalf as being patronising or intrusive. Sagittarians love their freedom and this aspect of their character can be expressed in a variety of ways. Some change career several times in the course of their lives, others move from place to place, or devote their spare time to travel and new experiences. Even in thought, the Sagittarian likes to give himself free rein; many are drawn to philosophy, esoteric studies or creative writing. But in spite of the potential for change, the Sagittarian is rarely half-hearted in his enthusiasm for his present occupation, hobby, or environment. Sagittarians are generally blessed with sound intuition and this can be very helpful when they are judging the possible outcome of any action they might take, but they are less likely to demonstrate sound financial sense and frequently have to suffer the consequences of rash overspending. Sagittarian children will be loving and fun, but their need for constant activity will present quite a challenge to their parents. They will make the most of new opportunities and enjoy the challenges of school, but may take time to accept the confines of routine and require a firm guiding hand to keep them grounded long enough to complete whatever task is at hand.

Personal relationships: Sagittarians make good friends and those who form a relationship with a Sagittarian will rarely be bored. There is always a risk, however, that when freedom calls, the Sagittarian might go. Sagittarians are likely to throw themselves enthusiastically into parenthood and try to bring their children up in an atmosphere of warmth and fun. They should guard against pushing too far with children who are introverted, shy, or lacking in self-confidence.

Career and business: A variety of careers suit Sagittarians. Their love of sport might lead them into an occupation that involves working out of doors, often with animals. Their natural good feeling towards their fellow men may be expressed in one of the caring professions, or the ministry. Sagittarians often thrive in managerial or consultant roles.

Health: Sagittarians are prone to problems with the hips and may also suffer from rheumatism or arthritis. They tend to overindulge in food and alcohol and risk suffering health problems related to this.

Colours: Orange or yellow.

Gemstones: Sapphire, amethyst.

Animals: Horse.

Flowers: Carnation, wallflower.

ST JOHN'S WORT A herbaceous plant of the family Hypericum, which is used in alternative medicine as an anti-depressant. In **OCCULTISM**, St John's Wort has a long history as an **AMULET** against demons and evil spirits.

SALAMANDER The name of one of the four categories of **ELEMENTALS**. Salamanders were associated with the **ELEMENT** of fire.

SALEM The name of a community which was established by English Puritan settlers in the 1620's in Massachusetts, USA, and which became, in 1692–3, the centre of a notorious episode of witch persecution. The episode was started by the claims of a number of young girls, including the daughter and niece of the Reverend Parris, the community's minister, that they had been bewitched. As investigations were made regarding the girls' claims, hysteria within the community mounted and the number of accusations and counter-accusations grew. Over a period of approximately one year, more than two hundred people were charged with crimes of witchcraft. A series of trials, presided over by a number of ministers from the colony, resulted in the execution of twenty people. When the furore eventually died down, the accused still remaining in prison were acquitted and released. Ten years later, the Massachusetts government, effectively admitting a terrible miscarriage of justice, granted amnesty to all those who had been accused and took steps to compensate the families of those who had been executed.

SALEOS A **DEMON** named in the **LEMEGETON**, appearing as a soldier mounted on a crocodile.

SALT A symbol of purity in religion and occultism worldwide. Salt is believed to repel evil and, in particular, the Devil. Salt, mercury and sulphur, both as physical substances and philosophical concepts, were central to the practice and intellectual study of **ALCHEMY**. In Christianity, salt is used in holy water for baptism and blessing. In **WICCA**, salt is used in many rituals, and is mixed with the water which is used to consecrate the **MAGIC CIRCLE** with the four **ELEMENTS**.

SAMHAIN, ALL HALLOW'S EVE or HALLOWE'EN An ancient fire festival which takes place on the night of October 31st, the eve of the Celtic New Year and the beginning of winter. It is one of the eight sabbats celebrated in **WICCA**. In Ireland it was also referred to as Féile na Marbh, or the Feast of the Dead. Samhain was the date by which the last of the year's crops had to be gathered in, to prevent them from becoming damaged by harmful spirits. Animals were brought in from pasture and those that were not to be kept for breeding were killed. Some of the meat would be eaten at a Samhain feast. Bonfires were lit on hilltops, a practice that has largely been replaced in modern times with the bonfires of Guy Fawkes night. Samhain was a time when the spirits of the dead could be contacted. It was also a time when evil spirits could roam freely and measures had to be taken to appease these forces and protect the home and family from them. There are many traditions associated with Hallowe'en. Several divinatory practices, particularly those concerning love and marriage, are associated with the festival. Turnip or pumpkin lanterns are still made and lit at Hallowe'en. The original purpose of lanterns like these was to warn away evil spirits. The popular children's Hallowe'en tradition of 'trick or treat', known in Scotland as 'guising', has its origins in propitiary **MAGIC**, bribing evil spirits with sweetmeats to keep them from causing harm. *See* **SABBAT**.

SANDERS, ALEXANDER (1926–1988) The founder of the Alexandrian Tradition of modern **WITCHCRAFT**. Sanders was born in Manchester, England, and claimed to have been initiated into the craft by his grandmother. He also claimed to have **PSYCHIC** powers, including the gift of healing. He was a flamboyant personality who dabbled in black **MAGIC** for some time, before devoting his energies to 'white' witchcraft. Along with his wife, Maxine Morris, he formed his own **COVEN**, which followed practices that were very similar to those of the Gardnerian Tradition (*see* **GARDNER**), although he had never been part of a Gardnerian coven. His efforts at self-publicity were very successful and he soon acquired a considerable following, both in Great Britain and abroad. Sanders proclaimed himself The King of the Witches, a title which was not universally accepted among practitioners of the Craft, but he is generally acknowledged as having had considerable influence and having kept general interest in witchcraft alive through his activities.

SASQUATCH A large, hairy, creature vaguely resembling a human, which allegedly inhabits remote regions of North-West America and Canada. Reports of sightings of this creature, which has a mythical status similar to the **YETI** and the **GREY MAN**, date back to the eighteenth century. It is also popularly known as Bigfoot, a name it was given after plaster casts were made of an enormous human footprint, which was believed to have been made by the creature.

SATAN A name by which the Devil, the supreme source of evil, is known.

SATANISM Devil worship, involving black **MAGIC**. Some satanic activities are thought to involve perversions of Christian religious worship, such as the **BLACK MASS** and the **BACKWARD BLESSING**. The majority of people who have an interest in **OCCULTISM** disassociate themselves from anything connected to Satanism.

SCORPIO (24 October–22 November) In **ASTROLOGY**, the eighth sign of the **ZODIAC**, represented by the sign of the scorpion. Scorpio is a **FIXED** sign, a **WATER** sign, and feminine. Its **RULING PLANET** is Pluto.

Character: Scorpions are energetic, inquisitive, perceptive, strong-willed and determined. They are not afraid to take risks. They can be very temperamental. They will generally be well aware of their own strengths and at times, because of this, they may seem arrogant. Their tenacity and strength of determination can, on occasion, seem obsessive. The typical Scorpio will have a magnetic personality and an unsettling ability to exert his will over other people with apparent ease. Scorpions can also be notoriously perverse. They are generally good actors, and quite capable of acting out a convincing and misleading role in public, either to impress or shock. Many Scorpions are fascinated by the occult and will often have psychic gifts. Scorpions make stimulating friends but be wary of crossing them, for the sting in their tail can be vicious. Scorpio children are energetic and daring, and may strain their parents' nerves with their physical exploits. They are generally very affectionate, but can be prone to outburst of temper, and may be quite melodramatic. They are competitive, but may be very poor losers.

Personal relationships: Scorpions are very perceptive and choose their friends and partners carefully. In love, they will be passionate and exciting, but partners should be wary of the Scorpion's tendency to be jealous and possessive. Scorpions will understand their partners very well, but are unlikely to let their partners have such an intimate understanding of them. They guard their privacy fiercely when it comes to their innermost thoughts.

Most Scorpions will be devoted parents, but they should guard against a tendency to be too controlling as their children grow up.

Career and business: The Scorpions' love of danger suits many of them for a career in the military services; their inquisitiveness and perceptiveness draw some to work in military intelligence. Scientific study of some sort, particularly research, might also satisfy the Scorpion curiosity, and many are drawn to medicine or surgery. Typically fascinated by the workings of other people's minds and perceptive to the emotions of others many Scorpions opt for a profession which can utilise these attributes; for example, psychology. The Scorpion magnetism and persuasiveness has produced many gifted courtroom lawyers.

Health: Scorpio subjects may be prone to a variety of physical injuries. Many suffer from skin problems, in particular those affecting the facial complexion. There is a tendency to suffer from depression.

Colour: Deep red or russet.

Gemstones: Opal, ruby.

Animals: Wolf, panther.

Flowers: Red geranium, chrysanthemum.

SCOT or SCOTT, REGINALD (1538–1599) English MP and author of *Discoverie of Witchcraft*. A country-dweller who is recognised as the author of the first treatise on hop-growing in England, Scot showed a clearness of thinking and compassion that was very much at odds with current popular opinion in England when he published Discoverie in 1584. The book was written in attempt to demonstrate that belief in witchcraft and magic was illusory. Discoverie contained a wealth of information about ancient and contemporary beliefs and superstitions regarding magic, sorcery, witchcraft and alchemy, and attacked the work of a number of contemporary writers on the subject, including **BODIN**. Scot was also highly critical of the Roman Catholic church, which he believed was responsible for the current popular obsession with witchcraft, and led to the cruel persecution of so many vulnerable people.

Scot's work was widely condemned, and King James I ordered all copies to be destroyed.

SCOTT, MICHAEL (c.1175–c.1230) Scottish scholar, astrologer and magician. Details of Scott's early life are uncertain, but it is thought that he may have been born either in the Scottish Borders or in Northern England, to Scottish parents. He was educated at Oxford and then continued his studies on the Continent, in France and Italy. He was appointed as court astrologer and tutor to Frederick II of Germany and wrote a number of works on astrology. He also translated some of the great works of Greek philosophy. During his lifetime, he acquired a reputation as a magician, which spread throughout Europe, and after his death, he became the central figure in a number of popular legends, one of which tells of him outwitting the Devil in a series of challenges.

SCOURGE A ritual tool which is used in some branches of **WICCA**. The scourge is not intended to be an instrument for inflicting pain. It is generally made from cords of silk and its use in most covens is confined to symbolic purification in initiation ceremonies. It may also be used, gently and rhythmically, to induce a trance-like state and raise psychic awareness.

SCRYING A term used to describe several methods of **DIVINATION**, most of which use reflective surfaces , such as mirrors, **CRYSTALS**, crystal spheres, pools of water, or ink. The scryer, following a period of intense concentration or meditation on the question to which an answer is being sought, gazes into the reflective surface, to see images, or visions, which will bring enlightenment. It is thought that these visions are essentially reflections of what is seen 'in the mind's eye', or in the subconscious. The reflective surface, or speculum as it is properly called, is therefore acting for the scryer in the same way as a film screen does for a projector.

SEAL OF SOLOMON A six-pointed star formed from two identical, equilateral triangles, one of which is inverted and superimposed over the other. It has been used as an amulet since the early Middle Ages, for protection against the EVIL EYE. Amulets inscribed with the Seal of Solomon, artefacts made in its shape, or drawings of it have also been used for hundreds of years in a large variety of magical rituals, particularly in the summoning of DEMONS. The Seal was believed to give the magician some protection against rebellious and vindictive spirits and to help him to gain control over them.

SEANCE A meeting of people with an interest in SPIRITUALISM, who have gathered together to try to communicate with the dead. The numbers of people attending seances rose considerably in Great Britain during the nineteenth century, when there was a rise in popular interest in all aspects of the supernatural. Seances were presided over by a MEDIUM, who served as a conducting channel for messages from the afterlife. Through the medium, the spirits of the dead could make their presence felt in a number of ways; spelling out names or messages on a OUIJA BOARD, RAPPING, causing objects to move, appear, disappear or levitate, or by possessing the body of the medium and speaking through him or her. The practice of holding seances was wide open to fraud as the meetings were commonly held in a darkened room, facilitating all sorts of trickery for the sake of profit. Not surprisingly, it fell into disrepute. There are still people who practise as mediums nowadays, albeit it a less flamboyant fashion, calling their meetings 'sittings' rather than seances. The messages these people give to the living from the dead, particularly to those who are grieving, can be of considerable comfort. There have also been murder investigations in which mediums have offered their services to the police in an effort to find a body or identify a killer. *See* PSYCHIC CRIMINOLOGY.

SECOND SIGHT An inborn ability to see into the future. The gift of second sight is particularly associated with the people of the Highands of Scotland. It may be, but is not necessarily, hereditary. People who have second sight may experience any number of visions during their lifetime, which may either hint at, or indicate in greater detail, events that will take place at some time in the near or distant future. The visions appear spontaneously and may give the seer premonitions of either good or evil. *See also* BRAHAN SEER.

SECRET COMMONWEALTH OF FAIRIES, THE A book written in the sixteenth century by the Reverend Robert KIRK, a minister of the Scottish Presbyterian church, concerning the world of the supernatural. The book was used as a reference by the Scottish witch-hunters of the period, for its detailed description of the WITCHMARK.

SEEING STONE A crystal or a stone with a reflective surface, which is used for SCRYING.

SEER, SEERESS A person who has the ability to see into the future. Someone who has the gift of **SECOND SIGHT**.

SEERE A **DEMON** named in the **LEMEGETON**, who was said to rule over the eastern regions of the world. He appeared as a handsome man, mounted on a winged horse and was said to have the power to circle the world in moments. He could be summoned as a messenger, or could be used to find hidden treasure and stolen goods.

SIDHE In Celtic lore, a race of spirit beings who were believed to inhabit an underground kingdom on earth.

SHAMAN A term for a person who performs a number of magical feats, usually for benevolent purposes such as healing, through direct communication with the spiritual world, usually in a state of trance. The powers of a shaman include healing, **DIVINATION**, prophecy and shape-shifting. The term 'shaman' is Siberian in origin, but forms of shamanism have been practised in a large number of cultures around the world, including Asia, North and South America, Australia and Africa, since ancient times. In some cultures it is believed that shamanistic abilities are hereditary, whilst in others, the first sign that a boy may become a shaman is exhibited around puberty, with the experience of visions, or some form of mental disturbance. In some cases, a shaman is seen as one who is possessed by the spirit of a dead predecessor. Common to all cultures is the belief that a shaman has to undergo a period of initiation, frequently involving a life-threatening experience, in order to prove his abilities and make the initial contact with the spirit world and with the spirit guide, or guides, (birds or animals) whom he can seek out in future for help. A shaman's spirit guide is either seen as an animal spirit which enters the shaman's body (*see* **POSSESSION**), or as one which gives the powers particular to its species to him. When a shaman enters into a trance, which may be induced through **CHANTING**, drumming, dancing or with the help of hallucinogenic drugs, it is believed that his spirit leaves his body and journeys in the spirit world. He may take on the form of his guardian animal or bird spirit to make the journey. (*See* **SHAPE-SHIFTING**.) On these journeys, he finds the answers to questions regarding all aspects of the life of the people to whom he belongs, he can find the causes of illness and intercede with the spirits that cause them, or bring back the spirit of a sick person from the other world, to restore life and health.

SHAPE-SHIFTING A term for the magical transformation of humans into animal form. The mythologies of many cultures refer to deities changing into animal or human form, and belief in the ability of some humans, in particular magical adepts, to perform such feats, was similarly widespread. This belief had particularly cruel consequences in Medieval Europe. Records of witchcraft trials contain several references to shape-shifting and many accused witches were said to have performed various acts of malefice after having taken on the forms of animals or birds. The bizarre confessions of several of those who had been accused gave further credence to people's beliefs. It is thought that shape-shifting is not necessarily a voluntary process. *See* **LYCANTHROPY**.

SHAX A **DEMON** named in the **LEMEGETON**, said to take the form of a dove with a hoarse voice. He could be commanded to take precious possessions from others.

SHROUD OF TURIN A piece of linen bearing the impression of a human body, which has been preserved as a relic in St John's Cathedral in Turin since 1578. It was believed to be the shroud in which the body of Christ was wrapped after the crucifixion. In the 1980's, carbon dating tests on the fibres of the cloth demonstrated that the shroud dates from no earlier than 1260.

SIBYL *see* **ORACLE**

SIMON MAGUS A Samarian sorcerer, who is mentioned in the New Testament in the Bible. Simon Magus tried to buy the power of the Holy Ghost from the apostles. He is said to have had possessed great magical powers, including **LEVITATION** and making himself invisible, and to have set himself up in competition to the apostles, inviting people to worship him as a spiritual leader and promising immortality to his followers.

SITRI A **DEMON** named in the **LEMEGETON**, said to have the rank of prince and possess power over the sexual desires of both men and women.

SITTING A **SEANCE**.

SIX-FINGERED HUMANOID A form of extraterrestrial being, which is said to have been sighted on earth and to have communicated with humans. Six-fingered humanoids are one among several forms of extraterrestrial entity that have become associated with **AREA 51** in the United States of America.

SKY-CLAD A term used in **WITCHCRAFT**, meaning naked. Although the practice is not universal, many Wiccans prefer to perform rituals sky-clad. *See* **WICCA**.

SORCERY Practical **MAGIC**, involving the use of **DIVINATION**, spells, **CHARMS** and invocations to influence events and change the environment. The term is frequently used synonymously with **WITCHCRAFT**, especially when referring to the practice of **BLACK MAGIC**.

SPEAKING IN TONGUES *see* **GLOSSOLALIA**.

SPECULUM *see* **SCRYING**.

SPIRITUALISM Belief in the existence of the human spirit as a non-physical entity, in the life of the spirit after bodily death and in the possibility of communication between the living and spirits of the dead.

SPONTANEOUS HUMAN COMBUSTION A term which came into being after a significant number of mysterious deaths were documented in which the victims appeared to have burned to death without any evidence to show how this had come about. The first cases recorded date back to the seventeenth century. In the majority of cases of spontaneous human combustion, no obvious source of ignition is in evidence. Typically, only small parts of the victims remain intact and apart from the confined area in which the body had been, there is no other evidence of fire to be found; furnishings, carpets etc. in the vicinity are undamaged. There may be body parts remaining, but the burning of the rest of the body is more complete than could be achieved in a crematorium. These cases have led to speculation that the victims have somehow burned from the inside out. A number of cases of apparent spontaneous human combustion have been witnessed. Witnesses typically report that flames appear to be coming out from within the victim; in most cases, either from the abdomen or from the face. The victim is typically motionless–presumably paralysed by pain–and makes no sound. Scientific experiments have been conducted to find an explanation for occurrences like these, which have been reported in a number of different places around the world. Most of these experiments have been carried out in an attempt to disprove that such as thing as spontaneous human combustion is possible and to demonstrate that all alleged cases have external causes. But the efforts of scientists to date have failed to prove beyond reasonable doubt that it is beyond the realms of possibility. Spontaneous human combustion is one of many strange and unexplained occurrences that are commonly referred to as **FORTEAN PHENOMENA**. (*See* **FORT**.)

STEINER, RUDOLF (1861–1925) Social philosopher, teacher and founder of Anthroposophy, Rudolf Steiner was born in Croatia and trained as a mathematician and scientist. His fascination with the spiritual world began when he was a young child and first began to experience visions. Through a combination of study and his own experiences, he became convinced that materialism and preoccupations with earthly pleasures had caused mankind to become divorced from its spiritual nature; that the sense of the divine which had once pervaded all aspects of human life had now been lost to the large majority of people. His life thereafter was to become dedicated to trying to reawaken man's spirituality; uniting science and the arts with religion, and imbuing all areas of human activity once more with spiritual consciousness. For a number of years, Steiner was associated with the Theosophical Society in Germany (*see* **BLAVATSKY, THEOSOPHY**), and although he kept a degree of independence from the movement, he devoted a large amount of time to teaching and lecturing to its members on spiritual matters. During this period he also wrote a number of works on Christianity, Theosophy and the occult. In 1913, following Annie Besant's controversial claim to have found, in KRISHNAMURTI, the reincarnated Christ, Steiner split from the Theosophists, founded his own movement of spiritual science, Anthroposophy, and built the Goetheaneum in Basle as a centre for the movement. Steiner based much of his spiritual teaching on the doctrines of the Christian religion, but also embraced the concepts of KARMA and REINCARNATION, believing that the human soul had to evolve through successive bodily incarnations in order to achieve perfection. Steiner's work was not confined to the theoretical. His spiritualism was essentially holistic; he believed it should inform all of human life. Practising what he believed in, Steiner extended his interests into agriculture, music and the arts, health therapies and children's education. The Waldorfschule education system, which he set up after the First World War, now has more than 400 schools in operation, offering an alternative to the traditional state education that has been welcomed by a great many people. The Camphill organization, which works on Anthroposophical principles of therapy and education, and has bases in Europe and the United States, has earned recognition and praise from families and care professionals alike for the work which is done in their residential communities to enable young people and adults who have special needs to reach their full potential.

Steiner continued to work tirelessly until his death, writing and lecturing. His philosophy and his ideas on education, organic farming and holistic medicine are still widely respected.

STIGMATA Wounds on a living person that replicate those suffered by Christ at the crucifixion. Stigmata are generally open wounds which appear spontaneously and are resistant to medical treatment; in some cases they can disappear (or heal) and reappear repeatedly. They are found on the hands, feet and torso, and sufferers are generally extremely devout Christians, the majority of whom are women. The appearance or reappearance of the marks is frequently associated with important days in the religious calendar, in particular Good Friday. The marks have also appeared on some people following periods of intense devout contemplation. The first documented evidence of the appearance of stigmata concerned St Francis of Assisi in the early thirteenth century. There have been several hundred reported cases since then, many of which have been photographed. Sceptics have tried to dismiss the appearance of stigmata as either fraud or a psychosomatic problem, but the authorities in the Roman Catholic Church have been convinced that in several cases, that of St Francis included, the stigmata have been an indicator or manifestation of the sufferer's extreme piety.

STOLAS A DEMON named in the LEMEGETON, said to appear either as a raven or as a man.

STONEHENGE A megalithic monument located on Salisury Plain, in Wiltshire, England. Stonehenge is one of many stone circles that can be found all over the British Isles, and is the largest of its kind. It is thought to have been constructed and modified in three major phases between the fourth millennium and second millennium BC. Originally, an earth bank (now destroyed) enclosed the outer circular ditch. The ditch surrounds another bank of earth. Within the circle of the bank are fifty-six burial holes. The bank encloses two concentric stone rings, the outer one of which originally had thirty sarsen pillars topped by linked lintels, the inner one originally a double circle of bluestone pillars. Inside the rings are two U-shaped formations, the outer formed from sarsen trithlons, the inner from stones which were taken from the bluestone rings in the third phase of modification. In the centre lies a single stone, known as the Altar Stone. The exact purpose of the monument is unknown, but the orientation of the entrance to the circles and the horseshoes suggests that it may have served as an astronomical observatory.

SUCCUBUS The term used to denote a devil or DEMON which was believed to be able to transform itself into a woman in order to have sexual intercourse with men as they slept. *See* INCUBUS, NIGHT DEMON.

SUMMERS, [ALPHONSUS JOSEPH-MARY AUGUSTUS] MONTAGUE English Roman Catholic priest, academic and writer, whose works include two important studies of WITCHCRAFT, The History of Witchcraft and Demonology (1926) and The Geography of Witchcraft (1927). The books were written from the standpoint of a man who had an abiding belief in witchcraft as an inherently evil practice.

SUN SIGN in ASTROLOGY, the name for the sign of the ZODIAC through which the sun is passing at the time of a person's birth. A person's sun sign is thought to determine aspects of his or her personality.

SWASTIKA An ancient symbol of good luck and prosperity recognised by many cultures around the world. The swastika is formed from a Greek cross, the arms of which are bent over at a right angle, all facing in the same direction, most commonly clockwise. It was adopted by the Nazis as their emblem, with arms pointing in an anti-clockwise direction.

SWEDENBORG, EMANUEL (1688–1772) Swedish scientist and mystic. The son of a bishop, Swedenborg was educated at the University of Upsala, and following graduation spent some time travelling in Europe expanding his scientific and technical knowledge. He then took up a post as assessor of the Swedish Royal Board of Mines in 1710. He was a brilliant academic, skilled in all sciences and fluent in several languages, and he also had a profound interest in spiritual matters. He wrote prolifically on science and philosophy. In 1734 he published *Opera Philosophica* *et Mineralia,* a three-volume work which combined science with philosophical theory regarding the creation and structure of the cosmos. In the early 1940's he underwent a form of spiritual crisis. He had already begun recording his dreams in a journal, in an attempt at self-discovery, when he experienced what he understood to be a direct vision of the spiritual world, communicated to him by God. Following this, he continued to have similar visions, entering trances, speaking with God and visiting the afterlife. He abandoned his scientific pursuits to document the religious revelations which these experiences had given him, along with scriptural interpretations made according to the revelations. He published a large number of works, including Divine Love and Wisdom (1763) and an eight-volume opus *The Heavenly Arcana* (1749–56). His writings earned him a sizeable following, and in 1787, English Swedenborgians founded the Church of the New Jerusalem in London. The Church's influence spread, and several other branches started up in other countries around the world, including the United States. The influence of Swedenborg's thinking can be found in the work of a number of English writers, including William Blake and Henry James.

SYLPHS The name of one of the four categories of ELEMENTALS. Sylphs were associated with the ELEMENT of air. They were believed to be tiny, winged, semi-translucent creatures.

SYMPATHETIC MAGIC A term for any form of MAGIC that works at a distance and is essentially imitative. The practice of sympathetic magic works upon the assumption that it is possible to bring about certain changes by performing a ritual that resembles these changes. Magical rituals using dolls to resemble people, whether for good or bad intent, are examples of sympathetic magic.

SYNCRETISM The fusion of different belief systems, or the combining of elements from different belief systems. Syncretism is a notable feature of occult practice in the twentieth century.

TALISMAN An object constructed from any one of a variety of materials, which is believed to be endowed with certain specific powers, sourced from deities, angels or demons, which may then be imparted to the carrier or wearer. The term 'talisman' is frequently used synonymously with AMULET, but most occultists differentiate between the two. Whilst the amulet is purely protective and, in a sense, passive, the power of the talisman is believed to be active and directed, intended to give its owner success in a particular sphere of activity, such as money-making, war or oratory.

TAROT A set of seventy-eight cards used for DIVINATION and fortune-telling. The Tarot has been in use in Europe since the early Middle Ages, when it is believed that the Crusaders brought the first sets back from the East. Although over the years theories have been put forward linking the Tarot with Egyptian, Indian, Celtic and Hebrew mysticism, none of these theories have been proven and its exact origins remain a mystery. There are many different Tarot packs in circulation, each with its own particular symbolism, and selection of a set for personal use is very much a matter of individual preference, although experts are agreed that there is considerable variation in the quality of the imagery. Some Tarot packs have been designed with particular cultures or groups of people in mind, with symbolic imagery relevant to these groups. The Tarot consists of two groups of cards; the Minor Arcana and the Major Arcana. There are fifty-six cards in the Minor Arcana, made up of four suits; Wands, Pentacles, Cups and Swords. Each suit has numbered cards Ace to ten and four face cards, King, Queen, Knight and Page. The pack of fifty-two playing cards used everywhere today is based on the Minor Arcana. The Major Arcana is made up of twenty-two cards, each of which has a title and a picture. One of the cards, the Fool, is either un-numbered or numbered zero. The other cards are numbered and named as follows:

1. The Magician
2. The High Priestess (or The Female Pope)
3. The Empress
4. The Emperor
5. The Hierophant (or The Pope)
6. The Lovers
7. The Chariot
8. Strength
9. The Hermit
10. The Wheel of Fortune
11. Justice
12. The Hanged Man
13. Death
14. Temperance
15. The Devil
16. The Tower
17. The Star
18. The Moon
19. The Sun
20. Judgement
21. The World

When the Tarot is being consulted, either all seventy-eight cards or the Major

Arcana alone may be used. A number cards are laid out, either according to one of hundreds of traditional patterns ('spreads'), or according to the personal choice of the reader. The interpretation of the spread will depend not only on the individual cards that have turned up, but also on their position in the pattern and their relationship to the other cards around them. When a Tarot reading is made by one person for another, the process involves questions and answers between reader and client which will also influence the interpretation of the cards. The Tarot designed by Aleister **CROWLEY** and illustrated by artist Frieda Harris is one of the most popular in use today. The symbolism contained in the cards reflects Crowley's belief that the Tarot was linked to the **KABBALAH**.

TASSEOMANCY A method of **DIVINATION** using tea-leaves. It is thought to have originated in China. Tasseomancy is generally used to answer specific questions of a personal nature. The questioner drinks tea made with loose leaves, from a tea cup. When the cup is almost empty, the reader swirls the dregs round three times before inverting the cup over the saucer and turning it round another three times. The patterns made by the tea leaves remaining in the cup can then be interpreted by the reader to find answers to the questions that have been asked.

TAURUS In **ASTROLOGY**, the second sign of the **ZODIAC**, represented by the figure of the bull. Taurus, is a **FIXED** sign, an **EARTH** sign, and feminine. Its **RULING PLANET** is Venus.

Character: Taureans are frequently 'home birds', who thrive on stability and security. This can make them very fixed in their habits and rather resistant to change. Their strengths lie in those same characteristics, however, for they are likely to be dependable, trustworthy, solid and reliable. They will tackle whatever challenges life throws up at them with a practical approach and a dogged determination to succeed. At home and at work, they will strive to promote harmony and security; their approach to finances cautious, but tempered by a natural generosity. They are generally imaginative and greatly appreciate beauty in nature and artefact alike. Many Taureans are creative either musically or artistically. Taureans are generally slow to anger, but once their temper is aroused, it can be quite formidable. Taurean children will thrive on routine and structure in their lives, along with kind and patient encouragement to help them to adapt to the unfamiliar.

Personal relationships: Taureans who are fortunate enough to find a compatible partner will invest a great deal of themselves in the relationship. As homemakers they excel, making every effort to provide a warm, comfortable and attractive living environment. These qualities can make them wonderful husbands or wives, but can be undermined by possessiveness. Taurean parents are likely to provide a loving, stable and secure home for their children to grow up in, but should be sensitive to the fact that some children might find such constancy restricting at times.

Career and business: Job security will be important to most people born under this sign. Taureans often find rewarding employment in well-structured careers such as banking or the civil service, but their practical nature, thoroughness and love of beauty might lead them into other avenues, such as gardening, painting, or the sciences. Their caring and homely characteristics can be used to good effect in the caring professions.

Health: Taureans are generally fairly robust, but may be prone to throat infections. They may also tend towards obesity.

Colour: Pink.

Gemstones: Emerald, sapphire, turquoise.

Animals: Bull.

Flowers: Rose, poppy, violet, foxglove.

TELEKINESIS *see* **PSYCHOKINESIS**

TELEPATHY Communication between the minds of two people, without the use of any form of physical communication such as speech, writing, facial expressions, body language, etc. Telepathic communication is particularly associated with people who have a strong emotional attachment or blood bond; for example, there are numerous documented cases of telepathic communication taking place between identical twins. Telepathy can apparently operate at a considerable distance, sometimes between two people who have been separated for a number of years. It may occur spontaneously and unintentionally, or deliberately. Telepathic messages may be received as visions, feelings, auditory hallucinations, etc. Typical examples of reported telepathic communication include numerous stories of one person being struck with a strong sensation that another (absent) person, with whom they have a strong attachment, is in pain, or ill. They make contact, and their feeling is confirmed. Many people believe that telepathy is possible between humans and animals. A smaller, but nonetheless significant number of people claim that it is can also take place between humans and extraterrestrials. *See* **ANIMAL ESP, ALIEN ABDUCTION.**

TEMPLARS *see* **ORDER OF THE KNIGHTS TEMPLAR.**

TETRAGRAMMATON In the philosophy of the **KABBALAH**, the true, hidden name of God, which was contained within the ten sepiroth. The Tetragrammaton was believed to be a **NAME OF POWER**, which, when uttered, had the potential to cause terrible havoc and destruction. Formed from the Hebrew letters, Yod, He, Vau, He, it is written as YHVH, and pronounced 'Yahweh' or 'Jehovah'. For many years the Tetragrammaton was held in such awe by the Jewish people that it was rarely uttered aloud, and only spoken in a whisper by high priests on Yom Kippur, the Jewish Day of Atonement. Names which were used in place of the Tetragrammaton included Adonai, Elohim and Shaddai.

THELEMITES The followers of **ALEISTER CROWLEY**.

THEOSOPHY A term, derived from the Greek theosophos, meaning 'wisdom in God', which was originally applied to wisdom gained through revelation or study regarding the nature of the supreme deity, or to the search for such wisdom through religious and philosophical study and contemplation. After the founding, in 1875, of the Theosophical Society (*see* **BLAVATSKY**), the term was used to refer to its doctrines, most of which were laid down in the writings of Madame Blavatsky, who founded the movement along with Colonel Henry Steel Olcott and William Q. Judge. Blavatky's ideas strove to unite humankind in brotherhood and common philosophical wisdom, which she believed had been handed down unchanged by wise men through the ages. This wisdom, she claimed, was not simply theoretical; it could be tested scientifically. Demonstrating similarities between the doctrines of different religions, Blavatsky claimed that all were derived from one original source. Much of her own knowledge, she claimed, had been gleaned from communication with the spirits of ancient wise men from the east. Blavatsky believed in spiritual **REINCARNATION** and **KARMA**, and hence, the importance of individual moral responsibility figured largely in Theosophical doctrine. A person's thoughts and deeds in one life would have an effect, not only on one's own experiences in the next incarnation, but also on the karma of others. The doctrines of the Theosophical society also emphasised the brotherhood of man regardless of sex, creed, race or colour. According to theosophical doctrine, all human souls are emanations from the same all-pervading, boundless, eternal and unchanging divine principle and as such, all humankind is one. Through successive incarnations, souls evolve from primitive life forms into animals and finally, into human form. In each incarnation thereafter, the soul may develop further, towards the spiritual realm. This can be achieved through a combination of study of the wisdom of ancient masters and conscious effort to live a life which shows compassion, care and active consideration of others. Divine wisdom is accessible to all who seek it, rather than to a select number of adepts.

Among the more controversial theories argued by Blavatsky was that of the existence of the lost lands of **LEMURIA** and **ATLANTIS**. Blavatsky believed that all mankind was descended from five **ROOT RACES**, the third and fourth of which dwelt in Lemuria and Atlantis respectively. Blavatsky's interest in the hidden psychic powers of humans was also controversial, and her willingness to demonstrate her own alleged powers of mediumship and clairvoyance ensured that the Theosophical Society, and she personally, attracted as many critics as followers. The Theosophical Society continued after Blavatsky's death under the leadership of Annie **BESANT**. Rudolf **STEINER**, who was associated with the German branch of the society for a number of years, eventually parted company with the Theosophists and founded his own movement of spiritual science, Anthroposophy. There have been other breaks within the Theosophical movement since then, and a number of other groups have formed with ideas that have been derived from Blavatsky's teachings, and developed along different lines. But the Theosophy of Blavatsky has not lost its vitality and continues to attract numerous followers in Europe and the United States.

THOTH The Egyptian god of wisdom, art, science and magic, the scribe of the gods who invented writing and mathematics.

THREEFOLD LAW In modern **WITCHCRAFT**, the belief that in magic, whatever is done to others, whether good or bad, will be returned three times over.

THULE SOCIETY A German occult organization which sprang from the **ORDER OF TEUTONS** and was founded in 1916 by a wealthy occult **ADEPT**, Rudolf Blauer, also known as Rudolf von Sebottendorff. The name of the organization was derived from the belief that there had once existed in the far north a land called Thule, which, like Atlantis, had been the home of a highly sophisticated race of humans. Members of the society believed that the secrets of the Nordic people who had dwelt in this lost land had been preserved by a number of ancient masters, who could be contacted through esoteric magical rituals. Under the guidance of these masters, initiates would, it was believed, be able to develop supernatural powers, which would enable them to re-establish a superior race of Aryan stock and ultimately vanquish or exterminate other, inferior races. The Thule Society rapidly became active in anti-communist and anti-Semitic politics. Thule Society members took a leading part in the foundation of the German Worker's Party, which later became the National Socialist German Worker Party, led by Adof Hitler. The **SWASTIKA**, which had been an emblem of the Thule Society, was adopted by the Nazi movement. Amongst the leadership of the Nazi party were a number of Thule Society members, including Hitler himself, and under Hitler's leadership, the racist doctrines of the society were transformed into a national movement towards the domination of Germany in world politics and the re-establishment of its people's identity as a supreme Aryan race.

TOTEM Any living thing or inanimate object that is revered for certain desirable qualities that it possesses or is believed to possess. Those who adopt something as a totem seek to become invested with the qualities associated with it. Since ancient times, totems have been adopted and revered by peoples in many different parts of the world, but they are most commonly associated with the North American Indian peoples.

TRANCE A state akin to unconsciousness, or sleep, in which a person becomes apparently unaware of their physical surroundings. Trance may be accompanied by feelings of ecstasy and allegedly, can alter one's consciousness in such a way that awareness of non-physical entities increases, or becomes possible. In a trance state, for example, some people claim to experience visions or to be able to communicate with spiritual beings. Trance states may be self-induced in a number of ways, including drugs, meditation, drumming, dancing and CHANTING, but may, allegedly, also occur spontaneously. People who use self-induced trance states as a means of gaining or enhancing spiritual awareness, or of increasing PSYCHIC powers, include mystics, mediums, shamans, ascetics and practitioners of magic. *See* MEDIUM, MYSTICISM, SHAMAN.

TREE OF LIFE *see* KABBALAH

TRIPLICITIES The name used in ASTROLOGY for the division of the twelve signs of the ZODIAC into four groups of three, according to each group's association with one of the four ELEMENTS. *See* AIR SIGNS, EARTH SIGNS, FIRE SIGNS, WATER SIGNS.

TUATHA Dé DANANN In Irish folklore, a race of people skilled in magical arts who ruled Ireland before the advent of the Celts. When the Celts arrived the Tuatha were driven underground, where they created a magical world of their own. The legend of the Tuatha is echoed in one of the theories that have been put forward regarding the nature of fairies. *See* FAIRY.

TWILIGHT ZONE *see* BERMUDA TRIANGLE.

UFO An Unidentified Flying Object. Reports of these phenomena have baffled scientists for many years and fuelled speculation about life on other planets. UFOs commonly manifest themselves as unexplained moving lights or saucer-shaped objects in the night sky and there are certain places worldwide where their appearance has been reported on numerous occasions by several people independently of each other.

UNCTIONS, or UNGUENTS Magical, greasy ointments, used in WITCHCRAFT and ceremonial MAGIC, the recipes for some of which may be found in the Medieval Grimoires. (*See* GRIMOIRE.) These ointments were typically made from a number of distasteful ingredients, including poisonous or hallucinogenic herbs, animal and human excretions and occasionally, body parts. Use of these ointments was limited to magical purposes, such as **FLYING** and **SHAPE-SHIFTING**. Some could also be used for killing by magic.

UNDINES The name given to one of the four categories of **ELEMENTALS**. Undines were associated with the **ELEMENT** of water and were believed to be tiny creatures with fin-like wings.

VALAC A **DEMON** named in the **LEMEGETON**, said to appear as a winged boy, mounted on a two-headed dragon. He had the power to find hidden treasure.

VALEFAR A **DEMON** named in the **LEMEGETON** and described as a lion with a man's head.

VALIENTE, DOREEN EDITH [née DOMINY] (1922–1999) English witch and author, who is widely regarded as the Mother of **WICCA**. Doreen Valiente was initiated into **WITCHCRAFT** by Gerald **GARDNER** in 1953, and eventually became high priestess of his **COVEN**. While she was practising with Gardner, she took upon herself the task of adapting and developing much of the writing in Gardner's **BOOK OF SHADOWS**. Valiente's contributions to the book are widely appreciated by most practitioners of **WICCA** for their poetic beauty. Doreen eventually parted company with Gardner in the 1960's. She was initiated into a hereditary coven run by Robert Cochrane, but separated from that, too, for ethical reasons. She devoted much of her time in the last thirty years of her life to writing, and in correspondence with fellow Wiccans. An ABC of Witchcraft (1973) and Natural Magic (1975) earned her widespread acknowledgement as an authority on Wicca. In the early 1980's, Valiente successfully tracked down the birth and death certificates of Dorothy Clutterbuck, the woman who initiated Gerald Gardner into witchcraft, proving to Gardner's critics that she had not been, as they claimed, a figment of Gardner's imagination. In 1995, she became a patron of the British Pagan Federation.

Valiente remained active in the Craft throughout her life. She was passionate in her belief that the ethics of Wicca should never be undermined by any of its practitioners, and was a teacher, source of inspiration and role model for a great many people who entered the Craft after her.

VAMPIRE In Eastern European folklore, one of the parasitic 'undead', who rise from their graves in the hours of darkness and nourish themselves by feeding on the blood of living victims. Modern perceptions of vampires have been heavily influenced by Bram Stoker's fictional creation, Count Dracula. Vampires are said to be repelled by **GARLIC**, and in some rural regions of Eastern Europe, strings of garlic are still hung outside some homes as **AMULETS**.

VAPULA A **DEMON** named in the **LEMEGETON**, said to appear as a lion with griffon's wings. He had the power to make men skilled in various crafts.

VASSAGO A demon, named in the **LEMEGETON** and said to have the power to predict the future and find lost objects.

VEPAR A **DEMON** named in the **LEMEGETON**, having the rank of duke and appearing as a mermaid. He had the power to cause storms at sea and cause men's wounds to become fatally infected.

VINE A **DEMON** named in the **LEMEGETON**, appearing as a lion riding a black stallion. He was said to have the power of **CLAIRVOYANCE**.

VIRGO (24 August–22 September) In **ASTROLOGY**, the sixth sign of the **ZODIAC**, represented by the sign of the virgin. Virgo is a **MUTABLE** sign, an **EARTH** sign and feminine. It **RULING PLANET** is Mercury.

People who are born under this sign are typically intelligent, blessed with a great deal of common sense, conscientious and thorough in their approach to everything. They are cautious and controlled in everything they do, more comfortable in the role of supporter than leader. This may mean, however, that they are perceived as being rather dull and they run the risk of being undervalued for their contributions to group activities. When travelling in a group, for example, the Virgoan will be the one who studies the timetables, routes and itineraries and takes precautions against every eventuality, sometimes incurring outbursts of impatience from others. Virgoans can be over-critical, both of themselves and others, and are also extremely sensitive to criticism and complaint from their friends, colleagues or superiors. They are likely to be shy and self-effacing. Their virtue lies in their adaptability; whatever their circumstances, Virgoans will generally act accordingly, falling into the role that is expected of them, so long as it suits their purpose. They will accept change calmly and readily, taking stock of unfamiliar situations objectively, rationally and sensibly. Their objectivity, however, can occasionally manifest itself in a certain cold-bloodedness of attitude when in pursuit of particular goals. They will act as part of a team towards their own ends, but are very much their own people and not often motivated by altruism alone or a desire to promote the communal good. Virgoans are not natural risk-takers and will shrewdly weigh up the pros and cons of any venture upon which they embark. They are methodical rather than intuitive, rational rather than imaginative. They can be perfectionist to the point of obsession. Virgoan children are less likely to clash with their parents on matters of routine and discipline; they will generally be quite compliant and willing to help at home, and diligent and quiet at school. They may lack self-confidence, and parents should be sensitive to this.

Personal relationships: Virgoans make loyal partners when they choose to enter into a long-term relationship, but many prefer to remain single. In relationships, their tendency to be hyper-critical and perfectionist can be a problem to some partners, but the trouble they take with all that they are involved in can provide a welcome sense of security and being cared for. The Virgoan family home may not be ostentatious, but it is likely to be pleasantly decorated and meticulously maintained. Virgo parents will provide a stable environment for their children, and although not wildly demonstrative, will be loving, reliable parents, perceptive to their children's emotional needs. Any tendency to be over-critical or to expect unreasonably high standards should be curbed.

Career and business: Their capacity for analytical work and their characteristic thoroughness and attention to detail opens up a wide spectrum of careers for Virgoans. Law, clerical work, editorial work, computer programming and scientific research are some fields that are particularly suitable. Security takes precedence over ambition on the whole, and most Virgoans are quite happy working under the management of others. Many Virgoans will become self-employed, but they are more likely to do so if they work alone, rather than as an employer of others.

Health: Virgoans are more prone than others to disorders of the lower digestive tract and their tendency to worry may manifest itself in irritable bowel syndrome. They may show hypochondriacal tendencies, and can be prone to addiction.

Colour: Green.

Gemstones: Cornelian, jade, diamond.

Animals: Squirrel

Flowers: Buttercup, cornflower.

VOODOO or VODOUN A magical cult originating in West Africa and imported to Haiti by the African slaves of the French colonists. Voodoo is popularly associated in other cultures with black, or harmful **MAGIC**, but its origins are in predominantly beneficial and protective practices. Voodoo combines African spirit worship with many elements of Roman Catholicism, which was introduced to Haiti by European settlers. Although the existence of a supreme god figure, the Grand Maitre or Bon Dieu, is acknowledged, religious practice in Voodoo revolves around the worship of a great number of deities, known as loas, who comprise deified ancestors, spirits of natural phenomena and a number of deities associated with different spheres of human life, such as death, dying, war, love, sex, agriculture, etc. Many of the loas are identified with Christian saints. Ruling over the loas is the serpent god, Damballah. In Voodoo rituals, offerings of food, wine and sometimes animal sacrifices are made to the loas, who are summoned for their assistance in various aspects of human activity. A priest (houngan) or priestess (mambo) presides over religious ceremonies, which may take place in a temple building, or in a less formal setting such as a room in a house. Dancing, drumming and music play a central part in all rituals, and are used to facilitate a trance-like state in devotees, who may then become possessed by the loas. When someone becomes possessed by a loa, he or she will display behaviours associated with that particular spirit. The loas are not necessarily benevolent spirits. They may be summoned, according to their individual characteristics and attributes, for whatever purpose the devotees choose, and their magical powers can be harnessed for good or for evil. A darker side of Voodoo does exist, and there are houngans who practise harmful magic. The former Haitian dictator, the late 'Papa Doc' Duvalier, used the popular fear of the darker side of Voodoo to his own political advantage, by promoting an image of himself as a powerful black magician who used the power of the dreaded Baron Samedi, the spirit of death, to bring death upon his enemies. *See also* **ZOMBIES**.

VRIL *see* **BULWER-LYTTON**.

VUAL A **DEMON** named in the **LEMEGETON**, said to appear either as a camel or a man and to have the power to find love for men.

WALPURGIS NIGHT The eve of the 1st of May, celebrated in German tradition in much the same way as **HALLOWE'EN** is celebrated in the British Isles. It was believed to be the night when evil spirits roamed the world and witches congregated in appointed meeting-places to take part in obscene revellries and Devil-worship. *See* **BROCKEN**.

WATER MONSTERS For many centuries, large stretches of deep water all over the world have provoked speculation that there may lurk within their hidden depths some form of mysterious and terrible creature. Legends of sea monsters have been told since ancient times. These legends may have arisen out of a logical fear of the dangers faced by those who travelled across unknown waters, prey to the unpredictability of waves and weather and unable to see the world beneath the surface. But even today, when scientific advances have provided man with the technology to see into and understand much more about the mysteries of the deep, reports of monstrous entities persist in cropping up from time to time. Whether the numerous alleged sightings of sea monsters are fraudulent, or genuine, or have arisen from fearful hallucination, is not clear. Inland lakes in many countries worldwide are the focus of similar tales. One of the most famous of all of these is Loch Ness, where the supposed existence of a monster affectionately known as 'Nessie' has brought sightseers and serious investigators in their hordes to its shores for almost a century. The alleged existence of a monster in Loch Ness was first documented many centuries ago; St Columba is said to have encountered it in the sixth century A.D.. The legend of the Loch Ness monster lived on quite quietly in the folklore of the area until the 1930's, when it suddenly grew considerably in stature. The number of alleged sightings increased between 1930 and 1935, and a photograph taken by Robert Wilson, an English doctor, successfully convinced many people that the creature really did exist. In the years since, numerous projects have been launched to try to find the illusive creature. Believers cannot prove beyond reasonable doubt that the monster exists, but neither can the sceptics prove that she does not. Nessie will not go away. Even if scientists were to demonstrate that the existence of such a creature is impossible, it is unlikely that their arguments will convince everybody. Nessie, and all other water monsters like her, may be phantom, fraud or fact, but most importantly, they are the embodiment of man's eternal fascination with the mysterious and unknown.

WATER SIGNS In **ASTROLOGY**, the signs of the **ZODIAC** associated with the **ELEMENT** of water: **CANCER, SCORPIO** and **PISCES**. They are also known as the Water Triplicity. People who are born under any of these signs are likely to be emotional and sensitive. *See* **TRIPLICITIES**.

WELLS Water is one of the four **ELEMENTS** central to occultism, and wells, as 'living' sources of water, have been associated with religion and magic since ancient times. In Christianity, water is symbolic of cleansing, healing and purification and wells or springs were frequently chosen as the sites for Christian churches. Many wells were said to have magical powers, some particularly associated with fertility, some chosen as sites for divinatory practices. South-running water was believed to have healing powers, and wells from which the water flowed in this direction were often used for healing rituals, which generally involved washing the garments of the sick person. Wishing wells and healing wells can be found throughout the British Isles.

WEREWOLF A man who metamorphoses into a wolf in the hours of darkness, or on nights when the moon is full, and who hunts down humans, killing them and eating them or feasting on their blood. The werewolf is a well-known figure in the folkloric traditions of a number of European countries, and belief in the existence of such a thing caused real fear in the Middle Ages, leading to the persecution of many unfortunate innocents. In countries where the wolf is not a native animal, similar legends exist relating to other were-creatures. *See* **LYCANTHROPY**.

WHITE LADY A commonly reported form of **APPARITION** which appears in ghost stories and reports of hauntings from several different countries. Some white ladies are seen as ghosts of identifiable figures from the past. Others are seen as ominous portents of forthcoming death.

WHITE MAGIC A general term to describe magical practices that are intended to be harmless or beneficial to others. *See* **WICCA**.

WICCA The name given to the practice of **WITCHCRAFT** in the Western World as a **NEO-PAGAN** religion, after its revival in the 1950's. Wiccans believe that their rituals and practices have their origins in pagan beliefs which pre-date Christianity, but practitioners also draw on other influences, such as **YOGA**, **ASTROLOGY**, shamanism and **PARAPSYCHOLOGY**, for inspiration. Wiccans try to work in close harmony with the forces of Nature and stress the benevolent aspect of the magic that they perform. *See* **GARDNER, VALIENTE, WICCAN REDE, WITCHCRAFT**.

WICCAN REDE The law, of unknown origin, that underlies all Wiccan practice:
'Eight words the Wiccan Rede fulfil;
    An' it harm none, do what ye will.'
    It is this law, more than anything else, that distinguishes **WICCA** from other forms of magical practice (and in particular, from black magic), as a craft which has entirely benevolent aims..

WICKER MAN A huge human effigy, which is believed to have been built at **BEALTAINE** by the **DRUIDS** of ancient times, in which humans and animals were ritually sacrificed by burning, to propitiate the gods.

WIDDERSHINS Anticlockwise movement, or movement against the sun. In sixteenth and seventeenth century Europe, dancing widdershins was associated with **WITCHCRAFT**, and hence with Devil worship. It is still associated with the rites of **BLACK MAGIC**. *See* **DEOSIL**.

WISHING WELL *see* **WELLS**.

WITCHCRAFT A general term for the practice of **MAGIC**. It is uncertain when the term 'witchcraft' first came into being, but in Great Britain it came to be used to denote a broad scope of activity, including the predictions of **SECOND SIGHT**, the use of spells, **CHARMS** and rituals, **HEALING**, love magic, protective magic, **SHAPE-SHIFTING** and a variety of harmful magic, such as **CURSES**, storm-raising and causing sickness and death. Magic in various forms has been practised throughout the world since ancient times. People of all cultures turned to seers, diviners, healers and sorcerers in their efforts both to understand their world better and to improve their circumstances. These people, in turn, sought the assistance of supernatural forces in order to bring about change. In Europe, as in other parts of the world, the existence of such people was accepted with a mixture of respect and fear. The advent of Christianity did not eradicate the practice of magic. Laymen and members of the clergy alike continued to resort to magical practices, although the church was growing increasingly uncomfortable about drawing a line between witchcraft or sorcery and heresy. The launch of the Papal Inquisition in the thirteenth century marked the beginning of a shift in attitude. From that time onwards, the line between witchcraft and heresy became increasingly blurred until it disappeared altogether. The perception of witchcraft in Europe as something essentially morally neutral gradually changed, and witchcraft was attacked by church and state alike as heretical and evil. By the fifteenth century, the persecution of witches, or those who were alleged to be witches, had begun in Europe, starting in Switzerland. A Papal Bull issued in 1484 authorised the killing of witches, but the witch-hunts were not confined to the Roman Catholic church. By the sixteenth century, the Protestant church had joined in the persecution with equal, if not more, ferocity. Publications such as the **MALLEUS MALICARUM**, published in Germany in 1486, which stressed the notion that witchcraft involved Devil worship and the making of a demonic pact, had a major influence on popular beliefs about witches in a number of countries, including Scotland and England. As representatives or servants of the Devil, witches were the human embodiment of evil and the enemies of the Christian faith. More than 3,000 witches were executed in Germany. In Spain and Italy, thousands of alleged witches faced the wrath of the Inquisition, but the vast majority of these escaped execution. In Great Britain, the first phase of witch persecutions began in the sixteenth century and did not die out until 1736, when the Witchcraft Act was repealed. Scotland was more badly affected than England. Although records are incomplete, there is evidence to suggest that more than 1300 witches were burned at the stake in Scotland during the witch-hunts. The panic spread to European colonies in the Americas. In **SALEM**, an English colony in Massachusetts, an outbreak of community witch hysteria between 1692 and 1693 resulted in a series of trials during which condemned twenty people were condemned to death. In all countries affected by the witch persecutions, the majority of those who were brought to trial were women.

The witch panic gradually subsided and finally, died out. How many of the people who suffered as a result of the persecutions saw themselves as witches, practised magic, or even participated in Devil-worship, will never be known. The popular fascination with magic appeared to wane, or at least, was driven underground. It was not until the end of the nineteenth century that a there was a resurgence of interest in occultism in general and in witchcraft in particular. The birth (or rebirth) of modern witchcraft, or **WICCA**, as a **NEO-PAGAN** religion, happened in the 1950's, and is attributable to the work of Gerald **GARDNER** and later, Doreen **VALIENTE**. Gardnerian Wicca, which Gardner viewed as a development of ancient pagan traditions that had survived since pre-Christian times, drew on a number of different influences; the written works of Charles **LELAND** and Geraldine **MURRAY**, Gardner's own experiences working with self-professed hereditary witches, his membership of **ORDER OF THE ORIENTAL TEMPLARS** and consequent interest in sexual magic, and his association with Aleister **CROWLEY**. The publication of his book,

Witchcraft Today, attracted many more followers to what has since become known as the Gardnerian tradition of Wicca. Since Garder's time, Wicca has grown and diversified into a number of different branches, including the Alexandrian Tradition, Seax Wicca, Wicca as a Science and Dianic Wicca. All forms of Wicca are pantheistic and polytheistic, involving worship of the **GODDESS** and the **HORNED GOD** in their different manifestations (with emphasis placed on the supremacy of the Goddess). All celebrate the pagan festivals which mark the changes in the seasons as the elements in nature die and are reborn. All adhere to the **WICCAN REDE**. But the practice of Wicca is fluid and adaptable, and there is considerable scope for individuality and innovation in the rituals which each group, or solitary practitioner, may develop for themselves.

WITCHES' SABBATH *see* **SABBAT**

WITCH-FINDERS A term used to describe people who were employed to identify witches in sixteenth and seventeenth century Europe, when witch persecution was at its height. Witch-finders were generally paid well for their skills and fraudsters frequently made considerable profits from this occupation. Witch-finders, either by **PRICKING** or observation, were supposedly skilled in finding the **WITCHMARK**, or Devil's mark, on a suspect's body. Although witch-finders were employed throughout the period of the witch persecutions, their practices were viewed with a growing sense of unease within the judicial system, and several witch-finders were exposed as frauds.

WITCHMARK or DEVIL'S MARK The mark, or blemish, by which it was once believed a person might be identified as a witch. There are various descriptions of the supposed appearance of such marks in documents and books which date from the fifteenth to seventeenth century, the period when witch persecution was prevalent in Europe. Witchmarks were believed to be the scars or blemishes left after the witch had been kissed, nipped or bitten by the Devil when he had claimed her (or him) as his own. Witchmarks might look like a wart, a mole, a birthmark or an unusual blemish and it was generally thought that they were most likely to be found somewhere hidden from normal view, for example, in the hair or under the clothes. In addition to these kinds of marks, some witches were accused of having an extra nipple (in all likelihood, a protuberant mole), from which they might suckle their **FAMILIARS**. Witchmarks were thought to be insensitive to pain and unlikely to bleed if pierced. *See* **KIRK, PRICKING**

WRAITH A form of **APPARITION**, the spectral figure of a living person, appearing somewhere distant from their physical body. It is commonly a sign of approaching death. Wraiths are similar to doubles (*see* **DOUBLE**), but are generally unnaturally pale and thin. According to popular belief, wraiths are most likely to be seen by people who have a close relationship with the person thus manifested. *See also* **BILOCATION.**

WYRD An Anglo-Saxon term meaning power and destiny, which is used to refer to a supernatural force believed to pervade the earth and all in it, shaping the destiny of men. 'The Web of Wyrd' is an expression which is used to depict the interconnectedness of everything within the scope of this force.

XENOGLOSSIA A psychic phenomenon whereby a person displays knowledge of an identifiable language which he or she has never had the opportunity to learn. Xenoglossia is sometimes associated with recollections of previous incarnations. *See* **PAST LIFE RECALL.**

YEATS, WILLIAM BUTLER (1865–1939) W. B. Yeats was born in Dublin. His family lived in London for twelve years of his childhood, but returned to Dublin in 1881. He progressed from school to Art College, where he realised that his real interest lay in literature. His fascination with the occult began at a relatively young age and he became a founder member of the Dublin Hermetic Society when he was only twenty. He pursued his interests when he moved again to London, and there he joined the magical society, the **ORDER OF THE GOLDEN DAWN**, becoming a high-ranking member. He proved himself rapidly to be a thoughtful and gifted writer, particularly of poetry. His writings, prose, drama and poetry alike, reveal his interest in mysticism, and he wrote a number of essays on occult subjects. Yeats's wife, Hyde Lees, shared his interest in the occult and experimented extensively with **AUTOMATIC WRITING.**

YETI *see* **ABOMINABLE SNOWMAN.**

YGGDRASIL In Norse mythology, the name of the mighty ash tree which grows through all levels of the cosmos, linking the human with the divine, and life with the afterlife. It was said to grow from beneath the underworld (**NIFLHEIM**), through the mid-level (**MIDGARD**) and up into heaven, the level of the gods (**ASGARD**).

YOGA An ancient system of Hindu philosophy which is believed to have been founded by Patanjali, a wise man who lived in the Indian state of Uttar Pradesh in the second century BC. Yoga, meaning 'union', was developed as a means of reaching a state of individual spiritual union with the supreme, divine being, through certain disciplined practices including asceticism, deep meditation and physical postures and exercises. There are several different forms of yoga, each of which is aimed at the individual reaching the final goal of samadh through specific techniques. Some are centred on meditative techniques, whilst others concentrate on achieving their aim through physical discipline. In all forms of yoga, the student progresses, over time, through a number of levels of increasing difficulty. Hatha Yoga, which involves breathing techniques and the adoption and maintaining of prescribed physical postures, known as asanas, has been absorbed into the West as a popular means of achieving a state of physical wellbeing and calm. Dhyana Yoga involves deep meditative techniques. Raja Yoga is regarded as the most superior of all. Other forms of yoga include Tantric yoga and **KUNDALINI** yoga.

YOGIC FLYING A form of **LEVITATION** which is achieved by some people who practise transcendental meditation.

ZAGAN A **DEMON** named in the **LEMEGETON**, said to appear as a bull with griffin's wings. He had the power to turn base metals into gold coins, and water into wine.

ZAR According to ancient beliefs in North-East African countries, a kind of spirit that can take **POSSESSION** of people, causing them to become sick.

ZENER CARDS A set of twenty-five cards on each of which are printed one of five simple symbols (circle, quadrilateral, triangle, cross and wavy lines), which are used in formal testing of **ESP**. One subject is shown the cards in random order, while another subject, out of sight and earshot, is asked to state which cards are being shown. Zener cards were developed by parapsychologist J.B.Rhine at the American Society for Psychic Research in the late 1920's.

ZEPAR A **DEMON** named in the **LEMEGETON**, said to appear as an armed soldier dressed in red, and to have the power of influencing matters of love among mortals.

ZODIAC An imaginary band in the sky through which the ecliptic passes, and which contains the paths of the sun, moon and planets. It is divided into twelve sectors of thirty degrees, each of which has a corresponding astrological sign. The twelve signs of the zodiac originally corresponded to constellations that once lay within each sector. Each sign corresponds to a period of approximately thirty days, as follows:

ARIES – 21st March–20th April
TAURUS – 21st April–21st May
GEMINI – 22nd May–21st June
CANCER – 22nd June–22nd July
LEO – 23rd July–23rd August
VIRGO – 24th August–22nd September
LIBRA – 23rd September–23rd October
SCORPIO – 24th October–22nd November
SAGITTARIUS – 23rd November–21st December
CAPRICORN – 22nd December–20th January
AQUARIUS– 21st January–18th February
PISCES – 19th February–20th March

See **ASTROLOGY, GROUPINGS, HOROSCOPE, HOUSES, PLANETS.**

ZOMBIE According to **VOODOO** belief, a zombie is a reanimated corpse or a living person deprived of a soul; one of the living dead. It is believed that zombies can be conjured from the dead by **MAGIC**, and will follow, unquestioningly and mechanically, the bidding of the master who has summoned them. In reality, 'zombies' are more likely to be people who have been poisoned with one or a number of toxic substances. One substance which is thought to have been used is tetradoxin, a nerve poison which is obtained from the puffer fish, and which induces a deep coma. In recovery, the victims, although able to move, remain in a trance-like state and are significantly mentally impaired, sometimes permanently.

ZOROASTER or Zarathustra A Persian prophet of the seventh century BC, founder of the religion known as **ZOROASTRIAMISM**.

ZOROASTRIANISM A dualistic religion founded in Persia by **ZOROASTER**, which is based on the belief in the existence of two opposing supreme beings, who are locked in conflict. One is **AHURA MAZDA**, the Creator, good and wise, living in eternal light and the other is **AHRIMAN**, the evil one, lying, deceitful and destructive, living in perpetual darkness. Zoroaster prophecied that ultimately, Ahura Mazda will triumph.